H A N D B O O K S

→ Columbine City Gorge
→ Powell's City of Books

PORTLAND

HOLLYANNA McCOLLOM

Contents

Maps

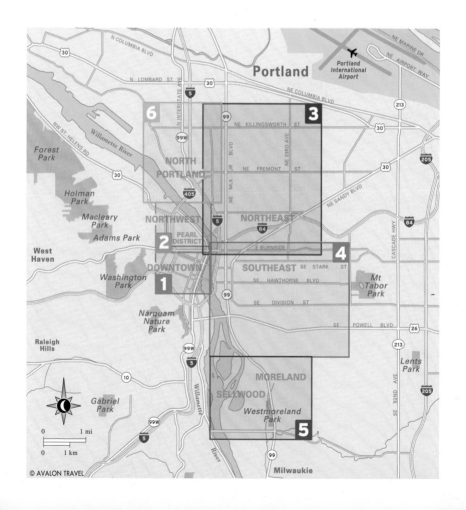

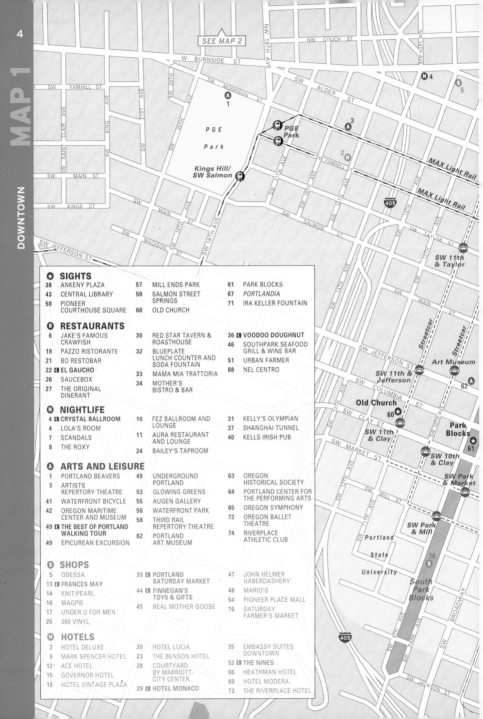

⊗ SIGHTS

38	ANKENY PLAZA	57	MILL ENDS PARK	61	PARK BLOCKS
43	CENTRAL LIBRARY	59	SALMON STREET SPRINGS	67	*PORTLANDIA*
50	PIONEER COURTHOUSE SQUARE	60	OLD CHURCH	71	IRA KELLER FOUNTAIN

⊗ RESTAURANTS

6	JAKE'S FAMOUS CRAWFISH	30	RED STAR TAVERN & ROASTHOUSE	36	▣ VOODOO DOUGHNUT
19	PAZZO RISTORANTE	32	BLUEPLATE LUNCH COUNTER AND SODA FOUNTAIN	46	SOUTHPARK SEAFOOD GRILL & WINE BAR
21	BO RESTOBAR			51	URBAN FARMER
22	▣ EL GAUCHO	33	MAMA MIA TRATTORIA	68	NEL CENTRO
26	SAUCEBOX	34	MOTHER'S BISTRO & BAR		
27	THE ORIGINAL DINERANT				

⊗ NIGHTLIFE

4	▣ CRYSTAL BALLROOM	10	FEZ BALLROOM AND LOUNGE	31	KELLY'S OLYMPIAN
4	LOLA'S ROOM	11	AURA RESTAURANT AND LOUNGE	37	SHANGHAI TUNNEL
7	SCANDALS			40	KELLS IRISH PUB
8	THE ROXY	24	BAILEY'S TAPROOM		

⊗ ARTS AND LEISURE

1	PORTLAND BEAVERS	49	UNDERGROUND PORTLAND	63	OREGON HISTORICAL SOCIETY
3	ARTISTS REPERTORY THEATRE	53	GLOWING GREENS	64	PORTLAND CENTER FOR THE PERFORMING ARTS
41	WATERFRONT BICYCLE	55	AUGEN GALLERY		
42	OREGON MARITIME CENTER AND MUSEUM	56	WATERFRONT PARK	65	OREGON SYMPHONY
		58	THIRD RAIL REPERTORY THEATRE	72	OREGON BALLET THEATRE
49	▣ THE BEST OF PORTLAND WALKING TOUR	62	PORTLAND ART MUSEUM	74	RIVERPLACE ATHLETIC CLUB
49	EPICUREAN EXCURSION				

⊗ SHOPS

5	ODESSA	39	▣ PORTLAND SATURDAY MARKET	47	JOHN HELMER HABERDASHERY
13	▣ FRANCES MAY	44	▣ FINNEGAN'S TOYS & GIFTS	48	MARIO'S
14	KNIT/PEARL			54	PIONEER PLACE MALL
16	MAGPIE	45	REAL MOTHER GOOSE	70	SATURDAY FARMER'S MARKET
17	UNDER U FOR MEN				
25	360 VINYL				

⊗ HOTELS

2	HOTEL DELUXE	20	HOTEL LUCIA	35	EMBASSY SUITES DOWNTOWN
9	MARK SPENCER HOTEL	23	THE BENSON HOTEL	52	▣ THE NINES
12	ACE HOTEL	28	COURTYARD BY MARRIOTT- CITY CENTER	66	HEATHMAN HOTEL
15	GOVERNOR HOTEL			69	HOTEL MODERA
18	HOTEL VINTAGE PLAZA	29	▣ HOTEL MONACO	73	THE RIVERPLACE HOTEL

NW 11th
& Couch
NW 10th
& Couch
North
Park
Blocks
SEE MAP 2
NW 5th/
Couch
Skidmore
Fountain
Burnside
Bridge

NW COUCH ST
NW 12TH AVE
W BURNSIDE ST
W BURNSIDE ST
W
BURNSIDE ST

SEE MAP 3

7 8
11
10
SW 6th/
Pine
25
24
26
Ankeny
Plaza
36 37
38
39
ANKENY ST

6
9
12
SW 10th
& Stark
23
22
SW 5th/
Oak
35
40
99W

13
Obryant
Park
21
20
18
27 28
41

14
SW 11th
& Adler
SW 10th
& Adler
16
17
19
Oak/
SW 1st
42

15
Galleria
SW 10th
Galleria
Shopping
Center
SW ALDER ST
29
30
31
32
33
34

Central
Library
45
Pioneer
Courthouse/
SW 6th
DOWNTOWN
Tom McCall
Waterfront
Park

43
Central
Library
44
Library/
SW 9th
Pioneer
Sq North
51 52
49
50
SW 5th/
Morrison
Morrison
Bridge

48
Pioneer
Courthouse
Square
Pioneer
Sq South
Pioneer
54
Place
Morrison/
SW 3rd

46
47
53
Pioneer
Place/
SW 5th
Mall/
SW 4th
55
56

South
Park
Blocks
66
65
Yamhill
District
Mill Ends
Park
57
SEE MAP 4

63
64
Lowns Dale
Square
58

SW 6th/
Madison
Portlandia
67
Chapman
Square
59
Salmon Street
Springs
99W

City Hall/
SW 5th &
Jefferson

68
69
SW 5th
& Market
71
Ira Keller
Fountain
72

PSU Urban
Center
Hawthorne
Bridge

PSU/SW 5th & Mill
SW 5th & Montgomery
PSU/
SW 6th &
Montgomery

Portland
State
University
Pettygrove
Park
Tom McCall
Waterfront
Park
73

SW 3rd &
Harrison

Lovejoy
Park

Willamette River

0   100 yds
0   100 m
DISTANCE ACROSS MAP
Approximate: 0.9 mi or 1.5 km

© AVALON TRAVEL

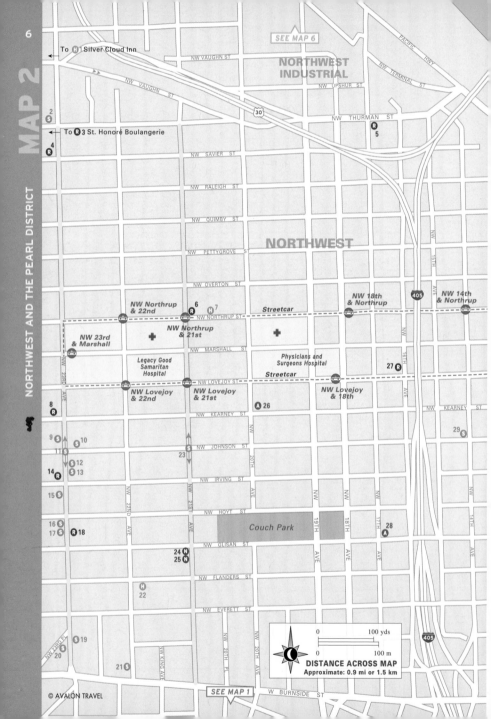

SEE MAP 6

NORTHWEST
INDUSTRIAL

NORTHWEST

NW VAUGHN ST

NW VAUGHN ST

NW UPSHUR ST

NW THURMAN ST

To 1 Silver Cloud Inn

To 3 St. Honoré Boulangerie

NW SAVIER ST

NW RALEIGH ST

NW QUIMBY ST

NW PETTYGROVE ST

NW OVERTON ST

NW Northrup & 22nd

NW Northrup & 21st

NW 23rd & Marshall

NW 18th & Northrup

NW 14th & Northrup

Streetcar

NW NORTHRUP ST

NW MARSHALL ST

Legacy Good Samaritan Hospital

Physicians and Surgeons Hospital

NW LOVEJOY ST

Streetcar

NW Lovejoy & 22nd

NW Lovejoy & 21st

NW Lovejoy & 18th

NW KEARNEY ST

NW KEARNEY ST

NW JOHNSON ST

NW IRVING ST

NW HOYT ST

Couch Park

NW GLISAN ST

NW FLANDERS ST

NW EVERETT ST

NW BURNSIDE ST

SEE MAP 1

W. BURNSIDE ST

DISTANCE ACROSS MAP
Approximate: 0.9 mi or 1.5 km

0   100 yds
0   100 m

SIGHTS

35	JAMESON SQUARE	37	UNION STATION	54	POWELL'S CITY OF BOOKS	73	PORTLAND VINTAGE TROLLEY	79	PORTLAND CLASSICAL CHINESE GARDEN
36	JEAN VOLLUM NATURAL CAPITAL CENTER	53	THE BREWERY BLOCKS	57	THE ARMORY	77	CHINATOWN GATE		

RESTAURANTS

3	ST. HONORÉ BOULANGERIE	8	TWO TARTS BAKERY	30	THE DAILY CAFÉ	48	50 PLATES	67	SWEET MASTERPIECES CHOCOLATE
4	BESAW'S	14	PAPA HAYDN	39	¡OBA!	62	CUPCAKE JONES	72	GILT CLUB
5	CARLYLE	18	MOONSTRUCK CHOCOLATE	40	ANDINA	64	ISABEL PEARL	78	HOUSE OF LOUIE
6	PALEY'S PLACE	27	LE HAPPY	41	BYWAYS CAFÉ				

NIGHTLIFE

24	BARTINI	38	WILF'S RESTAURANT AND BAR	59	DESCHUTES BREWERY AND PUBLIC HOUSE	61	TEARDROP COCKTAIL LOUNGE	81	DARCELLE XV SHOWCLUB
25	M BAR	43	TEAZONE AND CAMELLIA LOUNGE	60	JIMMY MAK'S	71	EMBERS	83	BOILER ROOM
33	METROVINO	45	VINO PARADISO			74	BACKSPACE	84	HOBO'S
						75	GROUND KONTROL	85	DANTE'S

ARTS AND LEISURE

26	COMEDYSPORTZ	47	ELIZABETH LEACH GALLERY	65	BEPPU WIARDA GALLERY	70	MUSEUM OF CONTEMPORARY CRAFT	80	OLD TOWN/ CHINATOWN PEDI CAB TOUR
28	THE MISSION THEATER	49	BULLSEYE GALLERY	69	BLUE SKY GALLERY			82	OREGON JEWISH MUSEUM
42	WATERSTONE GALLERY	58	PORTLAND CENTER STAGE						

SHOPS

2	STEVE'S CHEESE	9	LUSH COSMETICS	10	AMAI UNMEI	11	NW 23RD AVENUE	44	DIG GARDEN SHOP
						12	GILT	46	LEXI DOG BOUTIQUE AND SOCIAL CLUB
						13	KIEHL'S	50	MOULE
						15	ZELDA'S SHOE BAR	51	CARGO
						16	DUCK DUCK GOOSE	52	EVERYDAY MUSIC
						17	BLUSH BEAUTY BAR	55	SOLE
						19	THE DAPPER CAP	56	LUCY ACTIVEWEAR
						20	TWIST	63	HANNA ANDERSSON
						21	ELEPHANTS DELICATESSEN	66	URBAN FAUNA
						23	NW 21ST AVENUE	68	POWELL'S TECHNICAL BOOKS
						29	REI	76	UPPER PLAYGROUND
						31	LIZARD LOUNGE		
						32	FEZ STUDIO		
						34	PEARL SPECIALTY MARKET & SPIRITS		

HOTELS

1	SILVER CLOUD INN	7	THE INN AT NORTHRUP STATION	22	PORTLAND INTERNATIONAL GUESTHOUSE

BEAUMONT-WILSHIRE

To (S)25 Found on Fremont

CONCORDIA

Fernhill Park

Wilshire Park

ALAMEDA

VERNON

Alberta Park

SABIN

NORTHEAST

KING

Irving Park

SEE MAP 6

◊ SIGHTS
43 BEVERLY CLEARY CHILDREN'S
    SCULPTURE GARDEN/GRANT PARK
45 HOLLYWOOD THEATRE

◊ RESTAURANTS
1   THE GRILLED CHEESE
    GRILL
3   HELSER'S ON
    ALBERTA
7   ZILLA SAKÉ HOUSE
8   PETITE PROVENCE
9   CIAO VITO
12 SIAM SOCIETY
13 LA BONITA
14 TOUR DE CREPES
16 D.O.C.
17 ◀ BEAST
18 YAKUZA
19 KENNEDY SCHOOL
23 NED LUDD
24 BELLY
28 ◀ TORO BRAVO
34 MILO'S CITY CAFÉ
36 CADILLAC CAFÉ
39 CHEZ JOSE EAST
42 SWEET BASIL
44 CHAMELEON
    RESTAURANT & BAR
57 ◀ SCREEN DOOR
58 TABLA
61 NAVARRE

◊ NIGHTLIFE
4   EVERYDAY WINE
27 SECRET SOCIETY
    LOUNGE
29 WONDER BALLROOM
30 BILLY RAY'S
    NEIGHBORHOOD BAR
53 GALAXY
54 NOBLE ROT
59 WINE DOWN ON 28TH

◊ ARTS AND LEISURE
10 ONDA ARTE LATINA
20 KENNEDY SCHOOL
46 HOLLYWOOD
    THEATRE
47 PORTLAND
    WINTERHAWKS
48 PORTLAND TRAIL
    BLAZERS
50 THE PORTLAND
    BREW BUS
55 PORTLAND ROCK GYM
60 THE LAURELHURST

GRANT PARK

★ Beverly Cleary Children's Sculpture Garden/Grant Park

Grant Park

★ 43

HOLLYWOOD

45 46

Hollywood Theatre

Hollywood/ NE 42nd

R 44

44

R 42

41

O 40

O 38

R 39

IRVINGTON

O 37

R 35 36

R 34

32 33

31

N 30

51

SULLIVAN'S GULCH

Oregon Park

59 N
60 R 61
58

KERNS

56 O
57

SEE MAP 4

ELIOT

Dawson Park

Legacy Emanuel Hospital

47 48
Rose Garden
Rose Quarter

R R O 29
27 28

Holladay Park
Medical Center

A 50
Holladay West Park

Lloyd Center

LLOYD DISTRICT

NE 7th Ave
49

Lloyd Center/ NE 11th Ave

Buckman Field

54
52 53
55

Convention Center
Oregon Convention Center

Rose Quarter TC

Rose Quarter

Steel Bridge

SEE MAP 2

SEE MAP 1

Willamette River

Burnside Bridge

© AVALON TRAVEL

○ SHOPS

2	MABEL & ZORA	31	FOSTER & DOBBS
5	GREEN BEAN BOOKS	35	OH BABY!
6	GRASSHOPPER	37	FUREVER PETS
	ALBERTA	40	WELL SUITED
	ARTS DISTRICT	41	BELLA STELLA
22	POPINA SWIMWEAR	51	LLOYD CENTER
26	FOUND ON FREMONT	52	REDUX
26	AMENITY SHOES		

○ HOTELS

21	KENNEDY SCHOOL	38	PORTLAND'S
32	BLUE PLUM INN		WHITE HOUSE
	BED & BREAKFAST	49	DOUBLETREE
33	LION & ROSE		LLOYD CENTER
	VICTORIAN BED	56	EVERETT STREET
	& BREAKFAST		GUESTHOUSE

DISTANCE ACROSS MAP
Approximate: 2.7 mi or 4.3 km

0   500 yds
0   500 m

MAP 4

SOUTHEAST

SEE MAP 2

SEE MAP 3

KERNS

E BURNSIDE ST

St. Francis Park

BUCKMAN

Colonel Summers Park

Lone Fir Cemetery

Vera Katz Esplanade

Hawthorne Bridge

Marquam Bridge

Willamette River

Ladd Circle Square Park

Ladd's Circle and Rose Garden

Rose Garden

HOSFORD-ABERNETHY

SEE MAP 1

Ross Island Bridge

Ross Island

SOUTH PORTLAND

SEE MAP 5

Tom McCall Waterfront Park

Morrison Bridge

Burnside Bridge

SIGHTS
16 LONE FIR CEMETERY	27 VERA KATZ ESPLANADE	55 LADD'S CIRCLE AND ROSE GARDEN

RESTAURANTS
1	THE FARM CAFÉ	17	WILD ABANDON	34	SEL GRIS
2	LE PIGEON	18	KEN'S ARTISAN PIZZA	53	APIZZA SCHOLLS
8	LE BISTRO MONTAGE	19	BAMBOO SUSHI	62	DOT'S CAFÉ
10	CLARKLEWIS	33	CAFÉ CASTAGNA	65	CLAY'S SMOKEHOUSE

70	YOKO'S JAPANESE RESTAURANT
71	WY'EAST PIZZA

NIGHTLIFE
4	DOUG FIR	14	EASTBURN	54	SAPPHIRE HOTEL
9	LE BISTRO MONTAGE	20	THE GOODFOOT	57	ALADDIN THEATER
11	BEAKER & FLASK	25	HORSE BRASS PUB	59	BAR AVIGNON
12	HOLOCENE	30	LUCKY LABRADOR	60	NIGHT LIGHT LOUNGE
				61	REEL 'M INN

63	DOTS
67	THE EGYPTIAN CLUB
68	VICTORY BAR
69	HOPWORKS URBAN BREWERY

HOTELS
5	JUPITER HOTEL	32	THE CECILIA	36	HAWTHORNE HOSTEL	66	BLUEBIRD GUESTHOUSE

© AVALON TRAVEL

SEE MAP 3

LAURELHURST

Laurelhurst Park

SUNNYSIDE

RICHMOND

SEWallcrest Park

SOUTHEAST

Clinton Park

SEE MAP 5

DISTANCE ACROSS MAP
Approximate: 3.2 mi or 5.1 km

0   300 yds
0   300 m

To A 26 Mount Tabor

A ARTS AND LEISURE

6	CITYBIKES	29	WILLAMETTE JET BOAT
7	MILAGRO THEATRE		EXCURSIONS
26	MOUNT TABOR	31	NEWSPACE CENTER FOR
28	OREGON MUSEUM OF SCIENCE		PHOTOGRAPHY
	AND INDUSTRY	45	DO JUMP!

47 THE BAGDAD THEATER & PUB
64 CLINTON STREET THEATER

S SHOPS

3 CRAFTY WONDERLAND
13 FOOD FIGHT
15 MOXIE
21 MUSIC MILLENNIUM
22 POLLIWOG
23 NOUN
24 BELMONT SHOPPING DISTRICT
35 HAWTHORNE SHOPPING DISTRICT

37 MURDER BY THE BOOK
38 DOLLAR SCHOLAR
39 HOUSE OF VINTAGE
40 KIDS AT HEART
41 IMELDA'S AND LOUIE'S SHOES
42 LOCAL 35
43 JACKPOT RECORDS
44 PRESENTS OF MIND
46 BUFFALO EXCHANGE

48 GREG'S
49 PASTAWORKS
50 POWELL'S HOME AND GARDEN
51 MUSE ART & DESIGN
52 ELLA+SAM
56 WINN PERRY
58 EDELWEISS

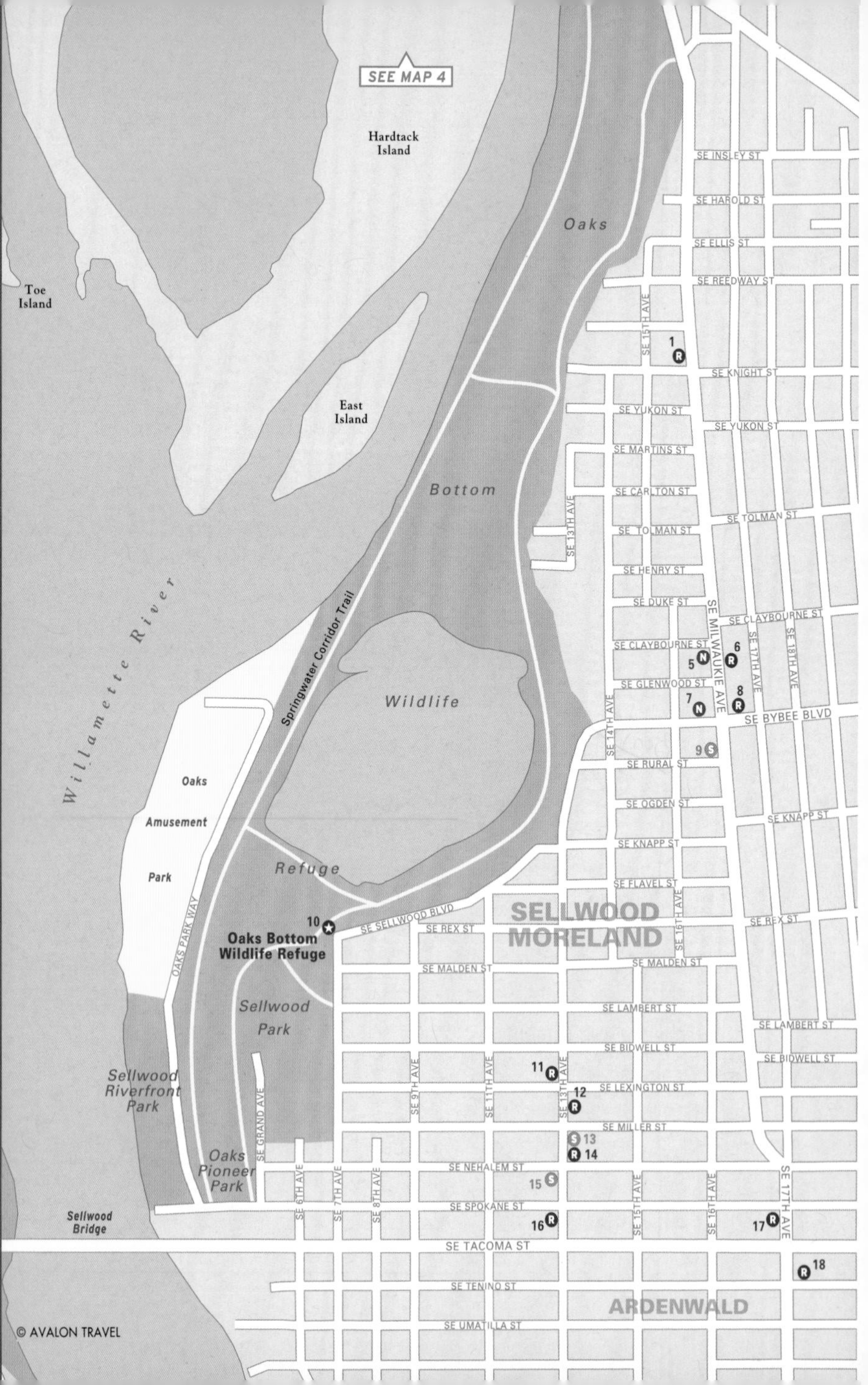

MAP 5

SEE MAP 4

Hardtack
Island

Oaks

Toe
Island

East
Island

Bottom

SE INSLEY ST

SE HAROLD ST

SE ELLIS ST

SE REEDWAY ST

1 R

SE KNIGHT ST

SE YUKON ST   SE YUKON ST

SE MARTINS ST

SE CARLTON ST

SE TOLMAN ST   SE TOLMAN ST

SE HENRY ST

SE DUKE ST

SE CLAYBOURNE ST

SE CLAYBOURNE ST

5 S   6 R

7 N   8

SE GLENWOOD ST

SE BYBEE BLVD

9 S

SE RURAL ST

SE OGDEN ST

SE KNAPP ST

SE KNAPP ST

SE FLAVEL ST

SE REX ST

**SELLWOOD
MORELAND**

Springwater Corridor Trail

Wildlife

Refuge

Willamette River

Oaks

Amusement

Park

10 ✪
**Oaks Bottom
Wildlife Refuge**

SE SELLWOOD BLVD

SE REX ST

SE MALDEN ST   SE MALDEN ST

*Sellwood
Park*

SE LAMBERT ST

SE LAMBERT ST

SE BIDWELL ST

SE BIDWELL ST

*Sellwood
Riverfront
Park*

11 R

SE LEXINGTON ST

12 R

SE MILLER ST

*Oaks
Pioneer
Park*

13 S
14 R

SE NEHALEM ST

15 S

SE SPOKANE ST

16 R

17 R

*Sellwood
Bridge*

SE TACOMA ST

R 18

SE TENINO ST

ARDENWALD

SE UMATILLA ST

SE 6TH AVE
SE 7TH AVE
SE 8TH AVE
SE 9TH AVE
SE 11TH AVE
SE 13TH AVE
SE 15TH AVE
SE 17TH AVE
SE 19TH AVE
SE GRAND AVE
OAKS PARK WAY
SE MILWAUKIE AVE

SEE MAP 4

REED

SE STEELE ST

99

SE 28TH AVE

SE 32ND AVE

SE 34TH AVE

SE INSLEY ST

SE HAROLD CT

SE 37TH AVE

SE 38TH AVE

SE 39TH S

Crystal
Springs Pond

Reed College

To R 4 Delta Café

SE WOODSTOCK BLVD

Crystal Springs
Rhododendron Garden

3

SE MARTINS ST

SE REED COLLEGE PL

SE 34TH AVE

SE MARTINS ST

SE 28TH AVE

SE CARLTON ST

SE MCLOUGHLIN BLVD

Crystal
Springs
Lake

SE 28TH AVE

SE CARLTON ST

SE TOLMAN ST

SE 23RD AVE

SE MARTINS ST

SE 29TH AVE

SE 31ST AVE

SE 32ND AVE

SE HENRY ST

SE 38TH AVE

Eastmoreland
Golf Course

SE TOLMAN ST

SE 30TH AVE

SE CLAYBOURNE ST

A 2

SE GLENWOOD ST

SE COOPER ST

Berkley Park

SIGHTS
3 CRYSTAL SPRINGS RHODODENDRON GARDEN
10 ◪ OAKS BOTTOM WILDLIFE REFUGE

RESTAURANTS
1   PAPA HAYDN
4   DELTA CAFÉ
6   FAT ALBERT'S
8   SABURO'S
11 GARDEN STATE
12 JADE TEAHOUSE & PATISSERIE
14 MEKONG VIETNAMESE GRILL
16 GINO'S
17 BERTIE LOU'S
18 MIKE'S DRIVE-IN

NIGHTLIFE
5   THE WOODS
7   OAKS BOTTOM PUBLIC HOUSE

ARTS AND LEISURE
2   EASTMORELAND GOLF COURSE
    AND DRIVING RANGE

SHOPS
9   HAGGIS MCBAGGIS
13 SPIELWERK COMMUNITY TOYSTORE
15 GREENLOOP
15 SOCK DREAMS

SE BYBEE BLVD

SE RURAL ST

SE OGDEN ST

SE KNAPP ST

SE FLAVEL ST

SE REX ST

SE MALDEN ST

SE 38TH AVE

SE 37TH AVE

SE NEHALEM ST

SE CRYSTAL SPRINGS BLVD

SE TENINO ST

Westmoreland
Park

SE 20TH AVE

SE 21ST AVE

SE 22ND AVE

SE 27TH AVE

SE MCLOUGHLIN BLVD

SE 21ST AVE

SE 22ND AVE

SE 23RD AVE

SE TACOMA ST

SE 28TH AVE

99

Tideman
Johnson
Park

0   300 yds

0   300 m

DISTANCE ACROSS MAP
Approximate: 2.2 mi or 3.5 km

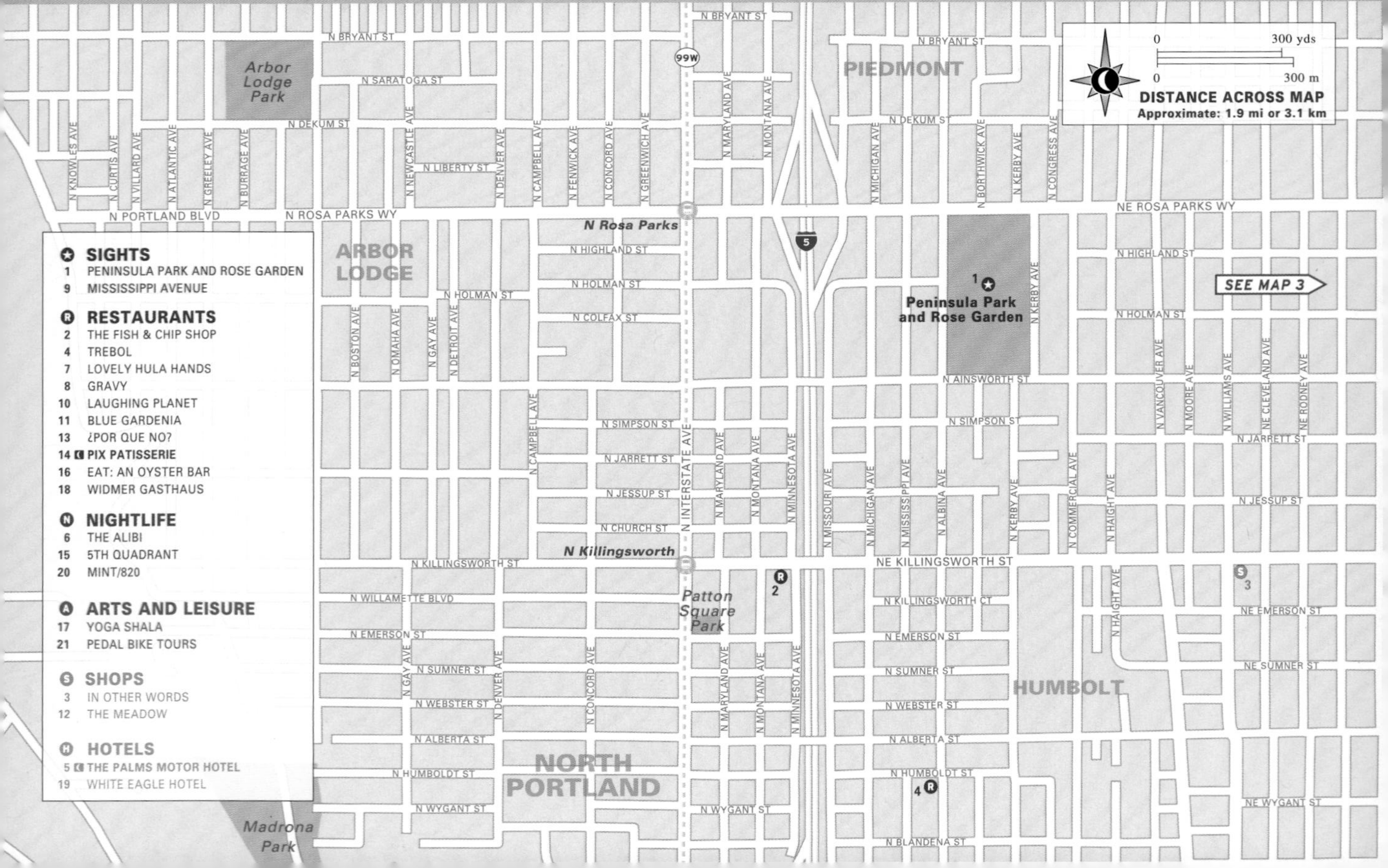

SIGHTS
1 PENINSULA PARK AND ROSE GARDEN
9 MISSISSIPPI AVENUE
RESTAURANTS
2 THE FISH & CHIP SHOP
4 TREBOL
7 LOVELY HULA HANDS
8 GRAVY
10 LAUGHING PLANET
11 BLUE GARDENIA
13 ¿POR QUE NO?
14 PIX PATISSERIE
16 EAT: AN OYSTER BAR
18 WIDMER GASTHAUS
NIGHTLIFE
6 THE ALIBI
15 5TH QUADRANT
20 MINT/820
ARTS AND LEISURE
17 YOGA SHALA
21 PEDAL BIKE TOURS
SHOPS
3 IN OTHER WORDS
12 THE MEADOW
HOTELS
5 THE PALMS MOTOR HOTEL
19 WHITE EAGLE HOTEL
0 300 yds
0 300 m
DISTANCE ACROSS MAP
Approximate: 1.9 mi or 3.1 km
SEE MAP 3
PIEDMONT
ARBOR LODGE
HUMBOLT
NORTH PORTLAND
Arbor Lodge Park
Peninsula Park and Rose Garden
Patton Square Park
Madrona Park
N Rosa Parks
N Killingsworth
99W
5
N BRYANT ST
N SARATOGA ST
N DEKUM ST
N LIBERTY ST
N PORTLAND BLVD
N ROSA PARKS WY
NE ROSA PARKS WY
N HIGHLAND ST
N HOLMAN ST
N COLFAX ST
N AINSWORTH ST
N SIMPSON ST
N JARRETT ST
N JESSUP ST
N CHURCH ST
N KILLINGSWORTH ST
NE KILLINGSWORTH ST
N KILLINGSWORTH CT
N WILLAMETTE BLVD
N EMERSON ST
NE EMERSON ST
N SUMNER ST
NE SUMNER ST
N WEBSTER ST
N ALBERTA ST
N HUMBOLDT ST
N WYGANT ST
NE WYGANT ST
N BLANDENA ST
N KNOWLES AVE
N CURTIS AVE
N VILLARD AVE
N ATLANTIC AVE
N GREELEY AVE
N BURRAGE AVE
N NEWCASTLE AVE
N BOSTON AVE
N OMAHA AVE
N GAY AVE
N DETROIT AVE
N DENVER AVE
N CAMPBELL AVE
N FENWICK AVE
N CONCORD AVE
N GREENWICH AVE
N INTERSTATE AVE
N MARYLAND AVE
N MONTANA AVE
N MINNESOTA AVE
N MISSOURI AVE
N MICHIGAN AVE
N MISSISSIPPI AVE
N ALBINA AVE
N BORTHWICK AVE
N KERBY AVE
N CONGRESS AVE
N COMMERCIAL AVE
N HAIGHT AVE
N VANCOUVER AVE
N MOORE AVE
N WILLIAMS AVE
NE CLEVELAND AVE
NE RODNEY AVE

SEE MAP 3

SEE MAP 2

ELIOT

ROSE

OVERLOOK

NORTHWEST

Unthank Park

Dawson Park

Lillis Albina Park

Overlook Park

Mississippi Avenue

Albina/Mississippi

Legacy Emanuel Hospital

Willamette River

N MISSISSIPPI AVE
N ALBINA AVE
N BORTHWICK AVE
N KERBY AVE
N GANTENBEIN AVE
N VANCOUVER AVE
N WILLIAMS AVE
N RODNEY AVE
NE CLEVELAND AVE
N HAIGHT AVE
N COMMERCIAL AVE
N MICHIGAN AVE
N MISSOURI AVE
N MONTANA AVE
N INTERSTATE AVE
N OVERLOOK BLVD
N MASSACHUSETTS AVE
N GREELEY AVE
N OVERLOOK TER
N OVERLOOK BLVD
N MASON ST
N SKIDMORE ST
N GOING ST
N PRESCOTT ST
N SHAVER ST
N FAILING ST
N BEECH ST
N FREMONT ST
N IVY ST
N FARGO ST
N KNOTT ST
NE KNOTT ST
NE STANTON ST
NE MORRIS ST
NE MONROE ST
NE FARGO ST
NE COOK ST
N GRAHAM ST
N RUSSELL ST
N PAGE ST
N ROSS AVE
N FLINT AVE
N RIVER ST
N CHANNEL AVE
N PRESCOTT ST
N SKIDMORE CT
N CONCORD AVE
N COLONIAL AVE
N LONGVIEW AVE
N GOING ST
RIVER ST
N PORT CENTER WAY
NW FRONT AVE
NW REED ST
NW NICOLAI ST
NW SHERLOCK AVE
NW 21ST AVE

5
405
99W
30

© AVALON TRAVEL

205

14

E PLAIN MILL BLVD

Lemon Island

NE AIRPORT WAY

NE MARINE DR

To 9 McMenamins Edgefield
and 10 Rooster Rock

84

205

8

NE GLISAN ST

NE STARK ST

SE STARK ST

213

11
The Grotto

To 36 Glendover
Golf Club

84

CASCADE HWY

Columbia River

Marine Park

Portland
International
Airport

30

30

Rose City
Golf Course

Washington
Oregon

NE COLUMBIA BLVD

NE KILLINGSWORTH ST

Portland

NE FREMONT ST

NE SANDY BLVD

Laurelhurst
Park

14

NE COLUMBIA BLVD

NE 33RD AVE

Hayden
Island

NORTH
PORTLAND

NE BROADWAY

E BURNSIDE ST

NORTHEAST

84

SE STARK ST

1

5

East
Delta
Park

Portland
Meadows
Race Track

NE MLK JR BLVD

99

5

Vancouver

50

30

30

5

N INTERSTATE AVE

99W

405

Smith
Lake

4
Multnomah
County
Fairgrounds

Portland
International
Raceway

6
Paul Bunyan
Statue

N LOMBARD ST

Willamette River

NORTHWEST

Heron Lakes
Golf Club 3

N COLUMBIA BLVD

Portland
17 18 Japanese
16 Garden

Bybee
Lake

N MARINE DR

30

University of
Portland

Forest
Park
4 13 14

Adams
Park

International 16
Rose Test
Garden

2

Smith
and Bybee
Lakes Park

30

Macleary
Park

Pittock Mansion 15

Holman 12
Park

NORTHWEST
HEIGHTS

Forest
Park

NW ST HELENS RD

West
Haven

30

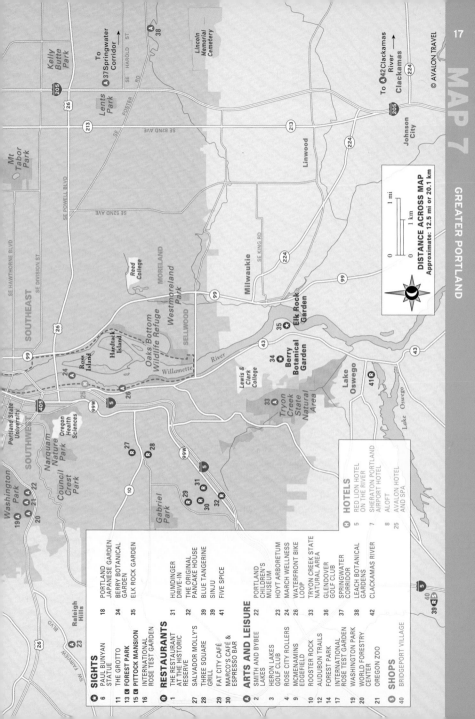

Discover Portland

"What's the deal with Portland?" That seems to be the question these days with everyone from the Food Network to the *New York Times* knocking on the door to the Rose City. *Travel + Leisure* magazine recently noted that Portland is a "peculiar utopia that believes in both unbridled sensuality and the notion that doing good actually makes people happy."

The truth is, Portland is a vibrant city full of passionate and creative people supportive of each other and the town's overarching artistic ecosystem. The motto of the city government is "The City That Works," which seems silly, but Portlanders really do know how to get things done.

People flock to the city to immerse themselves in the lively visual, music, and performing arts scenes. Artists, playwrights, actors, and musicians have made this city a bohemian playground, rich with color, opulence, and inspiration.

More and more, visitors are heading to Portland for its unique personality and hospitable style. Frankly, it's hard not to feel like a local when you visit P-Town. Thanks in part to its pioneering ancestors, Portland has all the stimulation and excitement of a big city and all the charm of a small town.

From the urban delights of the downtown Cultural District to the unspoiled wilderness of Forest Park, each corner of this DIY-centric city is bursting with that distinctive P-Town energy. From the coffee shops and thrift stores of Hawthorne to the lounges and boutiques of the Pearl District, each neighborhood possesses its own unique voice, all of which lend themselves to the whimsical carnival choir of this dynamic city.

Planning Your Trip

► WHERE TO GO

Downtown
Many of Portland's galleries and performing arts venues are in the heart of downtown, in an area known as the Cultural District. To the north, at the edge of downtown that abuts Washington Park, is Goose Hollow. To the south is Portland's oldest neighborhood, Old Town, home to a number of great nightclubs and restaurants, as well as Chinatown and the beautiful Classical Chinese Garden.

Northwest and the Pearl District
Whether you're in the Pearl District or strolling NW 23rd Avenue, the northwest side of Portland is a shopper's paradise and the city's most fashionable spot for galleries, restaurants, boutiques, and urban living. Farther north, you'll find the area interchangeably known as Nob Hill or the Alphabet District, an immensely walkable area that is home to a number of Portland's most chic boutiques and trendy restaurants.

Northeast
In the midst of modern condos snuggled nicely with historic Victorian homes is the Alberta Arts District, where there are blocks of art galleries, studios, and restaurants. The Irvington District is where you'll find the Rose Garden Arena, Lloyd Center, and the Oregon Convention Center. To the north is the Hollywood District, with an iconic Byzantine-style movie theater, several burger shops, and international restaurants.

Southeast
Home of the hipster set and much of Portland's "creative class," the Southeast is a vibrant and wildly diverse sector. Hawthorne and its sister street, Belmont, are chock full of restaurants and shops that are off the beaten path; Clinton Street, a six-block section of Southeast Portland, also houses a remarkably large number of locally favored stops.

This sign marks one of the many entrances to Portland's Saturday Market in Old Town.

Cathedral Park in North Portland, under the grand St. John's Bridge

Sellwood and Moreland

Rounding out the farthest edges of Southeast Portland are Sellwood and Moreland, two smaller areas collectively known as Antique Row, thanks to the large concentration of vintage and antiques shops that inhabit them.

North Portland

The newest P-Town darling, NoPo is the affordable, eclectic home to many of Portland's imaginative newcomers. The influx of artistic energy has made for some remarkable transformations in the area, bringing fun brewpubs, unique dining options, and several popular bars. A vibrant, youthful counterculture continuously injects the area with originality and enthusiasm.

▶ WHEN TO GO

Contrary to popular belief, it is not always raining in Portland. In fact, the metro area experiences less average rainfall per year than Atlanta, Birmingham, Houston, Indianapolis, or Seattle. If you want to avoid the rainy season, skip it in November, December, and January. If you don't mind getting a little wet, those months are great times to secure cheap hotel rates and catch seasonal attractions like ZooLights, Fall Crush, and the new works theater festival, Fertile Ground.

The best time for you to visit depends largely on what you plan to do when you are here. Ski season is often at its height between January and March, while summer (June through September) is a great time to come experience the city's open-air markets, gardens, and festivals, as temperatures tend to top out at 80–100°F (27–38°C) and days are often clear and dry.

The Willamette River is the dividing line between the east and west sides of the city.

Explore Portland

▶ THE THREE-DAY BEST OF PORTLAND

While you could easily spend a week in Portland without venturing over the bridge, you can pack a lot of the city's charms into a three-day sampler trip. Save money by skipping a rental car—you can access most of these places using public transportation or your own two feet.

Day 1

▶ Start your day with a crash course in Portland culture. First head to Mother's Bistro & Bar for some cornflake-crusted French toast, eggs Benedict, and Stumptown coffee.

▶ Next, embark on The Best of Portland Walking Tour from Downtown. The 2.5-hour tour will give you the lowdown on Portland's history, landscape, and most notable spots.

▶ Afterward, check out what can easily be considered the holiest of all holy for book

Powell's City of Books

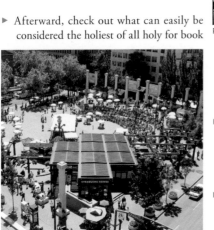
Thousands gather for a free lunchtime concert in Pioneer Courthouse Square.

lovers, Powell's City of Books. Pick up a book (or 12) and order a sandwich and a latte from the café downstairs.

▶ Just two blocks north, you will discover The Armory, home of Portland Center Stage, where you just might be able to catch a world premiere.

▶ Pick up tickets from the box office and then head out into the Pearl District for preshow dinner at 50 Plates, where they give classic American dishes a chic new life.

A cyclist makes his way across the Burnside Bridge.

Day 2

▶ Want to explore the weird side of Portland? Start your day by taking the MAX or walking down to SW 3rd Avenue to the little hole-in-a-brick-wall that is Voodoo Doughnut. Grab yourself a Portland (a.k.a. Boston) Crème or a Bacon Maple Bar and discover what they mean when they say, "The magic is in the hole."

▶ From there, you are mere steps away from the Portland Saturday Market, an open-air extravaganza that runs between March and December and operates on Sundays as well. Watch some live music as you grab lunch in the Saturday Market food court.

▶ After lunch, take a load off as you tour through Old Town and Chinatown in a PDX Pedicab, a rickshaw-style cab that is powered by street-savvy Portlanders.

▶ When the sun goes down, head to Le Pigeon, where being a carnivore is practically a religion. Sip on a glass of Belle Pente Pinot Noir as you dig into your beef cheek Bourguignon.

▶ After dinner, embrace the oddity of The Woods, a live music venue and bar converted from a funeral parlor.

Day 3

▶ What better way to spend your last day in the city than by getting out of it? Take a cab to NW 23rd Avenue and NW Thurman, or take the Portland Streetcar to NW 23rd and NW Marshall. Load up on coffee and pastries from St. Honoré Boulangerie.

▶ From there, there are many access points at which you can enter Forest Park and explore the numerous trails.

▶ After your hike, head back to NW 23rd Avenue, where you'll find some of the

THE ART OF PORTLAND

The Portland Art Museum is the oldest art museum in the Pacific Northwest.

- **Alberta Arts District:** A monthly art walk is a great opportunity to explore this area. Handmade accessories, trinkets, and art abound every few steps down Alberta Street.

- **Art in the Pearl:** This monthly art walk in the Pearl District is a perfect place to wander from gallery to gallery without feeling the pressure to buy something.

- **Bullseye Gallery:** Walk through the large wooden doors of this gallery and you will see some real eye candy. This gallery, which focuses on international artists in the field of kiln-formed glass, is filled with colorful, unique pieces.

- **Cargo:** This enormous import store just screams to be photographed. In every nook, you will find treasures, trinkets, fabrics, and art in a bold array of colors.

- **Museum of Contemporary Craft:** This museum is an awesome celebration of all things handmade. It is the sort of art you can touch, hold, and purchase. Explore both floors and then just try to suppress the desire to make art out of household objects.

- **Portland Art Museum:** There's a lot to see here, so take your time exploring the 112,000 square feet of art, sculpture, and exhibits that range from European Impressionism to contemporary pieces.

- **Real Mother Goose:** This store is devoted to American crafts like colorful art glass, gorgeous ceramics, jewelry, artisan furniture, and sculptural works. It's a great place to simply explore or purchase unique gifts, as everything is handcrafted and beautiful.

- **Redux:** If walking into this store – chock full of locally made jewelry, art, and accessories – doesn't inspire you to create, it will at least inspire you to up the ante on your style.

WHERE TO SPEND A RAINY DAY

Having fun while staying dry is no problem in a town that is used to about 36 inches of rainfall per year. When things get wet, Portlanders head for **Powell's City of Books** (1005 W. Burnside St., 503/228-4651, www.powells.com) and get lost among the million books. The friendly staff doesn't mind at all if you simply want to browse, read, and ride out the storm.

For those who would rather not sit still, there are plenty of options. Head to **Portland Rock Gym** (21 NE 12th Ave., 503/232-8310, www.portlandrockgym.com) if you're feeling like you might start climbing the walls lest you get some exercise, or to **Ground Kontrol** (511 NW Couch St., 503/796-9364, www.groundkontrol.com) if your idea of being active is getting to the 200th level of Galaga.

If you'd like to take in a little culture, spend the afternoon strolling through the 112,000 square feet of gallery space at the **Portland Art Museum** (1219 SW Park Ave., 503/226-2811, www.pam.org). Or catch an afternoon matinee at either **Portland Center Stage** (128 NW 11th Ave., 503/445-3700, www.pcs.org) or the **Artists Repertory Theatre** (1516 SW Alder St., 503/241-1278, www.artistsrep.org). Many of the area theater companies have afternoon showings for discounted prices, as do a number of the historic movie houses, such as **The Bagdad Theater & Pub** (3702 SE Hawthorne Blvd., 503/225-5555, www.mcmenamins.com), which allows you the luxury of watching a film while sipping beer or wine and noshing on pizza.

The Bagdad Theater & Pub

city's most unique shops and restaurants. Check out the bath bombs at Lush Cosmetics and imagine soaking your sore muscles later, or try on some killer heels at Zelda's Shoe Bar.

▶ When you are ready for dinner, Paley's Place on NW 21st Avenue is one of the best spots in town for fresh Northwest cuisine. Round out your meal with a bottle of Oregon Pinot Noir and the specially selected cheese course.

▶ If you aren't ready to call it a night, head across the street to Bartini for cocktails. When you're finished, you're just steps away from the streetcar stop that will take you back downtown.

SIGHTS

Mother Nature spoils us rotten in these parts. Native Portlanders are accustomed to a life alongside the lush and colorful backdrop of trees, flowers, and rolling rivers. However, that is not to say that we take it for granted. Most residents will tell you that one of the reasons they love this city so much is for its proximity to some of the nation's most beautiful scenery.

If you are a nature lover, you are in luck. Portland is home to a number of peaceful wildlife areas like Oaks Bottom and Forest Park. Cultural gardens provide tranquility amid the sort of art that can't be found in a gallery, and botanical retreats allow respite from the bustling city. These little pockets of nature are only part of what makes Portland so unique. It is a key facet of the city's sparkle, in fact, for life in Portland is not often defined by what people do, but by what they create. Ask someone what he or she does for a living and they are more likely to say, "I am a fire dancer," then they are to say, "I am an accountant." And since inspiration reigns supreme, it makes sense that art springs out of the grey city blocks in unexpected places like the Vera Katz Esplanade, Pioneer Courthouse Square, or the facade of a restaurant. When creativity is king, it makes sense that the historical mingles with the avant-garde and that one of the nation's largest urban forests is mere moments outside of downtown.

Of course, the star of the show in P-Town is the originality. The instinct to create something out of nothing is a feeling that dates back to the founders of the city, who valued

SIGHTS

HIGHLIGHTS

LOOK FOR ((TO FIND RECOMMENDED SIGHTS.

((**Best Place to Find a Zen Moment:** Right in the middle of Old Town, the **Portland Classical Chinese Garden** is an oasis of quiet beauty. The walled garden occupies approximately 40,000 square feet and was influenced by many of the famous classical gardens in Suzhou, China (page 32).

((**Best Place to Get Lost:** If heaven were a library, it would look a lot like **Powell's City of Books,** the independent bookstore that occupies an entire city block. With more than one million new, used, and rare books under one roof, you'll need a map to find your way through (page 32).

((**Best Place to Contemplate the Past:** Amidst the bustle of Southeast Portland, you will find **Lone Fir Cemetery,** a quiet, ethereal spot where more than 25,000 of Portland's dead have been lain to rest. More park than graveyard, the 30-plus acre arboretum holds some pretty dark secrets (page 35).

((**Best Place to Spot a Blue Heron:** Hawks, ducks, woodpeckers, and kestrels are just some of the wildlife that inhabit **Oaks Bottom Wildlife Refuge,** a 140-acre floodplain wetland that is considered a bird-watcher's paradise (page 36).

((**Best Place to Hug a Tree:** If you think Central Park in New York is big, check out **Forest Park,** which stretches across 5,100 acres of hills, trails, streams, and spots of old-growth forest, much of which overlooks the beautiful Willamette River (page 38).

((**Best Place to Develop House Envy:** The beautiful and stately **Pittock Mansion** is an amazing French Renaissance chateau in the West Hills of the city, and was the former home of the original publisher of *The Oregonian* (page 40).

© CHRISTOFFER JON

These steps lead up to a stone house which was once a public restroom, but is now a popular place to rest while hiking through the 5,100 acres of Forest Park.

imagination over the idea of building something on the backs of those who had come before them. Still today, Portlanders are known for their scrappy, do-it-yourself creative culture, and that instinct is reflected through all quadrants of the city in the form of art, nature, architecture, and urban planning. From the chilling beauty of Lone Fir Cemetery and the historical elegance of Pittock Mansion to the glittering opulence of the Pearl District and the wooded hills of Forest Park, Portland has a number of must-see sights.

Downtown   Map 1

ANKENY PLAZA

SW Ankeny St. and SW Naito Pkwy., 503/823-2223
HOURS: Daily, 24 hours
COST: Free

Before Pioneer Square became "Portland's living room," Ankeny Plaza was considered the heart of Portland commerce. Built by Captain Alexander Ankeny after an 1872 fire devastated the region, Ankeny Plaza (also known as Ankeny Square) has housed a number of retail businesses, public marketplaces, and performance spaces over the years. When first opened, it was known as the New Market Theater. The area is a popular spot for photographers hoping to capture some of Portland's most historic facades thanks to its ornate pilasters, pediments, and cornices. In fact, the Victorian Italianate masonry and grand cast-iron columns that surround the equally iconic Skidmore Fountain are considered to be largest and best-preserved group of such architecture in the American West.

CENTRAL LIBRARY

801 SW 10th Ave., 503/988-5123, www.multcolib.org
HOURS: Mon. 10 A.M.-6 P.M., Tues.-Wed. 10 A.M.-8 P.M., Thurs.-Sat. 10 A.M.-6 P.M., Sun. noon-5 P.M.
COST: Free

This Georgian Revival landmark was built in 1903 by A. E. Doyle and bears the names of famous historians, philosophers, scientists, and artists etched along its outer walls and benches, and the interior is no less impressive. Renovated in the mid-1990s, the library boasts a number of awe-inspiring elements, such as lofty, arched ceilings and windows and the grand, intricately etched black granite staircase. The Beverly Cleary Children's Library, named for the author who wrote her beloved Ramona books about growing up on Portland's Klickitat Street, houses a 14-foot bronze "Tree of Knowledge" sculpture by artists Dana Lynn Lewis and Barbara Eiswerth. Its trunk is a menagerie of toys, animals, storybook characters, and musical instruments that both children and adults love to explore while enjoying a little structured (or unstructured) story time. Climb the sweeping staircase to the third floor and you'll find the Collins Gallery, which hosts regular recitals, poetry readings, community events, and frequent educational and artistic exhibits.

True to its Oregonian style, however, the library is not only committed to preserving history, but also to protecting the environment. In 2008, Central Library also became the first library in Oregon to construct an "eco-roof," in response to the growing need for green spaces amid urban growth. Besides extending the overall life of the roof and providing a habitat for wildlife, the eco-roof reduces rain runoff by 70 percent. If you are interested in learning more, the library provides 20-minute guided tours of the eco-roof on Tuesdays and Saturdays. You can register for the tours online or by calling 503/988-5234.

IRA KELLER FOUNTAIN

SW 3rd Ave. and SW Clay St.
HOURS: Daily 5 A.M.-midnight
COST: Free

Just outside the Civic Auditorium is an enormous fountain built in honor of Ira C. Keller, a Portland civic leader and the first chairman of the Portland Development Commission (PDC), who is credited with pushing through much of the urban renewal work that happened during his time on the PDC. The grand two-level fountain is designed to mimic the falls and cataracts of the Cascade Range, and provide a peaceful white noise to diminish the sounds of the city. It's a popular spot for afternoon business traffic, where people go to unwind or just cool off.

MILL ENDS PARK

SW Naito Pkwy. and SW Taylor St.
HOURS: Daily, 24 hours
COST: Free

There are more than 9,000 acres of park space in the Portland metropolitan area—and some areas are so big you can forget that you are in the city. Mill Ends Park could be that kind of escape—providing you're the size of an ant. Noted in the *Guinness Book of World Records* as the world's smallest park, Mill Ends occupies only 452 square inches (yes, inches) and measures just two feet across. As the story goes, Dick Fagan, a columnist for the now defunct *Oregon Journal* spotted a leprechaun from his window that overlooked what is now Naito Parkway. He raced out to capture the creature and upon doing so, wished for a park of his own. The clever leprechaun granted the wish, but since Fagan had been unspecific as to the size of park he wanted, he was given the small patch of dirt upon which the capture had taken place.

Fairy tales aside, Mill Ends Park was named an official park on St. Patrick's Day in 1971. Over the years, a number of curious "contributions" have shown up, such as a tiny swimming pool (complete with diving board), a Ferris wheel, and several miniature statues.

OLD CHURCH

1422 SW 11th Ave., 503/222-2031, www.oldchurch.org
HOURS: Wed. noon-1 P.M., or by arrangement
COST: Free

The Calvary Presbyterian Church was erected in 1883, thanks to the help of architect Warren H. Williams, who donated his designs for the Victorian-style Carpenter Gothic building. It cost a total of $36,000 to build and included a number of elegant touches, like the ornate window traceries, archways, chimneys, buttresses, and spires. One key feature is the "wedding ring," which is nestled on the bell tower, and the recently rebuild porte cochere at the Clay Street entrance. Nowadays, the building is referred to simply as the Old Church, and serves as a secular place for meetings, weddings, concerts, and events. The building opens its doors each Wednesday for a free lunchtime concert, which is a great time to check out the cast-iron Corinthian columns, hand-carved fir pews, and elaborate stained-glass windows.

PARK BLOCKS

SW Park Ave. from SW Salmon St. to SW Jackson St. and NW Park Ave. from SW Ankeny St. to NW Glisan St.
HOURS: Daily 5 A.M.-10 P.M.
COST: Free

In the midst of Portland's Downtown Cultural District are the 18 collective blocks that make up the North and South Park Blocks. The area is sprinkled with some of Portland's most interesting pieces of public art, like the 12-foot-tall father-and-son elephant statue that honors a piece from the late Shang Dynasty (circa 1200–1100 BC) and the 18-foot-tall representation of Rough Rider Teddy Roosevelt.

The land to the south was donated to the public in 1852 by Daniel H. Lownsdale, who hoped that it would become a promenade, a "cathedral of trees with a simple grass floor." Nowadays, the area is a popular gathering place for Portland State University students or the downtown workforce who wish to eat their lunch under the 100-plus Lombardy poplars and elms. It is also the home of one of the city's popular farmers markets (www.portlandfarmersmarket.org) on Wednesdays and Saturdays.

To the north, you'll find six blocks lined with bigleaf maples, black locusts, and American elms. A popular place for both rest and recreation, the North Park Blocks contain a playground, basketball court, and bocce ball area, as well as a popular fountain, the *Portland Dog*

Bowl, designed by famed weimaraner photographer William Wegman.

PIONEER COURTHOUSE SQUARE

City block bounded by SW Morrison St., SW 6th Ave., SW Yamhill St., and SW Broadway, 503/223-1613, www.pioneercourthousesquare.org

HOURS: Daily, 24 hours

COST: Free

The true heart of Portland is the area affectionately known as "Portland's living room." Occupying 40,000 square feet of the downtown Cultural District, Pioneer Square is the nucleus where performance and function come together. It's a fashionable spot for locals on lunch breaks, who head for the square to grab a bite from one of the popular food carts, engage in some people-watching, or perhaps just unwind with a book.

The square also contains a number of art pieces, like the iconic P-Town statue entitled *Allow Me,* which features a well-dressed gentleman extending his hand to you while holding an umbrella, and the *Weather Machine,* which opens each day at noon to announce the weather amid trumpet fanfare and flashing lights.

Chess games often crop up on the Morrison corner of the square where, in 2003, Soderstrom Architects built three bronze chessboards atop what appear to be fallen columns. During the summer months, local chess clubs and game enthusiasts meet here (instead of at pubs and coffeehouses) for alfresco matches, and it's not uncommon for crowds to gather as they wait for the nearby MAX train.

Whether you're catching a concert, attending a festival, or just catching a glimpse of some of the locals at play, be sure to check out one of the lesser-known novelties of the square: the echo chamber. The chamber, on the western side facing Morrison, is really more like a tiny circular amphitheatre. If you stand on the small center circle (a.k.a. the Sweet Spot) and speak, your voice will reverberate back to you as if amplified to a massive stadium. Remarkably, the sound of your voice remains unchanged to anyone except you.

PORTLANDIA

1120 SW 5th Ave.

HOURS: Daily, 24 hours

COST: Free

Like a sentinel over the city, *Portlandia* sits as inconspicuously as a 35-foot-tall woman can. Based on the city seal of Portland, which bears a woman as a representation of commerce, *Portlandia* was designed by sculptor Raymond Kaskey and is thought to be the second-largest repoussé statue in the United States (after the Statue of Liberty). *Portlandia* can seem both menacing and welcoming in different light, and although she is an iconic figure for the city, her image belongs to the sculptor (which is why you will not see key chains and miniatures of her as you will of Lady Liberty).

A plaque at the base of *Portlandia* bears a poem written by Portlander Ronald Talney:

She kneels down/and from the quietness/of copper/reaches out/We take that stillness/ into ourselves/and somewhere/deep in the earth/our breath/becomes her city.

SALMON STREET SPRINGS

SW Naito Pkwy. at SW Salmon St.

HOURS: Daily 5 A.M.-midnight

COST: Free

This Waterfront Park centerpiece cycles through an impressive 4,924 gallons of water per minute at full capacity, pushing (recycled) water through as many as 137 jets at one time. It is regulated by an underground computer, which switches between the three phases of the fountain. In the first setting, a light mist covers the center of the fountain, as if luring unsuspecting kids into the fray and thus setting them up for disaster. The second setting involves three circles of water, shooting up to resemble a wedding cake. The final setting is by far the most amusing and most dangerous, as water jets around the perimeter of the fountain activate and shoot inwards, creating a huge shower of water in the middle. It's this setting that tends to catch passersby and parents with cameras off guard, soaking them and knocking children to the ground.

Northwest and the Pearl District   Map 2

THE ARMORY

128 NW 11th Ave., 503/445-3700, www.pcs.org

HOURS: Tues.-Sun. 10 A.M.-1 hour post-show, Mon. by appointment only

COST: Free

Built in 1891 to house the Oregon National Guard, the First Regiment Armory Annex (a.k.a. Portland Armory) served as a home to soldiers during the Spanish-American War and World War I. It was opened to the public in the early 1900s when the castle-like Romanesque Revival structure played host to operas, circuses, roller derbies, dances, boxing matches, and concerts. The building was one of only a few that could accommodate large crowds, as the truss system within the cavernous fortress allowed for unimpeded sightlines and free movement. Therefore, it served as the gathering spot where citizens heard speeches from the likes of Teddy Roosevelt, William Taft, and Woodrow Wilson.

In 2000, the Armory began a remarkable transformation when it was renovated (to the tune of $36.1 million) into an arts center that is now the permanent home of Portland Center Stage. Besides having two stages, a sprawling multilevel lobby, offices, work areas, and rehearsal spaces, the venue was the first on the National Register to receive platinum-level LEED certification for its sustainable design.

THE BREWERY BLOCKS

Between NW 10th Ave., NW 13th Ave., W Burnside St., and NW Davis St., www.breweryblocks.com

HOURS: Daily, 24 hours

COST: Free

One of Portland's many nicknames is Beervana, thanks in part to Henry Weinhard, who established his iconic brewery here in the mid-1850s. For years, the Blitz-Weinhard Brewery served as the cornerstone of this former industrial area; although it has been more than a decade since the sale of the brewery's property in 1999 ignited the development of Portland's glittering arts district, the Pearl, the beer giant's influence still shines through. The five blocks and 1.7 million square feet of gritty industrial space is now a mixed-use area sprinkled with luxury apartments, hip boutiques, and galleries, as well as a number of the city's favorite restaurants.

CHINATOWN GATE

NW 4th Ave. and W Burnside St.

HOURS: Daily, 24 hours

COST: Free

With its multiple roofs, 78 dragons, 58 mythical characters, and two huge lions, the Chinatown Gate represents more than 135 years of Chinese history in Oregon, and marks the official entrance to Chinatown. It's a popular place for photographs in an area that isn't always guidebook-presentable. The lions—Yin on the left side and Yang on the right—signify protection of the young and of the nation. The gate is both a beautiful landmark and a reminder of the era when Portland had the second-largest Chinese community in the United States. These days, Chinatown is compressed into just a few blocks, and with the exception of the gate, a few restaurants, shops, and grocery stores, much of the vibrancy the neighborhood saw in the 1890s is gone.

JAMESON SQUARE

810 NW 11th Ave., 503/823-7529, www.portlandonline.com/parks

HOURS: Daily 5 A.M.-midnight

COST: Free

When developers were planning the Pearl District in the early 1990s, they wanted to create a number of open gathering spaces within the urban sprawl. Located on the full city block between NW Johnson and NW Kearney, Jameson's real gem is the interactive fountain and tidal pool. It's a popular spot for families to gather in the heat of the summer. Children splash in the low pools and chase the ever-changing flow of water while their parents take advantage of the free Wi-Fi or chat with others.

WINTER SCHMINTER: 10 REASONS TO COME TO PORTLAND IN THE COLDER MONTHS

- **Coastal Storm-Watching:** Whether you head to the Columbia Gorge or the Oregon Coast, you're not far from some pretty spectacular storm-watching. Come January and February, there's nothing like holing up behind a grand picture window by a warm fire while Mother Nature puts on a show.

- **Fertile Ground Festival:** This annual festival of new works, which is held in January, is a fine example of why Portland is becoming a launch pad for creative and exciting new plays.

- **Holiday Ale Fest:** Toast the dark, cold month of December at the only beer festival in the Northwest to be held outdoors in Pioneer Courthouse Square. There are usually about 30–40 beers on tap, all of which are special-edition winter ales.

- **New Year's Eve with the Portland Winterhawks:** At the turn of every year, Portland's hockey team hosts the Seattle Thunderbirds in what can easily be categorized as a civil war. The game starts at 8 P.M. and is a good way to ring in the new year with the family.

- **Portland Jazz Festival:** The city of Portland has a long and vibrant jazz history. This annual multi-venue festival features headlining talent such as Wayne Shorter, McCoy Tyner, Dianne Reeves, Regina Carter, Tom Grant, and Eddie Palmieri, and a number of free showcase performances highlighting regional talent.

- **Santacon:** If you see hundreds of Santas parading the streets of Portland singing, shouting, and behaving badly, you have stumbled upon Santacon. This guerilla-style pub-crawl/march is all about creativity, spontaneity, and a little bit of harmless debauchery.

- **Ski Season:** Oregon has the longest ski season in North America thanks to all that precipitation. Putting up with a little rainfall in the city means an opportunity to carve some serious powder on the slopes of Mount Hood.

- **The Grotto:** More than half a million lights illuminate the National Sanctuary of Our Sorrowful Mother, a Catholic sanctuary that is more commonly called The Grotto. It's a breathtaking sight that you don't have to be Catholic (or celebrate Christmas) to enjoy.

- *The Nutcracker:* Every year, Portlanders know it's the holiday season when Oregon Ballet Theatre begins dancing *The Nutcracker.* The production is a holiday tradition that families flock to every year and is the only West Coast production of George Balanchine's version of the famous ballet.

- **ZooLights:** This annual holiday event is a delight. Each winter, the Oregon Zoo comes alive with thousands of lights, hundreds of musical groups, and the brightly lit Zoo Train. Stroll through after dark and see how active the animals are in the chilly night air.

The park is on the streetcar line and adjacent to a number of coffee shops, pizza joints, and other restaurants, so it's a great spot to grab a bite and do some people-watching—providing you like children, of course, since this park is a haven for shrieking, but happy, tykes.

JEAN VOLLUM NATURAL CAPITAL CENTER
721 NW 9th Ave., 503/227-6225, www.ecotrust.org/ncc

The Jean Vollum Natural Capital Center (also called the Ecotrust Building) was the first historic redevelopment in the United States to receive gold-level LEED certification from the U.S. Green Building Council. It's a mixed-use building that was originally built in 1895 and was redeveloped with a revolutionary focus on eco-friendly practices, materials, and design. Construction of this beautiful space was done with environmentally friendly materials like recycled paint, wheatboard cabinets, and rubber flooring made from recycled tires. Inside, you will find Patagonia, a clothing company that adheres to a strong environmental ethic, and a number of other like-minded businesses. It's a really pretty space and an innovative idea that has received a lot of attention. The public is welcome to wander through the atrium, mezzanine, and other public spaces, and visitors can also inquire about event space or ask about tours.

◖ PORTLAND CLASSICAL CHINESE GARDEN

NW 3rd Ave. and NW Everett St., 503/228-8131, www.portlandchinesegarden.org

HOURS: Apr. 1–Oct. 31 daily 10 A.M.–6 P.M., Nov. 1–Mar. 31 daily 10 A.M.–5 P.M.,

COST: $8.50 adult, $7.50 senior, $6.50 child, free for child under 5

Envisioned in 1988, when Portland and Suzhou, China, became sister cities, this Ming Dynasty scholar's garden opened in September 2000 and has since become an oasis for tranquility right in the heart of Old Town/Chinatown. A sanctuary devoted to the "five elements" (rock, water, flora, architecture, and words), the garden is an extraordinary landscape of blossoms, sculpture, and poetry that seems worlds away from the city. The majority of plants and materials contained within the garden's stone walls originated in China, including indigenous plants, limestone rocks from Lake Tai in Suzhou, and many types of fir, gingko, and China pine. The garden offers twice-daily guided tours at no extra cost and guests are encouraged to visit the Teahouse to experience Chinese tea presentations, along with traditional snacks and sweets.

PORTLAND VINTAGE TROLLEY

NW Glisan and NW 5th Ave., www.vintagetrolleys.com

HOURS: Sun. 10:33 A.M.–5:44 P.M.

COST: Free, donations accepted

If you would like to see the city for free, hop onto one of Portland's vintage trolleys. A 30-minute round-trip will take you from Union Station to Portland State University, hitting all the MAX stops along the way. The cars are newly constructed replicas of the streetcar that the J. G. Brill and Company supplied to Portland in 1904 and feature comfortable rattan seats with reversible backrests, carved oak interiors, brass handrails, and pull-down window shades. You can pick up the trolley at its 5th and Glisan stop, or at Portland State on SW 6th and Morrison.

◖ POWELL'S CITY OF BOOKS

1005 W. Burnside St., 503/228-4651, www.powells.com

HOURS: Daily 9 A.M.–11 P.M.

COST: Free

They don't call it a city of books for nothing. Occupying a full city block, Powell's is the largest independently owned new and used bookstore in the world. Within the walls of this bibliophile's dream, you can find a million new, used, rare, and out-of-print books. Grab a map as you enter or ask an employee to help you navigate the labyrinth of color-coded rooms. Grab a couple of locally produced zines or small press books and head to the on-site café for a cup of coffee. Whatever your preference, it is easy to lose hours exploring the shelves, listening to guest authors speak in the Pearl Room, or simply people watching. Since Powell's buys over 3,000 used books every day, they are almost guaranteed to have everything you are looking for and several things you didn't even know you wanted. The rare book room is especially inviting with its soft lighting, antique furniture, and dark wood shelves that house thousands of first editions, odd volumes, and books far older than Portland itself—some dating as far back as the 1400s.

UNION STATION

800 NW 6th Ave., 503/273-4865, www.amtrack.com

HOURS: Daily, 24 hours

COST: Free

In the early days of P-Town, Union Station served as a hub for import, export, and transportation, thus supporting the movement of livestock, timber, produce, and most

Ever since the early days, the clock tower at Union Station has urged Portlanders to "Go by Train."

importantly, people. New arrivals came to Portland and marveled at the beautiful, Romanesque and Queen Anne–style station with its elegant brick, stucco, and sandstone—and the iconic 150-foot clock tower that now urges passersby to "Go by Train."

Union Station still serves as the depot for all Amtrak and Greyhound service to and from Portland, and is worth a visit, especially for history buffs and train lovers. Look out for the markers that will guide you through a walking tour beginning on Broadway and Hoyt. As you walk up the Broadway Bridge, check out the yards and the expansive views of the Portland skyline before you descend the steps to Naito Parkway and continue on across the east station esplanade through the Yards. Climb the stairs to the Yards Plaza and cross the footbridge where you'll get an up-close overhead look at the station platform.

Northeast

Map 3

BEVERLY CLEARY CHILDREN'S SCULPTURE GARDEN/GRANT PARK

NE 33rd Ave. between Knott St. and NE Broadway, www.multcolib.org/kids/cleary

HOURS: Daily 5 A.M.-midnight

COST: Free

If you loved reading about the misadventures of the plucky, but not always well-behaved Ramona Quimby from the unforgettable children's series by Beverly Cleary, you'll want to visit Grant Park where Ramona, Henry Huggins, and Henry's dog Ribsy are immortalized in bronze. Off the street in a patch of trees there is a fountain where the statues were placed to honor the author who made some of Northeast Portland famous. Cleary grew up in the neighborhood and a number of her favorite childhood spots are remembered in the stories of Ramona and her sister Beezus. You can download a map from the Multnomah County website and take a self-guided walking tour of Ramona's/Cleary's neighborhood. You can see the homes where the author grew up or stroll

down Klickitat Street (yes, it's real and it's just four blocks from the park).

HOLLYWOOD THEATRE

4122 NE Sandy Blvd., 503/281-4215, www.hollywoodtheatre.org

HOURS: See website for showtimes

COST: $6.50 adult, $4.50 senior and child 4-12; Mon. evenings $4 all

A stroll through the Hollywood District wouldn't be complete without a look at the majestic Hollywood Theatre, which has one of the most ornate theater fronts in the Pacific Northwest. The Hollywood opened as a vaudeville house in the 1920s; back then, admission was only a quarter, and the films, which did not have sound yet, were accompanied by an eight-piece orchestra and an organ. The building might have fallen into disrepair if not for the volunteer group Film Action Oregon, which embarked on an aggressive campaign to renovate and save this old Portland landmark. Battling complications with water damage, asbestos, and

PINT-SIZED P-TOWN

Portlanders are known for keeping their kids in tow instead of opting for nannies or babysitters. It's no surprise then that the city offers a number of places that appeal both to the young and the young-at-heart.

Young and old alike will find themselves wanting to touch, twirl, poke, and examine things around every corner of the **Oregon Museum of Science and Industry** (1945 SE Water Ave., 800/955-6674, www.omsi.edu). You can ride the motion simulator, check out a flick in the incredible IMAX theater, tour a real U.S. Navy submarine, or visit the latest traveling exhibition. You can also find fun for all ages at **Oaks Amusement Park** (7805 SE Oaks Park Way, 503/233-5777, www.oakspark.com). Ride the Scream-n-Eagle, take a spin around the old-school skating rink, or have a picnic along the banks of the Willamette River. The rink is open most days and rides are operational on Saturdays and Sundays noon-7 P.M. and during special events.

Of course, the **Oregon Zoo** (4001 SW Canyon Rd., www.oregonzoo.org) is a big draw for families with its Asian elephants, adorable penguins, majestic polar bears, fascinating fruit bats, and a plethora of animals from all corners of the world. In fact, on any given day, there are 2,200 specimens representing 260 species of birds, mammals, reptiles, amphibians, and invertebrates. You can check out the daily keeper talks or ride the zoo train, which takes you around the zoo and shows off some of the pretty forested areas of Washington Park. Wintertime visitors can also check out ZooLights, when the zoo is transformed into a colorful wintry wonderland and hours are extended past dark.

A great day trip with the kids is the 20-minute drive out to Sauvie Island (www.sauvieisland.org), where there are a number of U-pick farms and wildlife areas to explore. A favorite in the fall is the **Pumpkin Patch** (503/621-3874, www.thepumpkinpatch.com), where kids can hop on a hayride out to the pumpkin patch. If you pick a pumpkin, you pay according to the size and weight, but otherwise, it's free. The produce market is full of fresh fruits and vegetables (as well as pumpkin carving

kits, fall decor, and other goodies) and you can pick up some hot buttered corn and homemade cider at the concession stands. While you're out there, visit the Maize (www.portlandmaze.com), a truly mind-boggling five-acre corn maze; and after dark, in October, the truly brave-hearted can traipse through the Haunted Field of Screams.

Saturday Market (503/222-6072, www.portlandsaturdaymarket.com) has long been a favorite for kids, especially since it's the place where elephant ears were invented. Portland's Elephant Ears is one of many carts in the market's food court, but this one is a particular favorite among the small set. The smell of those ginormous fried dough treats is hard to resist, especially when you can douse them in marionberries, apple butter, cinnamon and sugar, or whatever you like. Kids are also pretty fond of touring the merchant booths, as there are a number of vendors with things to touch, test-drive, or try on.

There are a number of great stops for the little reader in your life. **Powell's City of Books** (1005 W. Burnside, 503/228-4651, www.powells.com) has a truly jaw-dropping kids room. In fact, it has been dubbed the "largest children's book section on the West Coast." There are tables and chairs for impromptu story time and a staff person is on hand to help you or your child find exactly what you are looking for. Plus, they have a fun merchandise section with irresistible craft items, t-shirts, and cool educational toys. On the east side of the river, you'll find **Green Bean Books** (1600 NE Alberta St., 503/954-2354, www.greenbeanbookspdx.com), which has a fantastic collection of books for young readers and soon-to-be-bibliophiles. They also have an amusing collection of old vending machines that now distribute things like fake moustaches, finger puppets, and little fuzzy friends.

Many Portland hotels feature kid-focused packages. **Hotel Monaco** (506 SW Washington, 888/207-2201, www.monaco-portland.com), for instance, offers a "Mini DaVinci" deal with passes to the Portland Children's Museum, milk and cookies, and even paint sets and canvasses for you to keep.

general deterioration, the non-profit organization managed to save the structure and savor a little nostalgia, thanks to the help of donations, grants, and the unending passion of its volunteers. In addition to showing regular independent films, the building has also returned to its vaudeville roots to welcome the occasional live theatrical performance or concert.

Southeast   Map 4

LADD'S CIRCLE AND ROSE GARDEN
SE 16th Ave. and Harrison St.
HOURS: Daily 5 A.M.-midnight
COST: Free

Though his name may be cursed by drivers trying to navigate through the mystery that is Ladd's Addition, William Sargent Ladd was actually quite clever. He came West during the California Gold Rush and settled in Portland in 1851. The productive businessman and one-time mayor of Portland owned a 126-acre farm on Portland's east side, which he decided to subdivide in a manner similar to Pierre L'Enfant's plan for Washington DC. Ladd's design is based on a diagonal street system surrounding a central park and four diamond-shaped rose gardens located on the points of a compass. It was a radical departure from the common grid pattern of the expanding city and one that still confuses drivers who get stuck in a seemingly endless maze.

The central park was designed in 1909 by Park Superintendent Emanuel Mische, who planted camellias, perennials, and a lawn area, as well as numerous rose bushes with the intention of creating a stunning stained-glass effect. The garden is still quite lovely (if you can find it), with over 3,000 roses of 60 varieties that were popular in the early 20th century.

◖ LONE FIR CEMETERY
SE Morrison St. and SE 20th Ave., 503/797-1709
HOURS: Daily sunrise-sunset
COST: Free

Lone Fir Cemetery is a sometimes chilling, but always moving representation of Portland's mottled past. Buried among the some 25,000 known and 10,000 unknown souls are many of the city's founders, including Asa Lovejoy, Socrates H. Tryon, J. C. Hawthorne, and Portland's first axe murderess, Charity Lamb. There's a lot of history here (not all of it flattering) and a stroll around this 30-acre arboretum will expose the tales of Chinese immigrants, pioneers, politicians, and soldiers. It was discovered in 2004 that several hundred patients from the Oregon Hospital for the Insane (which Hawthorne founded) are buried here in unmarked graves.

The grounds are well kept and were it not for the gravestones, it would make a lovely park, speckled as it is with ginko trees, oaks, birches, firs, and dogwoods. If you visit in the summer months, you won't want to miss the Pioneer Rose Garden, where you'll find roses that were carried West with the pioneer women who made Portland their home. However, the memorials and grave markers are themselves worth the visit. Many date back to the mid-19th century and are surprisingly evocative of Portland's past.

VERA KATZ ESPLANADE
SE Water Ave. and SE Hawthorne Blvd., 503/823-2223
HOURS: Daily 5 A.M.-midnight
COST: Free

One of Portland's numerous nicknames is Bridgetown—and if you head down to the waterfront, it's easy to see why. For years, the land on the east side of the Willamette River was an undeveloped industrial mess. In the late 1980s, developers and city planners began to envision a walkway that would extend north from the Hawthorne Bridge, past the Morrison and Burnside Bridges, to the Steel Bridge, where it would then link across the river to the already popular Waterfront Park on the west side. The finished Esplanade contains a number of markers that enumerate some of the area's vibrant history—all artistically lit to make them visible even at night.

While the area is a hotbed of activity—with Portlanders strolling, biking, skating, or simply exploring the underbellies of the city's many bridges—it is also a carefully planned habitat for fish and wildlife. Beavers and herons swim near boat docks as they try to nab salmon and steelhead, while pigeons and ducks nest on the rocks.

Take a quiet stroll down the walk and check out some of the public art installations, such as the ethereal Echo Gate and the bronze statue that commemorates the former mayor for whom the esplanade was named. Climb the steps and cross to the west side or head down to the lengthy floating walkway and feel the ebb and flow of the Willamette beneath your feet.

Sellwood and Moreland   Map 5

CRYSTAL SPRINGS RHODODENDRON GARDEN

SE Woodstock Blvd. and SE 28th Ave., 503/771-8386

HOURS: Apr. 1-Sept. 30 daily 6 A.M.-10 P.M., Oct. 1-Mar. 31 daily 6 A.M.-6 P.M.

COST: Day after Labor Day-Feb. free; Mar.-Labor Day $3 adult, free for child under 12

It began as a "rhody" test garden in 1950, but now this 9.4-acre spot in the middle of Southeast Portland is a botanical oasis devoted to the flowering shrub that thrives better here than anywhere else. The cool, rainy Northwest climate is perfect for growing rhododendrons, but even when they are not in bloom, the garden is still a lush romantic retreat. Packed with trails, waterfalls, ponds, shaded nooks, and benches, it's a beautiful spot to take a stroll, have a picnic, or capture some great photos of flora and fauna. Mind the geese and ducks, though. They more or less run the ponds and have been known to be a bit temperamental.

When the rhododendrons are in full bloom (usually late spring), Crystal Springs is an explosion of color. The garden houses a remarkable variety of blooms, some of which you can take home if you visit during the annual plant sale held during Mother's Day weekend.

❰ OAKS BOTTOM WILDLIFE REFUGE

SE Sellwood Blvd. and SE 7th Ave., 503/797-1709

HOURS: Daily 5 A.M.-midnight

COST: Free

Oaks Bottom Wildlife Refuge is a 140-acre floodplain wetland on the east bank of the Willamette River that includes a number of trails for hiking and biking. The area is a favorite spot for bird-watchers, as more than 100 varieties of migratory birds manage to find their way to the refuge. You can hop on the trail at the SE Milwaukie Street entrance and head south along the edge of the pond, or opt for the paved Springwater Trail, which eventually connects to the south end of the Vera Katz Esplanade.

In 1969, the city blocked development of this area into an industrial park because it was one of the few remaining marshlands around. Now the area is maintained by a volunteer organization that not only cares for the land, but also works to restore the natural habitat of creatures such has wrens, raccoons, quails, kestrels, frogs, ducks, and the iconic blue heron.

North Portland   Map 6

MISSISSIPPI AVENUE

N. Mississippi Ave., between N. Fremont St.
and N. Skidmore St.

HOURS: Daily dawn-last call

COST: Free

Arguably one of the most walkable streets in Portland, Mississippi is still being quietly referred to as "one of the best-kept secrets in Portland," but it's not likely to stay hush-hush for long. What was once a haven for drug deals and debauchery is now a harbor for both shoppers and foodies, thanks to a recent (and much-needed) shot in the arm from the influx of creative souls looking to establish themselves in the Rose City. Unable to settle into the expensive Pearl lofts and unable to find space in the hotbed of the Alberta Arts District, artists and young entrepreneurs began to build their own neighborhood here, injecting into it their own ethos and style.

Mississippi Avenue is packed with some of the city's most creative restaurants, stylish bars, and quaint boutiques, but it's also a testament to Portland's commitment to sustainability. Near North Fremont Avenue stands the ornate dada-esque facade of The ReBuilding Center (3625 N. Mississippi, 503/331-1877), which hides a labyrinth of doors, windows, fixtures, and wood salvaged from homes all over the region and resold to locals who want to add unique touches to their home without creating a bigger carbon footprint.

PENINSULA PARK AND ROSE GARDEN

700 N. Rosa Parks Way, 503/823-2525

HOURS: Daily 5 A.M.-midnight

COST: Free

Designed in the early 1900s as part of the City Beautiful movement, this park is equal parts elegant formal garden and community gathering

With over 6,500 rose plantings in more than 65 varieties, it gets pretty fragrant at Penninsula Park and Rose Garden come June.

space. Enter the sunken rose garden on Albina Avenue and stroll among the 6,500 rose plantings, which include more than 65 fragrant varieties. The heart of this garden, which is bedecked with lantern-style lights and stone pillars, is where you'll find a historic fountain; it's been the centerpiece of the park for nearly 100 years and it is here that Portland's official city rose, Mme. Caroline Testout, was first cultivated and is maintained to this day.

Just past the formal garden, you'll find a grand octagonal gazebo, built in 1913 and preserved as a historic landmark, the last of its kind. Today, it is a popular spot for weddings and concerts. Beyond that are baseball fields, tennis courts, playgrounds, and a whimsical wading pool complete with a giant frog and flower sprinkler. At this end of the 16-acre park is also where you'll find Portland's first and oldest community center. The center, an Italian villa–-style structure, has a 33-yard outdoor swimming pool that is a popular retreat for locals—and once served as the home for a number of Humboldt penguins awaiting transport to Washington Park Zoo.

Greater Portland   Map 7

BERRY BOTANICAL GARDEN
11505 SW Summerville Ave., 503/636-4112,
www.berrybot.org
HOURS: Mon.-Fri. 9 A.M.-4:30 P.M. by reservation
COST: $5 adult, free for child under 12

The Berry Botanical Garden, a public non-profit garden, is really quite beautiful, with about 200 of approximately 5,000 regional native plants, and more than 2,000 rhododendrons representing 160 different species. The garden is the legacy of Rae Selling Berry, who obtained the seeds for her remarkable garden from explorers who specialized in flora, including Frank Kingdon-Ward, Francis Ludlow and George Sherriff, and Joseph Rock. Berry herself also collected plants from the Pacific Northwest, British Columbia, and Alaska. The garden hosts a series of classes, workshops, and events intended to bring information about plants and their importance to the community. The garden also hosts twice-yearly plant sales (held offsite) that help educate the public about plant management and the garden's programs.

ELK ROCK GARDEN
11800 SW Military Ln., 503/636-5613,
www.elkrockgarden.com
HOURS: Daily 8 A.M.-5 P.M.
COST: Free

The Garden of the Bishop's Close, known as Elk Rock, was created to show a collection of rare and native plants, magnificent trees, and remarkable views of the Willamette River and Mount Hood. It is a private garden and the home of Episcopal Bishop of Oregon. The family bequeathed the home to the church, leaving with it an endowment for the care and maintenance of the garden, and a requirement that it be left open to the public. It's a lovely, contemplative spot to visit, so long as you respect the rules. Dogs must be leashed; visitors may not bring picnics; and there is a prohibition against "frolicking," but nonetheless, it is a peaceful place to visit. You won't find any signage on Highway 43 indicating the garden is there, which makes it all the more of a treasure hunt, the reward of which is winding paths through magnolia trees, rhododendrons, giant sequoia, golden rain trees, gingko, witch hazel, and burning bushes.

◖ FOREST PARK
NW 29th and NW Upshur St.
HOURS: Daily 5 A.M.-10 P.M.
COST: Free

If you really want to get away from it all, go no farther than Forest Park, the 5,100-acre urban forest that sits just outside of downtown Portland in the Tualatin Hills. Featuring 70 miles of trails for hikers, bikers, bird-watchers, and horseback riders, the park provides a never-ending abundance of flora and fauna. The massive canopy of trees offers a safe and prosperous habitat for the 112 species of birds and 62 species of mammals that call the park home. Extending along the east ridge above the Willamette River, Forest Park is bounded by West Burnside Street on the south, and its juxtaposition to the Alphabet District in Northwest Portland makes it a popular retreat for those who seek peace and solitude without having to travel far.

At the southeastern end of the park, the popular Wildwood Trail passes Pittock Mansion and offers breathtaking panoramic views of Mounts Hood, St. Helens, Rainier, Adams, and Jefferson.

THE GROTTO

8840 NE Skidmore St., 503/254-7371,

www.thegrotto.org

HOURS: Apr. 1-Sept. 30 Mon. noon-7 P.M., Tues.-Sun. 10 A.M.-4 P.M.; Oct. 1-Mar. 31 Mon. noon-4 P.M., Tues.-Sun. 10 A.M.-7 P.M.

COST: Free, except evenings Thanksgiving Day-Dec. 31

The National Sanctuary of Our Sorrowful Mother, or the Grotto, as it is more commonly called, is a 62-acre botanical garden and Catholic shrine that is a sight to see, for anyone, be they Christians, agnostics, or followers of the Flying Spaghetti Monster. Towering fir trees and imposing basalt cliffs bend to the careful artwork of peace and tranquility. A highlight of the visit is Our Lady's Grotto, a shrine to Mary that was carved out of the black cliffs in 1925 and features a marble replica of Michelangelo's famed work, the *Pieta*. Take a tour (call ahead to schedule) or stroll through on your own and explore the statuary hidden among the trees, streams, and passageways. Buy a token from the gift shop for $3.50 and ride the elevator to the upper level, which sits atop a 130-foot sheer rock cliff and offers unequalled views of the Columbia River and Mount St. Helens.

In the wintertime, the Grotto is home to one of Portland's most popular holiday events, The Festival of Lights. Volunteers spend months installing over half a million lights, animated

displays, and fiber-optic representations of the holiday spirit. It is the only time of year when an admission fee is required, but tickets ($7.50 adult, $3 child, free for child under 2) include concerts in the cathedral-like 500-seat chapel, petting zoos, and theatrical performances.

INTERNATIONAL ROSE TEST GARDEN

400 SW Kingston Ave., 503/823-3636,

www.rosegardenstore.org

HOURS: Daily 7 A.M.-9 P.M.

COST: Free

Portland's famous rose garden in Washington Park is the oldest continuously operated test garden in the United States. While the primary purpose of the garden is to test and protect new rose hybrids (a tradition that began in the midst of World War I when people from around the world sent roses to Portland to keep them safe from bombing), the 4.5 acres of blooms are a shining example of why Portland is known as "The City of Roses." You can picnic in the Shakespearean Garden, where you'll find blooms that are named for characters in the bard's plays scattered among the benches, archways, and graceful trees. As you near the garden's edge and enjoy a panoramic view of the city, amble along the Queen's Walk, where the Rose Festival Queens are remembered with a plaque that bears their names and signatures. Next, stroll past the sprawling outdoor amphitheater (a perfect spot for a picnic), where you just might catch a summertime show or live music showcase.

PAUL BUNYAN STATUE

N. Interstate Ave. and N. Denver Ave.

HOURS: Daily 24 hours

COST: Free

Originally built to greet visitors to the Centennial Exposition for Portland's 100th anniversary on February 14, 1959, this big guy still looms tall over NoPo, as if watching over the adjacent Dancin' Bear, a famous local strip club. The legendary lumberjack of lore stands 31 feet tall and was recently added to the National Register of Historic Places.

Comprised mostly of steel, plaster, concrete,

SIGHTS

and paint, Paul is remarkably well constructed for his age (especially considering the fact that he was only intended to last six months). Thankfully, Paul has been lovingly cared for over the years by neighbors who saw him as a both a symbol of the lumberjacks of Portland's past and the working class of today.

◖ PITTOCK MANSION

3229 NW Pittock Dr., 503/823-3623,
www.pittockmansion.org

HOURS: Feb. 1-June 30 daily 11 A.M.-4 P.M., July 1-Aug. 31 daily 10 A.M.-4 P.M., Sep. 1-Dec. 31 daily 11 A.M.-4 P.M.; closed Jan. 1-31, Thanksgiving Day, Christmas Day

COST: $7 adult, $6 senior, $4 child, free for child under 6

One thousand feet above the city stands a monument to some Portland's most fundamental qualities: natural beauty, progress, civic enthusiasm, and historical preservation. The Pittock Mansion was built in 1914 by Henry and Georgiana Pittock, both active contributors to progressive mid-19th-century Portland. Henry (a newspaper man who developed what is now the *The Oregonian*) made his way to Oregon at the age of 19, penniless but driven. He and Georgiana married in 1860 and began a life of hard work, committing countless hours to community service, all the while building an empire from their real estate, banking, railroad, ranching, and mining investments. The Pittocks had six children and 19 grandchildren, many of whom were raised on the 46-acre estate—which was purchased by the City of Portland (and thereby saved from demolition) for a mere $225,000.

The home was designed by Edward Foulks (who also designed the Tribune Tower in Oakland, California) in the French Renaissance style and features a number of remarkably innovative features for its time, such as a central vacuum system, an intercom system, a walk-in freezer, and a Turkish smoking room. About 80,000 visitors tour the house each year (you can take a self-guided or docent-led tour) and then wander through the lush park-like gardens that blossom with rhododendrons and flowering cherries. There are also a number of trails through Pittock Acres Park (daily 5 A.M.–9 P.M.), which connect with the adjacent Forest Park and are popular with hikers and joggers for their verdant landscapes and spectacular views.

PORTLAND JAPANESE GARDEN

611 SW Kingston Ave., 503/223-5055,
www.japanesegarden.com

HOURS: Apr. 1-Sept. 30 Mon. noon-7 P.M., Tues.-Sun. 10 A.M.-7 P.M.; Oct. 1-Mar. 31 Mon. noon-4 P.M., Tues.-Sun. 10 A.M.-4 P.M.

COST: $8 adult, $6.75 senior and student, $5.75 child ages 6-17, free for child under 6

If the urban sprawl has you itching to find a much needed moment of peace and tranquility, seek it among the winding stone steps, wooden bridges, waterfalls, and koi ponds of the beautifully landscaped Japanese Garden. High above the city, the garden is encircled by stately Douglas fir and Western red cedar trees and the rolling green hills of Washington Park. Inside, the garden is divided into five spaces: the Sand and Stone Garden; the

COURTESY OF TRAVEL PORTLAND

a beautiful waterfall in the heart of the Portland Japanese Garden

Natural Garden; the Flat Garden; the Tea Garden; and the Strolling Pond Garden, with its exquisite Heavenly Falls and five-tiered pagoda lantern. It has taken years of cultivation to bring such serenity and authenticity to the gardens, but the efforts have certainly paid off. In 1998, Kunihiko Saito, the Japanese ambassador to the United States, declared this "the most authentic Japanese garden, including those in Japan."

The Portland Japanese Garden offers several guided tours daily between April and October and once daily on weekends between November and March. Reservations aren't necessary for these tours, but you can also call ahead to set up a private group tour.

RESTAURANTS

Portlanders have always known their fair city was a hotbed of fantastic chefs, master mixologists, and creative restaurateurs. The nation has finally begun to take notice as well. Suddenly, the names of P-Town favorites are showing up on the pages of the *New York Times, Bon Appétit, USA Today* and the *Wall Street Journal.*

Across the globe, people are buzzing about the local culinary scene, not just because of the food, but because of the way Portland chefs are doing it. In Portland, there is a joke that the "six degrees of separation" rule does not apply. Here we have only three degrees, and the same can be said for the food. Greens come from neighborhood gardens, beef from local farms, and it's likely that the mushrooms were picked by the chef. The coffee is fair trade and roasted by "that guy down the block." The wines are biodynamic and made from grapes grown in a vineyard you can drive to in less than an hour.

Chefs have flocked to Portland over the last 10 years, much in the same way the artists did 10 years before that, bringing with them a passion and energy that moved the city's culinary status from the underground. Suddenly, every quadrant of this town is positively bursting with restaurants, food shops, and pretty lounges, all devoted to the idea that fresh is best, local is key, and uniformity is passé. You won't find many chain restaurants in this city, and if you do, it won't be Portlanders in those seats. What you will find is a cadre of unique restaurants run by fascinating, energetic chefs with a mind on turning every meal into a story.

HIGHLIGHTS

LOOK FOR ◖ TO FIND RECOMMENDED RESTAURANTS.

◖ **Best Late-Night Snack:** One of Portland's most kitschy and beloved 24-hour indulgences lurks inside the rotating glass case at **Voodoo Doughnut,** where concoctions range from the tame Portland Cream to the wicked and wild Bacon Maple Bar (page 46).

◖ **Best Place Impress a Date:** No one knows how to make you feel like a VIP quite like **El Gaucho,** where the attention to detail borders on obsessive. This steakhouse leaves no potato unfluffed, no lap without a napkin (page 47).

◖ **Best Hot Spot:** The Pearl District's answer to fine Latin cuisine, **¡Oba!** really delivers, and service is almost always attentive and enthusiastic without being pushy. Stop in for happy hour nibbles or linger for the full dinner experience (page 53).

◖ **Best Six-Course Fine Dining:** Chef Naomi Pomeroy has been recognized in a number of national cooking magazines, and **Beast** is her baby. The 24-seat restaurant offers twice-nightly six-course dinners four nights a week, and reservations are a hot commodity. With such starters as a charcuterie plate that includes foie gras bonbons, each course is as unparalleled as the last (page 57).

◖ **Best Small Plates:** Tapas are popular in Portland and no place has received more attention than **Toro Bravo.** This Spanish-inspired restaurant is always bustling, but they run a tight ship. Plates come out hot and loaded with such treasures as squid-ink pasta, oxtail croquettes, and bacon-wrapped dates (page 60).

◖ **Best Breakfast: Screen Door** rocks in a town where breakfast is practically a religion. Their fried chicken and sweet potato waffles make any wait worthwhile (page 60).

◖ **Best Place to Sample the Whole Hog:** Meat eaters worship at the shrine of **Le Pigeon,** where chef Gabriel Rucker serves up some truly unbelievable (and occasionally adventurous) dishes. There's no part of the pig, cow, rabbit, or bird too strange to end up on this menu (page 62).

◖ **Best Ecofriendly Eats:** The first of its kind in the nation, **Bamboo Sushi** is a sustainable sushi restaurant that would do well even if they didn't employ all-green practices. The fish used to make their rolls, soups, and specialties must meet strict guidelines, so everything is about as fresh as if you plucked it from the sea yourself (page 62).

◖ **Best Comfort Food:** Open until the wee hours of the morning, **Le Bistro Montage** is a popular late-night spot that specializes in Cajun food and rich, creamy macaronis. The simplest one, Old Mac, has only four ingredients, but it is practically perfect (page 65).

◖ **Best Place to Satisfy a Sweet Tooth:** The French-inspired **Pix Patisserie** is more than just a bakery. This dessert house is also part coffeehouse and part bar, but it's the cakes, tortes, cookies, and sweets that make this place so magical (page 68).

© HOLLYANNA MCCOLLOM

The world famous jelly-filled Voodoo Doughnut can satisfy both your sweet tooth and your hankering for mischief.

Downtown

Map 1

RESTAURANTS

Downtown Portland, occasionally referred to as the Cultural District, has the fortune of being a hub for vacationers, theater-goers, and business travelers. Hotel bars abut late-night coffeehouses and everywhere there is a buzz of energy. No one is in a hurry, but they are not about to waste a moment on anything sub par. Because of this, the culinary scene is about as diverse as it gets. On one corner, a crowd of food carts offer quick, tasty bites, while one block away, a five-star chef garnishes a dry aged steak before sending it out.

AMERICAN
BLUEPLATE LUNCH COUNTER AND SODA FOUNTAIN $

308 SW Washington St., 503/295-2583,
www.eatatblueplate.com

HOURS: Mon.-Fri. 11 A.M.-5 P.M., closed Sat-Sun.

This tiny lunch spot fills up quickly around noontime, as it's a top choice among locals who want to grab a bite to eat on their break. BluePlate is only open for a few hours on weekdays and the service is oftentimes a bit hurried, particularly before 3 P.M. But somehow, the daily specials make it all worthwhile. BluePlate has only four regular entrées (all quite reliable) and a rotation of favorites like bacon mushroom mac and cheese, chicken-fried steak, and a meatball hoagie you'll need utensils to eat.

This place is also famous for its 1950s-style soda fountain, featuring house-made cane sugar sodas and incredible milkshakes. In fact, the chocolate peanut butter shake is so decadent, it's like reliving your childhood in a glass.

THE ORIGINAL DINERANT $$

300 SW 6th Ave., 503/546-2666,
www.originaldinerant.com

HOURS: Mon.-Thurs. 6 A.M.-10 P.M., Fri.-Sat.
6 A.M.-midnight, Sun. 6 A.M.-9 P.M.

While The Original can't seem to decide if it wants to be kitschy or swanky, nostalgic or modern, it does manage to have style with a capital S. The menu is chock-full of diner classics

PRICE KEY

$ Entrées less than $10

$$ Entrées $10-20

$$$ Entrées more than $20

like burgers, mac and cheese, chicken-fried steak, and fries. While none of those things are a surprising find at a restaurant that harkens back to the 1950s, everything has a slight twist. A burger can be sandwiched between glazed Voodoo doughnuts instead of a bun. Mac and cheese is made with lobster, mascarpone, and truffle. Fries can be ordered with cheese grits and gravy, a standard Canadian favorite called *poutine*—that is, until you add foie gras.

RED STAR TAVERN & ROASTHOUSE $$$

503 SW Alder St., 503/222-0005,
www.redstartavern.com

HOURS: Mon.-Thurs. 6:30 A.M.-midnight, Fri.
6:30 A.M.-1 A.M., Sat. 8 A.M.-1 A.M., Sun. 8 A.M.-11 P.M.

The best place to settle in at Red Star is one of the elevated booths in the bar. From there, you have a fantastic view of the restaurant and the enormous wall of booze that features one of the city's best collections of bourbons. The menu at Red Star tends to focus on classic American cuisine, with rotisserie meats as the main attraction. Chef Tom Dunklin likes to use organic and local products whenever possible, so the menu changes often, but always provides a healthy balance of vegetarian and carnivore-friendly dishes.

ASIAN
BO RESTOBAR $$

400 SW Broadway, 503/222-2688,
www.borestobar.com

HOURS: Sun.-Thurs. 5-11 P.M., Fri. 11:30 A.M.-2 A.M., Sat.
4 P.M.-2 A.M., closed Sun.

The pink neon "Bo" sign and sleek white

CARTOPIA: PORTLAND'S FOOD CARTS

Portland has a little culinary secret that might come as a great surprise. Some of the best food in the city doesn't come from fancy kitchens; it comes from food carts.

When you think about it, this makes sense. With such a strong focus on self-reliance and self-expression, the city is entirely welcoming of businesses that toss out the notion that a restaurant needs a brick-and-mortar building to be considered good and instead sets out to make the best waffle, taco, or French fries in town. There's even a website devoted to the phenomenon, **Food Cart Portland** (www.foodcartsportland.com), which provides details on locations, menus, prices, and hours. Across the city, countless Twitter pages and Facebook updates discuss the mobile culinary culture with an excitement otherwise reserved for major music festivals and show openings. The result is such that over a few short months of business, certain carts develop a cult-like following. While in some places, grabbing lunch or a late-night snack from a food cart might seem like slumming, in Portland, it's an indulgence and an adventure.

For one thing, the carts in P-Town have fixed locations and are usually clustered together, like miniature food courts. Downtown, there are a few clusters in areas such as Tom McCall Waterfront Park, Portland State University, and Pioneer Courthouse Square.

One major hub of carts is at SW 5th Avenue and Oak Street. Here you'll find **Jarochita** (503/421-9838), a Mexican food cart that serves standard burritos, tacos, and quesadillas. However, Jarochita makes the list of must-try carts because of its banana leaf-wrapped enchiladas (about $1.50 each) and huaraches, made with an oblong, fried masa base and stuffed with a cornucopia of toppings. Also in this area is **Tabor** (503/997-5467, www.schnitzelwich.com), home of the Schnitzelwich – a gorgeous sandwich made with breaded, fried pork loin on a ciabatta roll with sautéed onion, horseradish, and paprika-spiced pepper spread. It's authentic Czech cuisine with treasures like goulash, wild mushroom soup, and spaetzle on the menu. Another standout is **Brunchbox** (503/477-3286),

where the name just doesn't do the place justice. Yes, there are fantastic breakfast items, like egg sandwiches made with homemade English muffins, but it's the Black and Blue Burger that puts Brunchbox on the map. Arguably one of the best burgers in town, this beast of a sandwich has blackened Angus beef and creamy blue cheese crumbles. Brunchbox also has a fun kids menu with items like dino-shaped cheese or PB&J sandwiches for $1.50.

Another big gathering of carts can be found at SW 10th Avenue and Alder Street, where **Samurai Bento** (503/757-8802) sets up shop. Everything is made-to-order from scratch, so you'll get none of that fast-food warming light effect. Try the Okayoko-don with delicious sautéed chicken, onions, and egg on top; or nosh on veggie tempura as you amuse yourself with the humorous menu descriptions. If you're a fan of curry, give **Sawasdee Thai** (503/330-2037) a try. The pumpkin curry and green curry are stellar choices, but all of the dishes are well proportioned and balanced between veggies, meat, and sauce. Or, if it's a blustery day, head over to **Savor Soup House** (503/750-5634, www.savorsouphouse.com), where the star of the show is (naturally) hearty, belly-warming soup – like curried cauliflower and red lentil, broccoli and cheddar, or New England clam chowder topped with bacon. Also on the 10th and Alder block, **Ziba's Pitas** has received a lot of attention. This Bosnian food cart serves up flaky pitas stuffed with meat, cheese, spinach, or zucchini. Order a full plate and you'll get delicious sides like cucumber salad and *ajvar* (tasty fried bread balls with dipping sauces).

In North Portland, you'll find the drool-inspiring **Flavour Spot** (2310 N. Lombard St., 503/289-9866, www.flavourspot.com) and **Son of Flavour Spot** (N. Mississippi Ave. and N. Fremont), a pair of waffle carts that are re-inventing breakfast one gooey Black-Forest-ham-and-Gouda-stuffed waffle at a time. Lines form on the weekends as people hover waiting for their hangover remedy of coffee and waffles stuffed with Nutella and jam, or sausage and maple butter.

interior make Bo Restobar feel like it's going to be ostentatious. To a certain degree, it can be. Entrées, while tasty, can border on fussy, and cocktails can have so many ingredients that they begin to sound like an inventory list. But when it comes to small, shareable plates, Bo offers a number of super-affordable options with dishes like scallop cigars, squash dumplings, and sushi rolls. It's not exactly fill-your-belly fare, but it's cheap enough that you can order several plates, which gives you much more opportunity to mix and match. Bo usually serves up a happy hour cocktail of the day (weekdays 4–6 P.M. and 9 P.M.–midnight) for $5, but if that's not your bag, draft beers are $3 and wine is just $4 a glass.

SAUCEBOX ❸❺

214 SW Broadway, 503/241-3393, www.saucebox.com
HOURS: Mon.-Thurs. 11:30 A.M.-midnight, Fri.-Sat.
5 P.M.-midnight

Over the past 13 years, the folks at Saucebox have attempted to bring together fantastic food, perfectly crafted cocktails, exceptional music, and inspired decor to create an approachable chic nightlife atmosphere. In short, they have spent a long time cultivating a "place to be seen" cocktail lounge. Saucebox's dinner menu features sushi and a number of simple, but cautiously creative Pan-Asian dishes that put this place shoulder-to-shoulder with many of Portland's fine dining destinations. Plates arrive with the beautiful presentation you would expect of a place that seems to be all about appearance, but the use of fresh local and regional ingredients saves it from being too pretentious. You can order dim sum–style dishes like pot stickers, chicken dumplings, and salad rolls, or dig into a full-size entrée such as Korean ribs or grilled duck.

BREAKFAST AND BRUNCH
MOTHER'S BISTRO & BAR ❸❺

212 SW Stark St., 503/464-1122
HOURS: Tues.-Thurs. 7 A.M.-9 P.M., Fri. 7 A.M.-10 P.M., Sat.
9 A.M.-10 P.M., Sun. 9 A.M.-2:30 P.M.

With a name like Mother's, you can probably guess what sort of food owner Lisa Schroeder is

famous for serving up. Comfort is key here, and while you stare at the ample plates full of such belly-rich dishes as the near-infamous crunchy French toast, you can almost hear your mother whisper, "Eat! You look skinny!" The sun-drenched dining room is a fine place to start your day, but make sure you come back and hunker down in the richly appointed Velvet Lounge where "Mom's meatloaf & gravy" is served well into the night.

◖ VOODOO DOUGHNUT ❺

22 SW 3rd Ave., 503/241-4704,
www.voodoodoughnut.com
HOURS: Daily, 24 hours

After the bartenders announce last call and the waitresses swipe the empty glasses from all the tables of Portland's downtown bars, one late-night eatery is still going strong. Located in the Old Town neighborhood, Voodoo Doughnut has been a haven for creatures of the night since its opening in 2003. Owners Tres Shannon and Kenneth Pogson reject conformity by offering such doughnuts as the Dirt Doughnut, covered in vanilla glaze and crushed Oreos, and the Maple Blazer Blunt, a cinnamon doughnut rolled to look like an oversized joint with a red sprinkled tip. Voodoo doughnuts are good, but the real draw here is the peculiar atmosphere. Voodoo offers weekly Swahili lessons and late-night doughnut eating contests, and you can get legally hitched under the giant "Cruller Chandelier of Life."

ITALIAN
MAMA MIA TRATTORIA ❸❺

439 SW 2nd Ave., 503/295-6464,
www.mamamiatrattoria.com
HOURS: Mon.-Wed. 11:30 A.M.-2:30 P.M. and
5-9 P.M., Thurs. 11:30 A.M.-2:30 P.M. and 5-10 P.M., Fri.
11:30 A.M.-2:30 P.M. and 5-11 P.M., Sat. 5-11 P.M., Sun.
5-9 P.M.

Mama Mia Trattoria is not the place to find traditional Italian, but if you are looking for comfort, this is the spot. Owner Lisa Schroeder is famous for her pillow-soft gnocchi and her Sunday gravy, a sauce she simmers all day and serves with penne, sausage, pork, and a meatball the size of your fist.

Despite its proximity to Portland's Cultural District, this place seems to have gotten lost on its way to New York. It's in an elite class for Portland, which otherwise lacks for true Italian-American soul food. The food here seems like it was snatched from the kitchen of someone's nonna, yet surprisingly, Mama Mia's has a number of vegetarian options and will make many of their dishes vegan-friendly upon request. If you have room for dessert (or even if you don't) grab some out-of-this-world *zeppole* (fried dough balls sprinkled with powdered sugar) and a glass of Moscato before you go.

NEL CENTRO $$

1408 SW 6th Ave., 503/484-1099, www.nelcentro.com
HOURS: Mon.-Thurs. 6:30 A.M.-2:30 P.M. and 5-11 P.M., Fri. 6:30 A.M.-midnight, Sat. 8 A.M.-midnight, Sun. 8 A.M.-11 P.M.

The chic, contemporary decor at Nel Centro is the perfect backdrop for the simple menu, which leans toward the peasant-style cuisine found in the Italian Riviera. Utilizing fresh Pacific Northwest fish and produce, owner and chef David Machado serves up dishes—rich with seafood, walnuts, anchovies, and olives—that embrace the bounty of the Mediterranean region. The wine list here is a collection of elegant choices, particularly the whites and rosés, which pair nicely with the lighter fare. Since the menu doesn't rely on heavy pastas and gut-busting cream sauces, you can enjoy a hearty meal without worrying too much about your waistline. But if you're still worried, skip the appetizers and save room for dessert. Native Portlander and resident pastry chef Lee Posey has created a handful of perfectly balanced dishes—like the lavender-infused crème brûlée and the house-made ricotta fritters—that taste so good with a hot cup of Stumptown coffee.

PAZZO RISTORANTE $$$

627 SW Washington St., 503/228-1515, www.pazzo.com
HOURS: Mon.-Thurs. 7 A.M.-9 P.M., Fri. 7 A.M.-11 P.M., Sat. 8 A.M.-11 P.M., Sun. 8 A.M.-9 P.M.

Pazzo has been serving up classic, reliably satisfying Italian dishes with a Pacific Northwest influence since 1991. It's a popular place for lunchtime and dinnertime business traffic. Pazzo does the simplest things best, like a butternut squash ravioli in an unfussy brown butter sauce, or a salad of young greens with berries and balsamic vinaigrette. The bakery adjacent to the restaurant, Pazzoria, supplies all of the bread and baked goods, and if you're looking for a quick bite—a salad, sandwich, slice of pizza, or pastry—rather than a rich meal, that's where you will want to go.

STEAK AND SEAFOOD

◖ EL GAUCHO $$$

319 SW Broadway, 503/227-8794, www.elgaucho.com
HOURS: Mon.-Thurs. 5 P.M.-midnight, Fri.-Sat. 5 P.M.-1 A.M., Sun. 5-11 P.M.

El Gaucho is an anomaly among Portland restaurants. While most thrive on a balance of quality food with laid-back setting, the tuxedo-clad servers at El Gaucho will come just short of cutting your 28-day dry-aged Porterhouse for you. In fact, if you ask them to do it, they probably will. A meal here will run you a pretty penny, but the steaks are some of the best you can buy. Skip the sides and focus on their collection of stellar appetizers like the amazing (albeit ostentatious) seafood tower and the Caesar salad, which is prepared tableside. If you still have room, order the bananas Foster, also prepared tableside over an open flame.

JAKE'S FAMOUS CRAWFISH $$

401 SW 12th Ave., 503/226-1419, www.mccormickandschmicks.com
HOURS: Mon.-Thurs. 11:30 A.M.-10 P.M., Fri.-Sat. 11:30 A.M.-midnight, Sun. 3-10 P.M.

Jake's is a Portland legend that has been a city landmark for more than 100 years. From the exterior, it seems to be a modest pub, but inside the deep burnished wood booths and rich decor lend a touch of masculine luxury and class to the place. The menu at Jake's is printed daily (and occasionally reprinted) to incorporate fresh-caught fish and in-season specialties. While the seafood here is some of the best in the Northwest (and eventually launched an entire chain of restaurants for owners Bill McCormick and Doug Schmick), Portlanders love Jake's for its affordable and extensive happy hour—with nosh like the Jake's burger or shrimp ceviche for only $1.95. For that reason, it's a popular spot for locals to gather for post-work cocktails, Kobe beef sliders, and plate after plate of peel 'n' eat shrimp.

SOUTHPARK SEAFOOD GRILL & WINE BAR $$$

901 SW Salmon St., 503/326-1300, www.southparkseafood.com
HOURS: Sun.-Thurs. 11:30 A.M.-3 P.M. and 5-10P.M., Fri.-Sat. 11:30 A.M.-3 P.M. and 5-11 P.M.
Riding the edge between the Downtown core and the South Park Blocks, the exterior of Southpark Seafood Grill is deceptively unassuming. With little more of note than a statue of a bronze salmon bursting through the brick facade, the restaurant and wine bar seems like an innocuously quaint bistro. Inside, however, Southpark is a rock-solid example of Northwest cuisine, with an impeccable wine list and a staff knowledgeable enough to back it up. Of course, seafood is the forte, with fresh-caught crab, prawns, scallops, and fish starring on the menu. Daily specials are often fresh-from-the-sea, simple, and creative.

URBAN FARMER $$$

525 SW Morrison St., inside Nines Hotel, 503/222-4900, www.urbanfarmerrestaurant.com
HOURS: Sun.-Thurs. 5-11 P.M., Fri.-Sat. 5 P.M.-midnight
A new kid on the upscale block is Urban Farmer, a modern-style American steakhouse housed on the eighth floor of the Nines Hotel. Without any discernable walls, the restaurant seems to shrink into the vast open space of the overhead four-story atrium. While the scene evokes that of an elegant rooftop bar, the vibe is decidedly chill and the clientele characteristically eclectic. The menu is beef-centric here and there are plenty of choices to suit your taste, whether you prefer pasture-fed, corn-fed, or the oh-so-buttery Wagyu beef. After you order, your server will present you with a wooden box from which you may choose your own knife, and a tin can filled with a tasty loaf of pumpkin bread (their signature recipe). Wash it all down with one of their house-made moonshine cocktails.

Northwest and the Pearl District   Map 2

From the industrial swank of the Pearl District to the bustling energy of the Alphabet District and Nob Hill, Northwest Portland is a wonderfully walkable area with a dizzying array of culinary options. Stroll the Pearl for some of the newest darlings on the scene, for tapas bars, posh cafés, and elegant eateries. Or venture onto NW 23rd (also known as "Trendy Third"), where some of Portland's best restaurants have dwelled for years.

AMERICAN
GILT CLUB $$

306 NW Broadway, 503/222-4458, www.giltclub.com
HOURS: Mon.-Sat. 5 P.M.-2 A.M., closed Sun.
Moderately sized and unassuming from the outside, Gilt Club is bursting at the seams with fantastic eats, great atmosphere, and an impressive stable of infused spirits and specialty cocktails. Despite its stealthy presence on Broadway and Everett, Gilt has absolutely no problem drawing a crowd both in the dining room and the bar area, and oftentimes the outdoor seating is at capacity as well.

The menu, which owner Jamie Dunn likes to keep short and sweet, focuses on comfort and simplicity, using elegant strokes to create American favorites. Start with some Manchego fritters or foie gras *torchon* on toasted brioche with roasted apples. Gilt's pastas and gnocchi are always delicious and the Angus burger with house-cured bacon and Gruyère is quite popular as well. Be sure to sample one of the cocktail flights, a trio of tiny variations of one particular classic.

ASIAN
HOUSE OF LOUIE ❺
331 NW Davis St., 503/228-9898

HOURS: Daily 10 A.M.-10 P.M.

If you're a fan of dim sum, House of Louie will have you singing for your brunch because, here, the dim sum carts run daily. One of the most popular items here is *nor my gai* (pronounced "normy guy"), a gooey, sticky rice wrapped in lotus leaves and stuffed with little treasures like shrimp, Chinese sausages, chicken, and barbequed pork. Diners also love Louie's garlicky Chinese broccoli and the sautéed bok choy. For the kiddies—or the kiddies at heart—Louie's will swing around a cart that is toppling with Jello-filled parfait dishes adorned with colorful flags. It may seem daunting, but the best choice is the creamy, white coconut gelatin. It's not too sweet and the smooth texture is a nice finish to the meal. If you miss the dim sum hours (10 A.M.–3 P.M.) or if you can't bear to wait for an item to come around, you can order most of the dishes directly from the menu.

BREAKFAST AND BRUNCH
BESAW'S ❺❺
2301 NW Savier St., 503/228-2619, www.besaws.com

HOURS: Mon. 7 A.M.-3 P.M., Tues.-Fri. 7 A.M.-10 P.M., Sat. 8 A.M.-10 P.M., Sun. 8 A.M.-3 P.M.

It's not uncommon to see folks lining up outside a half-hour before this favorite weekend breakfast spot opens its door. Fortunately for them, Besaw's eases the anticipation by providing them with free Stumptown coffee while they wait. That neighborly hospitality is just one reason why Besaw's has been in business since 1903. It also supports local and sustainable farmers by exclusively using local organic beef, cage-free eggs, and hormone-free dairy, which goes a long way for locals. What really speaks volumes, though, is that Besaw's scrambles are some of the best in town. Try the wild salmon, tossed with three bright yellow eggs, cream cheese, and scallions, and served with Besaw's signature rosemary garlic roasted potatoes.

BYWAYS CAFÉ ❺
1212 NW Glisan St., 503/221-0011, www.bywayscafe.com

HOURS: Mon.-Fri. 7 A.M.-3 P.M., Sat.-Sun. 7:30 A.M.-2 P.M.

Byways has received a healthy helping of fame since the Food Network paid a visit, but locals have been flocking here for years to sample the omelets, scrambles, and corned beef hash. Byways is also famous for its blue corn pancakes, made with ground blue corn and served with honey pecan butter. The corn cakes are good, but nothing compares to the Amaretto French toast.

The weekend wait can be long here, as at many Portland breakfast joints. To make it more bearable, arrive early, bring something to read, and pick up something caffeinated on the way. Byways doesn't offer free sidewalk coffee, but they will take your drink order if you ask.

THE DAILY CAFÉ ❺❺
902 NW 13th Ave., 503/242-1916, www.dailycafeinthepearl.com

HOURS: Mon.-Tues. 7 A.M.-5 P.M., Wed.-Fri. 7 A.M.-9 P.M., Sat. 9 A.M.-9 P.M., Sun. 9 A.M.-2 P.M.

Sundays at the Daily Café are price-fix brunch days and the seats fill up fast. It's not much of a surprise when you consider the fact that the Daily has one of the cheapest (albeit quality) brunches in town. For about $14, you get your choice of appetizer and entrée as well as a basket of fresh baked goodies for the table. Have a bowl of Josie's "soon-to-be-famous" fruit and nut granola with a savory frittata, or nibble on some mascarpone rice pudding while you wait for your cornmeal-crusted trout and eggs. If you really do love the granola, you can take a bag home with you; just ask.

ST. HONORÉ BOULANGERIE ❺
2335 NW Thurman St., 503/445-4342, www.sainthonorebakery.com

HOURS: Sun.-Thurs. 7 A.M.-7 P.M., Fri.-Sat. 7 A.M.-8 P.M.

If your idea of a good breakfast is a smooth latte and a buttery pastry, St. Honoré is a great place to start your day. Named for the patron saint of bakers, St. Honoré takes its influences from the bakery ovens of Normandy. The

PHOTO COURTESY OF ST. HONORÉ

There's nothing like starting your day with a newspaper, a cup of coffee, and a fresh-baked goodie from St. Honoré Boulangerie.

traditional clay brick oven was imported brick by kaolin clay brick to Portland—where the earthen sides retain moisture and provide for more even baking (in other words, perfectly flaky croissants and custard-rich *canalets*). If you don't have much of a sweet tooth, ask for a slice of fresh-made quiche or the astounding croque monsieur sandwich (grilled brioche with black forest ham, Emmental cheese, Béchamel sauce, and Dijon mustard) and grab a seat at one of the sidewalk tables.

DESSERT
CUPCAKE JONES $

307 NW 10th Ave., 503/222-4404,
www.cupcakejones.net
HOURS: Mon.-Sat. 10 A.M.-8 P.M., Sun. noon-6 P.M.

It doesn't take a thinking man to figure out why cupcakes are suddenly so popular. They're sweet, portable, and provide infinite possibility for creative flavor combinations. Cupcake Jones is a perfect example of that. Their tiny Pearl District bakery sells cupcakes and only cupcakes, but it's not uncommon to see a line out the door of people waiting to get their hands on one of the daily specials. Three standard flavors are available every day (vanilla, chocolate, and red velvet), and there are three other unique offerings each day as well. Cupcakes can be ordered in miniature bite-sized treats or jumbo-sized filled cakes that are roughly the size of a softball.

MOONSTRUCK CHOCOLATE $$

526 NW 23rd Ave., 503/542-3400
HOURS: Mon.-Thurs. 8 A.M.-10 P.M., Fri.-Sat.
8 A.M.-11 P.M., Sun. 9 A.M.-9 P.M.

Moonstruck has three locations in Portland—and some of the best coffee drinks around. A Mexican mocha is less of a morning pick-me-up and more of a decadent treat, especially since you get a free coin of dark chocolate to nibble on with your drink. The cafés have all manner of hot drinks throughout the year, and when summer comes around, they break out some pretty unbelievable ice cream shakes. While the coffee, hot chocolate, and truffles—did I mention the truffles?!—are enough to send any chocoholic into cardiac arrest, there are also a variety of cakes to satisfy that sweet tooth.

PAPA HAYDN ❸❸
701 NW 23rd Ave, www.papahaydn.com
HOURS: Mon.-Thurs. 11:30 A.M.-10 P.M., Fri.-Sat. 11:30 A.M.-midnight, Sun 10 A.M.-10 P.M.

Papa Haydn has been in business in Portland for so long that it's practically a part of the background. Locals often forget about this staple, perhaps because they have been visiting here on birthdays or other special occasions for years. While it may be off the radar of the average Portlander, Papa Haydn is no less capable of turning out beautiful desserts than it was in 1983. Take the Boccone Dolce, for example, Swiss meringues drizzled with semi-sweet chocolate and layered with fresh seasonal fruit and chantilly cream; or the Cassata, a towering Kahlua- and espresso-soaked sponge cake with bittersweet chocolate-ricotta filling. You can expect a wait, especially on Friday and Saturday nights, but it will give you ample time to check out the dessert case.

SWEET MASTERPIECES CHOCOLATE ❸❸
922 NW Davis St., 503/221-0055, www.sweetmasterpiecechocolates.com
HOURS: Mon.-Thurs. 11 A.M.-11 P.M., Fri.-Sat. 11 A.M.-midnight, Sun. 11 A.M.-11 P.M.

This Pearl District café is a popular stop for the pre- and post-theater crowd, as well as the First Thursday art walk revelers looking to take a break and indulge themselves. The café specializes in chocolate and other scrumptious treats, but also serves a light lunch menu. If you dig chocolate, you can get your fix in the form of coffee, drinking chocolate, truffles, cakes, or tortes (and just about anything in between). You can even find vegan cheesecake, which is both puzzling and fun.

TWO TARTS BAKERY ❸
2309 NW Kearney St., 503/312-9522, www.twotartsbakery.com
HOURS: Tues.-Sat. 10:30 A.M.-7 P.M., Sun. noon-5 P.M.

When Portland lost one of its favorite food carts, a dessert cart known as The Sugar Cube, diehard fans followed its owner to Two Tarts, a bakery that already had a significant following of its own. Cookies run about $0.75 each or $7.50 for a baker's dozen. Once you sample the Cappuccino Creams, Hazelnut Bacis, Pecan Tessies, or Chocolate Chip Fleur de Sel cookies, you'll wish you had more.

FRENCH

LE HAPPY ❸
1011 NW 16th Ave., 503/226-1258, www.lehappy.com
HOURS: Mon.-Thurs. 5:30 P.M.-1 A.M., Fri.-Sat. 5 P.M.-2:30 A.M., closed Sun.

In one of the lesser-traveled areas of Northwest Portland is a tiny little café that specializes in the French equivalent of comfort food: the crêpe. Trust me now, these are nothing like your average pancake-chain crêpes. Besides being tasty and filling, the darn things are pretty versatile, too. You can order them savory or sweet in styles that range from elegant (such as the Saumon Fumé, with smoked salmon and white wine) to the downright trashy Le Trash Blanc (with bacon and cheddar, and an optional can of Pabst Blue Ribbon on the side).

On the sweeter side of the menu, some local favorites are the simple clover honey and lemon crêpe and the delectable Spectac, made with Grand Marnier, Nutella, and banana flambé.

PALEY'S PLACE ❸❸❸
1204 NW 21st Ave., 503/243-2403, www.paleysplace.net
HOURS: Mon.-Thurs. 5:30-10:30 P.M., Fri.-Sat. 5:30-11 P.M., Sun. 5:30-11 P.M.

Chef-owners Vitaly and Kimberly Paley are renowned in kitchens across the nation, having worked in some of the most illustrious restaurants on the map. Thankfully, the couple settled in Portland in the early 1990s because they loved that the Pacific Northwest is blessed with a bounty of ingredients. Years after opening their intimate 50-seat restaurant, the Paleys are still receiving national acclaim for their French-influenced dishes, such as seasonal risottos, crispy sweetbreads, and hearty cassoulets. After dinner, switch things up a bit

The dining room at Paley's Place is inside a Victorian-style home.

© JOHN VALLS

and ask for a cheese course instead of dessert. Pair it with a glass of local wine for a perfectly rounded meal.

LATIN

ANDINA $$$

1314 NW Glisan St., 503/228-9535, www.andinarestaurant.com

HOURS: Mon.-Thurs. 11:30 A.M.-2:30 P.M. and 4-11 P.M., Fri.-Sat. 11:30 A.M.-2:30 P.M. and 4 P.M.-midnight, Sun. 11:30 A.M.-2:30 P.M. and 4-11 P.M.

One of Portland's best restaurants, this Pearl District Peruvian tapas place has one of the most inspired and extensive small plates menus in town. You can order traditional entrées—like pork tenderloin or Pisco-brined Cornish hen—but a better bet is to order two or three *pequeño* (small) plates each and share. The empanadas, filled with slow-cooked beef, raisins, and olives, are a must—as is the yucca root stuffed with cheese.

Both floors of Andina get packed nearly every night, so expect a wait or book ahead online. Once seated, order a Sacsayhuamán

(Just say, "sexy woman") and soak in the atmosphere.

ISABEL PEARL $$

330 NW 10th Ave., 503/222-4333

HOURS: Daily 8 A.M.-9 P.M.

Isabel Cruz, the California-based chef and owner of this smallish Pearl District fusion café, draws influence from Puerto Rican, Cuban, Mexican, Japanese, and Thai cooking. While it might seem a little strange to set lettuce wraps and edamame alongside carnitas, Cruz manages to make it work. Her food is akin to spa food—elegant, colorful, and oftentimes quite good for you. Order Cruz's signature Crispy Dragon Potatoes as a breakfast entrée with eggs and bacon or as an appetizer. For dinner, the Big Bowls are always reliable.

Isabel originally opened as a breakfast and lunch spot and has since expended its menu and hours to include happy hour and dinner service. The reception has been warm, but the breakfast and lunch menus are still more extensive.

PHOTO COURTESY OF ANDINA

RESTAURANTS

The savory smell, warm atmosphere, and killer cocktails at Andina make you feel like you have stepped into a delicious Peruvian romance.

🍸 ¡OBA! 💲💲

555 NW 12th Ave., 503/228-6161,
www.obarestaurant.com

HOURS: Mon. 11:30 A.M.-2 P.M. and 4-10:30 P.M.,
Tues.-Wed. 11:30 A.M.-2 P.M. and 4-11 P.M., Thurs.
11:30 A.M.-2 P.M. and 4-11:30 P.M., Fri.-Sat. 11:30 A.M.-2 P.M.
and 4-12:30 A.M., Sun. 4-10:30 P.M.

Show up around happy hour at ¡Oba! and you'll see where many of the pretty Pearl District denizens hang out, sipping exotic cocktails and nibbling at pretty plates of ceviche. While the happy hour is popular for its affordability and its see-and-be-seen buzz, you should skip all that and splurge on the full dinner experience. The staff is usually very attentive and informed, and the dining room is warm and inviting, with a very conversation-friendly layout. It's a wonderful spot to linger and enjoy a long meal. Try the *queso fundido,* a traditional Mexican cheese dip that is served warm with tortilla chips. Follow it up with grilled ahi tuna, served with coconut rice and fresh mango salsa.

PACIFIC NORTHWEST

CARLYLE 💲💲💲

1632 NW Thurman St., 503/595-1782,
www.carlylerestaurant.com

HOURS: Mon.-Thurs. 5:30-9:30 P.M., Fri.-Sat.
5:30-10:30 P.M., closed Sun.

Tucked into a corner of the Alphabet District, Carlyle is one of the best-kept secrets in Portland. With a menu that incorporates local produce, meat, and seafood into French, Italian, and American dishes, Carlyle is difficult to categorize. Yet somehow, it all fits together. From the quiet luxury of the cherry wood bar to the rich rabbit and morel mushroom ragout and the carefully thought-out cheese menu, everything here seems to have received passionate attention. Because of that, Carlyle is a great place to relinquish control over your meal and try the tasting menu: five courses of the chef's choosing, which usually means a sampling of the best things on the menu.

Carlyle has a fairly extensive wine menu, but

you can also bring your own bottle (corkage is usually about $20).

50 PLATES ⑤⑤
333 NW 13th Ave., 503/228-5050, www.50plates.com
HOURS: Mon.-Thurs. 11:30 A.M.-11 P.M., Fri.-Sat. 11:30 A.M.-12 A.M., Closed Sundays
When it opened in 2008, 50 Plates crashed onto the swanky Pearl District culinary scene brandishing its "we-don't-need-no-stinkin'-fusion" attitude with pride. Critics around the city turned into lovesick schoolboys over the dirty rice beignets, silver dollar–sized sliders, and perfectly prepared pre–Prohibition era cocktails. Now that the dust has settled, 50 Plates is still a shining example of a restaurant doing it right. Redefining "American cuisine" to include dishes from all 50 states, this place is known for comforting classics like Yankee pot roast, molasses barbeque short ribs, and Southwest-inspired tamale pie. The menu changes often to reflect the seasons, but you can always expect to find something familiar and homey.

Northeast   Map 3

The Northeast section of town is easily the most diverse of all the Portland quadrants. From the vibrancy of Martin Luther King Jr. Boulevard to the stately elegance of Irvington and the historic Hollywood District, the cuisine here is just as diverse as the residents who call this area home. The quadrant's high residential base and unpretentious attitude make it a popular destination for families and those who prefer a mom-and-pop-style dining experience.

AMERICAN
BELLY ⑤⑤
3500 NE Martin Luther King Jr. Blvd., 503/249-9764, www.bellyrestaurant.com
HOURS: Tues.-Sat. 5-10 P.M., Sun. 10 A.M.-2 P.M.
Despite the odd location on the busy corner of MLK and Fremont, Belly has a laid-back vibe that lends itself well to the eclectic and occasionally unfocused menu. Everything is made from scratch here, with a focus on local ingredients. Don't miss the gnocchi, perfectly chewy potato pillows tossed with a creamy sauce and whatever is fresh from the farm—be it mushrooms, peas, or asparagus. Belly offers a three-course prix fixe meal for $25, which usually includes a salad, entrée, and desert. You can also take part in their "3 for $30" deal, a progressive meal in partnership with nearby restaurants Ned Ludd and Lincoln. Enjoy one course at each venue and walk off the extra calories between each place.

CHAMELEON RESTAURANT & BAR ⑤⑤⑤
2000 NE 40th Ave., 503/460-2682, www.chameleonpdx.com
HOURS: Tues.-Sat. 5:30-10 P.M., closed Sun.-Mon.
Don't let Chameleon's unassuming exterior fool you. True to its name, this place tends to disappear into the backdrop of the Hollywood District, but inside it's a real gem. Cool green drapes adorn the patio, which is lovely in the warmer months. Inside the dining room, white linens and soft amber lighting create a cozy and intimate ambiance. The menu changes regularly, reflecting the eclectic tastes of chef-owner Pat Jeung. The seafood dishes and Asian-inspired entrées are especially reliable, but Jeung's butternut squash ravioli, grilled rack of lamb with Merlot sauce, and *tom yum* soup are favorites among the regulars.

THE GRILLED CHEESE GRILL ⑤
1027 NE Alberta St., 503/206-8959, www.grilledcheesegrill.com
HOURS: Tues.-Thurs. 11:30 A.M.-9 P.M., Fri.-Sat. 11:30 A.M.-2:30 A.M., Sun. 11:30 A.M.-3 P.M., closed Mon.
Could anything be more inspired than building a restaurant solely devoted to that childhood favorite, the grilled cheese sandwich? This place

A menu based entirely around grilled cheese? Yes, please.

has Portland written all over it. Owner and grilled cheese enthusiast Matt Breslow turned an old Airstream trailer into a kitchen and set up picnic tables where hungry patrons can devour the cheesy delights. Somehow, even the most reticent adults get giddy as schoolchildren when they see the colorful school bus that has been redesigned into a cozy seating area. You can go for something basic, like a classic cheddar on white bread sandwich (with or without crusts), or get a little crazy with bacon, apples, blue cheese, and Swiss. If you're feeling particularly kinky, try the Cheesus Burger, a patty melt nestled between two grilled cheese sandwiches and garnished with lettuce, tomato, and grilled onion.

KENNEDY SCHOOL 💲💲

5736 NE 33rd Ave., 503/228-2192,
www.mcmenamins.com
HOURS: Daily 7 A.M.-1 A.M.

The McMenamin brothers, who own more than 55 pubs, hotels, and theaters around the Northwest, saved this old elementary school from almost certain destruction when they

decided to refurbish it and convert it into a hotel and restaurant. The old cafeteria is now the Courtyard Restaurant, where slimy spinach and overcooked beans-and-weenies are no longer on the menu. Instead, they offer hearty salads, fresh-baked pizzas and calzones, and generous burgers served alongside thin, shoestring fries. Grab a pint of McMenamins stellar Terminator Stout and check out the specials while you nibble on a basket of tater tots.

NED LUDD 💲💲

3925 NE Martin Luther King Jr. Blvd., 503/228-6900,
www.nedluddpdx.com
HOURS: Mon. 11 A.M.-2 P.M. and 5-10 P.M., Thurs.
11 A.M.-2 P.M. and 5-10 P.M., Fri. 11 A.M.-2 P.M. and 5-10 P.M.,
Sat.-Sun. 5-11 P.M., closed Tues.-Wed.

The rustic elegance of this Northeast Portland spot is immediately warm and inviting. With stacks of apple and pear wood tucked into corners, dishes piled high on every flat surface, and an open kitchen spilling over with market-fresh produce, this feels just like home—assuming you live in a beautiful cabin and know how to cook. Owners Benjamin Meyer

SUSHI AND SIPPY CUPS: DINING WITH KIDS

Portland is a town for foodies, and epicureans will find a number of places that offer kid-friendly dishes in a decidedly parent-pleasing atmosphere. Don?t worry, none of these places employ a chuckling cartoon mascot or maintain the belief that children should subsist solely on mac-and-cheese and peanut butter sandwiches.

If you're looking for some morning grub with the small fries, check out **Beaterville Café** (www.beaterville.com), a terrific option for breakfast and lunch. Beaterville is entertaining enough with its decor. Kids will love the various car parts and hub caps that adorn the walls, as well as the many photos of old cars and banged up beaters. The menu is just as whimsical, with many of the favorite dishes deriving their names from classic cars. Beaterville is a great place for vegans and vegetarians; besides having many meat-free options, they will also happily substitute tofu for eggs if you ask.

Laurelwood Public House (www.laurelwoodbrewpub.com) is another great dining option, and it happens to be one of the most popular breweries in town. The pub fare food sits well with picky palates and the playroom provides both entertainment for restless tots and respite for weary parents.

If your brood is more adventurous, take them to **MarinePolis Sushiland** (www.sushilandusa.com), where dinner comes around on a conveyer belt. Sushiland is a great kid-friendly option because there is immediate gratification. The sushi here is decidedly not the best in town, but kids can have their favorites in front of them within mere seconds of sitting down – and are mesmerized by the train of tiny plates as it goes spinning past the tables. Udon soup is often a kid favorite because of the slurpy noodles, but kids also seem to love the gyoza and the sweet fried bean curd. Most plates cost only $1-2, so it's affordable for the family to try new things here.

and Jason French have done something really special with their house-made charcuterie and pickle plates, but it's that enormous brick hearth in the middle of the kitchen that make this place so different.

Named after the guy that tech-hating Luddites are named after, Ned Ludd eschews fancy technology in favor of a good old-fashioned wood-fire oven. That means homey wood-fired meat pies, cherry-glazed game hens, and oven-roasted s'mores, all infused with the essence of fruitwood.

BREAKFAST AND BRUNCH
CADILLAC CAFÉ ❶❺

1801 NE Broadway, 503/287-4750
HOURS: Mon.-Fri. 6 A.M.-2 P.M., Sat.-Sun. 7 A.M.-3 P.M.

Cadillac Café is a breakfast standard around Portland, but not in the gritty, greasy spoon way. This is not a venue for nursing your Friday night hangover; rather, it's the sort of place where you might take your mom on Mother's Day. Cadillac is bright and clean

with a sprightly sort of attitude that makes you think the servers were nipping into the coffee long before the doors opened. If you have a sweet tooth, you won't want to miss the hazelnut-crusted French toast; otherwise, sink your fork into filet mignon and eggs or one of the hearty scrambles. Oh, and in case you were wondering, there is indeed a Cadillac in the Cadillac Café. A full-size 1961 Caddy in perfect condition is showcased in the center of the restaurant.

HELSER'S ON ALBERTA ❶❺

1538 NE Alberta St., 503/281-1477,
www.helsersonalberta.com
HOURS: Daily 7 A.M.-3 P.M.

If you go to Helser's for any reason, go for the German pancake (also known as a Dutch baby, but that seems a little macabre). The eggy puffed pancake is baked until it's golden brown and approximately the size of a bowler hat. One is enough to feed the entire table, especially if you order Scotch eggs on the side (hard-boiled eggs wrapped in bratwurst, breaded and fried). If that's not your cup of tea, try the brioche French toast or the smoked salmon hash topped with poached eggs and hollandaise. Order a mimosa made with fresh orange juice and you are well on your way to a food coma.

MILO'S CITY CAFÉ ❸❸

1325 NE Broadway St., 503/288-6456,
www.miloscitycafe.com

HOURS: Mon.-Fri. 6:30 A.M.-2:30 P.M. and 4:30-9:30 P.M., Sat.-Sun. 7:30 A.M.-2:30 P.M. and 4:30-9:30 P.M.

When you visit Milo's you might have the distinct feeling that you've been there before, not because it's familiar, but because everyone seems to treat you like a regular. The scrambles and omelets are superb and if you like a good Benedict, there are six for you to choose from. The crab cake Benedict with fresh Dungeness crab and béarnaise sauce is a neighborhood favorite—as is the Marianne, with cooked-to-order petite tenderloin. Make sure you arrive before 10:30 A.M. if you plan to have breakfast. They switch to their lunch menu at 11 A.M. and with the average wait time on the weekends exceeding half an hour, you may not get a chance to order before they stop serving.

FRENCH

❰ BEAST ❸❸❸

5425 NE 30th Ave., 503/841-6968,
www.beastpdx.com

HOURS: Wed.-Sat. dinner seatings at 6 P.M. and 8:45 P.M., Sun. brunch seatings at 10 A.M. and noon

Chef-owner Naomi Pomeroy is a legend in the Portland food scene. She was named one of the Best New Chefs of 2009 by *Food & Wine* and was featured in *Bon Appétit* within months of opening Beast. Pomeroy has drawn eyes thanks to her unabashed approach to "French grandma-style" cooking.

The prix fixe dinner is $60 per person for six courses, and it changes each week. Each meal usually begins with a delicate soup followed by a charcuterie plate stocked with such nibbles as foie gras bonbons, chicken liver mousse, and pickled seasonal vegetables. For the main course, you might find stuffed rabbit, braised duck, or pork cheeks (if you're lucky). As long as you are splurging, opt for wine pairings in addition to the meal ($35 for six small glasses).

PETITE PROVENCE ❸

1824 NE Alberta St., 503/284-6564,
www.provence-portland.com

HOURS: Sun.-Tues. 7 A.M.-6 P.M., Wed.-Sat. 7 A.M.-9 P.M.

Whether you stop by Petite Provence for breakfast or lunch, make sure you take away one of the buttery pastries in a bag for later. If you can get past the cream puffs, caramel tarts, and opera cakes, take a gander at the full menu, stocked with French egg dishes, grilled sandwiches, and country-style salads. The Colette Omelet is a neighborhood favorite, with its combination of basil and eggs topped with artichoke hearts, tomatoes, and mozzarella and then placed under the broiler until it's bubbly. For lunch, salads are a good bet. The goat cheese salad is simple enough, with medallions of cheese tossed with greens, onion, red peppers, roasted walnuts, and a light vinaigrette dressing. It's satisfying and refreshing, but still leaves room for a bowl of French onion soup and an almond croissant.

TABLA ❸❸❸

200 NE 28th Ave., 503/238-3777,
www.tabla-restaurant.com

HOURS: Tues.-Sun. 5-10 P.M., closed Mon.

Tabla calls itself a Mediterranean bistro, but its menu takes a big lesson from the French. The $24 three-course tasting menu allows you to choose three items from the regular menu; wine pairings are available with each course for just a bit more. Start off with a chilled vichyssoise or a warm haricot vert salad and move on to the tagliatelle with spicy pork sugo. Hopefully, you'll still have room for the fresh pan-seared salmon or halibut cheeks.

Tabla has long been one of the best restaurants in the area. Nowadays, there's a lot more competition from neighboring joints, but Tabla is still a reliable, chic choice in a comfortable, relaxed, and airy atmosphere. It can get a bit pricey, but you can save money by bringing your own bottle of wine and paying a $15 corkage fee.

TOUR DE CRÊPES ❺

2921 NE Alberta St., 503/473-8657,
www.tourdecrepes.blogspot.com
HOURS: Thurs. 10 A.M.–8 P.M., Fri. 10 A.M.–9 P.M., Sat. 9 A.M.–9 P.M., closed Mon.–Wed.

It's easy to miss this tiny crepe house if you aren't looking for it. Tiny, old, and reeking of character, this funky café serves up some really fantastic concoctions. Once you enter the colorful Carriage House you have to exit right out the back to order. The kitchen is located in an Airstream trailer behind the establishment. At the top of the list on this menu are the crêpe filled with prosciutto, chevre, and marsala-soaked figs and the decadent dark chocolate, poached pears, and white chocolate mascarpone delight. Tour de Crêpes also has a number of remarkably tasty vegan options such as fig-onion chutney, roasted garlic spread, almonds, and parsley all nestled inside a buckwheat crêpe. The wait can be long sometimes because the venue is understaffed, but the food is well worth it. There are no bathrooms on the premises but you can use the facilities at the coffeehouse next door.

ITALIAN
CIAO VITO ❺❺❺

2203 NE Alberta St., 503/282-5522, www.ciaovito.net
HOURS: Daily 5–10 P.M.

Ciao Vito is a diamond in the rough in the otherwise artsy, granola-crunching Alberta Arts District. The menu is a bit pricey, but includes simple, elegant, well-prepared dishes like pork sugo with crispy fried polenta, Bolognese ragu with fettuccini, and arguably the best beet salad in Portland. Start with the calamari and antipasti plate, served with bread from Ken's Artisan Bakery and spicy olive oil. When your entrée comes, don't be afraid to nibble at it and save room for dessert. Many of the heartier dishes here reheat well as leftovers and Ciao Vito's panna cotta with amarena cherry and caramel sauce is not to be missed.

D.O.C. ❺❺❺

5519 NE 30th Ave., 503/946-8592, www.docpdx.com
HOURS: Tues.–Sat. 6–10 P.M., closed Sun.–Mon.

If you think you've seen an open kitchen, you have never seen one like D.O.C.'s (Denominazione di Origine Controllata, the Italian food and wine control). Walk through the front door of this tiny establishment, just past the windows with red-checkered curtains and Mason jars stacked in the sills, and you will find yourself smack dab in the middle of the kitchen. It can be a bit disconcerting at first, but soon you will find yourself mesmerized by the tidiness and efficiency with which things are run. The restaurant opened in June 2008 and is already being recognized as one of the best in town, particularly when it comes to polished and chic, yet intimate dining. Chef Greg Perrault's cuisine nears perfection with dishes like tagliatelle, beef cheeks, and risotto. Order in courses or opt for the chef's tasting menu ($50), which gives you five courses, including dessert.

JAPANESE
YAKUZA ❺❺

5411 NE 30th Ave., 503/450-0893,
www.yakuzalounge.com
HOURS: Wed.–Thurs. 5:30–10 P.M., Fri.–Sat. 5:30–10:30 P.M., Sun. 5:30–10 P.M., closed Mon.–Tues.

A sushi restaurant named after the Japanese mafia? Well, not exactly. The term is a touchy subject, but the original meaning of the word *yakuza* was meant to describe people who aren't easily categorized. So the name is a surprisingly good fit for this Japanese joint, which seems to take what it likes from both the Japanese culture and the Pacific Northwest influence of owner Micah Camden. The dining room is sexy and sleek, with whimsical murals adorning the walls and large garage door windows. The menu is a good mix between traditional sushi and Asian-inspired hot dishes. Plan to order about three or four plates per person, as most items are served family-style and you'll want to sample a number of things. Panko-fried goat cheese is a must, as is the carpaccio and the spicy tuna roll. Be sure to try one of the signature cocktails as well. The Whiskey #1 is particularly tasty with Maker's Mark, brandied apricots, and a dash of nutmeg.

ZILLA SAKÉ HOUSE ❸❸

1806 NE Alberta St., 503/288-8372,
www.zillasakehouse.com
HOURS: Mon.-Sat. 5 P.M.-midnight, Sun. 5-10 P.M.

Zilla Saké House is pleasant, dark, and cozy, with high-backed booths and rain-colored walls adorned with funky decor. The staff is knowledgeable and helpful without a hint of pretentiousness. For that reason, and thanks to the sheer volume of options available, it is a great place to become a burgeoning sake drinker and sushi eater. If you like to nibble slowly, order the edamame, which is seasoned with ginger in addition to the traditional sea salt and pepper. The spicy *ika* (dried squid jerky) is a surprisingly delightful nibble, especially with wasabi mayo on the side. The sashimi, particularly the hamachi, is all quite good and served with real wasabi (which looks more like pesto than green paste).

MEXICAN

CHEZ JOSE EAST ❸❸

2200 NE Broadway St., 503/280-9888,
www.chezjoserestaurant.com
HOURS: Mon.-Thurs. 5-11 P.M., Fri.-Sat. 5 P.M.-midnight, Sun. 5-10 P.M.

This bustling Northeast family favorite is popular among locals for its kid-friendly atmosphere, top-shelf margaritas, and hearty Mexican fare. Kids under seven eat for free every night 5–7 P.M., so if you want to avoid the chaos, come in later or grab a seat in the back near the bar. Ask most people around you what to order and they are likely to be split between the butternut squash enchiladas with mushrooms, apples, jicama, onion, cheese, and peanut sauce or the lime chicken enchiladas with lime sour cream sauce. Both are equally delicious.

There's no need to order the large portions here, unless you are a big fan of leftovers. You can order à la carte or with rice and beans in single or double fashion. Word to the wise: the doubles are enormous and by the time you get

your order, you will have snacked heavily on chips, salsa and mole sauce.

LA BONITA ❸

2839 NE Alberta St., 503/281-3662
HOURS: Wed.-Thurs. 11 A.M.-9 P.M., Fri.-Sat. 11 A.M.-10 P.M., Sun. 11 A.M.-9 P.M., closed Mon.-Tues.

This little taqueria may not look like much from the outside, but the food is quick, inexpensive, and delicious—and the walls display the work of local artists. La Bonita is family-owned and claims to be "as authentic as Mexican gets." They come darn close with their *al pastor* tacos and unbelievably good carne asada. The burritos are enormous and run only about $6 each. If you stop in a little early or if you want to plan ahead for tomorrow, grab a breakfast burrito, filled with eggs, chorizo, and hash browns.

TAPAS

LOLO ❸❸

2940 NE Alberta St., 503/288-3400,
www.lolopdx.com
HOURS: Tues.-Sat. 5-10 P.M., Sun. 5-9 P.M., closed Mon.

Portlanders love small plates and while Toro Bravo gets a lot of attention, lolo is equally dependable and oftentimes less chaotic. There are a few vegetarian options on the tapas list; your server can provide you with a menu that details which items are safe and which ones can be made safe for non-meat eaters. Try the short rib empanadas, the salt cod cakes, or the ever-so-slightly spicy calamari. Better yet, try them all. You might be tempted to skip over the smaller things like the Spanish olives or the sea salt and herb potato chips. Don't make this mistake, as lolo really knocks it out of the park with simple dishes like these that allow great ingredients to shine.

NAVARRE ❸❸

10 NE 28th Ave., 503/232-3555,
www.navarreportland.blogspot.com
HOURS: Mon.-Thurs. 4:30-10:30 P.M., Fri. 11:30 A.M.-11:30 P.M., Sat. 9:30 A.M.-11:30 P.M., Sun. 9:30 A.M.-10:30 P.M.

The food at Navarre is like improvisational

RESTAURANTS

theater. You never quite know what you're going to get, but the off-the-cuff brilliance of it is impressive. Chef John Taboada builds his menu daily around the ingredients he gets from a nearby Community Supported Agriculture (CSA). If parsnips are in season, they might just get tossed into a warm crab salad. Fresh greens may be tucked under foie gras. Cauliflower is transformed into gratin. Green tomatoes are breaded and fried. Whatever you choose from the menu, make sure you order some bread (from Ken's Artisan Bakery down the street) to soak up all the bits of sauce and dressing from the other plates. Since it's technically a wine bar, Navarre has more than 50 different wines by the glass, so it's easy to pair a vintage with the eclectic array of plates on the table. Ask your server for recommendations if you get overwhelmed.

◖ TORO BRAVO 🄢🄢

120 NE Russell St., 503/281-4464,
www.torobravopdx.com
HOURS: Sun.-Thurs. 5-10 P.M., Fri.-Sat. 5-11 P.M.

Toro Bravo set Portland on its ear when it opened in 2007. Suddenly, everyone wanted to be there. Dinner here is an event, a whirlwind of noise and activity, a mish-mash of fast-moving plates and eager conversation. The general excitement here is palpable because everyone is waiting for their next little morsel to arrive.

The tapas here are expertly crafted right down to the last loving detail. Must-try dishes include the bacon-wrapped dates in warm honey, oxtail croquettes, and the delectable olive oil cake with caramel. The wait for a table can be agonizingly long, so be prepared. Don't come when you are ravenous. Reservations aren't offered for parties with fewer than seven people and aren't taken at all for Fridays and Saturdays. Come early and put your name on the list and then head upstairs to the Secret Society Lounge, where you can imbibe cocktails and snacks while you wait.

SOUTHERN AND CREOLE
◖ SCREEN DOOR 🄢🄢

2337 E. Burnside St., 503/542-0880,
www.screendoorrestaurant.com
HOURS: Tues.-Fri. 5:30-10 P.M., Sat. 9 A.M.-2:30 P.M. and 5:30-10 P.M., Sun. 9 A.M.-2:30 P.M. and 5:30-9 P.M., closed Mon.

One of the most secretly celebrated restaurants in Portland, Screen Door never takes itself too seriously. This is one of a few places in the city where you're likely to find off-shift chefs and bartenders. It's no coincidence. The menu spits in the face of the hoity-toity low-carb or raw food mentality, but still manages to use some of the best local ingredients in its soul-quenching dishes. This is food the way it was meant to be eaten. Crispy fried oysters dripping with gribiche sauce or fried green tomatoes with remoulade followed by some of the best fried chicken in the city will have you singing the praises of this quaint little Burnside joint. Will you wait for a table? Yes, you probably will. Will you clutch your belly in gluttonous joy as you roll yourself out the door? It's quite likely. Will it be worth every sticky, drippy, carb-laden bite? Absolutely.

This is another one of Portland's popular brunch spots. If you manage to get a table, don't walk away without sampling Screen Door's infamous praline bacon and equally notorious Bloody Mary.

THAI
SIAM SOCIETY 🄢🄢

2703 NE Alberta St., 503/922-3675,
www.siamsociety.com
HOURS: Tues.-Thurs. 11:30 A.M.-2:30 P.M. and 4:30-9 P.M., Fri. 11:30 A.M.-2:30 P.M. and 4:30-10 P.M., Sat. noon-2:30 P.M. and 4:30-10 P.M., Sun.-Mon. 4-9 P.M. Soi Cowboy lounge only

Even before you walk through the doors of this old electrical substation turned swank fusion restaurant, you somehow feel a bit more hip. Inside, the high cement ceilings, arched windows, candlelit tables, and curtained walls make you feel like you have stumbled onto the opulent set of *The King and I.*

The menu has a lot of creative items, so skip

© HOLLYANNA MCCOLLOM

The industrial-chic exterior of Siam Society hints at the menu inside.

the more traditional Thai items and opt for something more innovative, like the banana roasted pork shoulder or the pan-seared scallops in Brazilian red palm dende oil with coconut milk, garlic, and lime. Also, don't leave without having one of Siam Society's signature cocktails. They make their own infusions and the results are inspiring. Try a Soi Cowboy (tamarind pulp, bourbon, triple sec, and muddled mint) or a Hibiscus Mojito. Both are tasty and pair perfectly with the Asian flair of the menu.

SWEET BASIL $$

3135 NE Broadway, 503/281-8337,
www.sweetbasilor.com
HOURS: Mon.-Thurs. 11:30 A.M.-2:30 P.M. and 5-9 P.M.,
Fri. 11:30 A.M.-2:30 P.M. and 5-10 P.M., Sat. 5-10 P.M., Sun.
5-9 P.M.

Sweet Basil resides in an old Portland home

that has three cozy rooms and a large patio out back that's open in warmer months. They lean toward the traditional here, with delicate touches that make the dishes unexpectedly exciting. Start with a few appetizers while you wait for your entrées, or make a meal of appetizers, like the aptly named "O My God," a mix of crab, basil, and cream cheese wrapped in a tortilla, golden fried, and served with housemade plum sauce.

You must be accurate here about how spicy you want things. If you say you want it at level 10, they will kick it up with small Thai chilies, making your meal truly fiery. Thank goodness a side of black jasmine and white jasmine rice (charmingly, in the shape of a star and a moon) is served alongside the entrées.

Southeast   Map 4

Southeast Portland is fast becoming a home for great food, sassy presentation, and an adherence to artistic creativity—and less about the ever-popular but ironic dive bar. Since Southeast is home to the burgeoning area known as Distillery Row, where a number of craft distillers like House Spirits, New Deal, and Integrity have set up shop, the area has been imbued with passion for flavor, comfort, and delight. In other words, moderation isn't really part of the vocabulary here.

FRENCH
CAFÉ CASTAGNA $$

1758 SE Hawthorne Blvd., 503/231-9959, www.castagnarestaurant.com
HOURS: Mon. 5-11 P.M., Tues.-Sat. 11:30 A.M.-2 P.M. and 5-11 P.M., Sun. 5-10 P.M.

While the atmosphere at Café Castagna is a bit stark—with concrete floors and simple tables—the food is like a great big hug. Café Castagna can only loosely be categorized as French, but the coq au vin is phenomenal—it's not uncommon for them to run out of it—and so is the tarte aux pomme with Gruyére that's available on occasion. The real star, however, is the burger. While on the pricier side at around $11, it is as close to perfection as you can get. It's made with Painted Hills ground sirloin and cooked to your liking, and the pickles—which are sweet and seasoned with coriander, cumin, cloves, and cinnamon—merit almost as much attention.

❰ LE PIGEON $$$

738 E. Burnside St., 503/546-8796, www.lepigeon.com
HOURS: Mon.-Sat. 5-10 P.M., Sun. 5-9 P.M.

Portland has its fair share of vegan and vegetarian joints, but Le Pigeon ain't one of them. This place is all about indulgence, particularly the carnivorous kind. Chef Gabriel Rucker has achieved celebrity status for his use of classic French techniques with a modern twist. How about a pork belly salad or a foie gras

jelly doughnut? That's just for starters. The menu changes according to the chef's whim (and what's available at the local markets) but if you get a chance to try the beef cheeks, do not pass it up. The meat absolutely melts in your mouth.

This is a great spot if you're feeling adventurous, because it's not uncommon to find pig's tail, sweetbreads, and yes, even pigeon on the menu.

SEL GRIS $$$

1852 SE Hawthorne Blvd., 503/517-7770, www.selgrisrestaurant.com
HOURS: Mon.-Thurs. 5:30-10 P.M., Fri.-Sat. 5:30-11 P.M., closed Sun.

This bistro-style restaurant is a modish urban beauty with a bright, bustling open kitchen. Chef Daniel Mondok is a Portland legend and a winner of the Iron Chef Oregon competition several times over. Both the food and the presentation here seem to have a visceral effect on the patrons, who rock in their seats, hum, and cry out when sampling dishes like the fried calamari or risotto. The cuisine here is creative, but seemingly effortless, fabulous without being fussy. It is also carefully planned, right down to the last drizzle of sauce or sprinkle of salt.

Given the intimate nature of the venue and the bustle of the kitchen, Sel Gris isn't known for being a quiet dining spot. It's better to just accept it and enjoy the show. Or better yet, snag a seat at the chef's bar, which offers a front row seat of Mondok in action.

JAPANESE
❰ BAMBOO SUSHI $$$

310 SE 28th Ave., 503/232-5255, www.bamboosushipdx.com
HOURS: Daily 5-10 P.M.

There are a number of really great sushi restaurants in Portland, which is not surprising when you consider the proximity of the Pacific Ocean and the availability of some of the world's best salmon, crab, cod, halibut, and tuna. Bamboo Sushi made waves when it opened in 2008, not just because the sushi was top notch, but also because this was the first certified sustainable sushi restaurant in the world. The Green Machine is a vegetarian favorite with tempura asparagus, avocado, green onion, and cilantro sweet chili aioli; the Highway 35 (a critic favorite) has red crab, spicy sesame aioli, avocado, cucumber, and asparagus topped with sake-poached pears and eel sauce.

YOKO'S JAPANESE RESTAURANT ✖✖

2878 SE Gladstone St., 503/736-9228

HOURS: Daily 5-9:30 P.M.

Word to the wise: The wait at Yoko's is always long. Arrive mere moments after the doors open and you are still likely to wait an hour. To make the wait easier, leave your cell phone number on the sign-up sheet and head next door to C Bar, where the bartenders are happy to serve you a cocktail and offer you a sympathetic sigh.

Once inside the tiny sushi shack, peruse the extensive sake menu and order a number of rolls to share family-style. Yoko's is known for having creative, artful creations and that is where they really excel. If you just stick to the things you know like California rolls and spicy tuna, you might be disappointed. Try the Rainbow Roll or the popular Batman Roll, made with eel and cream cheese. Whatever you do, don't skip the Taka tuna, a local favorite.

PACIFIC NORTHWEST
CLARKLEWIS ✖✖✖

1001 SE Water Ave., 503/235-2294,
www.clarklewispdx.com

HOURS: Mon. 5-11 P.M., Tues.-Sat. 11:30 A.M.-2 P.M. and 5-11 P.M., closed Sun.

Deep in the gritty industrial area of Portland's inner southeast is an old loading dock that has been transformed into one of the city's swankiest restaurants. With small, elegant tables set into a cement and steel backdrop, the place is romantic without an overdose of femininity. In the cooler months, when the weather prevents them from opening the great garage-style doors

to let in light, the dinner hour can get downright dark. It's often so dark, in fact, that your server will bring you a tiny flashlight to read your menu by.

Your best bet is to chuck the menu altogether and go for the Chef's Choice, a prix fixe four-course meal ($55 per person). For an additional $55, wine pairings will accompany each course. Be sure to tell them if you have any allergies and then sit back and eat like an expert epicurean.

THE FARM CAFÉ ✖✖

10 SE 7th Ave., 503/736-3276, www.thefarmcafe.com

HOURS: Daily 5-11:30 P.M.

The Farm Café is a chic place that was converted from a farmhouse into a pretty little restaurant. The kitchen buys most of its ingredients direct from local farmers, so the menu is a fair reflection of Pacific Northwest bounty. Dishes are always remarkably presented and quite good. While the restaurant was remodeled during summer 2009 to include more space and a patio, it can still be tough to get a table, and reservations are available only for parties of six or more. You can, however, ride out the wait at the bar, which makes it all worthwhile.

WILD ABANDON ✖✖

2411 SE Belmont St., 503/232-4458,
www.wildabandonrestaurant.com

HOURS: Mon. 9 A.M.-2 P.M. and 4:30-10 P.M., Wed.-Fri. 9 A.M.-2 P.M. and 4:30-10 P.M., Sat.-Sun. 9 A.M.-2 P.M. and 5:30-11 P.M., closed Tues.

Wild Abandon is well known for its brunch menu with scrambles, Benedicts, and omelets for both vegetarians and omnivores. The brunch is good—so good, in fact, that it often overshadows the fact that this is a lovely place to catch a cozy, romantic dinner. The small venue does not lend itself well to large groups, but the bohemian decor and low lighting make it a great place to canoodle over a chocolate truffle tort.

While the menu changes often, it is not uncommon to find pan-fried oysters, grilled rib-eyes made from locally raised beef, or market-fresh Pacific fish among the entrées. Ask your server what the manicotti and risotto specials are; they change regularly and are often superb.

PIZZA
APIZZA SCHOLLS 🟊🟊
4741 SE Hawthorne Blvd., 503/233-1286,
www.apizzascholls.com
HOURS: Mon.-Sat. 5-9:30 P.M., Sun. 4-8 P.M.

When was the last time you waited an hour for a table to get a pizza? While it might seem crazy, Portlanders do just that almost every night at Apizza Scholls. In fact, it's not uncommon for folks to be lined up outside the place when the doors are unlocked. That's because Apizza has achieved that terrific balance that is required to make really good pizza. The crust is tantamount to pizza's success and this one is crispy on the outside, soft on the inside, and still maintains a flavor of its own that does not compete with the toppings.

KEN'S ARTISAN PIZZA 🟊🟊
304 SE 28th Ave., 503/517-9951,
www.kensartisan.com/pizza.html
HOURS: Tues.-Sat. 5-10 P.M., closed Sun.-Mon.

Ken's Artisan Pizza formed out of necessity when the bakery of the same name was flooded by requests for its hand-tossed, wood-fired pizzas—much like what you would find in Italy. The wait is long here. Reservations aren't accepted, and they won't seat a group larger than 10. To-go pizzas are occasionally done at the discretion of the staff (according to how busy they are) and are limited in number. Pizzas come in one size, which is perfect for one or two people, and there are a number of appetizers (try the lamb and pita) and salads to round out the meal.

WY'EAST PIZZA 🟊🟊
3131 SE 50th Ave., www.wyeastpizza.com
HOURS: Tues.-Sat. 4-8 P.M., closed Sun.-Mon.

Pizza from a trailer? Yup, especially when it's one of these 12-inch, made-to-order beauties. An outdoor trailer with a 800-degree oven in the middle of Southeast Portland is an oddity at best, but the service and quality of food continuously squash any questions about whether the owners know what they're doing. Wy'east (the Multnomah name for Mount Hood) always has a handful of pizzas to choose from, like the Zig-Zag Glacier, a delicious white pie with kalamata olives, arugula, and copious amounts of garlic. If you bike or walk there, you'll get a $1 discount, but no matter what, bring cash.

SOUTHERN AND CREOLE
CLAY'S SMOKEHOUSE 🟊🟊
2932 SE Division St., 503/235-4755,
www.clayssmokehouse.ypguides.net
HOURS: Wed.-Sun. 11 A.M.-10 P.M.

Portland has a number of barbeque spots, each with its own signature. At Clay's, you can smell the meat cooking for a three-block radius. All the meat is smoked on the premises—including the juicy brisket, chicken, and catfish—forming a carnivorous cloud around this quaint little block of Division Street. The meats are all fine, but oddly enough, Clay's also has remarkable salads. The spinach salad (with alder-smoked salmon, hazelnuts, pears, and white cheddar) is out of this world, and the grilled pork loin salad (with bleu cheese, spicy pecans, pepperoncini, tomatoes, croutons and balsamic vinaigrette) is a delight for those who want their greens, but just can't pass up a healthy portion of pig.

DOT'S CAFÉ 🟊
2521 SE Clinton St., 503/235-0203
HOURS: Daily noon-2 A.M.

Dot's Café has become a part of the Portland iconography. This is partly due to its location in the heart of the Clinton Street District, one of the smallest but most beloved (by locals) neighborhoods around—but it's also due to the fact that Dot's serves fantastically gut-busting fare until the wee hours of the morning. Dot's is like a 1950s diner, except you're more likely to hear Radiohead than Chubby Checker blasting through the sound system and you can't help but wonder if someone forgot to turn on the lights. While the velvet wallpaper and kitschy diner vibe lend to its charm, Dot's really wins with its menu, chock-full of things like chili cheese fries, Swiss and mushroom patty melts, burgers, and tuna melts. What's more, Dot's has a number of vegetarian options, like garden burgers, falafel wraps, vegan burritos, and hummus platters. Cash only.

LE BISTRO MONTAGE ⓒ$

301 SE Morrison St., 503/234-1324,
www.montageportland.com
HOURS: Mon. 6 P.M.-2 A.M., Tues. 11:30 A.M.-2 P.M. and
6 P.M.-2 A.M., Fri. 11:30 A.M.-2 P.M. and 6 P.M.-4 A.M., Sat.
6 P.M.-4 A.M., Sun. 6 P.M.-2 A.M.
Visiting Le Bistro Montage is almost a rite of passage for Portlanders. The service can be abrupt, abrasive, or almost absent, but the various "Macs" are cheap, filling, and worth any abuse you might suffer. It's tempting to try the oddities on the menu like frog legs and alligator linguini, but you're better off sticking with the Montage classics. The original macaroni and cheese recipe, Old Mac, was featured on the Food Network, and is a simple garlic, parmesan, and heavy cream delight. Another staple is the jambalaya, hearty and spicy with Cajun gravy and your choice of chicken, catfish, rock shrimp, crawfish, scallops, oysters, andouille sausage, or, yes, even alligator.

There are no boring doggie bags here. Instead, leftovers are wrapped in foil and sculpted into a veritable cornucopia of shapes like snails, flowers, swords, and cats.

Sellwood and Moreland   Map 5

RESTAURANTS

Deep in Southeast Portland, you'll find the quaint neighborhood of Sellwood, which is bordered by Westmoreland to the north, Eastmoreland to the east, and the city of Milwaukie to the south. The area has a small-town feel, and was once, in fact, its own city. Nowadays, Sellwood is home to a fine collection of friendly small businesses, mom-and-pop bars, and neighborly restaurants.

Moreland is split into distinctive halves. To the east, you will find Eastmoreland, the home of Reed College, Crystal Springs Rhododendron Garden, and a number of chi-chi independently owned boutiques. And while it is difficult to tell when you have crossed into Westmoreland, the neighborhood is known for its manicured yards, stately homes, and impressive mansions.

AMERICAN
MIKE'S DRIVE-IN ⓢ
1707 SE Tenino St., 503/236-4537
HOURS: Sun.-Thurs. 10 A.M.-10 P.M., Fri.-Sat.
10 A.M.-11 P.M.
A throwback to the days of old is Sellwood's Mike's Drive-In, where the shakes are often made with fresh, local ingredients like strawberries,

marionberries, and peaches; seasonal choices like pumpkin and eggnog; and a bevy of whimsical choices like marshmallow, orange Creamsicle, and Skor chocolate bars. But the list of options at Mike's does not end there. Like any good drive-in worth its salt, Mike's has an extensive menu filled with things that are fried, grilled, or covered with cheese, including a pretty good list of burgers, foot-long hot dogs, Reubens, and sandwiches made on soft pretzel buns.

PAPA HAYDN ⓒ$
5829 SE Milwaukie Ave., 503/232-9440,
www.papahaydn.com
HOURS: Mon.-Thurs. 11:30 A.M.-10 P.M., Fri.-Sat.
11:30 A.M.-midnight, Sun. 10 A.M.-9 P.M.
This chic but slightly more understated sister to the Papa Haydn in Northwest Portland is, of course, a fine place for desserts, but the elegant, airy atmosphere also makes it a nice place for a meal or Sunday brunch. If you go for dinner, start with the gorgonzola and fontina fondue, order some entrées to share, and then see if you have room for fresh berry cobbler or peanut butter mousse cake. It's best to head there early for quick seating; at both Papa Haydn

outposts, the dining room tends to fill up later in the evening when people come for dessert.

ASIAN
JADE TEAHOUSE & PATISSERIE $$
7912 SE 13th Ave., 503/477-8985,
www.jadeteahouse.com
HOURS: Tues.-Sat. 11 A.M.-9 P.M., Sun. 11 A.M.-5 P.M., closed Mon.

Do not be deceived into thinking that Jade Teahouse is a bustling fast-food place, despite the counter service. It's quite the contrary, in fact. This calm, peaceful restaurant invites lingering; and with countless excellent teas, free Wi-Fi, and some of the best Vietnamese food in town, it's easy to do so. The salad rolls are fresh and spicy, with a great balance of texture and flavors, and the French fries with truffle oil alone are worth the trip to this part of town.

MEKONG VIETNAMESE GRILL $
7952 SE 13th Ave., 503/808-9092,
www.mekonggrill.com
HOURS: Mon.-Sat. 11:30 A.M.-3:30 P.M. and 5-9 P.M., closed Sun.

This simple, yet spacious Vietnamese restaurant in Sellwood was named for the Mekong Delta, an area abundant with rice, vegetables, and fruit. The Sellwood neighborhood has long hungered for good Asian cuisine, particularly a good *pho*. Thankfully, this spot serves good takeout or dine-in fare that is both quick and healthy. The menu has a handful of grilled items, like salads and skewers of chicken, beef, pork, or tofu, as well as egg rolls and salad rolls, and rice and noodle entrées. Be sure to check out the daily specials, which often feature *pho*.

BREAKFAST AND BRUNCH
BERTIE LOU'S $
8051 SE 17th Ave., 503/239-1177
HOURS: Mon.-Fri. 7 A.M.-2 P.M., Sat.-Sun. 7:30 A.M.-2 P.M.
Bertie Lou's is the Estelle Getty of the breakfast world in PDX. She's tiny, colorful, and a bit rough around the edges, but oh boy, does she pack a punch. Bertie's offers a truly extensive collection of standard breakfast offerings like biscuits and gravy, Benedicts, scrambles,

and omelets with witty descriptions like, "if you're a little hungover…this one's for you" and "the things I do for money." Bike riders get a 10 percent discount, but breakfast will only run you about $6–10 anyway, so it's affordable even if you arrive in a gas-guzzler.

FAT ALBERT'S $
6668 SE Milwaukie Ave., 503/872-9822
HOURS: Mon.-Fri. 6 A.M.-2 P.M., Sat.-Sun. 7 A.M.-3 P.M.
You won't really want to linger at Fat Albert's. For one thing, there is a sign that discourages you from "camping." For another thing, there's probably going to be a horde of hungry people eyeing your table and drooling over every plate of home-style potatoes that goes by. It's not the sort of place that will fuss over you, so don't expect anyone to spread jelly on your toast or cut up your chicken-fried steak for you. This place is all about no-nonsense, good food. The portions are generous and the food is great, which is really all that matters on most days. Bring cash.

CAJUN AND CREOLE
DELTA CAFÉ $$
4607 SE Woodstock Blvd., 503/771-3101,
www.deltacafeandbar.com
HOURS: Mon.-Fri. 5 P.M.-midnight, Sat.-Sun. 9 A.M.-midnight
In the heart of the Woodstock neighborhood, Delta Café is a favorite haunt for nearby Reed College students on a carbohydrate binge and families who know that kids love nothing more than a bowl of ooey-gooey mac and cheese. If you can get past the appetizer menu—with its hushpuppies, cornbread, sweet potato fries, and catfish bites—settle into a plate of fried chicken or a bowl of crawfish étouffée; or simply order a sampler platter. Delta also has a fantastic cocktail menu that utilizes a variety of house-infused vodka, tequila, rum, and whiskey.

ITALIAN
GARDEN STATE $
7875 SE 13th Ave., 503/705-5273,
www.gardenstatecart.com
HOURS: Tues.-Sun. 11 A.M.-3:30 P.M., closed Mon.
While grab-and-go vegetarian food can be

difficult to find (even in a city that embraces it), Garden State is doing something right. The Sellwood food cart was featured in *Sunset* magazine thanks to its delicious chickpea sandwich and the rest of its Italian street food menu. Try the *arancine* (fried risotto balls) or the Sicilian potato fritters with tomato sauce. Both are pure, unadulterated comfort in a box. The menu changes with the seasons, but everything is delicious. Meat eaters won't go hungry at this cart, either. Garden State's take on the classic meatball hero or chicken saltimbocca are both superb.

GINO'S ❸❸

8051 SE 13th Ave., 503/233-4613,
www.ginossellwood.com

HOURS: Sun.-Thurs. 4-10 P.M., Fri.-Sat. 4-11 P.M.

Gino's is a great place to find traditional Italian soul food: good old-fashioned cioppino; hearty ravioli tossed with seasonal sauces; chicken marsala; and a simmered-on-the-stove-all-day tomato, pork rib, and beef sauce tossed over penne. If you're on a budget, skip the expensive steaks, which are good but not exceptional. Instead, opt for the hearty pastas and a family-size Caesar

salad. If you're dining on the bar side, there is also a very small, inexpensive bar menu that occasionally includes some specialty dishes.

JAPANESE
SABURO'S ❸❸

1667 SE Bybee Blvd., 503/236-4237,
www.saburos.com

HOURS: Mon.-Thurs. 5-9:30 P.M., Fri. 5-10:30 P.M., Sat. 4:30-10 P.M., Sun. 4:30-9 P.M.

There are some who would question why people line up outside this Sellwood spot for hours waiting for spicy tuna rolls or salmon belly nigiri. For those folks, Saburo's will toss a cell-phone sized sushi roll on their plate and say, "What do you think of that?" The fish here is always quite fresh and artfully prepared, but the real killer here is the portion control (or lack thereof).

Yes, the wait is long and the staff can be a bit brusque sometimes, but it's worth the wait. Order everything you think you might want at once, including dessert, because you will not be allowed to order again. But frankly, you would be hard pressed to leave here hungry with unagi rolls that measure eight inches long.

RESTAURANTS

North Portland | Map 6

Portland's newest little darling, NoPo (North Portland), started out as an inexpensive place for the city's creative class to set up shop. With their artistic influence, the area has developed into a veritable melting pot of ideas and tastes. This spirit is reflected in the cuisine here as well. Local, homey neighborhood spots reign supreme. On this side of the river, everyone takes their time and food is more of an art form than a means of sustenance.

AMERICAN
THE FISH & CHIP SHOP ❸

1218 N. Killingsworth St., 503/232-3344,
www.thefishandchipshop.com

HOURS: Mon.-Thurs. noon-3 P.M. and 5-10 P.M., Fri. noon-3 P.M. and 5-11 P.M., Sat. noon-11 P.M., Sun. noon-9 P.M.

If your idea of fish and chips normally involves

a heavily breaded and dry piece of fish, the Brit-born owner of this sparsely decorated but charming hole-in-the-wall shop wants to show you what you've been missing. You can choose from cod, red snapper, Dover sole, haddock, and halibut, or whatever else is fresh. The fish here is cut when you order it, so be prepared to wait as long as 30 minutes for your food. In true British style, they also have Scotch eggs, pasties, sausage rolls, mushy peas, and Heinz curry beans.

If you aren't already stuffed from that, they will fry you up some dessert as well. The banana and pineapple fritters are delightful, but it's the sinfully fabulous deep-fried Mars Bar that really tips things over the edge.

GRAVY 💲💲

3957 N. Mississippi Ave., 503/287-8800

HOURS: Tues.-Fri. 7:30 A.M.-2:30 P.M., Sat. 8 A.M.-3 P.M., closed Sun.-Mon.

A great spot for a good old American greasy spoon breakfast, Gravy is a testament to the joys of gluttony. Biscuits and gravy naturally get a lot of attention here and deservedly so. The biscuit is the size of a plate and smothered with a decidedly un-Atkins-approved portion of gravy. In fact, a single order is enough to share between two people. The weekday lunch menu leans to the Southern side: You can get a salad, but why would you when there are fried egg sandwiches, tuna melts, and gravy-soaked fries to consume?

Word to the wise: The wait can be long on the weekends, as it is for any Portland breakfast joint. Come prepared with a cup of coffee from one of the many nearby coffeehouses.

LOVELY HULA HANDS 💲💲💲

4057 N. Mississippi Ave., 503/445-9910, www.lovelyhulahands.com

HOURS: Tues.-Sun. 5-10 P.M., closed Mon.

Step inside Lovely Hula Hands and you are immediately warmed by the atmosphere. The rosy-hued walls, Victorian decor, mismatched china, and chandeliers make for a space that is alluring and cozy. It's a cross between grandma's house and a fairy cottage. It's the food, however, that brings Lovely Hula Hands to the top of everyone's list. The menu changes to reflect the seasons, but always includes dishes for both vegetarians and meat-eaters. Try a grilled rib eye with onion rings and garden lettuces, or short ribs braised in a red wine sauce and served over polenta. If you're vegetarian, try a leek and mushroom tart or perhaps an order of fresh-made penne with grilled seasonal vegetables.

The cocktail menu includes a number of 1920s-era drinks and some very pretty specialties. Critics are fond of Tallulah's Bathwater, with pomegranate molasses, tequila, lime juice, and sugar, as well as the Bee's Knees, which features spiced rum, honey, fresh-squeezed lemon juice, and soda.

DESSERT

BLUE GARDENIA 💲

3747 N. Mississippi Ave., 503/460-2583

HOURS: Mon.-Sat. 7 A.M.-6 P.M., Sun. 8 A.M.-5 P.M.

This tiny bakery and coffeehouse is nestled on a busy part of Mississippi Avenue, perfectly situated near a number of the strip's hottest restaurants. The folks at Blue Gardenia roast their own single-origin coffee. The coffee is strong and stout, which is a nice accompaniment to the adorable pastries (like tiny, but delicious bite-sized pies and pretty lemon tarts). If it's too early for homemade ice-cream sandwiches, chocolate tortes, or monster-sized cookies, grab one of the amazing cinnamon rolls, or better yet, buy frozen rolls so that you can take them home and fill your house with that "I know how to bake" smell.

◖ PIX PATISSERIE 💲

3901 N. Williams Ave., 503/282-6539, www.pixpatisserie.com

HOURS: Mon.-Thurs. 7 A.M.-midnight, Fri. 7 A.M.-2 A.M., Sat. 8 A.M.-2 A.M., Sun. 9 A.M.-midnight

Pix is a dessert place in the strictest sense of the word, and it's all about indulgence. Beautiful cakes and tarts that look like they belong on a wall in a gallery instead of on a cake plate sit in ordered, anticipatory silence. Colorful *macarons* (almond, not coconut) in flavors such as raspberry, rose, and passion fruit beckon to be touched and tasted. A signature dish here is the Amelie, an orange-vanilla crème brûlée that sits atop a glazed chocolate mousse with caramelized hazelnuts, praline crisp, and Cointreau génoise. Check the website for upcoming dim sum nights, wherein you may choose from over 20 different desserts as they make their rounds through the restaurant. Each dessert is $3 or less, and you can also sample beers for $1 and dessert wines for $3.

GERMAN

WIDMER GASTHAUS 💲💲

929 N. Russell St., 503/281-3333, www.widmer.com

HOURS: Mon.-Thurs. 11 A.M.-11 P.M., Fri.-Sat. 11 A.M.-midnight, closed Sun.

Sehr Gut! The Widmer Gasthaus has great

beer, of course, since it's brewed right across the street. The company is famous for its brews, not the least of which is its Hefeweizen—the first made in the United States. The menu is a fabulous assortment of German-inspired dishes, from the crispy and delicious chicken or pork schnitzel to the slow-roasted beef sauerbraten. It's all about comfort food, and while you could order a salad, why would you when there is goulash to be had? It's hard to hold back when there are bread chunks to be dipped in fondue and plates of sausage to be sampled.

MEXICAN
LAUGHING PLANET ❸

3765 N. Mississippi Ave., 503/467-4146,
www.laughingplanetcafe.com
HOURS: Daily 11 A.M.–9 P.M.

At Laughing Planet, the idea seems simple. Take great organic and local ingredients, then wrap them in a tortilla or put them in a bowl, and make it all really cheap. The burritos at Laughing Planet are big and hearty, but they are also remarkably healthy. Opt for a traditional-style wrap with beans, grilled chicken, Tillamook cheese, and brown rice, or try something with an international spin like the Che Guevara, which comes with plantains, sweet potatoes, and spicy barbeque sauce.

Laughing Planet serves beer and wine, in addition to fresh-squeezed organic juices (in varieties from apple to beet) and some pretty fantastic smoothies—like the PB&J with strawberries, bananas, organic peanut butter, and apple juice.

¿POR QUE NO? ❸

3524 N. Mississippi Ave., 503/467-4149,
www.porquenotacos.com
HOURS: Mon.-Thurs. 11 A.M.–9:30 P.M., Fri.-Sat.
11 A.M.–10 P.M., Sun. 11 A.M.–9:30 P.M.

If you're looking for cheap and sublime tacos, this is the place. Try the delicious and juicy carnitas with braised local pork in handmade tortillas or wild shrimp, sautéed and served with a dollop of *crema*. The ceviche (line-caught snapper and wild shrimp marinated in seasoned lime) is superb as well, and it's served with house-made tortilla chips. If you're thirsty (and you should be after that), try a pomegranate margarita, which tastes like summer ought to taste. Or order a glass of *horchata,* which is creamy, sweet, and delicious, especially when spiked with rum.

TREBOL ❸❸

4835 N. Albina Ave., 503/517-9347, www.trebolpdx.com
HOURS: Mon.-Thurs. 5–10 P.M., Fri.-Sat. 5–11 P.M., Sun.
11 A.M.–2 P.M. and 5–10 P.M.

Besides boasting the largest collection of tequilas in town, Trebol is also a really good Mexican restaurant that relies as much as possible on local and organic foods. The food is creative, pleasing to the eye, perfectly seasoned, crispy when it needs to be, and succulent whenever called for. The portions are generous but not gratuitously so. Try the taco sampler (wild boar, fish, and braised beef) with a tamarind margarita, or dig into some wild mushroom enchiladas and wash them down with a glass of sangria.

SEAFOOD
EAT: AN OYSTER BAR ❸❸

3808 N. Williams Ave., Ste. 122, 503/281-1222,
www.eatoysterbar.com
HOURS: Sun.-Wed. 11:30 A.M.–10 P.M., Thurs.-Sat.
11:30 A.M.–midnight.

Owners Ethan Powell and Tobias Hogan (the E and T of the restaurant's name) get a number of shipments each week from different oyster farms, making their bivalves just about the freshest you can find in town. A chalkboard on the wall announces the most recent arrivals from Oregon, Washington, and the East Coast. If you're new to eating oysters, ask your knowledgeable server for guidance. The freshness of the raw oysters, served on the half shell, really speaks for itself, but EaT also makes a mean oysters Rockefeller. Baked and topped with a puree of watercress, garlic, and spinach, and then finished with a touch of absinthe, they are remarkably rich and earthy.

Greater Portland
Map 7

There are a few places outside the core of the city that are worth a gander. If you're heading out to Bridgeport Village to do some shopping, you have a number of options that don't involve consuming food served on a stick. Also, traveling up into the deep western hills of Portland can be a pretty drive, but the weather doesn't always cooperate enough to allow picnicking. Fortunately, the outskirts of the city are populated with eclectic and interesting places to dine.

AMERICAN

HUMDINGER DRIVE-IN $

8250 SW Barbur Blvd., 503/246-8132

HOURS: Mon.-Sat. 10 A.M.-9 P.M., closed Sun.

Thick and delicious ice-cream milkshakes and fat burgers dominate the menu at Humdinger, which is located on Barbur Boulevard near Lewis and Clark College. If you like a good balance between meat, cheese, and bread, order a double (or more) and eat as much as you can—or split it. You will be happier with the overall flavor than if you get two single burgers. Side dishes—like krinkle-cut fries, deep-fried mushrooms, onion rings, and the very popular tater tots—are also stellar. Bring cash.

THREE SQUARE GRILL $$

6320 SW Capitol Hwy., 503/244-4467,

www.threesquare.com

HOURS: Tues.-Sat. 5-9 P.M., Sun. 9 A.M.-2 P.M.

Why come to Three Square Grill? Deep-fried pickles. Also, they have an adorable kids' menu—clearly designed by finicky kids—and a menu that was clearly designed for discerning adults. Delta-style crab cakes with lemon remoulade, smoked salmon hash, and roast chicken with chanterelle mushrooms are just a few of the popular dishes, but it's the sampler of fried pickles, okra, and hushpuppies that make this worth the drive out to the hills of Southwest Portland.

BREAKFAST AND BRUNCH

FAT CITY CAFÉ $

7820 SW Capitol Hwy., 503/245-5457,

www.fatcitycafe.net

HOURS: Daily 6:30 A.M.-3 P.M.

Fat City Café has won numerous awards for its quirky style and delicious food; for many locals, it's the perfect place to enjoy classic diner favorites in generous proportions. Cinnamon rolls the size of a baby's head are the big star at this neighborhood café, and the recipe hasn't changed since 1974. Breakfast is the specialty here and it's served all day, and there's also a terrific lunch menu full of burgers, sandwiches, and other such things.

MARCO'S CAFÉ & ESPRESSO BAR $$

7910 SW 35th Ave., 503/245-0199,

www.marcoscafe.com

HOURS: Mon.-Fri. 7 A.M.-9 P.M., Sat. 8 A.M.-9 P.M., Sun. 8 A.M.-2 P.M.

This quaint Multnomah Village café is a neighborhood favorite, which is why you don't hear much about it in the city. With its friendly service and reliably good breakfasts, this charming café is a well-guarded secret. The extensive menu has a heavy emphasis on scrambles, omelets, and Benedicts; everything is organic and fresh. If you're not a fan of egg-heavy breakfasts, opt for a hearty veggie breakfast burrito filled with brown rice, black bean chili, corn, tomato, avocado, and pepperjack cheese, or try the superb tofu scramble with mixed veggies in a tandoori or Korean barbeque marinade.

THE ORIGINAL PANCAKE HOUSE $$

8601 SW 24th Ave, 503/246-9007,

www.originalpancakehouse.com

HOURS: Wed.-Sun. 7 A.M.-3 P.M., closed Mon.-Tues.

The Original Pancake House has a number of locations around the country, but this is the original Original—and it is not to be confused with the "International" chain that we are all so familiar with. OPH has simple but fantastic breakfasts that include all the usuals, like waffles, corned beef hash, omelets, and of course, pancakes. It's all very classic and simple, with the exception of the Dutch baby and the German pancake. Both dinner plate–sized treats are oven-baked, enormous, puffy, and delicious. You'll wait a little longer to get one, but if you have a sweet tooth, it's worth the wait.

CARRIBEAN
SALVADOR MOLLY'S $$

1523 SW Sunset Blvd., 503/293-1790,
www.salvadormollys.com
HOURS: Sun.-Thurs. 11 A.M.–9 P.M., Fri.-Sat. 11 A.M.–11 P.M.

Salvador Molly's is just plain fun. They call it "pirate cookin'" because they have stolen cuisine concepts from all over the Seven Seas. You'll find Caribbean jerk chicken, Baja fish tacos, Hawaiian Kalua pork, and Creole jambalaya—and that's just a smattering of the eclectic entrées. There are some starters you won't want to miss, like the unforgettable Cheesy Poofs, fried mashed potato fritters with a touch of cheese and chipotle chiles. But if you really want an adventure, order the Great Balls of Fire. If you can manage to eat all five habanero cheese fritters with the sauce, you'll get your picture on the Wall of Flame.

JAPANESE
SINJU $$

7339 SW Bridgeport Rd., 503/352-3815,
www.sinjurestaurant.com
HOURS: Mon.-Thurs. 11:30 A.M.-2:30 P.M. and 5-9:30 P.M., Fri. 11:30 A.M.-2:30 P.M. and 5-10:30 P.M., Sat. 5-10:30 P.M., Sun. 5-9:30 P.M.

Sinju, like much of Portland, is sophisticated and casual at the same time. The decor is lovely and subdued and the chefs produce excellent-quality sushi and sashimi, particularly given the shopping mall location. Options abound on the menu, whether you opt for appetizers and sushi rolls or traditional cooked entrées like sukiyaki, chicken katsu, or grilled salmon with white miso. It's great to share here, especially if

everyone orders an appetizer and a roll or two. The Ahi Tower appetizer—with tuna tartare, crab, and avocado atop sushi rice that's been infused with creamy wasabi—is particularly impressive.

MEDITERRANEAN
BLUE TANGERINE $$

7361 SW Bridgeport Rd., 503/620-9734,
www.bluetangerinerestaurant.com
HOURS: Sun.-Wed. 11 A.M.–9 P.M., Thurs.-Sat. 11 A.M.–10 P.M.

Blue Tangerine offers good-quality Mediterranean food for a decent price. It's a great spot to hit for lunch while shopping at Bridgeport Village, especially because the wait at many of the other nearby restaurants can edge up to an hour or more during busy times. At Blue Tangerine, you order at the counter and wait at your table for the food. Make sure you order some hummus, which they will give you immediately. It's delicious and it will tide you over until your food comes.

PACIFIC NORTHWEST
THE RESTAURANT
AT THE HISTORIC RESERVE $$

1101 Officers Row, Vancouver, WA, 360/906-1101,
www.restauranthr.com
HOURS: Sun.-Mon. 11 A.M.-2 P.M., Tues.-Fri. 11 A.M.-9 P.M., Sat 5 P.M.-9 P.M.

This lovely slice of history is located in Vancouver, Washington, mere minutes from downtown Portland on I-5. The restaurant is housed in the historic Grant House, a gorgeous two-story home built in 1849 along Officers Row at the Vancouver National Historic Reserve. The Reserve is well maintained, and the building itself is quite pretty, with high ceilings, white linen tablecloths, and silver place settings. Meals are elegant, and dishes such as procuitto-wrapped chicken saltimbocca and wild salmon risotto with English peas are impressive—and cost less than $20. There are also wine tastings every Tuesday, where you can sample four two-ounce glasses with some nibbles for $15.

SEAFOOD
FIVE SPICE ⑤⑤⑤

315 1st Ave., Ste. 201, 503/697-8889,
www.fivespicerestaurant.com
HOURS: Mon.-Sat. 11:30 A.M.-10 P.M., Sun.
11:30 A.M.-9 P.M.

Five Spice in the nearby city of Lake Oswego has fantastic lake views and Pacific Northwest cuisine with an Asian flair that arrives looking so pretty that it almost rivals the landscape. The wine selection is excellent, with a number of French, Californian, and Northwest favorites, as well as a respectable collection of ports and dessert wines. Seafood is terrific, with Pacific treats like halibut with saffron potatoes or sturgeon with black rice risotto and shimeji mushrooms. Given its location in a bustling part of Lake O, this place gets crowded, so it's best to make a reservation by phone or email at least a day in advance.

NIGHTLIFE

Thanks in part to Portland's DIY youth culture, the city has a lot of spirit. For the most part, traditional clubs with packed dance floors and blaring Top 40 music are shunned in favor of more eclectic venues with attractive architecture, great cocktails, and comfortable gathering spaces. The music found at most popular venues is as varied as the personalities of the city itself. While some flock to hear the latest indie label band at McMenamins Crystal Ballroom, others will be sipping a martini and listening to some of today's hottest jazz at Jimmy Mak's.

The Pacific Northwest has long been considered a key player in the independent music scene. But long before bands like the Decemberists, Pink Martini, Modest Mouse, the Dandy Warhols, or the Shins called Portland home, it was still a favorite stop for many jazz, blues, and bluegrass players. These days, the music that first put Portland on the map is still an active part of its fabric, with annual festivals that draw thousands to see the likes of Etta James, B. B. King, Mel Brown and Bobby Torres.

If the music scene isn't your bag, you're still in luck. Portland is fast becoming a destination spot for the burgeoning "cocktail renaissance," with local bistros, taphouses, lounges, and watering holes being featured on television, in magazines, and in blogs across the country. Like legendary chefs in decades past, hometown mixologists are reaching cult star status, recognized for their particular tastes and their ability to encapsulate the perfect experience in a glass.

COURTESY OF PIONEER COURTHOUSE SQUARE

HIGHLIGHTS

LOOK FOR TO FIND RECOMMENDED NIGHTLIFE.

◖ Best Place to Grab a Pint: With arguably one of the best selections of draughts from around the globe, **Horse Brass Pub** holds the honor of being one of the most recognized British pubs (outside of Britain, of course) (page 75).

◖ Best Place to Walk on Air: For 90 years, music lovers have flocked to the **Crystal Ballroom** to dance on the legendary "floating" dance floor (page 78).

◖ Best Place to Dig That Crazy Beat: Rated as one of the top 100 jazz clubs in the world, **Jimmy Mak's** draws some of the best acts around (page 78).

◖ Best Place to Beat Your High Score in Galaga: Part bar, part well-appointed arcade, **Ground Kontrol** is a great spot to make the kid in you squeal with delight (page 81).

◖ Best Place to Sip a Classic: The house-made tinctures, infusions, tonics, and bitters at **Teardrop Cocktail Lounge** are only part of what make it a must for cocktail enthusiasts (page 84).

◖ Best Place to Meet Marvelous Dames: After 40 years, **Darcelle XV Showclub** is more than just a drag show. It's a Portland rite of passage (page 86).

Once the "floating floor" at the Crystal Ballroom gets moving, it's hard not to rock along.

© LIZ DEVINE

NIGHTLIFE

Brewpubs and Taphouses

BAILEY'S TAPROOM

213 SW Broadway, 503/295-1004,
www.baileystaproom.com
HOURS: Mon.-Sat. 4 P.M.-midnight, closed Sun.
COST: Free
Map 1

Bailey's Taproom is like a library for beers. The selection is extensive and constantly changing. In fact, the Taproom sends out Twitter and blog posts to let followers know what's new on the taps. They are open from 4 P.M. until midnight everyday except Sunday and while they don't serve food, they will allow you to bring in anything you like—or you can order from the Mexican joint next door and have the food delivered right to your table.

DESCHUTES BREWERY AND PUBLIC HOUSE

210 NW 11th Ave., 503/296-4906,
www.deschutesbrewery.com
HOURS: Thurs.-Sat. 8 P.M.-2 A.M., closed Sun.-Wed.
COST: $10 cover
Map 2

For more than 20 years, Deschutes Brewery has been hand-crafting ales that are popular all over the world, like Mirror Pond Pale Ale and Black Butte Porter. The Portland pub (sister to the flagship in Bend, Oregon) has become a favorite spot for folks to grab a pint before they hit the theater or galleries. Order a sampler tray and try six brews for just slightly more than the price of a single pint.

5TH QUADRANT

3901 N. Williams Ave., 503/228-3996,
www.newoldlompoc.com
HOURS: Daily 11 A.M.-1:30 A.M.
COST: Free
Map 6

The 5th Quadrant is part of the Lompoc family of brewpubs, most of which are favored by locals who appreciate fine, locally made beer. Sip on a glass of LSD (Lompoc Strong Draught) or sink into a hoppy C-Note Imperial Pale. If you don't know what you'd like, the servers here are equipped and more than happy to direct you toward the one that suits your taste. Happy hour (daily 4–6 P.M.) is a pretty good time to check it out, but if your budget is tight, head here on Tightwad Tuesdays, when pints are only $2.50.

HOPWORKS URBAN BREWERY

2944 SE Powell Blvd., 503/232-4677,
www.hopworksbeer.com
HOURS: Sun.-Thurs. 11 A.M.-11 P.M., Fri.-Sat. 11 A.M.-midnight
COST: Free
Map 4

Portland's first eco-brewpub, Hopworks Urban Brewery (HUB) makes organic brews from locally grown ingredients on-site in its sustainability-focused facility. This is where the beer snobs of Portland sit and debate the use of adjuncts (like raspberry, peach, or chocolate) in the brewing process. Try the boozy Hopworks float made with vanilla ice cream and the signature Organic Survival "Seven Grain" Stout.

◀ HORSE BRASS PUB

4534 SE Belmont St., 503/232-2022,
www.horsebrass.com
HOURS: Mon.-Fri. 11 A.M.-2:30 A.M., Sat.-Sun. 10 A.M.-2:30 A.M.
COST: Free
Map 4

Named one of the best bars in America by *Esquire,* this is a public house in the true sense of the term. The sprawling interior is welcoming and warm with wood paneling and decor that belie its Pacific Northwest location. Once inside, it's easy to believe you've hopped the pond. There are more than 50 beers on tap (and some of the best from around the world, at that), but the menu really hollers for a good nip of Scotch to wash down the delicious fish and chips or Scotch eggs. Even as brewpubs pop up all over the city, Horse Brass is still the best spot to toss a few darts or sip an IPA while

NIGHTLIFE

YEAST MEETS WEST:
AN A-Z GUIDE TO PORTLAND BREWPUBS

We won't make it all the way to Z, but with more than 70 microbreweries in and around Portland, there are plenty of pints to sip, sample, and savor. Here are a few favorites:

- Located in the eponymous Alameda district, **Alameda Brewhouse** (4765 NE Fremont St., 503/460-9025, www.alamedabrewhouse.com) has won a number of awards, particularly for its Black Bear XX Stout. The Klickitat Pale Ale — which shares a name with the real street made famous by Beverly Cleary's *Ramona Quimby* books — is another great beer with bold hops and a caramel finish.

- You won't want to forget this one. **Amnesia Brewing** (832 N. Beech St., 503/281-7708) is housed in a converted warehouse with a covered beer garden in one of the city's most up-and-coming neighborhoods. The lineup is consistently good to very good, and features mostly IPAs, pale ales, and ESBs.

- A longtime award-winner and staple in the local microbrew scene, **Bridgeport** (1313 NW Marshall St., 503/241-3612, www.bridgeportbrew.com) has a terrific ale called Blue Heron which was released in 1987 as a special tribute to the Audubon Society. The pale ale is round and soft on the palate, but finishes crisply. Of course, Bridgeport is probably better known for its IPA, a consistent Gold Medal winner in the World Beer Championship.

- Brewed in Bend, Oregon, **Deschutes** (210 NW 11th Ave., 503/296-4906, www.deschutesbrewery.com) has a number of beers that are recognized well beyond the Pacific Northwest: Black Butte Porter, Nitro Obsidian Stout, and Mirror Pond Pale Ale, just to name a few. That's reason alone to visit, but the Portland pub also features a 100 percent gluten-free Golden Ale, which is derived from sorghum, brown rice, and roasted chestnuts.

- **Hopworks Urban Brewery** (2944 SE Powell Blvd., 503/232-4677, www.hopworksbeer.com) is fairly new on the scene, but it has Christian Ettinger (formerly of Laurelwood) at its helm, which is basically a pedigree for success. Hopworks' beers are already winning a number of awards and turning the heads of beer snobs everywhere, and

---

sampling traditional British treats like bangers or shepherd's pie.

OAKS BOTTOM PUBLIC HOUSE

1621 SE Bybee Blvd., 503/232-1728,
www.newoldlompoc.com
HOURS: Daily 11:30 A.M.-midnight
Map 5

This addition to the Lompoc family was named for the Oaks Bottom Wildlife Refuge, which runs just west of the pub. This is everything a neighborhood pub is supposed to be: cozy, welcoming, and blessed with good beer. The expected Lompoc brews are available, but you can also find some very unique guest beers on tap. Regular patrons sing the praises of the limited but pleasing menu, which includes "Totchos," an unholy mash-up of tater tots and nachos.

since Hopworks is the first "Eco-Brewpub" to offer all organic handcrafted beers, it's really taking off.

- **Laurelwood Brewing Co.** (5115 NE Sandy Blvd., 503/282-0622, www.laurelwood-brewpub.com), a locally owned, certified-organic brewery and collection of pubs, is popular with many locals thanks to the stellar Tree Hugger Porter, Free Range Red, and especially the Workhorse IPA, which bears a larger-than-life hop flavor and a 7.5 percent alcohol-by-volume kick.

- This Portland darling has a number of locations, but the original is known as **The New Old Lompoc** (1616 NW 23rd Ave., 503/225-1855, www.newoldlompoc.com). The beers are almost all terrific, but it's LSD (Lompoc Strong Draft) with its smoked malt and generous hop flavor that's won most beer lovers' hearts.

- This brewpub also has a number of locations. A popular one is the southeast **Lucky Labrador Brew Pub** (915 SE Hawthorne Blvd., 503/236-3555, www.luckylab.com). You can bring your own four-legged friend and sip some fantastic craft brews, like Black Lab Stout, Hawthorne's Best Bitter, Königs Kölsch, Reggie's Red, Stumptown Porter, and Dog Day IPA. Even better, try your favorite brew from the nitro tap for a smoother, creamier experience.

- There's a pirate in every bunch and **Rogue Ales** (1339 NW Flanders St., 503/222-5910, www.rogue.com) is Portland's resident scallywag. Rogue has a truly impressive lineup of beers, but it does dark best. In particular, the Shakespeare Stout is rich, chocolaty, and earthy. Another popular one is the Dead Guy Ale, which is done in the German Maibock style — and you'll be sold on the packaging before you even taste it.

- **Widmer Brothers Brewery** (929 N Russell St., 503/281-2437, www.widmer.com) is probably the most widely recognizable Northwest brewer, thanks to its wildly successful Hefeweizen. Operating since 1984, the Widmer brothers have been doing it right for some time now. Sample the Hefeweizen, but move on to some of the other notable beers like Drop Top Amber Ale and Broken Halo IPA.

Live Music

ALADDIN THEATER
3017 SE Milwaukie Ave., 503/234-9694, www.aladdin-theater.com
HOURS: Mon.-Sat. 11 A.M.-6 P.M., closed Sun.
COST: Varies per show
Map 4

Since its days as a vaudeville house, The Aladdin has been host to some of the greatest performers of our time, particularly when it comes to blues, jazz, bluegrass, soul, and pop. The 600-plus-seat house lends intimacy to the experience, whether it's a quiet sit-down show, a screaming punk show or the monthly Live Wire! Radio Show. Arrive early and grab some food and a pint at The Lamp (get it?) next door if you don't have your tickets already, because the lines often snake around the block for this venue.

BACKSPACE
115 NW 5th Ave., 503/248-2900, www.backspace.bz
HOURS: Mon.-Wed. 7 A.M.-11 P.M., Thurs.-Fri. 7 A.M.-midnight, Sat. 10 A.M.-midnight, Sun. 10 A.M.-11 P.M.
COST: $6-10
Map 2

Part Internet café, part gallery, part music venue, Backspace is especially popular with the crowds who wish to (or must, by nature of age) avoid the bar scene. With a calendar that skips all the way from acoustic guitar performances to hip-hop DJs, the music is pretty varied, but so is the venue. Whether you're there to see an art opening, attend an open mic, play some chess, or sink into the welcoming arms of a plush chair while catching a concert, make sure you pick up a cup of Stumptown coffee.

◖ CRYSTAL BALLROOM

1332 W. Burnside St., 503/225-0047, www.mcmenamins.com
HOURS: Box office Mon.-Fri. 11:30 A.M.-6 P.M., later for shows; show times vary
COST: Varies per show
Map 1

The McMenamin brothers have made a name for themselves in the Pacific Northwest for breathing life into some pretty remarkable historic venues. The Crystal Ballroom is no exception. It has seen a lot of action in its 90 years: dance revivals, police raids, fabled rock concerts and even near demolition. It is even rumored that Little Richard once fired Jimi Hendrix mid-concert on the Crystal's stage. Despite all that, what people can't seem to stop talking about is the floor. One of only a few like it in the country, the dance floor moves on ball bearings, giving a whole new meaning to the phrase "dance on air."

DANTE'S

1 SW 3rd Ave., 503/226-6630, www.danteslive.com
HOURS: Daily 11 A.M.-2:30 A.M.
COST: Varies per show
Map 2

Spend an evening at Dante's and you can practically hear "In a Gadda Da Vida" seeping through the walls. Dante's has a long and sordid history having been a brothel, flop house, punk club, and gambling hall. These days, it's the home of two must-see weekly events: Sinferno Cabaret, a weekly mash-up of fire dancing, burlesque, and debauchery; and Karaoke From Hell, where wanna-be rockstars can sing with a live band.

◖ JIMMY MAK'S

221 NW 10th Ave., 503/295-6542, www.jimmymaks.com
HOURS: Mon.-Wed. 4 P.M.-1 A.M., Thurs.-Sat. 4 P.M.-2 A.M., closed Sun.
COST: Free-$15
Map 2

This place is slick. Somehow, you walk in and just *feel* cooler. There's really not a bad seat in the house and while the drinks are reliably strong, the music is hands down the reason to go. *Down Beat* magazine named Jimmy Mak's one of the top 100 places in the world to hear jazz and they weren't kidding around. The venue draws some of the biggest names in the business, who love its dark intimacy and nostalgic air.

KELLY'S OLYMPIAN

426 SW Washington St., 503/228-3669, www.kellysolympian.com
HOURS: Daily 10 A.M.-2:30 A.M.
COST: Free-$7
Map 1

If Portland has a biker bar, this is it. In the heart of downtown, Kelly's seems like a kitschy neighborhood diner by day, chock-full of motorcycle memorabilia and fully-restored bikes; by the time night falls, however, it becomes a hot venue to catch local punk, indie, and underground rock shows. You won't see many hipsters here, but you will find a lot of post-work bartenders and servers, actors, and retail denizens. And why not? Besides a line-up of great music, Kelly's has all the elements of a good dive bar: stiff drinks, hot bartenders, and a plethora of fried late-night nosh.

WILF'S RESTAURANT AND BAR

800 NW 6th Ave., 503/223-0070, www.wilfsrestaurant.com
HOURS: Mon 11:30 A.M.-2 P.M., Tues.-Thurs. 11:30 A.M.-11 P.M., Fri. 11:30 A.M.-midnight, Sat. 5 P.M.-midnight, closed Sun.
COST: $5 cover
Map 2

If you picture a piano bar (the elegant kind, not the cheesy kind), you'll get an idea what an evening at Wilf's is like. High-backed red chairs and the dark, deep-colored surroundings make for a swank affair. In fact, Wilf's somehow manages to feel like an awful lot like an affair: secretive, romantic, and unpredictable. The talent is reliably great and it is not uncommon to feel as though you have stumbled into *A Star is Born.*

WONDER BALLROOM

128 NE Russell St., 503/284-8686,
www.wonderballroom.com
HOURS: Show nights 5 P.M.-midnight (for Under Wonder Lounge)
COST: Varies per show
`Map 3`

Easily one of the top concert venues for big acts, the Wonder has only recently become an active part of the live music scene. The 1914 ballroom was beautifully restored in 2005 and now plays host to big name bands, fashion shows, and raucous charity events. There's a fairly spacious dance floor, and the balcony (if it's open) is a fine place to escape and have a drink while you rest your feet. While you're there, make sure you check out the Under

Wonder Lounge downstairs, where the food is delicious and never more than $10.

THE WOODS

6637 SE Milwaukie Ave., 503/890-0408,
www.thewoodsportland.com
HOURS: Mon 7 P.M.-1:30 A.M., Tues.-Sat. 8 P.M.-2:30 A.M., Sun. 6 P.M.-12:30 A.M.
COST: Varies by show
`Map 5`

If you are dying to get out and see some of the latest local and regional bands, head to The Woods. The pun was intended because this bar has been converted from an old funeral parlor and despite the fact that there is lots of space—a number of side rooms, a big outdoor area, and plenty of seating—the place still bears a strong resemblance to its former self. From the street, it's difficult to tell that the space is anything but a funeral parlor. That may change after the place has been open for a while, but for now, it's a fun place to sip beer and wine while catching some low-cost live music shows in the former chapel. The Woods also hosts regular comedy events and karaoke.

Dance Clubs

AURA RESTAURANT AND LOUNGE

1022 W. Burnside St., 503/597-2872,
www.auraportland.com
HOURS: Wed. 5-10 P.M., Thurs.-Sat. 5 P.M.-2:30 A.M., closed Sun.-Tues.
COST: $8 on Sat., free otherwise
`Map 1`

This is where the pretty people go to dance. Aura is an "upscale dance club" that primarily plays hip-hop and techno beats. There are several bars on two levels and while it can get crowded on a Saturday night, there are plenty of places to linger and people watch. The bathrooms are a particular pleasure—one-way mirrors into the bar allow you to people-watch while you do your business.

FEZ BALLROOM AND LOUNGE

318 SW 11th Ave., 503/226-4171,
www.fezballroom.com
HOURS: Tues.-Sat. 8 P.M.-2 A.M., closed Sun.-Mon.
COST: Free-$10
`Map 1`

This hip Persian-themed venue sits atop a seemingly endless flight of stairs. It's particularly popular on Friday nights for its Shut Up and Dance party, which features 1980s tracks—the likes of Depeche Mode and Madonna—with a distinctly electric twist. Check out the monthly Andaz event every last Saturday, where DJ Anjali and The Incredible Kid spin international music and practically transform the place into a Bollywood movie.

NIGHTLIFE

THE GOODFOOT

2845 SE Stark St., 503/239-9292,
www.thegoodfoot.com

HOURS: Daily 5 P.M.-2:30 A.M.

COST: Free upstairs, $1-15 downstairs

Map 4

The Goodfoot is like the Odd Couple subletting a bar together. Upstairs, there's the tidy and bright Felix with his art and carefully arranged pool tables; in the basement it's Oscar, with his windowless, squat space filled with duct-taped benches and odd-tiled floors. Surprisingly, both atmospheres are ideal for their purpose. The music downstairs is some of the best and least predictable in town, particularly the Soul Stew spins on Friday nights with DJ Aquaman.

HOLOCENE

1001 SE Morrison St., 503/239-7639, www.holocene.org

HOURS: Wed.-Thurs. 8 P.M.-2:30 A.M., Fri.
5 P.M.-2:30 A.M., Sat. 8 P.M.-2:30 A.M., closed Sun.

COST: Varies by show

Map 4

Holocene has a stark industrial feel to it and despite the fact that it seems spacious at the outset, the open spaces fill up quickly some nights. They play some great music here and have some of the city's most fashionable DJs spinning every week. One of the most popular events is Double Down, a hot and sweaty queer-friendly dance party held on the last Saturday of each month. Holocene is definitely at home among the artsy, swanky bars in Portland and they get big props for the sunken projection-lit dance floor that looks like a living room in the midst of a gritty industrialized loft.

LOLA'S ROOM

1332 W. Burnside St., 503/225-0047,
www.mcmenamins.com

HOURS: Mon.-Sat. 8 P.M.-2 A.M., closed Sun.

COST: $5 Fri., otherwise varies per show

Map 1

Lola's is one of the top spots in town to get your groove on, especially if you're not looking to hear the Top 40. Named for the first Portland policewoman who tried to pull a *Footloose* on the city by ridding it of sinful practices such as dancing, Lola's (on the second floor of the Crystal Ballroom) hosts the popular '80s Video Dance Attack! on Fridays, when VJ Kittyrox spins the stuff we knew from back when MTV still had videos.

Bars

THE ALIBI

4024 N. Interstate Ave., 503/287-5335

HOURS: Mon.-Sat. 11 A.M.-2 A.M., Sun. 11 A.M.-1 A.M.

Map 6

Comfortable as an old sweater—complete with holes—and as friendly and helpful as a Smurf, The Alibi tops many a local's list for after-work drinks, happy hour, and, of course, karaoke. Sure, it's a bit kitschy, but maybe that's why we like it. After a full day of doing whatever it is we do around PDX, what we need is a drink—and maybe some $2.50 chicken strips—served up with a "Hey, how are ya?" kind of smile. Plus there is the added charm of feeling like you're drinking in the Tiki Room at Disneyland.

BILLY RAY'S NEIGHBORHOOD BAR

2216 NE Martin Luther King Jr. Blvd., 503/287-7254

HOURS: Mon.-Sat. 11 A.M.-2:30 A.M., Sun.
2 P.M.-2:30 A.M., later for shows

Map 3

Billy Ray's is about as unassuming as it gets. It's the sort of bar you could drive by for months and never think twice about, which may be part of its charm. Billy Ray's is like that accidentally hot, soft-spoken friend you've had for years who suddenly grows on you. There's nothing outside to claim it as "Billy Ray's" or to announce that *Playboy* named it one of the top dive bars in America, but frankly, they are just too cool and mysterious to make a fuss.

© HOLLYANNA MCCOLLOM

NIGHTLIFE

You don't need an excuse to cut loose at The Alibi, strong tiki drinks and nightly karaoke are reason enough.

EASTBURN

1800 E. Burnside St., 503/236-2876, www.theeastburn.com

HOURS: Mon. noon-2 A.M., Tues.-Sat. 11 A.M.-2 A.M., Sun. 11 A.M.-midnight

Map 4

When it comes to hang-out spots for Portlanders, EastBurn is at the top of the list. Is it the skee-ball? The year-round patio with mosaic fire tables, outdoor heaters, and chair swings? The fact that they call their happy hour "recess"? It's probably all those things, coupled with the fact that EastBurn has a great selection of locally produced beer and wine as well as a menu with favorites such as the Grover's Mackin' Cheese. Round up as many as nine of your friends for a birthday party and you will all drink for free for one hour after 9 P.M. EastBurn's laid-back, sports bar style makes it a great place to watch a game or just catch a drink and some great conversation while swinging on the patio.

GROUND KONTROL

511 NW Couch St., 503/796-9364, www.groundkontrol.com

HOURS: Daily noon-2:30 A.M.

Map 2

What could be more appealing to your inner geek than an arcade full of classic games from the 1970s, '80s, and '90s, like Galaga, Pac Man, Mario Brothers, and Street Fighter? How about an arcade that also serves cocktails and hosts regular Dance Dance Revolution and Rock Band tournaments? Thought so. Ground Kontrol is a time warp into the bygone days of Atari, Pumas, and Apple II Es...but with beer. While it's basically a hands-on museum to the bleep, bleep, whirr digital past, it's also a really fun way to spend a date or an evening out with friends when you tire of playing pool for the umpteenth time.

KELLS IRISH PUB

112 SW 2nd Ave., 503/227-4057, www.kellsirish.com

HOURS: Mon.-Fri. 11 A.M.-2 A.M., Sat. 9 A.M.-2 A.M., Sun. 9 A.M.-1 A.M.

Map 1

If you're out roving for a pint, Kells Irish should be the direction in which you point your feet. With a fantastic collection of beers on tap (including Guinness, of course) and a fine collection of whiskey to round out the well-stocked bar, Kells can be a lot of fun. They have live Irish music on many nights, but it's also a fine place to sit and chat or watch a soccer game. Hand your server a dollar and a couple of quarters and ask to see "the dollar trick." You'll lose the dollar, but it's for a good cause.

LUCKY LABRADOR

915 SE Hawthorne Blvd., 503/236-3555, www.luckylab.com

HOURS: Mon.-Sat. 11 A.M.-midnight, Sun. noon-10 P.M.

Map 4

There are few things Portlanders love more than their beer and their dogs—and at Lucky Lab, you can sip a pint with your pup at your side. Absolutely unpretentious and packed with some of the most laid-back native Portlanders, it's a great place to linger on the patio, munch on hand-tossed barley flour pizza, and a glass of Stumptown Porter.

NIGHT LIGHT LOUNGE

2100 SE Clinton St., 503/731-6500, www.nightlightlounge.net

HOURS: Daily 3 P.M.-2:30 A.M.

Map 4

At the edge of the Clinton Street, a tiny neighborhood that still ranks as favorite for the DIY youth culture of the city, sits an unspoken outpost for Portland's artistic scene. Writers, musicians, artists, and the like flock to the Night Light, crowd into the dark booths or huddle into the couches and sip on PBRs while engaging in the (only partially) accidental task of seeing and being seen. The Night Light makes great cocktails (try the Art Snob) and the food menu is both elegant and affordable.

REEL 'M INN

2430 SE Division St., 503-231-3880

HOURS: Daily 9 A.M.-2:30 P.M.

Map 4

This Clinton-area dive bar has cheap stiff drinks, brassy female bartenders, and a constant stream of neighborhood regulars. There's also free pool, an online jukebox, and poker machines to entertain you. So what sets this dive bar apart from the rest of them? They have the best fried chicken in town, that's what. It's cheap and served with enormous Jo-Jos and a six-pack of dipping sauces. It's a good lubricant for whichever form of alcohol you decide to consume with it. The drinks are strong and inexpensive.

SHANGHAI TUNNEL

211 SW Ankeny St., 503/220-4001, www.shanghaitunnel.com

HOURS: Tues.-Sat. 4 P.M.-2:30 A.M., Sun.-Mon. 8 P.M.-2:30 A.M.

Map 1

Learn a little about Portland's history and you'll understand why Shanghai says it's to "bars what Bruce Campbell is to horror films." The dark, seedy journey into the bowels of Old Town is part of the novelty. But truth be told, it's also a pretty good bar. Skip right past the first level and head down the narrow staircase to the basement, where the cocktails are stellar and you can play pool for $0.50 a pop. Shanghai isn't classy, but that's okay because it never means to be.

Karaoke

BOILER ROOM
228 NW Davis St., 503/227-5441,
www.boilerroomportland.com
HOURS: Mon.-Fri. 7 P.M.-2:30 A.M., Sat.-Sun.
8 P.M.-2:30 A.M.
Map 2

Seven nights a week beginning at 9 P.M., the Boiler Room begins rolling out the karaoke. There's no stage to speak of, but singers have the pleasure of being surrounded by an entourage of dancers as they rock the mic. It can get crowded, so it's a good idea to get here early and get your songs in. While you wait, play some pool or belly up to the bar. The drinks here are both strong and reasonably priced, which goes a long way towards making you sound like Joan Jett.

GALAXY
909 E. Burnside St., 503/234-5003,
www.devilspointbar.com
HOURS: Mon.-Fri. 11 A.M.-2:30 A.M., Sat.-Sun.
5 P.M.-2:30 A.M.
Map 3

All things considered, this is one of the best karaoke joints in town, particularly if you can't tolerate another rendition of Janis Joplin's "Me and Bobby McGee"—or the off-key girl singing it, who is probably way too young to remember it. Galaxy has a great sound system and a song list that is heavy on rock selections and decidedly light on things you have heard at every other karaoke bar from here to Japan. The drinks are reasonably strong and swift here, even more so if you treat your server (who has seen it all) with respect and gratitude.

Lounges

BARTINI
2108 NW Glisan St., 503/224-7919,
www.urbanfondue.com
HOURS: Sun.-Thurs. 4 P.M.-midnight, Fri.-Sat.
4 P.M.-1 A.M.
Map 2

If your normal drink of choice involves something serious like bourbon, brandy, or top-shelf whiskey, go ahead and walk right past Bartini. There might be a few things on the menu to satisfy you, but truthfully, the name of the game here is creative, colorful cocktails with giggle-worthy names like Snickertini, a concoction of vanilla-infused vodka, Crème de Cocoa, and Frangelico shaken with cream and topped with caramel. This is a particularly popular spot with the ladies because there is a veritable fruit basket of cocktails to sample, like the hot-sweet Spicy Mango Martini and the Blueberry Smash with rum, blueberries, and mint.

BEAKER & FLASK
727 SE Washington St., 503/235-8180,
www.beakerandflask.com
HOURS: Mon.-Wed. 4 P.M.-midnight, Thurs.-Sat.
4 P.M.-1 A.M., closed Sun.
Map 4

When word got out that Kevin Ludwig would be opening his very own restaurant and bar, cocktail enthusiasts were aflutter with anticipation. Ludwig has a long history in Portland as one of the most inventive mixologists in town—and in the Pacific Northwest at large. Beaker & Flask is all about fresh ideas and creative collaboration. The focus is not specifically on classic cocktails, although there is a definite nod towards the pre-Prohibition approach to crafting the perfect drink.

NIGHTLIFE

MINT/820

820 N. Russell St., 503/284-5518,
www.mintand820.com

HOURS: Mon.-Thurs. 4-10 P.M., Fri.-Sun. 4-11 P.M.

Map 6

There's a reason why Mint/820 keeps showing up on top of everyone's list of places to imbibe. Cool, swanky, and casually intimate, it's the perfect spot to take a date or anyone else you want to impress. The drink list is smashing, and the Avocado Daiquiri, in particular, is to die for. A surprisingly perfect balance between creamy and tart, it leaves all those other overdone super-sweet blender nightmares in the dark. It's no wonder that the drink is owner and mix-goddess Lucy Brennan's signature cocktail.

SAPPHIRE HOTEL

5008 SE Hawthorne Blvd., 503/232-6333,
www.thesapphirehotel.com

HOURS: Mon.-Fri. 4 P.M.-2 A.M., Sat. 9 A.M.-2 A.M., Sun. 9 A.M.-midnight

Map 4

There's something about the soft, red ambience of The Sapphire that makes everyone feel a bit more romantic and beautiful. The space was once the lobby of a rather questionable motel that saw more than its fair share of lurid behavior. These days, the hotel is no longer operational, but the lobby continues to be a gathering place. The cocktail menu is full of tongue-in-cheek references to the bar's sordid past, like Going Up?, made with Serrano pepper–infused tequila that has been muddled with cilantro, lime juice, and sweet and sour.

SECRET SOCIETY LOUNGE

116 NE Russell St., 503/493-3600,
www.secretsociety.net

HOURS: Mon.-Thurs. 5 P.M.-midnight, Fri.-Sat. 5 P.M.-1 A.M., closed Sun.

Map 3

With its rich decor, low lighting, and classic cocktail menu, the Secret Society Lounge makes you feel hipper than you are. Try the Corpse Reviver (Aviation gin, Lillet, lemon juice, and absinthe), a lounge favorite. The Moscow Mule and the Chrysanthemum

© JOHN VALLS

Rainy nights don't keep Portlanders inside, not when there are tasty cocktails to be had at Mint/820.

cocktail are also lovely. If you're a lady, check out the bathroom, as the "ladies lounge" is almost cooler than the bar.

◖ TEARDROP COCKTAIL LOUNGE

1015 NW Everett St., 503/445-8109,
www.teardroplounge.com

HOURS: Mon.-Sat. 4 P.M.-midnight

Map 2

This is the spot for classic cocktails with a DIY Portland twist. The owners infuse booze, make their own bitters, and stock some stuff you can't possibly find in the liquor store. The menu changes regularly to reflect the season and what ingredients are locally available. If you need proof that these guys know what they are doing, just look around at the clientele; chances are, most of them are bartenders themselves.

TEAZONE AND CAMELLIA LOUNGE

510 NW 11th Ave., 503/221-2130, www.teazone.com
HOURS: Mon. 8 A.M.-7 P.M., Tues.-Fri. 8 A.M.-midnight,
Sat.-Sun. 10 A.M.-midnight, Sun. 10 A.M.-8 P.M.
Map 2

Before you belly up to the bar at Camellia Lounge and ask to try one of the infamous tea cocktails, you had better check the menu. No, the menu doesn't read like $5 Long Island night at the local meat market. Instead, it's a surprisingly creative array of cocktails for bourbon, vodka, rum and gin drinkers alike, most of which contain some form of tea. Sample the Southern Honey—a Manhattan made with bourbon that's infused with vanilla-rooibos tea, Southern Comfort, and muddled orange—and you'll see why this marriage works so well.

VICTORY BAR

3652 SE Division St., 503/236-8755,
www.thevictorybar.com
HOURS: Mon.-Sat. 5 P.M.-1 A.M., Sun. 5 P.M.-midnight
Map 4

If you're not all that familiar with Belgian beer, the list of options here can be a bit intimidating. In fact, *Imbibe* magazine rated Victory as one of the best places in the United States to have a beer. That is reason enough to go, but the dark, cozy, ambient environment helps—as does the impressive cocktail list, with such classics as the Corpse Reviver, Old Fashioned, and French 77. The bar is not shy about saying that it's a "bartender's bar," and they have a following of industry leaders to prove it.

Late-Night Bars

DOTS

2521 SE Clinton St., 503/235-0203
HOURS: Daily noon-2 A.M.
Map 4

The Clinton Street district (all six blocks of it) has so much charm. Much of this can be blamed on the high concentration of youthful artists who frequent the bars along this stretch—and find their way to Dots come midnight to make a last effort at chili cheese fries or hearty helpings of comfort food before committing themselves to bed. The food here is great and the drinks (especially the Lime Rickey) are delightful, but the real star here is the late-night people-watching.

DOUG FIR

830 E. Burnside St., 503/231-9663,
www.dougfirlounge.com
HOURS: Daily 7 A.M.-4 A.M.
Map 4

Also one of the area's most popular live music venues, Doug Fir is the place to be when the bartender calls last call. With a fascinating collection of nocturnals and a menu that spans from gut-busting breakfast to the cheeky Fir Burger, Doug Fir is the perfect salve after an evening of heavy dancing. Because the plucked-from-the-'50s diner is connected to the Jupiter Hotel and guests often spill into the outdoor fire pits and smoking lounges, the party at Doug Fir has been know to rage on long after the restaurant stops serving eggs.

LE BISTRO MONTAGE

301 SE Morrison St., 503/234-1324,
www.montageportland.com
HOURS: Mon.-Sat. 11:30 A.M.-2 P.M., Sun.-Thurs. 6
P.M.-2 A.M., Fri.-Sat. 6 P.M.-4 A.M.
Map 4

It's more or less a part of becoming a Portlander. For natives, sitting in the wee hours of the morning consuming large bowls of garlicky Old Mac is just a part of being a Stumptown inhabitant. Ask any resident and they're not likely to recall why this is so. The service is decidedly coarse and the ambiance has all the intimacy and gentleness of unexpected cannon fire. And yet, there's nothing like the crowd come 1 A.M., buzzed with enthusiasm, indifferent to mistreatment, and desperate for hot bowls of jambalaya and alligator linguine.

NIGHTLIFE

COURTESY OF JUPITER HOTEL

With its adjacency to the Jupiter Hotel, Doug Fir is a popular late-night spot to grab food and gather around a fire.

THE ROXY

1121 SW Stark St., 503/223-9160
HOURS: Tues.-Sat. 24 hours, closed Mon.
Map 1

There are a few things in life that are constant. The promise of rain in Portland? Yes, we can pretty much count on that. Around here, we have the comfort of knowing that the rain will always return and The Roxy will always bring you sweet, fantastic French toast and bacon at 2 A.M. (unless it's Monday). The food is surprisingly good here, especially after a night spent sweating to the sounds of 1980s pop. Check out the decidedly irreverent t-shirt collection and tip your server well (who else will bring you chili cheese fries at that hour?).

Gay and Lesbian

◖ DARCELLE XV SHOWCLUB

208 NW 3rd. Ave., 503/222-5338, www.darcellexv.com
HOURS: Wed.-Thurs. 6-11 P.M., Fri.-Sat. 6 P.M.-2:30 A.M.
COST: $15
Map 2

"That's no lady, that's Darcelle!" She's an icon in Portland and has been for more than 40 years. The girls at Darcelle's perform weekly shows that are full of bawdiness, humor, and sparkle. Make reservations before you go and catch the late Saturday show if you can. It's followed by a stripped-down and sexy performance by The Men of Darcelle at no additional charge.

LATE-NIGHT FOOD CARTS

Portland food carts have a cult-like following, but none quite so unwavering as that of the carts that occupy the corner of SE 12th Avenue and SE Hawthorne. After last call, hungry Portlanders flock to the food carts that sing out a collective siren song of something delicious swimming in the deep fryer. Most of the carts on this corner are open until 3 A.M., which provides ample time to replenish after working off all those calories on the dance floor. Make sure you bring cash. Like most food carts in town, these carts do not take cards.

The big daddy of them all is **Potato Champion** (www.potatochampion.com), a colorful cart that serves up fries in small or large paper cones. These fries are not the sort of greasy, soggy mess you're likely to find at some state fair. The fries at Potato Champion are hot, salty, and crispy on the outside, while still being soft and warm on the inside. They're good on their own, but just for kicks, PC offers an array of dips like rosemary ketchup, sweet hot mustard, tarragon anchovy mayonnaise, and remoulade. If you're feeling really indulgent, try the *poutine,* a Canadian treat that involves smothering fries with cheese grits and gravy.

Another great late-night cart is **Yarp?!** (971/275-6538), a delicious, inventive, and satisfying pasta place. Finding Yarp?! open can be a challenge. But, it's the nature of the food cart business, where a small handful of people (sometimes just the owners) work back-breaking hours in a cramped, hot space and still sometimes can't quite make ends meet. Nonetheless, Yarp?! is worth the quest once you have sampled the roasted red pepper spaghetti, pork tenderloin on vermicelli with jalapeno cream sauce, or spicy noodle bowl with pork heart.

If you want something gooey, melty, and rich, make a beeline for **Peierra Creperie** (www.facebook.com/perierra). Maybe it's the microbrews talking, but the consensus is that this crepe stand makes amazingly crisp and delicious pockets of joy with creative combinations of fillings like bananas and Nutella; pears and gorgonzola; gruyere and ham; and salmon, cream cheese, and arugula. Peierra also has vegan options and, in summer months, occasionally adds milkshakes to the menu.

For those carnivorous types who want nothing more than a big ol' healthy portion of meat to round out their evening, **Crown-Q** (503/806-2908) is the place to be. This cart serves up some pretty mean barbeque with all the smoky, spicy or sweet and sticky stuff you could want. If they're out of pulled pork sandwiches (they sell out fast), grab an unapologetically huge barbequed turkey leg, dig in, and get messy.

Crashing onto the scene with an almost immediately rabid following, **Wiffles** (www.whiffies.com) is a fried pie cart that tends to bring out the giggly kid in everyone. This is portable food at its best; and they've got the goods, whether you are in the mood for something savory like barbeque beef, brisket and cheese, or chicken pot pie; or something sweet like cherry, peach, or marionberry. The menu changes regularly, but with everything priced under $5, it's easy to sample your way through it and find a favorite.

THE EGYPTIAN CLUB
3701 SE Division St., 503/236-8689,
www.eroompdx.com
HOURS: Mon.-Fri. 1 P.M.-2:30 A.M., Sat.-Sun.
4 P.M.-2:30 A.M.
COST: Free-$5
Map 4

The Egyptian (or the E-Room) is basically three bars in one. The Front Lounge is where you'll find pool tables, darts, and big-screen televisions. Behind that, lovely ladies pack into The Room to belt out karaoke every night beginning at 9 P.M. In The Tomb, they hold special events and weekly dance parties complete with light shows. The drinks are cheap and the company can be especially fun.

EMBERS

110 NW Broadway, 503/222-3082,
www.emberspdx.com
HOURS: Daily 9 A.M.-2:30 A.M.
COST: Free-$6

It's practically a Portland icon, with its dual-purpose venue housing a stage on one side and a small but vibrant dance floor on the other. The music is loud and fast—mostly combos of house music, 1980s songs, and Top 40 hits—but it's the spirit of the place that gets you dancing. It's just so darn joyful. Plus, it's hard to resist the opportunity to do a little cage dancing or take a spin on the catwalk.
Map 2

HOBO'S

120 NW 3rd Ave., 503/224-3285, www.hobospdx.com
HOURS: Daily 4 P.M.-2:30 A.M.
COST: $10
Map 2

Had Old Blue Eyes and the rest of the Rat Pack been gay, this is where they would have hung out. Dark and comfortable, each table feels a little bit private and with the addition of the flickering candlelight and the soft piano, it's downright romantic. The Hobo's staff is friendly and attentive and it's an elegant choice for anyone seeking clandestine conversation over cocktails and delectable entrées.

SCANDALS

1125 SW Stark St., 503/227-5887,
www.scandalspdx.com
HOURS: Daily noon-2:30 A.M.
COST: Free
Map 1

Scandals has been around for about 30 years now, launching onto the scene many years ago as the first gay bar in the area. Nowadays it's a favorite haunt for pretty boys and sassy girls who like cheap, strong drinks, and a more laid-back, hospitable crowd than many of the popular meat markets nearby. Scandals is a great spot to sit and linger before heading off to dance or see a show and it's also a perfect place to decompress afterward.

Wine Bars

BAR AVIGNON

2138 SE Division St., 503/517-0808,
www.baravignon.com
HOURS: Mon.-Sun. 4 P.M.-midnight
Map 4

In this sleek, simply appointed bar, the focus is all about imbibing. Owners Randy Goodman and Nancy Hunt have a long history in the Portland restaurant business and they seem to have hit it out of the park here. Bar Avignon is a perfect spot for a slow evening conversation over dessert with a gently sparkling glass of Moscato or a cheese board served with a soft French red.

EVERYDAY WINE

1520 NE Alberta St., 503/331-7119,
www.everydaywine.com
HOURS: Tues.-Sat. 2-10 P.M.
Map 3

Everyday Wine is about as laid-back as it gets for a wine bar. There's no wine list here; simply choose a bottle from the shelf and it will be popped open for you. Drink it by the glass or share the whole bottle with friends. It's really up to you. They don't serve food there, but you're welcome to bring your own—and with the selection of restaurants on Alberta Street, there's plenty nearby to choose from. If you go on a Friday, ask about the Friday Night Flights, where you can sample several wines for just $12.

M BAR

417 NW 21st Ave., 503/228-6614

HOURS: Daily 6 P.M.-2:30 A.M.

`Map 2`

Arguably one of the smallest bars in Portland (think big closet, but with wine, beer, and sake), M Bar packs a lot of charm into its tiny space. The selection is simple and the happy hour prices (which last until 8 P.M.) are laughably low. There are no fussy menus here; a chalkboard mounted above the bar declares the choices for the day.

METROVINO

1139 NW 11th Ave., 503/517-7778,

www.metrovinopdx.com

HOURS: Mon.-Sat. 4-10 P.M., closed Sun.

`Map 2`

This is the high-tech version of a wine bar. MetroVino is equipped with an Enomatic machine, which is basically a futuristic vending machine that dispenses tastes or full glasses one at a time. Immediately after the pour, the system automatically injects an oxygen-buffering layer of argon into the top of the bottle, stopping oxidation in opened bottles. What all that means for you is that you can choose from a truly impressive selection of wines by the glass, including a number of wines you won't find anywhere else.

NOBLE ROT

1111 E. Burnside St., 503/233-1999, www.noblerotpdx.com

HOURS: Mon.-Fri. 5-11 P.M., Sat.-Sun. 5 P.M.-1 A.M.

`Map 3`

If your wallet is a little light, but you still want to sip some great wines, Noble Rot is your new best friend. The mark-up on bottles here is only $7 more than the retail cost. The selection of wine flights at The Rot changes almost on a nightly basis—as does the extensive tapas-style menu, which includes a number of items accented by greens grown on the rooftop garden. The 3,000-square-foot garden (which you can tour if you ask) is just one example of The Rot's eco-friendly focus.

NIGHTLIFE

COURTESY OF METROVINO

MetroVino uses modern technology to offer more than 80 wines and sparkling wines by the glass at any time.

VINO PARADISO

417 NW 10th Ave., 503/295-9536,
www.vinoparadiso.com

HOURS: Tues.-Sat. 4-11 P.M., Sun. 3-9 P.M., closed Mon.

Map 2

Cool and beautiful without being pretentious, Vino Paradiso has the signature swanky style of its owner, Timothy Nishimoto, who is a vocalist and percussionist for Pink Martini. Try a Northwest-focused flight, or order a bottle from the cellar. To its credit, Vino always has a great selection, but guests aren't expected to be especially clever about wine. If you aren't sure what you will like, don't be afraid to ask. They won't make you feel silly for wondering if Viognier goes with pheasant.

WINE DOWN ON 28TH

126 NE 28th Ave., 503/236-9463,
www.winedownpdx.com

HOURS: Sun.-Thurs. 4:30-11 P.M., Fri.-Sat. 10 P.M.-1 A.M., closed Mon.

Map 3

The small bar here has only a half-dozen seats and it's a good spot to sit and try a flight. The atmosphere here is warm, cozy and welcoming, so it's perfect for romantic dates or for small gatherings of friends. Wine Down has possibly one of the best selections of port by the glass in town, boasting more than 70 varietals. The food is reliably good here as well, but best enjoyed during happy hour when the prices are more affordable.

ARTS AND LEISURE

Portland's ever-increasing influx of creative souls has transformed the once sleepy town into a sparkling community of artists, performers, writers, and patrons eager to soak up their imaginative spirit. Even for a native, the city is full of surprises because the landscape and the community are constantly reinventing themselves. Blame it on the city's pioneering ancestors, but Portlanders just feel better when they are making something new.

You might think the weather would be prohibitive. After all, the Northwest skies are often so grey you'd think that Eeyore from *Winnie the Pooh* had taken up permanent residence. But the locals seem to take it in stride. It's the price one must pay to live in state so rich with hiking trails and rivers, a state just begging to be biked, hiked, climbed, fished, and explored.

It's like my old babysitter used to say when we would sit on her porch whining about the rain, "If you want trees to climb, you gotta get a little wet."

On any given night, there is likely to be a play being performed for the first time. Simultaneously, at the opening of a music festival, an up-and-coming band plays old-school rap songs on a banjo and mandolin (to the delight of the crowd). Mere blocks away, it is standing room only at a gallery opening where 30 artists have created 30 pieces of art, each of which will sell for $30. Where else can you find such a celebration of self-expression? Where else can you attend a gay pride festival, plunder with pirates, and ride your bike naked through the streets all in one day? Where else can you hike through a forest on your way to

HIGHLIGHTS

LOOK FOR ☾ TO FIND RECOMMENDED ARTS AND ACTIVITIES.

☾ **Best Theater Performance:** Portland's biggest and second-oldest theater company, **Portland Center Stage,** is known for balancing its season between daring new works and classic plays (page 98).

☾ **Best Cheap Flick in Classic Style:** Movies may be cheap (about $3) at **The Bagdad Theater & Pub** on Hawthorne, but the theater isn't. The Colonial Revival–style building with the oft-photographed marquee is both a Portland landmark and a great cheap date (page 100).

☾ **Best Place to Get Hoppy:** If you love beer, the **Oregon Brewers Festival** will seem like Nirvana. The annual event, which features 80-plus craft brewers, live music, food, and demonstrations, is quite popular in brew-loving Portland (page 104).

☾ **The Best Festival:** The annual **Portland Rose Festival** is a big bash indeed. With parades, music, rides, and special events scattered throughout the two-week event, there is no end to entertainment (page 104).

☾ **Best Place to Embrace Your Inner Geek:** Where else but the **Oregon Museum of Science and Industry** can you experience an earthquake, visit the Milky Way, climb aboard the USS *Blueback* submarine, and trip out in the OMNIMAX theater all in one day (page 110)?

☾ **Best Portland Crash Course:** In just a few hours, **The Best of Portland Walking Tour,** will give you more than enough fodder about strange landmarks, fun facts, and city history to outwit a local (page 118).

COURTESY OF TRAVEL PORTLAND

The Bagdad Theater & Pub is a stunning relic of Hollywood's Golden Age that just happens to serve local microbrews.

work? Portlanders want to do it all; and if "it" doesn't exist yet, "it" is created. Maybe that's why so many artists, writers, master chefs, and performers flock here. In this town, there is an assumed license to reinvent, redefine, or completely obliterate the boundaries of normalcy. It's terribly comforting and exhilarating all at the same time.

The Arts

With all its natural beauty, and its emphasis on self-expression and independent thinking, it's no wonder that Portland is a destination spot for creative thinkers. The energy of young artists, playwrights, poets, and musicians injects the city with vibrancy and color. One of the most compelling things about the arts scene in Portland is the expectation that whatever you are is exactly what you should be, so long as it brings you inspiration and pleasure. Artists in Portland tend to thrive on a mutual respect, rather than competition. There is pretty much room for everyone in the Portland arts scene. No one is any more or less weird than anyone else, and all of it—the theater, visual arts, dance, music—comes together to create rich environment for imagination to thrive.

MUSEUMS
HOYT ARBORETUM
4000 SW Fairview Blvd., 503/865-8733, www.hoytarboretum.org
HOURS: Visitors center Mon.-Fri. 9 A.M.-4 P.M., Sat. 9 A.M.-3 P.M., closed Sun.; grounds daily 6 A.M.-10 P.M.
COST: Free
Map 7

Part park, part museum of trees, the Hoyt Arboretum has miles of hills and trails that showcase tree life from all over the world. There are hours to be lost exploring all the 10,000 individual trees and shrubs, and sometimes, even with a map (provided outside the visitors center) it is quite easy to become disoriented. If you don't mind getting a little bit lost, the walk is beautiful and full of lovely secluded places to think, explore, or have a woodland picnic. There are a number of mapped-out self-guided tours that you can take in one-, two-, and four-mile segments, portions of which have paved and ADA-accessible paths.

MUSEUM OF CONTEMPORARY CRAFT
724 NW Davis St., 503/223-2654 or 503/223-2654, www.museumofcontemporarycraft.org
HOURS: Tues.-Sat. 11 A.M.-6 P.M., closed Sun.-Mon., first Thurs. 11 A.M.-8 P.M.
COST: Free
Map 2

Founded in 1937, the Museum of Contemporary Craft has long been dedicated to celebrating and showcasing excellence and innovation in craft from the early 20th century to the present. The museum takes a more active approach to its subject than a traditional gallery often does, pointing out that "craft is engaged as a verb as well as a noun." The 4,500-square-foot exhibition space spans two levels. There is an emphasis on the re-imagination of the place of craft in contemporary society, using physical interaction with objects, dynamic exhibitions, educational programs, and performances. In addition to interesting exhibits, the museum frequently hosts events to bring artists and the community closer together.

OREGON HISTORICAL SOCIETY
1200 SW Park Ave., 503/222-1741, www.ohs.org
HOURS: Tues.-Sat. 10 A.M.-5 P.M., Sun. noon-5 P.M., closed Mon.
COST: $11 adult, $9 student (with ID) and senior, $5 child, free for child under 5
Map 1

The Oregon Historical Society (OHS), founded in 1898, is Oregon's premiere history museum. OHS is home to a permanent exhibit on the history of Oregon: "Oregon My Oregon," which occupies 7,000 square feet of the museum. There are two theaters, interactive displays, and several re-created environments, such as a Hudson Bay Company ship hull, a 19th-century explorer's tent, and a store stocked with 1940s-era merchandise from the Hood River Yasui Brothers Mercantile. OHS also presents major traveling exhibitions on a variety of themes, such as the history of Claymation, American development, and Northwest traditions.

ARTS AND LEISURE

OREGON JEWISH MUSEUM

310 NW Davis St., 503/226-3600, www.ojm.org

HOURS: Tues.-Fri. 10 A.M.-3 P.M., Sun. 1-4 P.M., closed Mon.

COST: $3

Map 2

The Oregon Jewish Museum is the only Jewish museum in the Pacific Northwest, and therefore serves as a museum for historical materials from all over the entire region, not just Oregon. At any time in the museum there is a wide array of Jewish art, cultural pieces, and historical artifacts. They also have a surprisingly extensive collection of organizational records, family papers, photographs, and ephemeral materials dating from 1850 to the present—the largest collection of the documented and visual history of Oregon's Jews, which is available to researchers, students, and scholars.

OREGON MARITIME CENTER AND MUSEUM

115 SW Pine St. in Waterfront Park, 503/224-7724, www.oregonmaritimemuseum.org

HOURS: Wed.-Sun. 11 A.M.-4 P.M., closed Mon.-Tues.

COST: $5 adult, $4 senior, $3 child, free for child under 6

Map 1

To get a real understanding of the significance Portland played in maritime travel and commerce in years past, you'll want to visit this intriguing museum. Housed on the steam-powered *Portland,* which was called out of retirement to be moored at Tom McCall Waterfront Park, the floating museum's exhibits feature navigation instruments, model ships, photographs, memorabilia, and artifacts from vessels of the region's maritime past. Other attractions include "Mom's Boat," a fishing boat from the late 1920s, and the barge *Russell.* Lectures and educational programs are often offered, and there is a gift shop on-site.

PORTLAND ART MUSEUM

1219 SW Park Ave., 503/226-2811, www.pam.org

HOURS: Tues.-Wed. 10 A.M.-5 P.M., Thurs.-Fri. 10 A.M.-8 P.M., Sat. 10 A.M.-5 P.M., Sun. noon-5 P.M., closed Mon.

COST: $12 adult, $10 student (with ID) and seniors, free for those under 17

Map 1

The Portland Art Museum (PAM) was founded in 1892, which happens to make it the oldest art museum on the West Coast and seventh oldest in the United States. At 240,000 square feet, it is also one of the 25 largest art museums in the United States. It all begins with European Impressionism and transitions as you walk to more current pieces, and whichever major traveling exhibit is being shown at the time. The permanent collection is constantly changing (usually because something goes out on loan), the collection usually has more than 42,000 works of art, with a center for Northwest art, Native American art, Asian art, African art, and contemporary art, sculpture, and photography. PAM is also home to the Northwest Film Center.

WORLD FORESTRY CENTER

4033 SW Canyon Rd., 503/228-1367, www.worldforestry.org

HOURS: Daily 10 A.M.-5 P.M.

COST: $8 adult, $7 senior, $3 child, free child under 2

Map 7

This 20,000-square-foot museum has a number of interactive exhibits about the trees here in the Pacific Northwest and all over the world. So why go to a museum to learn about trees when you could just go to a forest? Well, the Forestry Center has a lot to say that those trees won't say themselves, like how to approach forest sustainability and how the intricate systems, structures, and cycles within the forests affect each other and us every day. Plus, it's fun, since you can take a simulated ride down Class IV rapids, practice being a smokejumper, and try your hand at logging.

ON DISPLAY: A GUIDE TO PORTLAND ART WALKS

Each of the city's quadrants has its own personality. Spend a month in Portland, and you can see just how different they are. **First Thursday in the Pearl** (www.firstthursdayportland.com) is one of the most popular and well-attended art walks. Most of the galleries launch new exhibits on this day, hosting receptions with free wine and goodies, where you can meet the artist in person and listen to live music. Generally, the hours are 6–9 P.M., but some parties can last well into the night. There is no real need to have an agenda unless there are particular galleries you want to visit. Otherwise, it is fun to simply stroll through the streets and stop at whichever gallery, shop, or restaurant calls to you.

If you aren't spent the next day, you can head over to the **Central Eastside Arts District First Friday Art Walk** (www.firstfridayart.com). The event is less of a walk and more of an opportunity to check out the launch of some new exhibits, as it is scattered as far north as NE Broadway, and as far south as Sellwood. A good area to hit is East Burnside Street, where you will find a few galleries and a number of restaurants to relax in while you suss out where you want to go next. There's a lot to see, but with it being spread out across much of the city's inner core, it can be a bit of a scavenger hunt. The website provides a map of galleries, shops, restaurants, and bars that are participating.

Between April and December, you can attend the **Lower Fremont Second Friday Art Walk and Sidewalk Sale** (www.lowerfremont. com), where more than 40 artists and crafters display and sell their work along NE Fremont at 13th and 14th Avenues. It usually runs 5–9 P.M. and features music and specials at a number of the area restaurants and boutiques.

Third Thursday in Kenton (www.kentonbusiness.org) started in July 2009. It's the first art walk for the north side of town. The Kenton neighborhood has been growing and changing for some time now, all the while developing a true sense of style. The neighborhood (which is home to the giant Paul Bunyan statue) has seen a significant influx of new restaurants and shops along North Denver Avenue, but still maintains a homey, small-town feel. The monthly art walk is a great chance to explore boutiques, cafés, and galleries that are new on the scene.

Finally, **Last Thursday on Alberta** (www.artonalberta.org) is the splashy, wild child in the bunch. Year-round, the crowds on Last Thursday are thick with people searching for affordable art, a little nip of wine, or just a good time. They close down about 15 blocks of NE Alberta Street between 10th and 30th Avenues, which alleviates some of the crowding. It's a good thing, because the real focus is the street vendors who set up their art on sidewalks, tables, trees, patches of dirt, or chain-link fences. Locals like to toss some coffee or wine in a portable mug and hit the streets for some unparalleled people-watching. It is not uncommon to see an impromptu parade, a live band on someone's porch, or a stilt-walker strolling by.

GALLERIES
AUGEN GALLERY
817 SW 2nd Ave., 503/224-8182,
www.augengallery.com
HOURS: Tues.-Sat. 10:30 A.M.-5:30 P.M., closed Sun.-Mon.
COST: Free
Map 1

The building that houses Augen Gallery was erected in 1894, and the gallery now occupies 10,000 square feet on two floors. The 110-year-old building stands in the Yamhill Historic District, which is three blocks from the center of the business district and two blocks from the Willamette River. There's a second gallery in the Desoto Building arts complex, which houses four galleries and the Museum of Contemporary Craft. Both galleries are worth a visit, especially if you can make it out for expanded First Thursday hours (until 8:30 P.M.).

BEPPU WIARDA GALLERY

319 NW 9th Ave., 503/241-6460,
www.beppugallery.com
HOURS: Wed.-Sun. 11 A.M.-6 P.M., closed Mon.-Tues.
COST: Free
Map 2

Opened in 2005, the beppu wiarda gallery was named (the lowercase is intentional) for owners Stan and Gail Beppu and Stephanie Wiarda. It's a fine place to find contemporary and contemplative works from an array of approaches, including paintings, works on paper, and sculpture. Most of the work represents an intimate group of established and emerging artists, and reflects the owners' passion for the evolutionary art scene in Portland and their considerable history in the art world. The Beppus owned and operated the Beppu Gallery on the central coast of Oregon for 15 years, and Wiarda was the director of Blackfish Gallery for eight years, as well as the Northwest Print Council.

BLUE SKY GALLERY

122 NW 8th Ave., 503/225-0210,
www.blueskygallery.org
HOURS: Tues.-Sun. noon-5 P.M., closed Mon.
COST: Free
Map 2

Blue Sky Gallery, which is also known as the Oregon Center for the Photographic Arts, is a nonprofit space that focuses on educating the public about photography. You may not already know the work of local, national, and international artists that are on display at Blue Sky, but you will soon. Blue Sky has been credited with having the best record of discovering new photographers of any artists' space in the country. As a non-profit, Blue Sky is largely supported by grants and by membership program, which costs as little as $40 and comes with a gaggle of incentives and gifts.

BULLSEYE GALLERY

300 NW 13th Ave., 503/227-0222,
www.bullseyegallery.com
HOURS: Tues.-Sat. 10 A.M.-5 P.M.
COST: Free
Map 2

Bullseye Glass Company has been a maker of colored glass for art and architecture since 1974, and was the first company in the world to formulate and manufacture glass that is factory-tested for fusing compatibility. Chances are, if you know of an artist who works with glass, she gets some of her materials from Bullseye. They have also supported individual artists and art-school programs by developing new materials technologies that have helped change the field of kiln-formed glass artistry. As part of Bullseye Glass Company, Bullseye Gallery works with a group of international artists in the field of kiln-formed glass, and showcases some of the most dynamic of the artists in this field through exhibitions and projects.

ELIZABETH LEACH GALLERY

417 NW 9th Ave., 503/224-0521,
www.elizabethleach.com
HOURS: Tues.-Sat. 10:30 A.M.-5:30 P.M.
COST: Free
Map 2

Established in 1981 and considered the second oldest gallery in Portland, the Elizabeth Leach Gallery offers a fairly comprehensive selection of contemporary fine art. It is definitely a high-caliber place, with excellent work on display that will particularly delight serious collectors. The gallery occupies a 4,000-square-foot space in the Pearl District, and features a video and light installation by Portland light artist Hap Tivey titled *Light on the Horizon*. Leach has a background in art history and has long been active in Portland's art community. She was at one time the President of the Portland Art Dealers Association, and has been on the board of several arts organizations such as Pacific Northwest College of Art, Portland Center for Visual Arts, and the Portland Institute for Contemporary Art.

NEWSPACE CENTER FOR PHOTOGRAPHY

1632 SE 10th Ave., 503/963-1935,
www.newspacephoto.org
HOURS: Mon.-Thurs. 10 A.M.-10 P.M., Fri.-Sat. 10 A.M.-6 P.M.
COST: Free
Map 4

Newspace Center for Photography is a complete

photography resource center that offers classes, gallery exhibits, digital lab, darkroom, and lighting studio access, artists' lectures, and portfolio reviews. It also serves as community hub for students, working artists, professional photographers, educators, and photo enthusiasts of all types. The gallery at Newspace launches about 12 exhibits each year, usually featuring one or two artists at a time, with the occasional group show or juried exhibition. While exhibits can be quite varied, an emphasis is placed on modern, fine art, and documentary photography.

ONDA ARTE LATINA

2215 NE Alberta St., 503/493-1909, www.ondagallery.com
HOURS: Wed.-Sat. 11 a.m.-6 p.m., closed Mon.-Tues.
COST: Free
Map 3

Onda Arte Latina is part gallery and part store, both of which come together to celebrate the art of Latin America. The gallery, located in the Alberta Arts District, shows fine art from painters and sculptors, and the shop brings you hand-crafted, Fair Trade and sustainable ceramics, textiles, glass, and wood for home decor, clothing, and gifts. Owner Pablo Merlo Flores and curator Allan Oliver have gathered a fine collection of unique pieces that simply burst with creativity, color, and design. Flores, a native Argentinean with European ancestry, has brought the romance and rich history of the Latin American and European arts to Portland through Pampeana, an online wholesale art business that supports Fair Trade and sustainability.

WATERSTONE GALLERY

424 NW 12th Ave., 503/226-6196, www.waterstonegallery.com
HOURS: Wed.-Sat. noon-6 P.M., Sun. noon-4 P.M., closed Mon.-Tues.
COST: Free
Map 2

Waterstone Gallery was founded in 1992 by four established artists who believed that an artist-run gallery would provide uniquely intimate interaction with their clientele. Today, Waterstone still offers clients the opportunity to have direct contact with the artists who own and operate the space—though it has grown to include 14 nationally and internationally known artists. You will still find creative, contemporary, original art that is carefully crafted and beautifully presented.

THEATER
ARTISTS REPERTORY THEATRE

1515 SW Morrison St., 503/241-1278, www.artistsrep.org
HOURS: Tues.-Sat. noon-6 P.M., closed Sun.-Mon.
Map 1

Formed in 1982, Artists Repertory Theatre (ART) is Portland's oldest, continuously run theater company. In the early days, ART (which is *never*, by the way, pronounced "art," but always as "A-R-T") performed in a 110-seat venue in a YWCA building. The company has come a long way and now has its own two-stage venue (which has been recently renovated to allow easier access between their two stages). ART has survived as long as it has in part because it has committed since its inception to performing new, innovative works and taking dramatically different approaches to classics.

MILAGRO THEATRE

525 SE Stark St., 503/236-7253, www.milagro.org
Map 4

Miracle Theatre (otherwise known as Teatro Milagro) produces a broad array of work that focuses on celebrating Latino culture and language, sometimes bridging it with American theater traditions. The company is consistently—and delightfully—different, whether presenting a vibrant Dia de los Muertos (Day of the Dead) combination of dance, music, and theater or a dark, compelling historical piece. Miracle manages to keep things fresh, all the while keeping its Latino heritage in mind. The company occasionally performs in Spanish (usually with super-titles projected), but even if you don't understand the language, the performances are full of heart and compelling to watch. You can purchase tickets online, by

ARTS AND LEISURE

phone, or in person at the Hollywood Theatre (4122 NE Sandy Blvd.) daily 1–9 P.M.

PORTLAND CENTER FOR THE PERFORMING ARTS

1111 SW Broadway, 503/248-4335, www.pcpa.com
HOURS: Mon.-Sat. 10 A.M.-5 P.M., closed Sun.
Map 1

The Portland Center for the Performing Arts (PCPA) is actually three separate buildings: the Keller Auditorium, the Arlene Schnitzer Concert Hall, and Antoinette Hatfield Hall (formerly called the New Theatre Building), which houses the Newmark and Dolores Winningstad theatres, and Brunish Hall. Portland Center Stage used to occupy much of the calendar in Hatfield Hall, but now that they have their very own venue, PCPA has an even wider array of performances that occur on almost any night of the week. In fact, there are 21 resident companies that call PCPA home, among them are Portland Opera, Oregon Ballet Theatre, Oregon Symphony Orchestra, Oregon Children's Theatre, White Bird Dance Company, and Broadway in Portland.

◖ PORTLAND CENTER STAGE

128 NW 11th Ave., 503/445-3700, www.pcs.org
HOURS: Fri.-Wed. noon-5:30 P.M., Thurs. 10 A.M.-5:30 P.M.
Map 2

The sparkling (and super-sustainable) renovation of its home, the Gerding Theater at the Armory, would be reason enough to make Portland's second-oldest theater company worth a visit. The circa-1895 Armory became the first historic renovation and the first theater to achieve a LEED Platinum certification for green building practices. The result? An airy, visually stunning lobby (complete with Wi-Fi and a café) and two state-of-the-art performance spaces. On the 599-seat Main Stage, you'll find hit musicals like *Cabaret* mixed with national bestsellers like *Frost/Nixon* and *Doubt,* plus world premieres like Ken Kesey's *Sometimes a Great Notion.* The downstairs studio space, the 200-seat Ellyn Bye Studio, leans toward smart, cutting-edge performances that are scaled for the stage's more intimate advantage.

THIRD RAIL REPERTORY THEATRE

121 SW Salmon St., 503/235-1101, www.thirdrailrep.org
Map 1

Third Rail Repertory Theatre burst on the scene in 2003 with a core group of actors, each of whom was already known for solid, dynamic performances. As the company began to evolve, putting together progressively risky and exciting works, everyone kept expecting—but dreading—the moment when this group would stumble. In fact, the company has finally sidled right up against the two top companies in town—and has managed to remain a darling among the temperamental and often obstinate local theatre critics. The company performs at **The World Trade** Center downtown, and you can purchase tickets online, by phone, or in person at the **Hollywood Theatre** (4122 NE Sandy Blvd.) daily 1–9 P.M.

DANCE

DO JUMP!

1515 SE 37th Ave., 503/231-1232, www.dojump.org
Map 4

Do Jump! calls its performers "actorbats." It is a fitting term because their work is a unique blend of theater, dance, aerial work, acrobatics, dynamic visuals, and live music that defies categorization. The company was established in 1977 as a group of volunteers under the direction of Robin Lane. Today, Do Jump! has progressed into a troupe of salaried players with Lane still at the helm. Many of the company members also serve as teachers for Do Jump!'s Movement Theater School, which offers classes in trapeze, acrobatics, and aerial yoga.

OREGON BALLET THEATRE

Keller Auditorium at 222 SW Clay St., 503/227-0977, www.obt.org
Map 1

Oregon's premiere classical dance company, Oregon Ballet Theatre (OBT) was the product of a 1989 merger of Ballet Oregon and Pacific Ballet Theater. At the time, James Canfield, a former dancer with Joffrey Ballet served as artistic director, and under his direction, the company repertoire grew to comprise over 80 ballets, from evening-length works to contemporary pieces. Every holiday season, the company performs the West Coast production of George Balanchine's *The Nutcracker*, which includes OBT's full company and nearly 100 students from the OBT School.

PENDULUM AERIAL DANCE THEATRE
Various venues, www.pendulumdancetheatre.org
Boundaries are tested and then distinctly ignored by Pendulum Aerial Dance Theatre. Using various aerial apparatuses such as the trapeze, a hoop, aerial silks, and ropes, and darn near anything they can suspend themselves from, the multi-talented and captivating company puts on quite a show. In some moments, the movements are so smooth and controlled, it is as if they are underwater. At the core of their physically demanding performances is sheer physical prowess and strength, and a whole new concept of dance that is one part circus, one part burlesque, and a whole lot of imagination.

WHITE BIRD
Various venues, 503/245-1600, www.whitebird.org
White Bird brings established and emerging companies and choreographers to Portland that audiences here wouldn't otherwise see. It has commissioned several new works, developed numerous partnerships, thought up some otherwise unimaginable collaborations, and retained a strong relationship with the performing arts community right here in Portland. Since 1997, partners Walter Jaffe and Paul King have presented more than 118 companies from all over the world and given Portland audiences a pretty remarkable helping of modern dance. As the audience has grown more sophisticated, so has White Bird, bringing in increasingly more complex and compelling companies and challenging returning companies to perform more innovative works.

MUSIC
OREGON SYMPHONY
1037 SW Broadway, 503/228-1353,
www.orsymphony.org
`Map 1`
The Oregon Symphony has a long history in Portland, stretching all the way back to 1896, when it was known as the Portland Symphony Society. These days, the orchestra entertains some 225,000 people per season with classical concerts, pops concerts, shows geared specifically for children, and a number of special guest shows. Arrive one hour early for any of the classical series concerts and hear 30-minute conversations between the music director, conductor, and symphony musicians as they chat live on the radio about the music, the composers, and the history of the piece that will be performed.

PORTLAND BAROQUE ORCHESTRA
Various venues, 503/222-6000, www.pbo.org
Presenting mostly 17th- and 18th-century music, the Portland Baroque Orchestra performs baroque and classical music on centuries-old instruments or truly authentic replicas—thus creating music on the instruments from when the music was composed. Using the lute, harpsichord, lirone, and many others, they can play the music in a way that modern orchestras can't—namely, the way it was intended. Their approach brings a whole new complexity to Beethoven, Handel, Vivaldi, and Bach, and the results are particularly noticeable when you hear them play a piece that is still heard a lot today, like Handel's *Messiah*.

PORTLAND CELLO PROJECT
Various venues, www.portlandcelloproject.com
This "indie cello orchestra" is about as hip as it gets, oftentimes collaborating with the likes of the Dandy Warhols, the Builders and the Butchers, Loch Lomond, and 3 Leg Torso. Their repertoire contains everything from Bach and Beethoven to Britney Spears and Led Zeppelin, and when the 8–16 cellists get together, they are just as likely to play any of those songs as they are to invent something completely new. With their quirky attitude and undeniable ability to attack any song with the passion and fervor of a moth around a porch light, it's no surprise that they have a rock star following in Portland.

THIRD ANGLE NEW MUSIC ENSEMBLE
Various venues, 503/331-0301, www.thirdangle.org

Third Angle tends to turn the traditional concept of chamber music on its ear with its modern and inventive expressions of the work from 20th- and 21st-century composers. They have presented over 90 programs of contemporary music, commissioned more than 20 new works, and released five recordings to much critical acclaim. The ensemble produces three to five programs each year interspersed between recording projects and educational outreach projects. Over the years, the company has garnered a well-deserved reputation for musical excellence and interesting, positively electric performances.

COMEDY
COMEDYSPORTZ
1963 NW Kearney St., 503/236-8888,
www.portlandcomedy.com
Map 2

If you are familiar with shows like *Whose Line is It Anyway?* then you are familiar with ComedySportz. The troupe of sketch comedians have been performing fast-paced, hilarious (but clean) comedy in Portland since early 1993 and they are still going strong. During the show, two teams of comedians take turns making up scenes, playing games, and singing songs. There's a lot of audience participation, and at the end, it's the audience who decides which team they like the best. On select Sundays, the group performs a ComedySportz 4 Kids show, where they focus the games and suggestions of the 12-and-under crowd, and even give a bunch of the audience members a chance to be in the spotlight.

HISTORIC MOVIE HOUSES
◖ THE BAGDAD THEATER & PUB
3702 SE Hawthorne Blvd., 503/225-5555,
www.mcmenamins.com
HOURS: Mon.-Thurs. 11 A.M.-midnight, Fri.-Sat.
11 A.M.-1 A.M., Sun. noon-midnight
Map 4

One of Portland's most notable historic theaters, which was immortalized in the 2004 film *What the Bleep Do We Know!?*, the Bagdad Theater & Pub was built in 1926 with the help of Universal Pictures and was designed using Middle Eastern influences, which were popular at the time. It was intended to be a vaudeville house, but by the early 1930s, vaudeville was dead. The site then became a cinema-only venue divided into a triplex. Mike and Brian McMenamin, the brewery brothers who have single-handedly redefined local renovation, purchased the building in 1991 and began serving beer and pizza alongside film screenings. In February 2006, the brothers converted the unused backstage space into a bar that stretches seven stories up. The space, now appropriately known as the BackStage Bar, was large enough to house a full fly system for the theater's vaudevillian past, but now it houses an enormous mural that depicts the building's theatrical beginnings.

CLINTON STREET THEATER
2522 SE Clinton St., 503/238-8899,
www.clintonsttheater.com
Map 4

Clinton Street Theater was built in the early Craftsman style in 1914, and it is said to be the oldest continuously operating movie house west of the Mississippi. In 1945, the name was changed to the 26th Avenue Theater, and then in 1969 it briefly became the Encore Theater before reverting back to Clinton Street Theater in 1976. The theater plays host to a number of underground and independent movies and festivals, such as Filmed by Bike, a festival devoted to bike-themed independent shorts and the Portland Underground Film Festival (PUFF). The theater is best known, however, for playing the *Rocky Horror Picture Show* every Saturday night since 1978. Fans of the cult classic line up for the midnight showing in full costume armed with rice, toast, newspapers, and other appropriate props to wield or throw as they scream, sing, and dance along with the movie.

HOLLYWOOD THEATRE
4122 NE Sandy Blvd., 503/281-4215,
www.hollywoodtheatre.org
HOURS: Daily 1-9 P.M.
Map 3

Built as a 1,500-seat vaudeville house in 1926, The Hollywood still stands as one of the most ornate theater fronts in the Northwest, with a beautiful Byzantine, rococo tower. When the theater first opened, admission was only a quarter and the films, which did not have sound yet, were accompanied by an eight-piece orchestra and an organ. The theater is currently split into three venues, each capable of screening films. There is a 468-seat main auditorium, which was the original orchestra level, a 180-seat venue (one-half of the original balcony), and a 190-seat venue (the other half of the original balcony). The theater was purchased in 1997 by the non-profit Film Action Oregon (FAO), which has been on an aggressive campaign to renovate and save this old Portland landmark. The Hollywood has also returned to its vaudeville roots to welcome live theatrical performances, concerts, and lectures.

KENNEDY SCHOOL
5736 NE 33rd Ave., 503/249-3983,
www.mcmenamins.com
HOURS: Mon.-Fri. 5 P.M.-close, Sat.-Sun. 11 A.M.-close
Map 3

When this elementary school was built in 1915, it was as rural as it got. In fact, most residents who lived beyond this point lived without electricity, running water, or telephones. After closing in 1975 due to low enrollment, the building served as a community center, but was then threatened with demolition. With the help of the community and the Portland Development Commission, the building was successfully spared, and the McMenamin brothers began putting their signature style on the space in 1997. Gone are the boring assemblies about not being a bully; instead, the school's auditorium now lets you grab a slice and watch great movies from the comfort of some pretty cushy couches. Hey, you might

still get an education, but at least you can have a beer while you do it.

THE LAURELHURST
2735 E. Burnside St., 503/232-5511,
www.laurelhursttheater.com
HOURS: Mon.-Fri. 4 P.M.-close, Sat.-Sun. 1 P.M.-close
Map 3

The owners of the beautiful art deco Laurelhurst Theater, Prescott Allen and Woody Wheeler, had been regulars of the Bagdad Theater on Hawthorne when Allen discovered a run-down old theater that needed new life. The space was built as a single-screen venue in 1923 and was equipped with an orchestra pit and grand organ. In the 1950s, Laurelhurst was adorned with a small retail space and a soda fountain—which is now an additional screening room. The venue was renovated in 2001, and now offers four screens that show modern, independent, and classic films for about $3 per ticket. Concessions, most of which are provided by local businesses, include pizza, microbrews, and wine. Certainly, the Laurelhurst has come a long way since its inception; despite its classic Hollywood look, this surprisingly environmental gem now runs on wind power.

THE MISSION THEATER
1624 NW Glisan St., 503/223-4527,
www.mcmenamins.com
HOURS: Mon.-Fri. 5 P.M.-close, Sat.-Sun. 2 P.M.-close
Map 2

Probably the most varied past of the McMenamin brothers' kingdom—which they call their empire, seriously—belongs to the Mission Theater. Built in 1912, the site once housed the Portland Swedish Mission Covenant congregation. Church services on Sundays often brought in 500–700 people to gather, communicate, and socialize. As a community, the congregants were very focused on mission work, a task that took them all over the world. By 1954, however, the community had outgrown the space, largely due to the fact that the neighborhood had become a lot more commercial. When the gentle Swedes moved out, dockworkers moved in and the venue became a hiring hall

ARTS AND LEISURE

for longshoremen. The McMenamins opened the Mission Theater and Pub in 1987, the first of what would become a long list of pub-based theaters. The success of the cheap movie concept was staggering and the Mission still stands as a community-based gathering place, also hosting concerts and television showings in addition to second-run movies.

Festivals and Events

Portlanders love a good festival, particularly if it celebrates beer, bikes, music, and that favorite local pastime—devouring delicious treats. Late spring and early summer is festival season, when throughout the city, you can hear the twang of a band warming up, feel the hum of the parade passing by, and smell the waffle cones toasting. In fact, if you listen carefully, you'll hear the faint, "shhhhhh" of a new keg being tapped.

But we're not exactly sitting on our thumbs through the winter waiting for the sun. With venues like the Oregon Convention Center, the Expo Center, and the Rose Quarter, Portland has plenty of places to celebrate the bounties of the region, no matter what time of year it is.

SPRING
CINCO DE MAYO FESTIVAL
Waterfront Park, www.cincodemayo.org
The largest Cinco de Mayo festival in North America heats up in the first days of May with all the colors, cuisine, arts, music, and folklore of Mexico—more specifically, Guadalajara, Portland's sister city. The four-day fiesta usually kicks off bright and early with a ribbon-cutting ceremony followed by a naturalization ceremony. After that, it's time to enjoy all manner of music, food, and entertainment, and a magnificent fireworks display come nightfall. There's an interactive children's area and Guadalajara artisans and jewelers who demonstrate their crafts on-site and sell their wares.

FAUX FILM FESTIVAL
4122 NE Sandy Blvd., www.fauxfilm.com
It's all about spoofs and satire at the annual Faux Film Festival, where feature films and shorts from the United States, Canada, Russia, Belgium, Australia, Germany, Scotland, and the United Kingdom offer a much-needed humorous break from the daily grind. So what can you expect to see at the Hollywood Theatre during the festival? Counterfeit commercials, phony movie trailers, mockumentaries, and all manner of fake, phony, and funny stuff. The festival is basically a great big thumb in the eye of highbrow festivals like Sundance. It lasts three nights (admission is $7 per night) and culminates with an award show—where they hand out a bizarre mish-mash of cast-off bowling, little league, and karate trophies.

PORTLAND INDIE WINE FESTIVAL
2621 NW 30th Ave., 503/224-5778,
www.indiewinefestival.com
Here's your chance to support craft winemaking. The Portland Indie Wine Festival is a delicious chance to see, sip, and savor wines from 40 of Oregon's top artisan wineries. The festival is a good opportunity to meet the next generation of winemakers from promising wine cellars all over the region. You will not find most of these wines on the grocery store shelves, as most are very limited in production and not widely available. The festival is your chance to buy the ones you like from the winemaker himself and sample small plates from a dozen or so of Oregon's top chefs.

RED DRESS PARTY
Various venues, www.reddresspdx.com
What started out as a party in the basement of a North Portland home has blossomed into one of the most anticipated fundraising events to grace our city. Over the years, the Red Dress Party has raised more than $87,000 for charities that work with youth, adults, and seniors living with HIV and AIDS. The event seeks to

entertain party-goers with hosted food, beverages, red cocktails, fire spinners, and music. There's just one rule: Everyone, yes, *everyone* must wear a red dress to get in.

SPRING BEER & WINE FEST

Oregon Convention Center, 777 NE Martin Luther King Jr. Blvd., www.springbeerfest.com

More than 80 different beers and 25 wineries can be found at the Spring Beer & Wine Fest, which annually turns the Oregon Convention Center into a mecca for brew connoisseurs and vino aficionados alike. A wide assortment of breweries—like Full Sail, Bridgeport, and Deschutes—serve up frosty mugs of their most popular hoppy concoctions, while wineries the likes of David Hill, Hip Chicks Do Wine, and Arcane Cellars will gladly pop a cork of their latest vintage for your imbibing pleasure. Of course, there's a variety of food to sample as well, from barbeque to seafood—not to mention artisan cheeses, specialty chocolates, and chef's demonstrations. Admission is free noon–2 P.M., and $5 thereafter. You must also purchase souvenir beer or wine glasses and tokens to fill your glass with the beverage of your choice.

SUMMER

ART IN THE PEARL

Northwest Park Blocks, between W. Burnside and NW Glisan at NW 8th Ave., www.artinthepearl.com

Rounding out a Portland summer filled with as much inspiration and entertainment as can be packed into the warm months, Art in the Pearl is a lovely gathering of artists, entertainers, and art lovers in the northwest Park Blocks. Here, you can dance to world music, sample delicacies from around the globe, and check out the jury-selected work of 130 artists from across the United States and Canada. You can also work on building your art collection, as there are usually well over 100 artists showing and selling works ranging from jewelry to furniture at very reasonable prices.

THE BITE OF OREGON

Waterfront Park, www.biteoforegon.com

In August, food lovers drop their triple cream brie and put away their reduction sauce to come out for Bite of Oregon, a festival that celebrates the bounty of fantastic restaurants, breweries, and wineries in the Northwest. Lots of great entertainment, celebrity chefs, and the annual Iron Chef Oregon competition make it worth the price of admission, but the real draw here is the plethora of food, wine, and beer. Plus, the event benefits the Special Olympics, so you're eating that deep-fried asparagus for a reason, right?

BRIDGE PEDAL

Citywide, www.providence.org/bridgepedal

Even in bike-friendly Portland, it can be a pretty harrowing experience to navigate some city streets. Oh, the narrow bike paths, car doors swinging open, and missed signals! And that's just in the streets—never mind making your way across some of our many bridges. For one day in August, cyclists of all walks and all ages get a rare chance to ride freely over many of the bridges than span the Willamette River—including such forbidden territory as the Fremont and Marquam Bridges (which are basically freeways). It's a popular event and the city works hard to keep traffic moving in a reasonable fashion by shutting down only portions of the bridges to vehicles and only for short durations. A portion of the proceeds from the event goes to the Bicycle Transportation Alliance and to the Providence Hospital Heart and Vascular Institute.

GORGE GAMES

Columbia River Gorge, www.gorgegames.net

We're all about the adventure sports around these parts—and it's no wonder, considering our landscape. The Gorge, in particular, is ripe for adventure. If you like to tear it up (or watch someone else do it), then you'll love the Gorge Games. After a three-year break, the festival—which largely focuses on windsurfing, sailing, and kayaking—returned in 2008 with a new vision, which included all-green practices and electricity and new events like skateboarding. In fact, the new games features world-class athletes competing in over 30 different events, as well as classes, live music, vendors, food, a beer garden, and lots of kid-friendly fun. The event is also a perfect opportunity to take in the beauty of the Gorge and even get cozy with the landscape—especially with the addition of a two-acre campground right on the Columbia River.

LPGA SAFEWAY CLASSIC TOURNAMENT
www.safewayclassic.com

If you would rather watch someone else knock the ball around than chase your own through the trees, the LPGA Safeway Classic might just do it. Every August, 144 of the ladies of the LPGA compete for a $1.7 million purse in the oldest continuous event on the LPGA tour. The event is also an annual fundraiser for children's charities like the Boys and Girls Club, Easter Seals, and Trillium Family Services. In 2009, the tournament moved from Columbia Edgewater Country Club to Pumpkin Ridge Golf Club in Hillsboro, which hosted the event on the public Ghost Creek course and on the members-only Witch Hollow.

◖ OREGON BREWERS FESTIVAL
Waterfront Park, www.oregonbrewfest.com

If there is anything we truly love in Portland, it's beer. It's no wonder, then, that we would host an entire festival in its honor. The annual Oregon Brewers Festival is regarded by many as one of the finest craft beer festivals you can find. In years past, more than 60,000 people have attended the event—and the numbers climb each year for beer lovers of all walks seeking a sampling of local favorites, new brews, and micros from all over the nation. Food is provided by a number of local restaurants, and there's always live entertainment. Admission is usually free—unless, of course, you want to drink. A souvenir mug (required for tasting) will cost you $5 and you can buy as many $1 tokens as you'd like (but it will take about four to fill a mug.)

PEDALPALOOZA BIKE FESTIVAL
Citywide, www.shift2bikes.org

Each year, Pedalpalooza features an unbelievable line-up of events ranging from family-friendly events (like a tricycle race or the Kidical Mass) to the adventuresome (like Unicycle Polo). There are even a number of bike crawls that will take you on tours of pubs, vegan restaurants, or spoken-word joints. Or, if you really want to see a spectacle, check out Cirque du Cycling—part circus, part parade—which lights up Mississippi Avenue. Cirque du Cycling events in the past have included parades, races, biker performers, and even occasional impromptu naked rides.

PORTLAND PRIDE FESTIVAL
Waterfront Park, www.pridenw.org

If you really want to see a party, head down to the waterfront in June and check out the Portland Pride Festival. The event is intended to encourage and celebrate the positive diversity of the lesbian, gay, bisexual, trans, and queer communities, and allow an opportunity to gather together and celebrate with music, entertainment, food, demonstrations, and exhibits in Tom McCall Waterfront Park. The whole shebang lasts only one weekend and builds up to a fantastic and colorful parade through the streets of downtown on the last day of the event. If you miss that, however, there are a number of other fun events around the city during the festival and in the weeks before and after it. The Portland Drag Race, for instance, brings new meaning to the phrase "running in heels"; as the name implies, participants are encouraged to dress in drag or at the very least, wear something outrageous. There is also a pet parade, chock-full of rainbow-colored pooches. With mixers and parties and parades galore, the whole celebration is more fun than a barrel of sequins and a bottle of spray glue.

◖ PORTLAND ROSE FESTIVAL
Waterfront Park, www.rosefestival.org

The big daddy event for Portland is the Rose Festival, held every year from the end of May through the first two weeks of June to celebrate the riches of the Pacific Northwest heritage and environment. It's all about bringing the city together, but also about extending a hand to communities across the world. The spectacular

Grand Floral Parade, which is the centerpiece of the festival, is the second-largest floral parade in the nation and the biggest spectator event in the state of Oregon. But the festival has number of events that are worth checking out bedsides that. Kids are released from school early to march through the Hollywood District in the Junior Parade. After the sun goes down, the Starlight Parade, which winds through the streets of downtown, is always fun, and the party is always raging at Tom McCall Waterfront Park, with music, vaudeville acts, exhibits, acres of food, and Funtastic rides.

SCOTTISH HIGHLAND GAMES

Mount Hood Community College, 26000 SE Stark, www.phga.org

It's not everyday that you get to see bagpipes, kilts, and Scottish heavy games all in the same place—at least not on this side of the world. The Highland Games is hosted each year on the third Saturday in July by Mount Hood Community College, and somehow, it manages to bring the Scotsman out in everyone. But it's a lot of fun to don a kilt and slip into a series of bad Mike Meyer impressions as you take in world-class Scottish athletic championships, highland dance competitions, traditional Scottish music, the Kilted Mile Race, genealogy workshops, children's activities, traditional wares, and, of course, beer and bangers.

WATERFRONT BLUES FESTIVAL

Waterfront Park, www.waterfrontbluesfest.com

It's one of the largest blues festivals in the nation (second only to Chicago), attracting more than 120,000 blues lovers from all over the world. Fans show up to catch just a few of the 150 performances that happen on the festival's four stages. Proceeds from the festival benefit the Oregon Food Bank, a non-profit organization that provides food to low-income people in Oregon and southwest Washington. With such fantastic performances from such legends as Etta James, Marcia Ball, Keb' Mo, and Isaac Hayes, the festival is able to raise

© VALERIE K. DAVIS

ARTS AND LEISURE

The Waterfront Blues Festival is the largest blues festival on the West Coast and the second largest blues festival in the nation, with more than 150 performances on four stages.

$500,000 and more than 80,000 pounds of food (by collecting donations of money and non-perishable foods at the gate). If the crowds are a bit much for you, consider taking one of the Blues Cruises on the *Portland Spirit,* which sails down the Willamette to Oregon City. On board, you'll be treated to live music and a no-host hors d'oeuvres buffet and full bar.

FALL

H. P. LOVECRAFT FILM FESTIVAL
Hollywood Theater, 4122 NE Sandy Blvd., 281-4215, www.hplfilmfestival.com

Twentieth-century American author Howard Phillips (H. P.) Lovecraft has a name synonymous with blood-curdling screams, night terrors, and noisome monsters like "the green, sticky spawn of the stars." His stories dominated the literary scene with a new genre labeled "weird fiction," which encompassed horror, myth, and science fiction. In 1995, producer, author, and avid fan Andrew Migliore founded the H. P. Lovecraft Film Festival so that professional and amateur filmmakers could transport to the screen what Lovecraft had so brilliantly put on page. There's no better way to kick off the month of October than attending this festival, where goose bumps are a guarantee and horror is a form of art. The festival takes place at the historic Hollywood Theatre, lending a creep factor that is likely to make you believe that Cthulhu himself could crawl out of the balcony.

MUSIC FEST NORTHWEST
Citywide, www.musicfestnw.com

What started as North by Northwest—a smaller, grungier version of Austin's annual South by Southwest Festival—has blossomed into a pretty exciting event. These days, the festival, now called MusicFest Northwest (MFNW), is Portland's multi-day extravaganza of rock music, and it brings in some pretty stellar acts from all over the nation. As interest begins to build around Portland as a music town, more and more big acts are adding their names to the roster, which gives fans a great opportunity to see them play in a more

intimate setting. The festival also manages to give a platform to the lesser known, hard-working local musicians that keep Portland's music community feeling so alive. During the festival, acts perform on stages all across the city (like the Doug Fir, the Crystal Ballroom, Mississippi Studios, and Rotture), giving attendees a glimpse of some of the best venues in town.

NORTHWEST FILM AND VIDEO FESTIVAL
1219 SW Park Ave., www.nwfilm.org

With so many eyes and cameras on the Northwest these days, it is not surprising that we need our own film festival just to behold a portion of it. For more than 30 years, the Northwest Film and Video Festival has presented feature length, short, and documentary films that showcasing Northwest talent. Typically, there are about 50 films that are shown over the course of a week, all of them made by artists from Oregon, Washington, British Columbia, Montana, or Idaho. The festival is a showcase of what's on the minds of Northwest filmmakers, and an opportunity to seek inspiration and connections. The Northwest Film Center, which hosts the festival and is part of the Portland Art Museum, was established as a resource for media arts in the region. It offers a variety of film and video exhibitions in addition to education and information programs throughout the year and during the festival.

PICA'S T:BA FESTIVAL
Citywide, www.pica.org/tba

Stimulate your senses all over the city at the Time-Based Art Festival (T:BA), an exploration of every form of contemporary art—including dance, music, new media, and visual. Unique to Portland, T:BA provides a forum for contemporary as well as emerging artists from Portland and from around the world. With well over 100 workshops, installations, lectures, and performances, this 10-day festival is packed with opportunities to experience art as you have never seen it before. Since the festival happens all over the city, you can buy a pass that will allow you access to more than you can possibly see—or you can buy tickets to individual performances and events, available on the day of the show at the venues themselves.

PORTLAND FASHION WEEK

www.portlandfashionweek.net

Portland has garnered quite a name for maintaining a high standard of eco-friendliness, and that attitude is creating a buzz in the fashion industry these days, too. In October, the annual Portland Fashion Week rolls out the (bamboo) runway. Eco-designers from across the world unveil their upcoming spring and summer collections. For several years, Portland Fashion Week (PFW) has been illuminating the Northwest style scene with sustainable venues, organic food and drink, eco-friendly fabrics, and now, the world is paying attention—and not just to chuckle about a show that features only fleece and hiking boots. Suddenly, with PFW veteran Leanne Marshall riding out her *Project Runway* win, and a world-class showcase of emerging talent each year, it's not so funny anymore. Attendees can choose from a variety of tickets ranging from a one-night soiree to a whole-week affair and from VIP seating to general admission.

PORTLAND LESBIAN & GAY FILM FESTIVAL

Cinema 21, 616 NW 21st Ave., www.plgff.org

The Portland Lesbian & Gay Film Festival has been around unofficially since the early 1990s, but officially began in 1997 when the first annual festival was launched. By the third year, things really started to take shape with sold-out screenings, world premieres, Oscar-winning features, and emotionally moving forums. Each year, the festival showcases feature, documentary, and short films from all over the world that are made by, about, or of interest to the lesbian, gay, bi, and trans community. Films are selected based on the quality of storytelling, uniqueness, and overall appeal. The festival now works through a partnership with Film Action Oregon.

PORTLAND PIRATE FESTIVAL

Various venues, www.portlandpiratefestival.com

September 19 is International Talk Like a Pirate Day, which incidentally, was started by a couple of guys in Oregon. It seemed only natural that Portland should have a festival to celebrate this and all things Yar-worthy. What no one expected was that even in its first year (2005), thousands of festival-goers would show up costumed, enthusiastic, and raring for some good swashbuckling fun. Often held at St. John's Cathedral Park, there's fun aplenty for the whole family with cannon shows, sword fights, gallons of grub and grog to go around, and musical performances by local scallywags such as B.O.O.M. (Brothers of Oceanic Mercenaries), Captain Bogg & Salty, and Brothers of the Baladi. Little ones can head over to Scupper Monkey Island, where there are inflatable rides, puppet shows, crafts, games, and a climbing wall. If you are not properly outfitted, you can check out the Marauders Market and Tortuga Market for the latest in pirate fashion.

WINTER

ANNUAL PORTLAND GOLF SHOW

Oregon Convention Center, 777 NE Martin Luther King Jr. Blvd., www.portlandgolfshow.com

Kicking off the annual Pacific Northwest golf season, the Portland Golf Show gives enthusiasts a chance to get their swing into shape. You can try out the latest technology in clubs in the Green Demo Room, take the 50-foot putting challenge, get some free lessons from some of the area's top instructors, and shop the 5,000-square-foot clearance center, where you can replace all those balls you lost in a lake for a fraction of what you paid the first time. There's even a kiddie area where pint-sized golfers will receive a custom-made club and a mini lesson for free.

CHRISTMAS SHIP PARADE

Citywide, www.christmasships.org

The Christmas Ship Parade started back in 1954 when one guy with a sailboat decked the bow with lights and sailed the Willamette. Each year since then, the fleet has grown

ARTS AND LEISURE

and now it averages 55–60 boats between the Columbia and Willamette River fleets. The displays are elaborate and brightly lit, and can be seen from bank to bank on each river, which is a real treat for those dining, staying, or strolling riverside. Book well in advance if you want to witness this event from the warmth of a restaurant or hotel room. The skippers pay for their own fuel, decorations, and other expenses, so they welcome donations to keep the tradition going. The website provides a means for donations, plus gives an overview of hotels, restaurants, and viewing spots that offer a good vantage point.

FERTILE GROUND FESTIVAL

Citywide, www.fertilegroundpdx.org

Alright, so January in Portland isn't exactly a "showcase" month. Tourism is down, the skies are grey, and the weather is, at best, unpredictable. It's tempting to sulk about the house, but frankly, a whole month indoors is just not natural for most Portlanders. Thank goodness this city is full of creative folks who are not willing to give up on January. Thanks to them, the city suddenly has a reason get out of its collective pajamas and experience something truly original. In 2008, Portland launched its first citywide performing arts festival devoted entirely to new works. More than two years in the making, this ambitious 10-day event unites more than a dozen performing arts groups to present a series of world premiere productions. Portland has always been a "fertile ground" for playwrights and premiere performances, so it's no surprise that so many companies are consistently able to develop their seasons around the idea of producing something new and groundbreaking during this event.

FESTIVAL OF LIGHTS AT THE GROTTO

8840 NE Skidmore St., 503/254-7371,
www.thegrotto.org

For more than 20 years now, the Grotto, a 62-acre Catholic shrine and botanical garden, has hosted the Festival of Lights, which is open nightly from around Thanksgiving through December 30 (except for Christmas Day). The spectacle features 150 musical performances, more than 500,000 lights, petting zoos, puppet shows, carolers, family entertainment, and more. Local choirs perform at the Chapel of Mary, a remarkable cathedral constructed of rock quarried from a cliff; it's an awe-inspiring display of polished marble, magnificent statues, and beautiful murals, and the acoustics are said to rival some of Europe's finest cathedrals. During the festival, the Grotto is open nightly 5–9:30 P.M. Parking is free and admission runs $7.50 for adults and $3 for children ages 3–12.

HOLIDAY ALE FESTIVAL

Pioneer Courthouse Square, www.holidayale.com

Who says you can't have a beer festival in December? The Annual Holiday Ale Festival features some of the season's best craft beers (with names like Auld Nutcracker, Lumpa Coal, Ebenezer, and Sled Crasher). Held at Pioneer Courthouse Square, the event manages to get pretty heated, despite the chilly temperatures. A large, clear tent keeps patrons dry, but allows views of the city. Beer lovers sample robust brews, listen to seasonal music, and warm themselves by the gas heaters that surround the city's enormous holiday tree. Don't miss the third annual Brewers Brunch (tickets can be purchased on the website), where breakfast and local and imported beers not otherwise available at the festival are served.

INTERNATIONAL FILM FESTIVAL

1219 SW Park, www.nwfilm.org

Portland International Film Festival (PIFF) annually draws an audience of over 35,000, making it the biggest film event in Oregon. The festival premieres over 100 international shorts and feature films to film-loving audiences each February and hosts a number of visiting artists and talkback sessions throughout the one-week event. This is often a great place to catch foreign films that are creating an Oscar buzz, or check out Short Cuts, a program of experimental films presented by Cinema Project and the Northwest Film Center. In addition to films, there are also a number of parties and special events surrounding the festival, a full schedule of which can be found on the website.

OREGON SEAFOOD AND WINE FESTIVAL

Oregon Convention Center, 777 NE Martin Luther King Blvd, www.eventsnw.net/enw/seafoodandwine

While you are busy savoring all the bounties that the Northwest has to offer, you'll want to save some room for when the Oregon Seafood & Wine Festival comes to town. Stop in at the Oregon Convention Center to taste some of the state's most savory seafood and most veritable vinos, all while enjoying some local live music. Show up early and be one of the first 500 people through the door and you'll receive a commemorative wine glass to sip from all year long. Food prices start at $1 and wine samplings at $0.50.

PROVIDENCE FESTIVAL OF TREES

Oregon Convention Center, 777 NE Martin Luther King Blvd., www.providence.org/festivaloftrees

The Providence Festival of Trees is your opportunity to stroll through nearly 50 decorated trees, as well as wreaths and holiday vignettes created by the city's top designers, businesses, and volunteers. The Festival lights up the season in style and raises funds to support critically needed health care services at Providence Hospital. The public show features children's activities, including the adorable Teddy Bear Hospital and Santa's Workshop, live entertainment, model trains, gingerbread houses, and a holiday bookshop. Tickets can be purchased at the door, and there are often coupons on the festival website that will save you money at the gate.

REEL MUSIC FESTIVAL

1219 SW Park, www.nwfilm.org

Reel Music, the Northwest Film Center's celebration of music on film, is a cinematic love letter to music's most intriguing artists (both legendary and unknown). Not limited to any particular genre, the festival highlights jazz, rock, reggae, bluegrass, bossa nova, and indie rock. Featuring everything from vintage performance clips to new documentary and dramatic films, to cutting-edge music videos and animation, it's an interesting way to explore the ways sound and images play off each other to affect the human experience.

ZOOLIGHTS FESTIVAL

4001 SW Canyon Rd., 503/226-1561, www.oregonzoo.org

Every evening (except Christmas Eve and Christmas Day) from November 28 until December 28, the Oregon Zoo transforms to a holiday fairyland for its annual Zoolights Festival. It's a spectacular event for the entire family. Decorated with nearly a million lights, this winter wonderland is a more whimsical display than your traditional holiday light show, with swinging monkeys instead of snowmen, slithering snakes instead of nodding reindeer. Sip some cocoa from the Zoo Café or ride the special Christmas train, brightly decorated and aglow with lights, as it winds through the zoo.

Recreation

Around here, we don't always wait for the sun to start shining in order to enjoy a bit of recreation outdoors. We are lucky enough in Portland to have access to more than 290 municipal parks that are perfect spots for walking, jogging, cycling, or simply enjoying a little rest and relaxation. If you are more the active sort, you would be hard pressed to find a city more suited for cycling or hiking than Portland. Portlanders are all about living the two-wheeled or two-legged lifestyle and the sheer number of bike lanes, trails, and pedestrian bridges in town is a testament to that fact.

FUN FOR KIDS

◖ OREGON MUSEUM OF SCIENCE AND INDUSTRY

1945 SE Water Ave., 503/797-4000, www.omsi.edu
HOURS: Tues.-Sun. 9:30 A.M.-5:30 P.M., closed Mon.
COST: $11 adult, $9 child and senior, free for child under 3
Map 4

Oregon Museum of Sciences and Industry (OMSI) is considered one of the top science centers in the world. It offers a variety of exhibits and activities that are guaranteed to entertain and engage both children and adults. Take a tour of the U.S. *Blueback,* the U.S. Navy's last non-nuclear, fast-attack submarine, which appeared in the movie *The Hunt for Red October* (claustrophobics, beware). Watch a film on the five-story domed IMAX projection screen. Watch a laser light show in the Kendall Planetarium, or explore your way through some of the most exciting exhibits that are touring the world today. Admission to the Omnimax theater, planetarium, submarine, and the museum's multi-sensory motion simulator are not included in admission, and parking will cost you $2.

OREGON ZOO

4001 SW Canyon Rd., 503/226-1561, www.oregonzoo.org
HOURS: Spring daily 9 A.M.-6 P.M., summer daily 8 A.M.-7 P.M., fall and winter daily 9 A.M.-4 P.M.
COST: $10.50 adult, $9 senior, $7.50 for ages 3-11, free for child under 2
Map 7

The Oregon Zoo has a lot of great animal exhibits, like the Red Ape Reserve, where you will find orangutans and gibbons, and the African Savannah, where you will see giraffes, zebras, hippos, and rhinos. The polar bears, penguins, sea lions, otters, and the African Rainforest are always big winners, with underwater viewing tanks, the later of which contains slender-snouted crocodiles. Over at the Asian elephant exhibit, you can learn about Packy the pachyderm and find out why she is Portland's little sweetheart; or visit the zoo's exciting exhibit that feature predators of the Serengeti like lions, cheetahs, African wild dogs, African rock pythons, and caracals.

PORTLAND CHILDREN'S MUSEUM

4015 SW Canyon Rd., 503/223-6500, www.portlandcm.org
HOURS: Daily 9 A.M.-5 P.M.
COST: $8 adult and child, $7 senior
Map 7

This is a fun museum, especially if you are traveling with very small children. Kids over eight might find it a bit boring, but then again, even adults have been amused by the Water Works or the Building Bridgetown exhibit. In Bridgetown, kids can panel a wall, connect plumbing fixtures, take measurements, work the "button and latch" board, and build with blocks on the custom-designed building table. It's a lot of fun, especially if you have a block lover in tow. Water Works features a 12-foot-high waterfall, a hand-cranked "conveyor belt" that carries water in little recycled objects, a twirling collection of kitchen mops, and a number of instruments that kids can play by spraying the water cannon. They provide waterproof smocks for this exhibit, which you will most definitely want.

PARKS AND GARDENS

INTERNATIONAL ROSE TEST GARDEN

400 SW Kingston Ave.
HOURS: Daily 7:30 A.M.-9 P.M.
COST: Free
Map 7

This is where it all started. The City of Roses, the Rose Festival, the Royal Rosarians; it's all thanks to the Portland Rose Society, founded in 1889 as a means to educate budding gardeners and encourage them to plant roses. In the midst of World War I, when rose enthusiasts began to fear the negative effects that bombing might have on the various seemingly irreplaceable species of roses that grew so well in Portland, they established a garden to grown and cultivate them. Soon rose plantings were arriving from all over the world to be raised in the rich Northwest soil. Today, there are over 6,800 rose bushes representing 557 varieties.

LEACH BOTANICAL GARDENS

6704 SE 122nd Ave., 503/823-9503,
www.leachgarden.org

COST: Free

Map 7

If you head deep into Southeast Portland, you'll discover hidden treasure at the Leach Botanical Gardens. Named for Lilla Leach—who is famous for botanical research, her exploration of the Siskiyou and Klamath mountains, and discovering five plant species new to science—and her husband, this combination of forest and garden offers a woody feel. The original Leach residence is still on the property and serves as one of several entries to the garden's nine acres of walkable land. This botanical garden—or living museum—sits next to Johnson Creek and offers 2,300 planted species, a rock garden, physics garden, fern collection, wildflowers, and even a composting demonstration center.

WASHINGTON PARK

400 SW Kingston Ave.

COST: Free

Map 7

Washington Park is a sprawling, public park that is home to the Oregon Zoo, the World Forestry Center, Hoyt Arboretum, the Children's Museum, an outdoor amphitheatre, an archery range, tennis courts, and 40 acres of forest, trails, playgrounds, and gardens. Washington Park is also home to the oldest continuously operated public test garden, where more than 550 varieties of roses are cultivated and judged every year at the Portland Rose Festival. Take the MAX out to Washington Park and you will see the deepest transit station in North America, and Portland's only underground stop. Despite being 260 feet below ground, the elevators can carry 35 people up to street level in about 20 seconds.

WATERFRONT PARK

SW Naito Pkwy. between SW Harrison St.
and NW Glisan St.

HOURS: Daily 5 A.M.-midnight

COST: Free

Map 1

On the west bank of the Willamette River, stretching the length of most of downtown, you will find Tom McCall Waterfront Park, named for Oregon Governor Tom McCall. After a sea wall was installed in 1920 to protect the downtown area from rising winter waters, city planners began to reexamine ways to provide access to the riverbanks and green spaces. Rather than allow development to consume the area, they constructed walkways and open park spaces along the river, which gained particular popularity in the mid-1980s, when McCall was governor.

Between NW Davis and SW Naito Parkway, you'll find the Japanese American Historical Plaza, which was built to honor the citizens who were deported to internment camps during World War II. At the intersection where Salmon Street meets the park, the Salmon Street Springs is a popular fountain for children (of all ages) to cool off in the summer heat. The three cycles of the fountain are called misters, bollards, and wedding cake, and at full capacity, the fountain recycles 4,924 gallons of water per minute, through as many as 137 jets at once.

BIKE TRAILS

MOUNT TABOR

SE 60th and Salmon St.

HOURS: Daily 5 A.M.-midnight

COST: Free

Map 4

Mount Tabor Park is named for the eponymous dormant volcanic cinder cone that it surrounds. It wasn't until 1912, many years after the neighborhood and the park had been established at its base, was it discovered that the mountain was actually a volcano (extinct for 3,000 years). The beautiful 195-acre park was designed by the Olmsted Brothers, and includes basketball courts, picnic areas, play areas, dog off-leash areas, horseshoe pits, a stage, tennis courts, and volleyball courts. It's a popular spot for many reasons, but the numerous paved and unpaved trails make it a great ride for cyclists and dirt bikers alike.

ARTS AND LEISURE

COURTESY OF TRAVEL PORTLAND

Mount Tabor is actually an extinct volcano that has become one of the most popular places in southeast Portland to hit the trail on your bike.

SPRINGWATER CORRIDOR

SE Reedway and SE 124th Ave.

COST: Free

Map 7

Springwater Corridor is a small segment of a 40-mile loop that begins in Southeast Portland and includes Oaks Bottom Wildlife Refuge, Tideman Johnson Nature Park, and Powell Butte Nature Park. The Springwater Trail follows a former railroad route of the same name that ceased service in 1989. Most of the trail is paved and is bordered by fields and trees; though the trail does span some busy streets, most are equipped with crossing lights. In the summer of 2006, construction of three new bridges allowed cyclists access from the trail to the Eastbank Esplanade. The trail can get crowded on the weekends, particularly as you near the Esplanade, but the less populous areas are abundant in flora and fauna.

WATERFRONT BIKE LOOP

Begin on either the east or west bank of the river

COST: Free

Map 7

This 12-mile loop on both sides of the Willamette River is a great way to see the city without having to dodge through a bunch of cars. Access on the west side can be found in Tom McCall Waterfront Park, along the seawall and bollards. On the east side, it's best to enter along the Eastbank Esplanade. If you would like to do a shorter route and stick with the spectacular views of downtown, you can loop between the Hawthorne Bridge and the Steel Bridge. If you want to do the full route, which will take you as far south as the Sellwood Bridge, download a map in the "Getting Around" section of www.downtownportland. org by clicking on "PDOT Bike Maps." The map will show you the exact route, telling you about places where you should be cautious of traffic, children, and narrow passages.

BIKE RENTALS AND TOURS
CITYBIKES
734 SE Ankeny St., 503/239-6951, www.citybikes.coop
HOURS: Mon.-Fri. 11 A.M.-7 P.M., Sat.-Sun. 11 A.M.-5 P.M.
Map 4

Citybikes is a worker-owned shop that specializes in repairs, so their rental bikes are always in tip-top condition. They have a handful of hybrid bicycles available (call ahead) for rent, which are great for city riding and light off-road use. Each rental comes with locks, helmets, and maps, and goes for about $35 a day, and $10 for each additional day. Citybikes also has a number of new and used bicycles for sale. They are particularly known for refurbishing bikes into some pretty amazing customized rides.

PEDAL BIKE TOURS
2249 N. Williams Ave., 503/916-9704,
www.pedalbiketours.com
HOURS: Mon.-Thurs. 11 A.M.-7 P.M., Fri. 11 A.M.-6 P.M.,
Sat.-Sun. 11 A.M.-5 P.M.
COST: $49-89 per person
Map 6

Pedal Bike Tours is a bike rental place and tour guide company rolled into one. They have a variety of tours that range from simple rides around the city to a nine-mile ride through the Columbia River Gorge. Tours are themed and include the bike rental, helmet, and all the other equipment you might need on your trip. Take a trip through historic areas of downtown and old town, take an eco tour, or do the Coffee Crawl, where you will learn about the roasting process at one coffee shop, take a tour of one of Portland's most famous roasting facility, and ride over to Stumptown Coffee's cupping room, where you will learn how to select the best beans using the methods of a professional coffee buyer.

WATERFRONT BICYCLE
10 SW Ash St., 503/227-1719, www.waterfrontbikes.net
HOURS: Daily 10 A.M.-6 P.M.
Map 1

If you're looking to rent a cruiser for a little downtown exploration, Waterfront Bicycle has pretty top-notch equipment and service.

They have hybrid bikes, cruisers, and road bikes, all of which come with a helmet, bike bag, map, and lock. Road bike rentals also come with blow-out bags and a pump for fixing any flats that may occur. For kids in tow, they have trailers, trailer bikes, and kid-sized rides, and if there are two of you, you can rent a tandem cruiser, which always looks adorable, by the way.

HIKING
AUDUBON TRAILS
5151 NW Cornell Rd., www.audubonportland.org
HOURS: Daily dawn-dusk
COST: Free
Map 7

This 150-acre nature sanctuary, nestled against Forest Park, is only five minutes from downtown, but feels miles away. Chock-full of native flora and fauna, it has over four miles of forested hiking trails. At various times during the year, you can find over 40 species of birds and 60 species of mammals making their home in this sanctuary. You can pick up a trail guide at the Audubon House, which will provide you with a look at all three trails. The Pittock Bird Sanctuary trailhead is most accessible from the parking lot, but try finding the Founders Trailhead first (across the street). It offers a more exercise and lovely forest scenery as well as a view of Oregon's native plants unfettered by the invasive effects of English ivy and other non-native plants.

FOREST PARK
NW 29th Ave and Upshur St. to Newberry Rd.,
www.forestparkconservancy.org
HOURS: Daily dawn-dusk
COST: Free
Map 7

Whether you're looking for you quick hike without leaving the city, or want to lose yourself in midst of the inclines, tall trees, moss, flowers, birds, and quiet, this is your park. There are numerous trails to select, and you can make it as challenging or simple as you like. What is really spectacular is the feeling of escape once you're in the park. As the largest urban park in the world, Forest Park's peaceful surroundings make it hard to imagine that there is a city just outside its perimeter.

If you're feeling ambitious, you can take a 12-mile jog from the Leif Erickson Drive entrance, which is conveniently metered at each quarter-mile with a white pole sign. There are some spectacular views along the way, especially at Mile 3, where you get a great view of the city. Another picturesque trail is the Lower Macleay Trail, which you can find at Macleay Park (near NW Thurman and NW 29th). It's a really pleasant short hike through shady trees and small streams. Stick to the trail and you'll end up at the Audubon Society, which has its own circuit of beautiful trails.

TRYON CREEK STATE NATURAL AREA

11321 SW Terwilliger Blvd., www.tryonfriends.org

Map 7

Tryon Creek State Natural Area is a 645-acre park that lies between Boones Ferry Road and Terwilliger Boulevard in Southwest Portland. The park includes a number of hiking trails and horse trails, and a paved bicycle path that runs along the east edge of the park toward Lake Oswego. The park once belonged to pioneer settler Socrates Hotchkiss Tryon, Sr., who left the land to his family when he died. Years later, the land was sold, and the few decades were spent logging the cedar and fir trees, until the infamous Columbus Day Storm blew down most of the remaining trees. In 1969, Multnomah County bought 45 acres in the hopes of establishing a municipal park. Citizens banded together to help and eventually formed the non-profit Friends of Tryon Creek, which to this day helps raise fund, purchase land, and maintain the beauty and health of the reserve.

These days, the land is beginning to thrive as Douglas firs, Western red cedars, and big leaf maples tower over trilliums and sword ferns. As you stroll, it's not uncommon to see owls, woodpeckers, blue herons, and deer, as well as steelhead trout, coho salmon, salamanders, banana slugs, and beavers.

GOLF
Full Course
EASTMORELAND GOLF COURSE AND DRIVING RANGE

2425 SE Bybee Blvd., 503/775-5910,
www.eastmorelandgolfcourse.com
HOURS: Daily dawn–10 P.M.
COST: $13-37 per 18 holes
Map 5

Eastmoreland's golf course is a fun, short course, with wide fairways that are lined with low-limbed trees. A few of the holes require a bit of strategy, as some have significant doglegs, and one of them plays over a ravine. The driving range has two different levels, with 17 tees on the lower level and 17 tees on the upper level. The driving range is lit and covered and it's pretty cheap too, since it will run you less than $10 for 100 balls.

GLENDOVEER GOLF CLUB

14015 NE Glisan St., 503/253-7507,
www.golfglendoveer.com
HOURS: Daily 6:30 A.M.–9 P.M.
COST: $31-37 per 18 holes
Map 7

Glendoveer has 36 holes and when it's in tip-top shape, it's considered by many to be the best public course in the city. Many regular users prefer the East Course because it's hillier and more heavily treed, which presents interesting challenges depending on how the wind picks up over the hills. The West Course is easier for most because it lacks the tight, tree-lined passages and does not have any water hazards. The weekends can get crowded and require more patience while you wait for your opportunity to hit, so book on a weekday or during off-hours if you can. This course also has a jogging trail (open to the public) that circles the greens. With all the huge, old trees and rolling greens, it makes for a really beautiful walk or run, whether or not you golf.

HERON LAKES GOLF CLUB

3500 N. Victory Blvd., 503/289-1818,
www.heronlakesgolf.com
HOURS: Daily 6 A.M.–8 P.M.
COST: $13-42 per 18 holes
Map 7

Heron Lakes has two 18-hole, par 72 courses: Greenback and the Great Blue. There's water everywhere, so bringing a handful of extra balls is not a bad idea. The Great Blue is a traditional links-style track where you will find the par 4, 466-yard 8th hole, which has a 90-degree dogleg left and a dangerous slough. Greenback is a better course for beginners, but comes with plenty of challenges for more seasoned players as well (like numerous trees that must be avoided). Tee times can be booked online through the website or over the phone.

Miniature Golf
GLOWING GREENS

509 SW Taylor St., 503/222-5554,
www.glowinggreens.com
HOURS: Mon.-Thurs. 3-10 P.M., Fri. 3 P.M.-midnight, Sun. noon-midnight
COST: $7 adult, $6 child and senior
Map 1

Glowing Greens is a putt-putt course like no other. The underground course, in the midst of downtown, is like a radioactive mash-up of *Pirates of the Caribbean* meets *Alice in Wonderland*. Only in Portland would you find an indoor black light 3D miniature golf course (yes, 3D). With animated creatures, psychedelic sea scenes, and stimulating sound effects, this place pretty much turns your average putt-putt on its butt-butt. Opt for the 3D glasses, but don't be afraid to take them off. They're trippy and fun, but not exactly helpful when making a shot—and likely to make you motion sick if you wear them for too long.

MCMENAMINS EDGEFIELD

2126 SW Halsey St., 503/669-8610,
www.mcmenamins.com
HOURS: Vary seasonally
COST: $12-18
Map 7

There are many reasons to head out to Edgefield and meander through the stately property, and the Pub Courses are at the top of the list. There are two separate pitch-n-putt courses, including a 20-hole course (West) and a 12-hole course (East). The holes range about 40–80 yards throughout, and there is one set of mat tees for all hitters. The newest portion, which opened in the spring of 2008, was modeled after Burningbush, the fantasy fairways from Michael Murphy's *Golf in the Kingdom,* and includes 15 holes. It's a good place to practice your short game or simply entertain yourself while gathering with friends and drinking some of the famous McMenamins beer.

SPECTATOR SPORTS
PORTLAND BEAVERS

PGE Park, 1844 SW Morrison St.,
www.portlandbeavers.com
Map 1

The Beavers are a minor league team that represent Portland in the Pacific Coast League (PCL). While the current club has been in Portland only since 2001, the team has a long history with Portland that began back in 1902 when it was announced that a Portland and Seattle team would be joining the California League, thus creating the PCL. When PCL joined the National Association of Professional Baseball Leagues (NAPBL) in 1904, Portland's club became a Class A baseball team, which was briefly renamed the Giants until a newspaper contest called upon them to be renamed the Beavers, after Oregon's state animal. The newly dubbed Beavers won their first PCL pennant in 1906, finishing 19.5 games over the Seattle Rainiers. Fast forward through about a century of name changes and league classifications and the Beavers are back in Portland, playing primarily out of PGE Park. Portland fans are a bit odd in their support of the team, however. For the most part, they are enthusiastic and encouraging, but they are, overall, indifferent about winning or losing. For the fans in PGE Park, the experience of attending the game seems to take precedent over team wins.

ARTS AND LEISURE

PORTLAND TRAIL BLAZERS

Rose Quarter, 1 N. Center Court St.,
www.nba.com/blazers

`Map 3`

Love them or hate them, the Portland Trail Blazers have been an active part of professional basketball since the franchise began in 1970. Through it all, they have been a Portland team. As fans, Portlanders tend to be loyal in their support, but fickle in their devotion. Blazer fever, of course, kicks in with a vengeance whenever the team is successful, but when the team is failing, the same pseudo-fans are rather nonplussed. That was all different in 1976, when Bill Walton lead the team into a 49–33 season and the 1977 Championship. Blazer mania peaked again in the early 1990s shortly after billionaire Paul Allen purchased the team. With team legend and sentimental favorite Clyde "The Glide" Drexler as the team's charismatic forward and a starting lineup that included Buck Williams, Jerome Kersey, and Kevin Duckworth, the team was back in its fans' good graces. What followed a decade later is what most Portlanders refer to as the "Jail Blazers" era. Every day it seemed that another player was facing arrest. Players such as Rod Strickland, Isaiah Rider, Ruben Patterson, and Qyntel Woods seemed to get more press time for their off-court behavior than their game skills. Hot-headed Rasheed Wallace was repeatedly ejected from games. Despite the fact that the team was continuing to win, fans were giving up on the Blazers in droves. These days, the fans are slowly starting to regain trust in their team. With a number of strong (and well-behaved) players like Brandon Roy, Rudy Fernandez, and Greg Odin, the team is starting to remind Portlanders of the days when the song "Rip City Rhapsody" (a team spirit song written for and recorded by the 1990s-era Blazers) was on everybody's brain.

PORTLAND WINTERHAWKS

Memorial Coliseum, 300 N. Winning Way,
503/238-6366

`Map 3`

The Portland Winterhawks are a major junior ice hockey team that plays in the Western Hockey League, which is based in Western Canada and the Pacific Northwest. It is one of three leagues that make up the Canadian Hockey League, the highest level of non-professional hockey in the world. Most home games are played at the Memorial Coliseum, though typically a few games each season are also played in Rose Garden Arena. A great number of Winterhawks have graduated to play in the National Hockey League, including Mike Vernon, Gary Yaremchuk, Clint Malarchuk, Ray Ferraro, Adam Deadmarsh, Steve Knowalchuk, Glen Wesley, Pratt, Byron Dafoe, Brendon Morrow, Jozef Balej, and Richie Regeh. The Winterhawks have won the Memorial Cup twice, once in 1983 and again in 1998. They are known for doing a number of fundraising events, like the Teddy Bear Toss, wherein fans toss brand new bears onto the ice—which will then be donated to children's charities by the team. Portland broke the record in 2006 for most bears donated on one night, and then broke it again in 2007 when they collected 20,372 animals in one night.

ROSE CITY ROLLERS

Portland Expo Center, 2060 N Marine Drive,
www.rosecityrollers.com

`Map 7`

The Rose City Rollers, a collection of roller derby divas, have been tearing up tracks in Portland since 2004. Sure, they have tongue-in-cheek names like Madame Bumpsalot, Layla Smackdown, and Rocket Mean (their co-founder and executive director), and their costumes often involve fishnet stockings under their knee pads, but once the skates go on, they take their sport pretty seriously. At the derby, teams battle it out for points, with five girls from each team on the track at any given time. While one player fights her way through the crowd, earning one point for every member of the opposite team that she passes, her teammates try to ensure that she can stay on her feet, all the while endeavoring to stop the opposition from passing. Basically, it's a whole lot of elbows, shoulders, and knees, flying about at (literally) breakneck speed. Rose City Rollers events often draw as many as 2,500 spectators, and oftentimes sells out the seats of the Expo Center.

GYMS AND HEALTH CLUBS
MARCH WELLNESS
3303 SW Bond Ave., 503/418-6272,
www.marchwellness.com
HOURS: Mon.-Fri. 5 A.M.-10 P.M., Sat.-Sun. 7 A.M.-7 P.M.
Map 7

At the base of the Aerial Tram, you'll find March Wellness, which is housed in the first two floors of the Center for Health and Healing at Oregon Health and Sciences University. The center offers trainers and health coaches, a pool, cooking classes, and yoga. The programs follow a scientific approach designed to improve overall health and healing and promote long-lasting results.

PORTLAND ROCK GYM
21 NE 12th Ave., 503/232-8310,
www.portlandrockgym.com
HOURS: Mon., Wed., Fri. 11 A.M.-11 P.M., Tue. and Thurs. 7 A.M.-11 P.M., Sat. 9 A.M.-7 P.M., Sun. 9 A.M.-6 P.M.
COST: $14 adult, $7 child ($10 on weekends)
Map 3

If you like the idea of climbing but aren't quite keen on the idea of doing it on an actual rock, hit the walls at Portland Rock Gym. It's the largest rock gym in Oregon and includes a 40-foot lead climb, a second gym devoted to bouldering, a weight room, cardio machines, and yoga classes. The gym offers both private and group lessons, and offers both daily and monthly passes in addition to annual memberships. There are a large variety of routes on the walls that range from beginner's level to advanced. During the winter, the gym get can pretty crowded, particularly on the lead wall, but the bouldering area is spacious and oftentimes less crowded.

RIVERPLACE ATHLETIC CLUB
0150 SW Montgomery St., 503/221-1212,
www.therac.com
HOURS: Mon.-Fri. 4:30 A.M.-10 P.M., Sat. 7 A.M.-8 P.M., Sun. 8 A.M.-8 P.M.
Map 1

The RiverPlace Athletic Club, located near the waterfront downtown, is a membership-based club that offers free trial memberships without obligation. They have a variety of cardio equipment, weight machines, and Nautilus machines, as well as a pool, a luxury spa, an award-winning café, classes, and trainers. If you're traveling with little ones, there's an in-house childcare center, which will keep the little tyke busy for up to three hours a day at a pretty reasonable rate. They also offer kids' classes like yoga and swimming for kids that want a bit more structure. RiverPlace is clean and affordable (essentially free), with a friendly staff and enough equipment to go around, providing you avoid the weekend and post-work rush hours.

YOGA SHALA
3808 N. Williams Ave., 503/963-YOGA,
www.yogashalapdx.com
Map 6

Yoga Shala is dedicated to the sacred practice of Hatha yoga in a variety of different styles, so you are sure to find a class here that suits you, regardless of experience or ability. They even have classes for moms-to-be, moms and babies, as well as anatomy and philosophy classes to better understand the practice. If you really want to dive right in, try one of their three- to four-week immersion classes. Or, if it's your calling, they also offer advanced study and teacher training.

WATERSPORTS
CLACKAMAS RIVER
24101 S. Entrance Rd., Clackamas, 503/630-7150,
www.oregonstateparks.org
Map 7

There are a number of rivers and streams that are fun spots to float, swim, or soak when the weather gets warm. Estacada's Milo McIver State Park on the lower Clackamas River is a great spot for inner tubing or raft floating. It's a state park, so it will cost you about $3 per car; flotation devices can be purchased at most outdoor stores, Fred Meyer stores, or tire shops. There are some mild rapids along this river, so wearing a life vest is always a good idea—as is

ARTS AND LEISURE

avoiding any alcohol until after you're out of the water. The Upper Clackamas is a much more advanced rafting experience with Class III and IV rapids, and famous heart-pumping action spots like Carters Bridge, Sling Shot, Hole in the Wall, Toilet Bowl, and Bob's Hole.

ROOSTER ROCK

Corbett exit off I-84, 503/695-2261
COST: $3-5 per day
Map 7

Along a beautiful stretch of the Columbia River is one of the largest swimming areas near Portland. Rooster Rock also has the distinction of being the country's first officially designated clothing-optional beach. The beach is named for a column of basalt that rises from the Oregon side of the Columbia River Gorge in a natural obelisk; given the lax clothing rules and phallic nature of the rock, the park has acquired some rather unsavory nicknames over the years. Nonetheless, the area is beautiful and the area of the beach where nudity is allowed is completely separate and not visible from the clothing-required area of the large park. The non-nude area also has two disc golf courses, picnic shelters and tables, and a boat dock. The park is currently managed by Oregon Parks and Recreation, and requires a day-use fee for entry.

SMITH AND BYBEE LAKES

5300 N Marine Dr., 503/797-1850
COST: free
Map 7

The Smith & Bybee Wetlands Natural Area, consisting of around 2,000 acres of protected wetlands, is the largest of its kind within an American city. Surrounded by industrial areas in North Portland, this fragile ecosystem was developed for waterborne activities such as paddling. There's also a short trail with wildlife-viewing platforms from which you can spot beaver, river otters, and one of the largest Western painted turtle populations in the state.

WILLAMETTE JET BOAT EXCURSIONS

1945 SE Water Ave., 503/231-1532,
www.willamettejet.com
Map 4

If you are not the floating and paddling sort, maybe you would rather see the Portland waterfront whiz past you while you enjoy sights, history, and scenic beauty from the seat of a jet boat. On the tour, you will see giant ships, bridges, elegant riverfront homes, historic Oregon City, and the majestic Willamette Falls. Each boat holds about 50 passengers, and there are both one- and two-hour excursions available. Reservations are highly recommended, particularly in the height of summer. Oh, and by the way, wear sunblock and expect to get a little bit wet.

GUIDED TOURS
◖ THE BEST OF PORTLAND WALKING TOUR

701 SW 6th Ave., 503/774-4522,
www.portlandwalkingtours.com
Map 1

Did you know that Clark Gable once worked in the Meier & Frank tie department? Or that the local Elk Lodge boycotted the unveiling of the elk statue in the Plaza Blocks because they considered it an abomination of art? How about the fact that Portland was named as a result of a coin-flip between Asa Lovejoy and Francis Pettygrove. Pettygrove won, but had he lost, we would've been named after Lovejoy's hometown, Boston, and we'd all be talking about the "Pahk Blocks" instead of the Park Blocks. The guides that take you on this Portland 101 tour are equipped with all the inside tips, history snippets, rumors, and realities that you need to get to know the real Portland. Reservations are required, but the Best of Portland Tour, like many of the Portland Walking Tours, departs from the Pioneer Square Visitor Information Center at exactly 10 A.M. daily, or any time your private group wants.

EPICUREAN EXCURSION

701 SW 6th Ave., 503/774-4522,
www.portlandwalkingtours.com

Map 1

The Epicurean Excursion is a simply delight-ful tour through Portland's tastiest places. On the tour, guests taste any number of treats, like Oregon wine and imported mustards, gelato, sorbet, cheese, pizza, chocolate, and bread. As you sample and savor, you will also learn about how things are made, how sustainable practices work, and what Portland is doing differently that makes everything taste so good. Make sure you don't wear open-toed shoes for this one, because you will be traipsing through some kitchens.

OLD TOWN/CHINATOWN
PEDI CAB TOUR

NW 3rd Ave. and NW Everett St., 503/733-4222,
www.pdxpedicab.com

Map 2

Eco-tourism is a word that has a lot of buzz right now and Portland's very own zero-emis-sions tour guide is certainly doing it right. Beginning at the Japanese-American Historical Plaza in Waterfront Park, this 45-minute tour winds through Historic Old Town, Japantown, and New Chinatown, touring through the streets where Shanghai tunnels once reigned supreme. There's lots of history to take in with several points of interest along the way. The podcast audio tour of Old Town tells you all about the people who first occupied the area and who made the city what it is today.

THE PORTLAND BREW BUS

1000 NE Multnomah St., 503/647-0021,
www.brewbus.com

Map 3

Get ready to sample some of Portland's finest

as you visit places like Amnesia Brewing, Lucky Lab, Portland Brewing, and Widmer Brothers Brewing. This tour bus takes you around Portland to three or four breweries, where you can have samples different beers, tour several locations, and ask questions of the resident brewers. The tour is a fun, ed-ucational tour of Portland and the history of craft brewing. You'll hear about differ-ent styles of beer (ales, lagers, porters, stouts, etc.) and learn why Portland is the home of craft brewing.

UNDERGROUND PORTLAND

701 SW 6th Ave., 503/774-4522,
www.portlandwalkingtours.com

Map 1

The Underground Portland Tour, or "Worst of Portland Tour" as it is wont to be called, shines an unflattering light on the prostitution, gam-bling, racism, and shanghaiing of days gone by. Drunken sailors would pass out or be drugged and wake up on a boat miles out to sea before they even knew what happened to them. One of the more notorious shanghaiers, or crimp-ers, was Mary Boggs, who had a barge parked on the Willamette complete with a saloon and bordello. Most of this tour takes place in Old Town and Chinatown, so you will also get a good peek at what life was like for the numer-ous Asian Americans who lived in Portland at a time when they were facing near constant banishment and ridicule. And no story about Portland's dirty underbelly would be complete without a few ghosts, like those in the base-ment of Old Town Pizza, where ghosts are ru-mored to walk the halls.

SHOPS

A mantra for many Portlanders is "Shop Local." While you will find a handful of malls, department stores, and chains scattered about the city, most citizens prefer to purchase everything from the shoes on their feet to the paint on their walls from people in their own backyard. Because of this, P-Town has become known for unique boutiques, stylish designers, and creative concept stores. Over the past several years, the city has earned a reputation as a shopping mecca because of its indisputable style and personal touch. It's not only about buying local for Portlanders, they also want to know the story behind the food they buy and the clothes they wear. For years, NW 23rd Avenue led the pack as the foremost shopping district in town; now other neighborhoods, like Mississippi Avenue and the Alberta Arts District, are developing a distinct flair and presence all their own.

In the past few years, the fashion world has started noticing the many up-and-coming designers that first set their roots down in Portland—even before Portland darling Leanne Marshall won the fifth season of *Project Runway*. There has always been a sense that Portland fashion was built on the back of its DIY roots; and for many locals, the core motivation is the idea that if someone else can make something, it can done better and more ecologically right here in Portland. The garment industry has taken this notion and run with it. Since individuality and creativity reign supreme here, designers have taken it upon themselves to create the kind of fashions that reflect that principle—and the world is paying attention.

HIGHLIGHTS

LOOK FOR (TO FIND RECOMMENDED SHOPS.

(**Best Place to Begin Your I Dos:** Buying that all-too-important engagement ring can be stressful, but at **Gilt** you are likely to find something that is not only one-of-a-kind, but also has a history that bears repeating (page 122).

(**Best Place to Buy a Unique Gift:** Every Saturday and Sunday, a truly mind-boggling number of artists bring their jewelry, paintings, photographs, clothing, and sculptures out to **Portland Saturday Market.** It's the largest continuously operated market in the United States (page 124).

(**Best Place to Dig for Rare Vinyl:** One of the largest independent record retailers in the United States, **Music Millenium,** has been a favorite of Portlanders since the 1960s. With such a remarkable selection of used and new CDs, vinyl, and DVDs, as well as posters, memorabilia, and t-shirts, it's no wonder *SPIN* magazine ranked it one of the best indie stores in America (page 126).

(**Where to Find Your Inner Child:** Even the most straight-laced adult has a hard time not squealing for joy or sighing with nostalgia at **Finnegan's Toys & Gifts,** where the phrase "child's play" takes on a whole new meaning (page 130).

(**Best Book Store for Kids:** One of the best things about being a kid is using your imagination to become someone else. The game gets easier at **Green Bean Books,** where you will find customized retro vending machines that dispense tattoos, beards, and moustaches (page 130).

(**Best Place to Buy a Raincoat:** Portlanders tend to favor raincoats over umbrellas, so look for one that is both stylish and practical at **Lizard Lounge.** The outdoor and casual wear retailer has a hip Pearl District shop that really is a lounge with free wireless, an iMac bar, and Stumptown coffee on hand at all times (page 133).

(**Best Local Designer Boutique:** Portland's fashion scene is thriving, thanks to the influence of a number of art-centric designers who call the city home. You can find a number of their designs at **Frances May,** a mother-daughter owned shop that specializes in clothing and accessories for men and women (page 135).

© KIM NGUYEN

Portland's legendary Saturday Market is still one of the best places in town to find locally made gifts and trinkets.

The adherence to shopping local and the focus on individuality is not about elitism, it's about allowing each person to express their innermost desires and whimsies. That is why neighborhood boutiques and mom-and-pop stores thrive in this town. There is a little something for everyone. If you don't find it in one shop, just walk two doors down.

Accessories and Jewelry

Things are pretty casual around Portland, and it is not uncommon to see the jeans and t-shirts crowd alongside the skirts and suits. The current that runs through both manners of dress is the adherence to accessorizing as a means of self-expression. Portland is a hotbed of jewelry designers, haberdashers, and handbag artists who are all about giving you the icing for your cake.

THE DAPPER CAP

128 NW 23rd Ave., 503/719-5509,
www.thedappercap.com
HOURS: Mon.-Fri. 11 A.M.-8 P.M., Sat. 10 A.M.-8 P.M., Sun.
10 A.M.-6 P.M.
Map 2

Carrying around an umbrella in Portland's fickle weather can be a bother, which is why Portlanders really love wearing hats. The Dapper Cap has hats for men, women, and children at reasonable prices in brands like Bailey's of Hollywood, Stetson, and Kangol. The have more than 2,500 hats to choose from, so come prepared to try a few things on. The best time to come is on a Thursday night when they have a laid-back sale with free beer and a DJ who cranks out tunes for the shoppers.

▐ GILT

720 NW 23rd Ave., 503/226-0629,
www.giltjewelry.com
HOURS: Mon.-Sat. 11:30 A.M.-6 P.M., Sun. noon-5 P.M.
Map 2

If you are in the market for a unique engagement ring, or one-of-a-kind piece of jewelry, Gilt is likely to have something you can't live without. The cozy boutique has an immense selection of vintage and antique jewelry, mostly purchased from estate sales. Many of the rings here hail from the 1880s to the 1940s, and each piece has a story. Find a wedding set that belonged to high school sweethearts who were married for 60 years, or try on a cocktail ring that adorned the finger of a flapper.

Upstairs, Gilt has a selection of new, locally made jewelry and accessories, like chunky rings from Loving Anvil and fused glass pendants from Sunup.

JOHN HELMER HABERDASHERY

969 SW Broadway, 503/223-4976,
www.johnhelmer.com
HOURS: Mon.-Fri. 9:30 A.M.-6 P.M., Sat.
9:30 A.M.-5:30 P.M., closed Sun.
Map 1

For about 80 years now, the Helmer family has been outfitting the heads of Portland with some pretty distinguished styles. Focusing on menswear, accessories, and tailoring, they are above all things a haberdashery. Whether you are the sort to don a leather driving cap or sport an English derby, chances are they have a style that will work for you. They have a very small selection of ladies hats (particularly around the Kentucky Derby season), but they are primarily a men's shop. Shopping at John Helmer is like stepping back into a time when hats, scarves, and sock garters were de rigueur. The staff is still mostly Helmers (second and third generation), and just as knowledgeable and friendly as the originals.

REDUX

811 E. Burnside St., 503/231-7336, www.reduxpdx.com
HOURS: Tues.-Sat. 11 A.M.-7 P.M., Sun. 11 A.M., closed Mon.
Map 3

Walk into Redux and you are likely to feel like you've just stepped into a candy dish. From every wall and hook hang some of the most fascinating pieces, many of which were repurposed from other items like typewriters, PBR cans, or bicycle chains. Owner Tamara Goldsmith stocks jewelry designed by many local folks and has artwork on display by a number of great local artists. Ladies, grab a pair of delicate earrings made from real leaves or a set of leather cuffs made from a recycled belt. For guys, check out the quirky silk ties and wallets from db Clay. Everything is unique and the prices at Redux are remarkably affordable for such distinctive pieces.

SOCK DREAMS

8005 SE 13th Ave., 503/234-0885, www.sock-dreams.com
HOURS: Daily 11 A.M.-4 P.M.
Map 5

A longtime cult favorite on the web, Sock Dreams opened its Southeast store in a location that seemed ridiculous at first. At the east edge of the Ross Island Bridge in an unassuming and easy-to-miss building, Sock Dreams was far away from any other retail traffic. The purpose for this location was to house their enormous warehouse of merchandise, which includes a dizzying array of toe socks, stripy

socks, thigh highs, garters, leg warmers, tights, and more.

Their new Sellwood boutique has a more modest collection of socks than the website does, but here you can touch them and compare colors. If you don't find what you like, the staff can order it for you and they will ship anywhere in the United States for free.

TWIST

30 NW 23rd Pl., 503/224-0334, www.twistonline.com
HOURS: Mon.-Sat. 10 A.M.-7 P.M., Sun. 11 A.M.-6 P.M.
Map 2

Twist has two Portland locations (the other is in Pioneer Place Mall) and another in Seattle. Since the company was founded in 1980, they have been known to embrace elegant, high-end pieces of jewelry with striking elements like knots of coral, amber eggs, or clusters of cognac-colored diamonds.

Twist also carries a number of gallery-quality items for the home or for gifts, like hand-carved wood boxes, candles, pottery, and glassworks. It's a great place to wander through and admire, but things can get a little spendy here, so be careful what you covet.

Arts and Crafts

One of the most used phrases in Portland is "do it yourself," except everyone simply says, "DIY." You don't have to drive out to a strip mall to get craft supplies because nearly every neighborhood has some boutique devoted to a particular craft, and nearly every weekend there is some indie craft fest or workshop. Hang out and drink wine with the girls at a knit shop while learning their special techniques. Chat with a calligrapher at the Saturday Market, or learn how to make buttons with the ladies of Portland who consider craft a religion. That's just the way it goes in this town. There's something around every corner that is hoping to inspire you.

CRAFTY WONDERLAND

830 E. Burnside St., www.craftywonderland.com
HOURS: Second Sun. of every month, 11 A.M.-4 P.M.
Map 4

Once a month, the basement of Doug Fir Lounge is converted into a market that is not unlike Etsy.com come to life. Here you will find jewelry, T-shirts, greeting cards, retro aprons, miniature shrines, kitschy barrettes, stuffed robots, handmade candles, and more. Everything here seems to possess that inexplicable Portland charm. Come early before the crowd gets too thick.

If you get inspired to get a little crafty yourself, belly up to the DIY table, where the experts will teach you how to make a different project each month. Past projects have included making buttons, beaded earrings, pop-up cards, Father's Day can cozies, and even decorating cupcakes.

KNIT/PEARL

1101 SW Alder St., 503/227-2999, www.knit-pearl.com
HOURS: Mon.-Wed. 10 A.M.-7 P.M., Thurs. 10 A.M.-9 P.M., Fri.-Sat. 10 A.M.-6 P.M., Sun. noon-5 P.M.
Map 1

The area surrounding Knit/Pearl was referred to in *Sunset* magazine as the "Fiber Arts District," thanks to the cluster of shops devoted to fabric crafts. Knit/Pearl is an upscale knitting store lined with cubbies that are positively bursting with skeins of luxurious yarns from all over the world. While the price point may be slightly higher than some of the other knit shops in town, the selection can't be beat, particularly if you are looking for Koigu and ShiBui sock yarns. Check out the "Knit and Sip" event on Thursday nights, when they keep the doors open late so folks can gather as they knit and sip champagne.

Knit/Pearl is also conveniently located right next to Josephine's Dry Goods, a purveyor of beautiful silks, laces, and other high-end fabrics, as well as a number of pretty notions.

MUSE ART & DESIGN

4224 SE Hawthorne Blvd., 503/231-8704, www.museartanddesign.com
HOURS: Mon.-Sat. 11 A.M.-6 P.M., Sun. noon-5 P.M.
Map 4

This independently owned art supply store on Hawthorne is well stocked with all the pastels, paints, brushes, paper, sketchbooks, and printing supplies you need to keep your inner muse satisfied. The hole-in-the-wall shop is a nice place to venture into and seek out inspiration, whether it's from the blank canvases, colorful pots of ink, or from one of the workshops in the "Muse Room." Stimulate your creative juices by checking out the "Word to Draw," a random word chosen daily by the staff. It's fun to mull over and then check out what other people have created around the theme.

The staff at Muse is pretty unassuming. In fact, if they assume anything it's that you will ask for help if you need it. Otherwise, they are likely to leave you to explore on your own.

🌙 PORTLAND SATURDAY MARKET

South Waterfront Park and Ankeny Park, 503/241-4188, www.portlandsaturdaymarket.com
HOURS: March-Dec. Sat. 10 A.M.-5 P.M., Sun. 11 A.M.-4:30 P.M.
Map 1

Portland Saturday Market is the nation's largest open-air craft market. Each week on Saturdays and Sundays, artists haul their paintings, sculptures, lawn art, clothing, and jewelry down to Old Town and assemble one of the best displays in town. Stroll through row after row of handmade items and talk to the artists who made them. Visit the iconic Spoonman and see what you would look like with a wrench through your head. The east side of the market is where you will find the best handmade merchandise. Every artist on this side was chosen by a jury. If you are short on time, skip the other side, which is an international import market that focuses on jewelry, clothing, incense, tapestries, and other such things.

Books and Music

Yes, Portland is home to the granddaddy of all bookstores, Powell's City of Books, and the empire that encompasses it, but there are a number of amazing bookstores and record stores that don't seem to mind the competition. Why is that? Because every store has its own personality, and since Portland is a city that thrives on music and words, everyone is just happy to keep the music going (or the pages turning, as the case may be).

EVERYDAY MUSIC
1313 W. Burnside St., 503/274-0961,
www.everydaymusic.com
HOURS: Daily 9 A.M.-midnight
Map 2

Everyday Music has two locations in Portland (the other is at 1931 NE Sandy Blvd.), and true to its name, it's a great outlet for everyday music. This is not the place to go if you are looking for an obscure Townes Van Zandt recording, but you're likely to find great new releases, indie favorites, and some popular classics—it's easily one of the largest collections in town.

Everyday Music buys used CDs, DVDs, and records, so check out the used bins for some really great deals. The newest ones are sorted alphabetically according to when they were brought in, so check the same-day bins first and work your way down through the week to the more picked-over days. If you're going to luck out on that obscure recording, this is probably where you'll find it.

JACKPOT RECORDS
3574 SE Hawthorne Blvd., 503/239-7561,
www.jackpotrecords.com
HOURS: Mon.-Thurs. 10 A.M.-7 P.M., Fri.-Sat.
10 A.M.-8 P.M., Sun. 11 A.M.-6 P.M.
Map 4

This independently owned music store has two locations in Portland (the other is downtown at 203 SW 9th Ave.), and is popular among those seeking indie labels, rock, and metal.

The jewel cases are kept behind the counter and CDs are filed with their inserts into plastic sleeves, the color of which denotes whether it is a new or used album. While the method irks some music store purists, who enjoy the "clack clack" of searching the bins, it means you will find a greater selection thanks to the added space and it means you can check out the liner notes before you purchase the CD.

IN OTHER WORDS
8 NE Killingsworth St., 503/232-6003,
www.inotherwords.org
HOURS: Mon.-Fri. 10 A.M.-9 P.M., Sat. noon-6 P.M.,
closed Sun.
Map 6

This mash-up of bookstore and community center is the kind of place where you somehow feel smarter just walking in. In Other Words is the only surviving non-profit women's bookstore in the entire country and they seem to

© DANIEL ROOT

Portlanders love their music, and Jackpot Records is a popular, independently owned spot.

be fueled almost entirely by passion. Besides offering a comprehensive collection of books, magazines, and zines that embrace feminist and queer studies, erotica, sexuality, transgender studies, and spirituality, the store also hosts a number of community events. There are yoga classes in both Spanish and English, children's playgroups, feminist film nights, and the wildly popular Dirty Queer Open Mic, a no-holds-barred poetry reading every second Friday.

MURDER BY THE BOOK

3210 SE Hawthorne Blvd., 503/232-9995, www.mbtb.com
HOURS: Mon.-Sat. 10 A.M.-6 P.M., Sun. 11 A.M.-5 P.M.
Map 4

Murder by the Book (MBTB) is an independent bookstore devoted to mysteries. The store is divided into cleverly named sections like "Once Upon a Crime" for historical novels, "The Young and the Restless" for children's mysteries, and "A Sight for Sore Eyes,"

the section which holds the store's collection of large-print books. Check out the events calendar to catch a reading and make sure you visit the "Through a Glass Darkly" section, where you will find some truly stellar classic noir books.

MUSIC MILLENNIUM

3158 E. Burnside St., 503/231-8926, www.musicmillennium.com
HOURS: Mon.-Sat. 10 A.M.-10 P.M., Sun. 11 A.M.-9 P.M.
Map 4

You know those bumper stickers that appeal to everyone to "Keep Portland Weird"? It all started here. What began as a public awareness campaign to keep local businesses alive and boost independent thinking has become a mantra for the Rose City way of life. Music Millennium gets it, and they always have. This independent seller of used and new CDs, DVDs, and vinyl has been a staple since 1969, in part because of its impeccable knowledge and taste, but also because of the constantly

They don't call it a "City of Books" for nothing. With nine color-coded rooms and more than 3,500 sections, Powell's occupies an entire city block.

evolving selection. Music Millennium holds regular in-store concerts and events and also sells advance tickets to shows at the Doug Fir Lounge.

POWELL'S HOME AND GARDEN

3747 SE Hawthorne Blvd., 503/228-4651,
www.powells.com

HOURS: Mon.-Sat. 9 A.M.-9 P.M., Sun. 9 A.M.-8 P.M.

Map 4

Located just two spaces down from Powell's Southeast location is an outpost devoted to books on home and gardening. The cookbook section is fun, well organized, extensive, and inspiring, especially given its proximity to Pastaworks, the specialty market located just next door. They have a wide range of books on crafts like knitting, jewelry making, and woodworking, and often host readings from crafting experts and chefs.

This Powell's is also a great place to pick up trinkets and gifts. They have a marvelous collection of candles, garden tools, dishware, tablecloths, and art.

POWELL'S TECHNICAL BOOKS

33 NW Park Ave., 503/228-4651, www.powells.com

HOURS: Mon.-Sat. 9 A.M.-9 P.M., Sun. 11 A.M.-7 P.M.

Map 2

Arguably one of the best places in Portland to geek out, Powell's Technical Books houses books on everything from computers to clockmaking. There are sections for high-level mathematics, physics, electronics, telecommunications, metallurgy, and all the engineering disciplines.

In the fall of 2010, Powell's Technical Books will be rejoining the City of Books upon completion of a construction project that will add as many as three floors to the already enormous store.

360 VINYL

214 SW 8th Ave., 503/224-3688, www.360vinyl.com

HOURS: Mon.-Thurs. 11 A.M.-7 P.M., Fri.-Sat. 11 A.M.-8 P.M., Sun. noon-6 P.M.

Map 1

A go-to spot for DJs who want to expand their library, 360 Vinyl is still a hub for music enthusiasts who have a soft place in their heart for LPs. Owner Aaron Marquez (a.k.a. DJ KEZ) stocks the place with all the newest in hip hop, break beats, soul, jazz, funk, reggae, and an enviable number of classic gems. In addition to the stacks of wax, 360 also sells CDs, DJ equipment, magazines, and books. Ask the employees about upcoming local shows and pick up tickets, or if you're lucky, catch an in-store artist performance from the likes of Ohmega Watts, Vursatyl, or DJs Rev. Shines or Dundiggy.

Bath and Beauty

Portlanders tend to opt for the clean, natural look when it comes to beauty. Unfortunately, maintaining a sunny, natural glow in a city that tends to be a little grey can be a challenge. Thankfully there are terrific shops that can promise that cherubic glow, while still appealing to the average Northwesterner's desire for all-natural, eco-friendly lines—and a good number of shops that cater to those who don't mind spending a little more to look their best.

BLUSH BEAUTY BAR

513 NW 23rd Ave., 503/227-3390,
www.theblushbeautybar.com

HOURS: Mon.-Sat. 10 A.M.-7 P.M., Sun. 11 A.M.-6 P.M.

Map 2

This adorable little boutique in the Alphabet District promotes the idea of shopping local and still carries a fairly extensive selection of top-of-the-line cosmetics and skincare products (from brands like Nars, Bare Escentuals, Lorac, and Mario Badescu). The prices are not inflated, as you might suspect they would be in this neighborhood, and the staff is knowledgeable and can provide makeup application, skin treatments, and hair removal via waxing or threading.

Book a makeover during one of the popular "Flirty Friday" events and one of the team members will teach you all the tricks you need and walk you through the products. It costs $30, but the entire cost can be redeemed in products.

FEZ STUDIO
205 NW 10th Ave., 503/227-2226, www.fezstudio.net
HOURS: Mon.-Sat. 10 A.M.7 P.M., Sun. 11 A.M.-5 P.M.
Map 2

Determined to avoid the "makeup counter experience" that keeps so many women from asking for help, esthetician and stylist Brendan "Fez" Vartan opened his boutique with the intention of providing skin and makeup services without pressure, guilt, or pretentiousness. Since then, he and his staff have developed a reputation for taking a refreshingly honest approach. The studio carries a number of products that are otherwise difficult to find like Arcona and Kevyn Aucoin.

If you would like to have them test a few colors to help you find the right lipstick or shadow, there is no charge for that. A full makeup application will run you about $45.

KIEHL'S
712 NW 23rd Ave., 503/223-7676, www.kiehls.com
HOURS: Mon.-Sat. 10 A.M.-7 P.M., Sun. 11 A.M.-6 P.M.
Map 2

Keihl's is a Portland favorite for its apothecary-style line of lotions, cleansers, shampoos, shaving creams, and lip balms that are made with natural ingredients. This is a great spot for men because the Kiehl's line has a simple, no-nonsense approach to skincare with results that far exceed that sticky bar of soap that's melting into the soap dish. The lab coat–clad employees are always friendly and more than happy to send you away with a handful of free samples.

If you don't want to deal with parking in the congested Alphabet District, just call ahead; they'll happy to bring your purchases right to your car.

LUSH COSMETICS
803 NW 23rd Ave., 503/228-5874, www.lush.com
HOURS: Mon.-Sat. 10 A.M.-7 P.M., Sun. 11 A.M.-6 P.M.
Map 2

It's hard to miss Lush when you can smell it from about a block away. This bath and body shop is loaded with handmade bath bombs, body butters, creams, soaps, shampoos, and lotions. If you are new to the line, explore the bath bombs first. They're a fragrant and luxurious treat to use in a hotel bath or carry home with you as gifts. While Lush isn't a Portland-based company, the ideology behind it certainly fits with the Portland dogma, since all the products are fresh, eco-friendly, and never tested on animals.

The sales team can be quite helpful (sometimes overly so) in helping you find the products that will best suit your needs. Don't be afraid to tell them that you just want to explore and will ask if you have questions.

Children's Stores

While only about 40 percent of Portlanders have children, the ones that do seem deeply devoted to promoting their progeny's sense of self. For that reason, Portland is home to a number of awesome kids' stores that can turn any tot into the hippest kid on the block.

CLOTHING
BELLA STELLA
2751 NE Broadway, 503/284-4636,
www.bellastellababy.com
HOURS: Mon.-Sat. 11 A.M.-5 P.M., Sun. noon-4 P.M.
Map 3

This little store has everything you could want in terms of brand name and locally made clothing, organic slings and accessories, and imaginative toys. It's a fun place to shop for boys if you are tired of fire trucks, action heroes, and bugs. Bella Stella is both a resale and traditional retail store, so you can find new and used merchandise that is hip, bohemian, and affordable. Check out the eco-friendly marriage between cloth and disposable diapers, G-Diapers, or explore the extensive collection of carriers.

Just down the street is Bella Stella's big sister store (2635 NE Broadway Ave., www.bellastellaresale.com), where they sell clothing, toys, and accessories for kids sizes 5–14.

DUCK DUCK GOOSE
517 NW 23rd Ave., 503/916-0636,
www.shopduckduckgoose.com
HOURS: Mon.-Sat. 10 A.M.-6 P.M., Sun. 11 A.M.-5 P.M.
Map 2

This spendy shop in Portland's trendy Alphabet District has an irresistible collection of frothy dresses, tutus, and matching boy-girl outfits that are kiddie couture compared to most children's apparel. Priced out of the everyday play clothes market, Duck Duck Goose is a perfect place to go if you are shopping for a special occasion like Easter, a wedding, or a christening. They carry a number of European and domestic brands that are next to impossible to find and will have your kids looking runway-ready.

Sale prices can make otherwise frivolous purchases more practical, but be certain of what you choose as sale items are not returnable.

HAGGIS MCBAGGIS
6802 SE Milwaukie Ave., 503/234-0849,
www.haggismcbaggis.com
HOURS: Mon.-Sat. 10 A.M.-6 P.M., Sun. noon-5 P.M.
Map 5

Kids can blow through a pair of shoes faster than ice cream melts in July, but the shoes at this Sellwood shop are built with durability in mind. They are experts at fitting and measuring tiny feet, so you won't have to rely on guessing and poking at the toes to determine fit. It's an especially good place to check out if you have a little one who is transitioning into walking, as the shoes here are intended to be good for the feet. Feel free to send your kids off to the play area and slide while you check out the merchandise. In addition to kids' shoes in brands like See Kai Run, Naturino, Geox, and Keen, you will also find a selection of comfortable grown-up-sized shoes, kids' clothing, and colorful accessories.

HANNA ANDERSSON
327 NW 10th Ave., 503/321-5275,
www.hannaandersson.com
HOURS: Mon.-Fri. 10 A.M.-6 P.M., Sat. 10 A.M.-5 P.M., Sun. noon-5 P.M.
Map 2

When you want high-quality clothes that are extremely durable, this is the place. While many think this company—which specializes in cotton togs in a rainbow of colors—is a Swedish business, they were founded right here in Portland. Every button, stitch, zipper, and swath of fabric undergoes rigorous eco-testing to guard against chemicals and harsh radicals. Hanna stocks a number of soft and comfy sweaters, leggings, sweatpants, and dresses (with some matching mommy-and-me outfits) in styles and colors that are designed to last through generations of hand-me-downs.

POLLIWOG

2900 SE Belmont St., 503/236-3903,
www.polliwogportland.com
HOURS: Mon.-Sat. 10 A.M.-6 P.M., Sun. 11 A.M.-5 P.M.
Map 4

This whimsical shop stocks the sort of baby clothes that make almost anyone wish they had a little girl to dress up. The clothes can be a little pricey, but it's worth it if you want to find something unique. Send the kids to play in the back corner while you check out the Glug tees' cute urban chic designs. Service can be a bit aloof sometimes, but this edgier–than–The Gap store is full of fun children's clothing, like bright baby hats, striped PJs, and appliquéd onesies, as well as slings, wonderful wooden toys, and shoes.

TOYS AND GAMES

DOLLAR SCHOLAR

3279 SE Hawthorne Blvd., 503/235-2222,
www.thedollarscholar.org
HOURS: Daily 10 A.M.-8 P.M.
Map 4

Playtime is a priority at this quirky store. One of the owners is likely to greet you as you enter and beckon you over to show you the latest arrival. This isn't a high-pressure sales pitch, it's sheer enthusiasm over the ooey-gooey slime balls, spinning dinosaur tops, whoopee cushions, and silly whistles. Whimsy is the name of the game here, and they insist that you play with anything and everything. Open the packages; test out the poo-shaped pen; throw a rubber egg at the window; or visit with Dollar, the resident dog.

This is a discount store only in the sense that you won't pay more than a dollar for anything; the goods are well-chosen, often practical, and almost always fun.

🌑 FINNEGAN'S TOYS & GIFTS

922 SW Yamhill St., 503/221-0306,
www.finneganstoys.com
HOURS: Mon.-Sat. 10 A.M.-6 P.M., Sun. 11 A.M.-5 P.M.
Map 1

Spacious but stuffed to the rafters with smiling penguins, wind-up birds, colorful trains, and every game under the sun, Finnegan's is truly a gem. Find classic and collectable toys like Raggedy Ann, Playmobil, Curious George, and Radio Flyer, as well as fun new-fangled robots and crazy building sets from Zoob, K'Nex, and Lego. There is a train table in one corner to keep little hands busy and when it's time to leave, there are a number of small, inexpensive trinkets to distract them from that expensive toy they are likely to cling to. Finnegan's is a popular spot for families to stop in and play, thanks to its proximity to the Multnomah County Library and the MAX line.

There is also a smaller Finnegan's around the corner. It's devoted to novelties and toys for grownups and has a photo booth complete with kooky glasses to try on.

GRASSHOPPER

1808 NE Alberta St., 503/335-3131,
www.grasshopperstore.com
HOURS: Sun.-Mon. 10 A.M.-5 P.M., Tues.-Sat.
10 A.M.-6 P.M.
Map 3

Nestled in the midst of artsy Alberta Street, Grasshopper has a nice selection of organic and American-made clothes, funky rain boots, diaper bags, and bibs. They also have a unique collection of playthings that are non-toxic and not found on the shelves of any big-box store. The carefully selected array of amusing and colorful toys, games, and books are both stimulating to the imagination and wildly collectable.

The all-female staff is very sweet and willing to help you find that special something for a gift—and will even gift-wrap it for free.

🌑 GREEN BEAN BOOKS

1600 NE Alberta St., 503/954-2354
HOURS: Tues.-Fri. 11 A.M.-6 P.M., Sat. 10 A.M.-6 P.M., Sun.
10 A.M.-5 P.M.
Map 3

When schoolteacher Jennifer Green looked at the plethora of beloved children's books she had collected over the years, she didn't pack them up and haul them off to Goodwill. She opened a bookstore that specializes in new and used children's books in English and a multitude of other languages. Exploring all the nooks and crannies of this charming Alberta Street shop can be a lot of fun, especially when you discover the custom-made vending machines. One dispenses finger puppets (made by the owner); another offers temporary tattoos. An old gumball machine hands out pom-pom pets and what looks suspiciously like an old sanitary napkin dispenser is now an "Instant Disguise Machine" that distributes fake beards and moustaches for a quarter.

KIDS AT HEART

3445 SE Hawthorne Blvd., 503/231-2954, www.kidsathearttoys.com
HOURS: Mon.-Sat. 10 A.M.-7 P.M., Sun. 10 A.M.-6 P.M.
Map 4

Kids at Heart is a locally owned shop that specializes in toys and games that are creative and educational. That means you won't find any mega-blasters or current movie merchandise crap here, but you will find adorable puppets, plush robots, sticker books, magical costumes, and science kits. The books room has a number of new releases and old favorites for newborns

and readers up to young adults. The store is a wee bit on the small side compared to some of the other toy shops and bookstores in the region, but they seem to make up for their size in judicious selection and knowledgeable service.

SPIELWERK COMMUNITY TOYSTORE

7956 SE 13th Ave., 503/736-3000, www.spielwerk.net
HOURS: Mon.-Sat. 10 A.M.-6 P.M., Sun. 11 A.M.-5 P.M.
Map 5

The name of this store is German for "play work," a term they mean to imply that children have the very important job of playing. For that reason, the objects in this store are designed to engage, develop, and thrill. Instead of simply entertaining kids, these hand-carved, hand-painted, or hand-sewn toys are meant to promote positive brain activity.

The store also hosts regular "WerkShops," where young ones can learn how to do a number of imaginative things like build a fairy garden, paint silk scarves, or make their own hula hoops. If you can't make it over to Sellwood, you can visit the SpielWork store in The Hub on Williams Street, a food and lifestyle–focused retail space in North Portland.

Clothing and Shoes

Not everyone in Portland wears fleece, anoraks, and Birkenstocks; and not everyone is clad in the typical hipster uniform of skinny jeans, white belts, and ironic t-shirts (though depending on the neighborhood, you might see a lot of that). These days, the fashion industry in Portland is booming, and the concentration on making and wearing locally designed and produced fashions has become the norm, not the exception. In fact, shopping magazines like *Lucky* and *Cosmopolitan* are clamoring to understand the full scope of the community, as boutiques continue to spring up in Portland's most popular districts offering one-of-a-kind frocks and the latest trends.

MEN'S CLOTHING
GREENLOOP

8005 SE 13th Ave., 503/236-3999, www.thegreenloop.com
HOURS: Tues.-Sat. 11 A.M.-6 P.M., closed Mon.
Map 5

Greenloop is a style-savvy, eco-conscious company that stocks sustainable apparel and accessories for men and women. The brands carried by Greenloop all employ responsible practices in production, recycling, waste-reduction, and the use of renewable energy in addition to using eco-friendly, sustainable materials. They have a great collection of stylish art-focused t-shirts and sweatshirts here, Loomstate jeans, and Fair Trade, sweatshop-free sneakers. The selection ranges from relaxed to rebellious clothing and

CHEAP TRICKS: STUMPTOWN BARGAIN SHOPPING

Fortunately for Portlanders, there are a lot of bargain shopping outlets out there. Unlike many cities, the idea of "thrift shopping" doesn't carry much of a stigma in PDX. Maybe it's our DIY spirit or maybe it's our devil-may-care attitude, but from clothing to furniture, books to building supplies, P-Towners love to save whenever they can. Call it "junking," "thrifting," or simply "smart shopping;" no matter what, there are ways to survive today's economy without losing your sense of style.

One of the weirdest spots to find some bargains is **City Liquidators** (830 SE 3rd Ave., 503/238-4477, www.cityliquidators.com). Affectionately called "City Licks," this retail spot nestled under the Morrison Bridge is home to some great deals on everything from dishtowels and candles to lava lamps and micro-fiber sectionals. The merchandise at City Liquidators is so wildly diverse, it's downright entertaining to simply walk through.

Goodwill Outlet (1750 SE Ochoco St., 503/254-4795, www.meetgoodwill.com) is simply referred to as "The Bins." This is bargain shopping at its most hardcore – it's the *Jackass* of thrifting. Row after row of plastic bins are positively heaped with items you can't even begin to imagine, all sold for no more than $1.99 per pound. (The more poundage you buy, the cheaper it gets.) There are both horror and glory stories about the items found while digging through the bins. On one trip, you might find a pair of True Religion jeans, a Prada clutch, a bag of cool vintage bakelite bangles, and a retro neon diner-style clock. On another trip, you may find a used diaper. That said, it's wise to wear gloves while excavating your treasures (you'll be glad you did).

When it comes to clothing, there's no end to the vintage, thrift, and consignment stores, such as hipster favorites **Red Light Clothing Exchange** (3590 SE Hawthorne Blvd., 503/963-8888, www.redlightclothingexchange.com) and **Buffalo Exchange** (1420 SE 37th Ave., 503/234-1302, www.buffaloexchange.com), where they will take your clothing donations in exchange for cash or credit. They're pretty selective about the items that they pick, which means that their racks are filled with interesting, often one-of-a-kind pieces that are remarkably affordable.

One of Portland's oldest vintage clothing stores, **Avalon** (410 SW Oak St., 503/224-7156) has been in business since the 1960s – although it's unclear what would qualify as vintage back then (what would a vintage store be without bell-bottoms?), there's a reason why they are still in business. Most vintage stores have a fantastic selection of women's wear, but Avalon also boasts a pretty impressive array of men's clothing. For guys who want to find unique vintage suits and ties, Avalon has them in spades.

Another place to find affordable one-of-a-kind style is **Ray's Ragtime** (1021 SW Morrison St., 503/226-2616, www.raysragtime.com). The shop can easily overwhelm because sparkly gowns, vintage tees, shoes, and pillbox hats are literally spilling out of every corner. The downtown store is a destination for many Portland costumers; in fact, the wares at Ray's have been featured in a number of major films including *Mr. Holland's Opus* and *My Own Private Idaho*.

If you can't bear the idea of pre-worn fashions, but really want to find those designer deals, check out **Nordstom Rack** (401 SW Morrison St., 503/299-1815, www.nordstrom.com), the off-price version of Nordstrom where they carry items from the regular retail stores at 50-70 percent off the original prices. They get new merchandise daily and are a reliable spot to shop when you are looking for jeans, shoes, and formal wear in particular.

Finally, if you're looking to save a little on edible treats, venture over to the **Grocery Outlet** (4420 NE Hancock St., 877/478-2897, www.groceryoutlet.com) in the Hollywood District. They have close-out prices on everything from basic supplies (like crackers, chocolates, cheese, and pasta) to quirky never-made-it-to-the-shelves items. It's a bit like "The Island of Misfit Toys," only for food. The real find in this store is the wine section, where most bottles are less than $10. It is not uncommon to find a delightful Spanish red for $3.99 that may be selling for $18.99 at a wine shop just down the street. However, if you are shopping for groceries, it's best to pay attention to the sell-by dates on the packaging. It's not uncommon to spot the occasional expired good.

accessories, but there are a number of basics as well.

LIZARD LOUNGE

1323 NW Irving St., 503/416-7476,
www.lizardloungepdx.com
HOURS: Mon.-Thurs. 10 A.M.-7 P.M., Fri.-Sat.
10 A.M.-8 P.M., Sun. 11 A.M.-7 P.M.
Map 2

Lizard Lounge is a local hang-out, especially during First Thursdays when they have live music, free beer or wine, and art showings. If you miss the monthly event, it's still a great place to grab some free Stumptown coffee, play some ping pong, or make use of the free Wi-Fi or iMac station while you browse through stylish, laid-back, and earth-conscious clothes. As should be with any great lounge, the staff is friendly, stylish, accommodating, and chances are, they know something about every piece or designer in the shop. Lizard Lounge stocks a bunch of Horny Toad apparel and its high-end, Portland-based, eco-friendly line, Nau. The clothing can be a little pricy, so check for sales or be prepared to pay a little more for something durable and guilt-free.

LOCAL 35

3556 SE Hawthorne Blvd., 503/963-8200,
www. local35.blogspot.com
HOURS: Sun.-Wed. 10 A.M.-6 P.M., Thurs.-Sat.
11 A.M.-7 P.M.
Map 4

Local 35 has an excellent selection of contemporary clothes from small designers and it's clear that the owner has a good eye for fashion. Focusing on street wear, this is a great spot to find high-end sneakers, denim, hoodies, and tees. Items are expensive, but high-quality brands like Nudie, B.Son, Obedient, and Anzevino and Florence make it a worthwhile investment and the sales at Local 35 are epic. Considering this and the plethora of stylish accessories they have on hand, it's no surprise that they were featured

in *Playboy* in 2009 as one of the best stores in the United States.

UNDER U FOR MEN

507 SW Broadway, 503/274-2555,
www.underU4men.com
HOURS: Mon.-Thurs. 10 A.M.-6 P.M., Fri. 10 A.M.-9 P.M.,
Sat. 10 A.M.-6 P.M., Sun. noon-5 P.M.
Map 1

This is a small boutique that offers every kind of men's underwear, sleepwear, and swimwear that you could hope to find, from basic to exotic. Underwear comes in a multitude of colors, shapes, material, and support levels, turning this store into a hipper, sportier version of Victoria's Secret—for men. Whether you prefer boxers, briefs, bikinis, no-show bikinis, or thongs, they've got them in everything from silk to bamboo.

The items here are comfortable, athletic, and sexy enough to make anyone blush, but don't expect such style to come cheap. You can expect to pay about $20–30 for each pair of underwear and considerably more for sleepwear and swimwear.

UPPER PLAYGROUND

23 NW 5th Ave., 503/548-4835,
www.upperplayground.com
HOURS: Mon.-Sat. 11 A.M.-8 P.M., Sun. noon-6 P.M.
Map 2

Upper Playground is a hybrid between an urban-chic clothes source (selling t-shirts, hoodies, and hats) and an art gallery. Street and graffiti art adorns the walls, and there's a full-blown gallery in the back. This place has screen-printed shirts by metro artists Alex Pardee, Chris Lee, Cody Hudson, and Jeremy Fish. They have a number of Portland-themed shirts, which make great gifts for people who want a little piece of Portland with more character than your average tourist-trap buy.

If you don't mind a crowd, stop by on First Thursday. You can shop, sip beer or wine, check out the newest art in the gallery, and listen to a DJ spin some tunes.

WELL SUITED

2401 NE Broadway, 503/284-5939,
www.wellsuitedpdx.com
HOURS: Tues.-Sat. 11 A.M.-6 P.M., closed Sun-Mon.
Map 3

If you are in need of a suit but don't have the money to shell out for one at the usual designer store prices, Well Suited may be able to save you a lot of time and money. The unassuming storefront hides a remarkable selection of high-end suits by designer labels like Prada, Hugo Boss, and Armani—as well as some beach-style shirts and basic business-casual wear. Since the store is a consignment shop, you can find a great suit for about 50–80 percent what you might pay anywhere else.

If you find the perfect suit, but it doesn't fit quite right (or you already own a suit that needs tailoring), have it tailored right on the spot. The in-store tailor is one of the best in town and his prices are quite reasonable.

WINN PERRY

2505 SE 11th Ave., Ste. 102, 503/922-1298,
www.winnperry.com
HOURS: Tues.-Sat. 10 A.M.-6 P.M., Sun.-Mon. by appointment
Map 4

Winn Perry is the only retailer in town who provides exclusive space for Duchess Clothier's fantastic men's custom-made and ready-to-wear suits in nostalgic two- and three-piece styles. You can also find gentlemanly effects like sock garters, collar stays, overshoes, badger hair shaving brushes, soaps, ties, and hats. If this store had a theme song it would be ZZ Top's "Sharp Dressed Man," but perhaps only if it could be played by a grand orchestra while Gene Kelly spun a lovely girl around the dance floor and Frank Sinatra sipped champagne in the corner.

If you are particularly fashion challenged, just put yourself in their capable hands. Owner Jordan Sayler practically wrote the book on how to dress like a gentleman and is well equipped to advise you on simple changes you can make to look your best.

WOMEN'S CLOTHING

AMAI UNMEI

2275 NW Johnson St., 503/274-0026
HOURS: Tues.-Sat. 11 A.M.-6 P.M., Sun. noon-5 P.M.
Map 2

Known for smart, stylish coats and elegantly simple bridal designs, Amai Unmei (pronounced ah-MY oon-MAY) designer Allison Covington drew influences from *tsutsumi*, the Japanese high art of gift wrapping, wherein the wrapping is considered very much a part of the gift. Amai Unmei is a regular participant in Northwest fashion shows and the line garners a lot of respect for Covington's feminine but unfussy designs. When news traveled that Amai Unmei's first brick-and-mortar boutique would open just off of trendy 23rd Avenue, fashionistas were excited to see what this much-loved line would do with their new endeavor. Since then, things have only gotten better. Covington's beautiful designs, sensational silhouettes, and adherence to working only with naturally sustainable silks make her poised to become the future of Northwest fashion.

BUFFALO EXCHANGE

1420 SE 37th Ave., 503/234-1302,
www.buffaloexchange.com
HOURS: Mon.-Sat. 10 A.M.-8 P.M., Sun. 11 A.M.-7 P.M.
Map 4

Buffalo Exchange is a great spot to find one-of-a-kind pieces, locally made t-shirts and dresses, as well as second-hand high-end brands like Joe's Jeans, Rock & Republic, Anna Sui, BCBG, Betsey Johnson, and Nicole Miller. The store seems to cater to the young, hipster crowd of Portland, so you are likely to find odd vintage blouses, punky leather pieces, and earthy organic cotton dresses. While there is a second Buffalo downtown (1036 W. Burnside St.), the Hawthorne location is superior, if only because the racks are easier to navigate.

◖ FRANCES MAY

1013 SW Washington St., 503/227-3402,
www.francesmay.net
HOURS: Tues.-Sat. 11 A.M.-7 P.M., Sun. noon-6 P.M.,
closed Mon.
Map 1

Owned by a grandmother-granddaughter team,
Frances May blends modern-day panache with
sweet, old-fashioned whimsy. In addition to
having a handful of amazing one-of-a-kind vintage pieces, they carry the latest from a number
of hot local designers like Church+State, Emily
Katz, and Moth Love. Throughout the season,
you can also find vintage-inspired jewelry from
Anna Korte and a timeless collection of shoes
and belts by Rachel Comey.

Francis May has always been a Portland favorite for fashion-forward women's clothes, and
they now carry a slick selection of menswear
as well.

LUCY ACTIVEWEAR

1015 NW Couch St., 503/226-0220, www.lucy.com
HOURS: Mon.-Sat. 10 A.M.-7 P.M., Sun. 11 A.M.-6 P.M.
Map 2

Launched in 1999, this Portland-based company specializes in cutting-edge women's athletic wear. It's a great place to check out if you
are looking for some yoga basics or bright, colorful alternatives to your usual gym attire. The
company was started by former Nike executive
Sue Levin with the intention of creating active
gear for women that has a sense of style and a
fit that is both flattering and comfortable. Stop
by on "Fitness Fridays," where you can meet
fitness professionals who offer training advice
and hold short classes.

MABEL & ZORA

1468 NE Alberta St., 503/335-6169,
www.mabelandzora.com
HOURS: Mon.-Sat. 11 A.M.-7 P.M., Sun. noon-5 P.M.
Map 3

This sweet little Doris Day–themed boutique
is owned by husband and wife team Cory and
Tiffany Bean, a pair that knows quite a bit
about style. They stock a number of pretty,
feminine, and retro-edged brands like Tulle,

Sweet Pea, Trina Turk, Joe's Jeans, French
Connection, Michael Stars, and Hanky Panky.
They also have a number locally produced,
handmade garments, jewelry, and accessories
from some of Portland's favorite designers.
Everything here seems to have a lot of perk and
personality, from the apparel and the darling
luggage sets to the staff behind the counter.

If nothing else, stop by the boutique to meet
the owners and their staff. They are not only
exuberant and helpful, they are pretty fun as
well.

MARIO'S

833 SW Broadway, 503/227-3477,
www.marios.com
HOURS: Mon.-Sat. 10 A.M.-6 P.M., Sun. noon-5 P.M.
Map 1

Mario's is to a department store like Kobe
beef is to an overcooked sirloin. The service
is intended to be attentive and hospitable instead of merely advantageous. The first floor
of this downtown shrine to excess is devoted to
menswear; ladies will find their haven upstairs,
where sales associates offer a glass of wine or
champagne to sip while you shop.

If you are looking for labels, this is where
you want to go. Mario's has all the drool-worthy ones, like Prada, Pucci, Vera Wang, Dolce
& Gabbana, and Christian Louboutin. Yes, the
prices are high, but the sales are spectacular.

MOULE

1225 NW Everett St., 503/227-8530,
www.moulestores.com
HOURS: Mon.-Sat. 11 A.M.-7 P.M., Sun. 11 A.M.-6 P.M.
Map 2

This bright boutique in the Pearl District is
a bit of an odd duck. The selection is quirky,
but they have a spectacular collection of
women's clothing, including owner Rachel
Gorenstein's pretty and polished line, Rachel
Mara. Gorenstein's elegant designs have been
featured on *Sex and the City*, and in magazines
such as *Lucky* and *InStyle*—and it's not surprising, since her slinky dresses and soft silhouettes
fit quite well alongside top lines like Michelle
Mason, Rag & Bone, and Habitual.

The shop has a number of oddities as well, like men's clothes, *Playboy* collector books, baby clothes that sometimes tip the edge of appropriateness, and kitschy housewares. For all the randomness, they make browsing fairly easy with clean lines, pretty decor, and well-spaced racks.

MOXIE
2400 E. Burnside St., 503/296-6943,
www.moxiepdx.com
HOURS: Sun.-Thurs. 9 A.M.-7 P.M., Fri.-Sat. 9 A.M.-5 P.M.
Map 4

Moxie is a term usually applied to someone who is tremendously spirited or courageous, who has the guts to color outside the lines. Moxie the boutique is no less spirited than the flappers who were often referred to as possessing the quality during the time the word was popularized. The collection of clothing here is an eclectic mix of big-name brands, independent labels, and local designs, with a few select vintage pieces thrown in. Some of the clothes and accessories are distinctly feminine, with girl ruffles and floral accents; other items (like bold earrings and necklaces and casual t-shirts) are quite a bit more rocker-chic.

ODESSA
410 SW 13th Ave., 503/223-1998,
www.odessaboutique.com
HOURS: Mon.-Sat. 11 A.M.-7 P.M., closed Sun.
Map 1

This quaint little boutique packs a powerful punch with designer clothing from the likes of Jeffrey Monteiro, Jill Stuart, AF Vandervorst, Comme des Garçons, and Isabel Marant. The eclectic but sophisticated boutique is a favorite for casual urbanites who don't mind paying a little extra for exquisite apparel. In fact, the stocklist rivals that of boutiques you'd find in Los Angeles or New York. Established in 1996, Odessa has garnered a loyal following. Truthfully, the collection does include things that are otherwise impossible to find in Portland (at prices that don't seem to imply that getting them here was hard work). You'll find a little bit of everything here, from jeans and

cocktail dresses to coats and cashmere scarves. Warning: Just try to leave without buying some luxurious bedding from Kerry Cassill.

OH BABY!
1811 NE Broadway St., 503/281-7430,
www.ohbabyforyou.com
HOURS: Daily 10 A.M.-6 P.M.
Map 3

This is where good girls go to be naughty and naughty girls go to be even naughtier. This award-winning lingerie boutique is filled to the bedposts with lingerie in sizes 32A to 42G for all shapes and tastes. No really. At the center of the shop, you will find a four-poster bed, strewn with pretty panties in satin and lace. The girls who work here are experts at fitting and can no doubt put you in a bra that will make you wonder how you ever got along without it. They specialize in bridal lingerie and corsets, which you are welcome to try on in the private fitting room outfitted with floor pillows and enough room for an audience of one. If you're a little out of your element amidst all the ribbons and lace, the staff will help you pick out something fabulous that would make a perfect bridal shower or bachelorette gift, or just a self-indulgent treat.

POPINA SWIMWEAR
4831 NE 42nd Ave., 503/282-5159,
www.popinaswimwear.com
HOURS: Tues.-Wed. 10 A.M.-6 P.M., Thurs. 10 A.M.-7 P.M., Fri. 10 A.M.-6 P.M., Sat. 10 A.M.-5 P.M., Sun. noon-5 P.M.
Map 3

I know what you're thinking. A swimwear store in Portland? Yes, despite the fact that it rains nine months out of the year in these parts—or maybe because of it—we occasionally need to chuck the raincoat and head off to sunny Mexico or Hawaii. Heck, sometimes we'll settle for a dip in one of the nearby hot springs or even a friend's Jacuzzi. Whatever the reason, if Portlanders need a swimsuit, they go looking for something with panache. Enter Pamela Levenson, a swimwear designer who specializes in retro-styled suits. Try on one of the many suits she carries in her shop located

IT'S EASY TO BE GREEN, AND FASHIONABLE!

According to *Popular Science*, Portland is ranked number one among the greenest cities in the world. Half of its power comes from renewable sources; more than a quarter of the workforce commutes by bike, mass transit, or carpool; and recycling is done as a matter of principle, and not as an ecological statement. More and more business are following suit by remodeling their buildings or altering their practices and products to embrace the green standard.

Portland fashion designers jumped on that bandwagon years ago and are leading the industry in designing beautiful, sustainable clothing. **Idom** (827 NW 23rd Ave., 503/477-6818, www.idomdesigns.com) owner and designer Modi Soondarotok opened her boutique in 2006 with an emphasis on bold, fashion-forward clothing with an influence from her native Bangkok, Thailand. Her clothing made a big statement, but not a big footprint. The boutique (the name is "Modi" spelled backwards and pronounced like "item") stocks clothing that is made from personally sourced, hand-loomed silks and cottons. Each item is then sewn by a small handful of homemakers that Soondaratok pays enough wages to allow them to work from home and spend time with their families.

Similarly, **Pie Footwear** (2916 NE Alberta St., 503/288-1999, www.piefootwear.net) is saving the earth one foot at a time with their smart and stylish shoes that are socially responsible to boot. The store is vegan friendly and stocks a number of eco-conscious socks, hats, and bags. **Olio United** (1028 SE Water Ave., 503/542-5000, www.oliounited.com) is also an eco-fashionista's dream with environmentally groovy threads for men, women, and children, as well as jewelry, home decor, and art.

If you are looking to relax, but don't want to fret about the impact your pampering might have on the environment, check out **Blooming Moon Wellness Spa** (2050 NW Lovejoy St., 503/222-2391, www.bloomingmoonspa.com). The spa only uses all-natural products that are never tested on animals; adheres to a recycling and sustainable energy plan; and encourages employees and guests to bike or take the streetcar to the spa. Book a Sore Muscle Relief package (foot bath, acupuncture, and massage) and you just might need to call a taxi to get you home.

Speaking of home, **Tropical Salvage** (2455 SE 11th Ave., 503/236-6155, www.tropicalsalvage.com) makes some truly amazing furniture out of wood that was salvaged from demolition sites, or pulled from landslides, lakes, and rivers. They can also take old, sometimes diseased trees culled from coffee plantations, or dredge up trees buried by centuries-old volcanic eruptions, clean it, cut it, kiln-dry it, and then turn it into some pretty impressive cabinets, tables, beds, dressers, and chairs. There are a number of local places, like **ECOpdx** (2289 N. Interstate Ave., 503/287-8181, www.ecopdx.com) and **Ten Thousand Villages** (914 NW Everett St., 503/231-8832, www.portlandvillages.com) where you can purchase this salvaged wood furniture.

Finally, if you want to find some environmentally friendly gourmet treats, check out **Cork** (2901 NE Alberta St., 503/501-5028, www.corkwineshop.com), where the focus is on supporting sustainable producers by stocking certified organic and biodynamic wines. Look for the green signs describing products that are certified organic, biodynamic, salmon-safe, or Low Input Viticulture and Enology (LIVE) certified.

just off of Alberta Street; if it doesn't fit perfectly, they will alter it for you at a surprisingly small cost.

REI

1405 NW Johnson St., 503/221-1938, www.rei.com

HOURS: Mon.-Sun. 10 A.M.-9 P.M., Sun. 10 A.M.-7 P.M.

Map 2

If you are unaccustomed to the Northwest weather, or if you plan to explore the Oregon wilderness while you're here, take a trip by this Pacific Coast–based retailer. The gear and apparel here are high quality and are designed and sold by people with an expertise and a passion for outdoor recreation. Shopping here can be especially invigorating for women who may have felt overlooked or simply nonplussed about the bland athletic-wear options at other retailers.

SHOES

AMENITY SHOES

3430 NE 41st Ave., 503/282-4555,
www.amenityshoes.com

HOURS: Mon.-Fri. 10 A.M.-7 P.M., Sat. 10 A.M.-6 P.M., Sun. 11 A.M.-5 P.M.

Map 3

Established in 2005, Amenity Shoes is a locally owned and operated resource for comfy shoes that don't look like they came out of grandma and grandpa's closet. The owners have a background in art and shoe manufacturing, which is evident the selection. From colorful, embroidered flats to classy patent-leather t-strap sandals, they seem to choose the kind of footwear that is cute, modern, and comfortable all at once. The stock of men's shoes is equally well balanced and modern, with brands like Sole, Kenneth Cole, and Fly London leading the pack.

IMELDA'S AND LOUIE'S SHOES

3426 SE Hawthorne Blvd., 503/233-7476,
www.imeldasandlouies.com

HOURS: Mon.-Fri. 10 A.M.-7 P.M., Sat. 10 A.M.-6 P.M., Sun. 11 A.M.-6 P.M.

Map 4

Like moths to a flame, the shoe addicts in Portland keep coming back to Imelda's & Louie's to get their fix. The styles here range from functional work shoes to date night pumps and everything in between—with many pairs boasting buttery leathers or eco-friendly materials. This is a great source of shoes for both men and women. The shoes are expensive, but well made, colorful, and beautifully designed. Sizes are sometimes limited because the store is fairly small, but if you fall in love with something, don't fret. They are oftentimes able and more than happy to order a pair for you in your size.

SOLE

1033 NW Couch St., 503/222-7653, www.4mysole.com

HOURS: Mon.-Sat. 11 A.M.-7 P.M., Sun. 11 A.M.-6 P.M.

Map 2

If ever there was a siren song for shoe lovers, then Sole is singing it. The drool-worthy display of delicious heels, pretty sandals, and cute accessories is enough to draw in anyone (especially if you have two X chromosomes and a credit card). The selection at Sole is trendy and reasonable priced, with most pairs checking in at around $100–150. The staff is ready with suggestions or sizes, but not likely to pressure you.

ZELDA'S SHOE BAR

633 NW 23rd Ave., 503/226-0363,
www.zeldaspdx.com

HOURS: Mon.-Sat. 11 A.M.-6 P.M., Sun. 11 A.M.-5 P.M.

Map 2

In 2009 Zelda's Shoe Bar merged with the adjacent high-end clothing store, Elizabeth Street. In Zelda's space, the smaller of the two, there is some apparel like French Connection blouses and ultra-versatile Butter by Nadia dresses, but the collection does not quite compare to that of Elizabeth Street. No one is complaining, however, because the shoes are what keep the serious collectors and curious onlookers coming back. Given the way that shoes are displayed here, you can tell that they take it seriously. Each shoe is treated like a piece of art. If you are a sucker for well-made heels, boots, flats, and sandals that err on the practical side, Zelda's is a good place to get your fix.

Gifts and Home

Looking for the tools or know-how to start an urban farm? Portland has a number of places where you can find everything you need from a shovel to a garden gnome. Whether you want to find a one-of-a-kind accent for your home or a gift for someone who can't possibly be impressed by a gift certificate, there is a boutique that has the exact hand-blown glass vase or monkey-shaped lamp you've been looking for.

CARGO
380 NW 13th Ave., 503/209-8349, www.cargoinc.com
HOURS: Daily 11 A.M.–6 P.M.
Map 2

Longtime purveyors of imported artifacts and antiques, Cargo is a veritable treasure trove of trinkets, oddities, jewelry, furniture, decor, and more. Their Pearl District warehouse is just a few shouting vendors away from being an Asian street market, with baubles and beads adorning statues, colorful displays, and teak wood furniture stacked high. Cargo specializes in garden statuary, folk art, religious memorabilia, carpets, vibrant glassware, and propaganda art, as well as antique and custom-designed furniture, all with a heavy emphasis on Asian designs. This place is huge and there is something eye-catching at every angle, so allow yourself time to get lost for awhile. Also, Cargo always has a free knick-knack that they give away just to thank you for your visit. So, make sure you pick up your free Chinese finger trap (or whatever it might be).

DIG GARDEN SHOP
425 NW 11th Ave., 503/223-4443,
www.diggardenshop.com
HOURS: Tues.-Fri. 11 A.M.–6 P.M., Sat. 11 A.M.–5 P.M., Sun. noon–5 P.M.
Map 2

If you are lucky enough to have hung out on one of the many rooftop gardens or terraces in the Pearl District, chances are it was designed by Dig Garden Shop owner Tom Adkisson. The professional landscape architect has made a name for himself when it comes to urban renewal and the art of transforming otherwise austere places into comfortable but bold living spaces. The shop reflects Adkisson's adherence to urban design, art, and modern touches. There are a number of contemporary containers that a perfectly suited for the Northwest weather and art to make the concrete jungle (or a simple garden) seem a little less stark.

ELLA+SAM
4314 SE Hawthorne Blvd., 503/517-9942,
www.elsasam.com
HOURS: Tues.-Fri. noon–6 P.M., Sat. 11 A.M.–5 P.M., Sun. noon–4 P.M., closed Mon.
Map 4

If you are the kind of person who gets all fluttery in the heart at the sight of colorful dishes stacked like pies in a cooler, or knows the difference between engraved and etched glass, you are going to want to move into this adorable shop. It is here that you will find pretty porcelain tea sets; ceramic plates emblazoned with old-fashioned revolvers; and stunning mouth-blown, engraved crystal martini glasses. It's a great place to find a unique wedding or shower gift or something to give that person who has everything. Because really, how could they possibly have a handmade serving plate with winged skulls already?

FOUND ON FREMONT
4743 NE Fremont St., 503/284-4804,
www.amyhollands.typepad.com
HOURS: Mon.-Fri. 11 A.M.–6 P.M., Sat 11 A.M.–5 P.M., Sun. noon–5 P.M.
Map 3

Found on Fremont is a great little vintage gift boutique that has a number of sweet handmade cards, kitschy housewares, mid-century furniture, and terrific vintage hats. The ladies who owned Vestiges Storefront, Ruby Cushion, Flea, and Poppy & Ivy joined forces to open this place, which is bedecked with jewelry and crafts created by local artists, and a number of one-of-a-kind treasures that were likely snatched up from an estate sale mere moments before being given a loving, but temporary home in the store.

This is a great place to find gifts for crafty friends who can draw inspiration from vintage cookbooks, craft kits, or subversive embroidery projects from Sublime Stitching.

GREG'S
3703 SE Hawthorne Blvd., 503/235-1257
HOURS: Daily 10 A.M.-6 P.M.
Map 4

Greg's is filled with everything you could possibly want, but nothing you need. On every shelf and wall, you'll find tschotschkes, cards, posters, bags, housewares, wind-up toys, and more—much of it from Northwest designers and craftspeople. You may not need three different sizes of mirrored disco balls, but you will want them. The same goes for the Virgen de Guadalupe candles, the googly-eyed stuffed monkey, or avenging narwhal play set. This is a terrific spot to find a gift for someone back home as proof-positive that Portland is a very weird place.

PRESENTS OF MIND
3366 SE Hawthorne Blvd., 503/230-7740,
www. presentsofmind.tv
HOURS: Daily 10 A.M.-7 P.M.
Map 4

Presents of Mind has an eclectic mix of amazing locally made jewelry, bags, and clothes, along with hilarious gag gifts and stationery. It's a fun place to pick up a killer diaper bag or a onesie for the newborn in your life, or a retro apron for a bridal gift, or a yodeling pickle. You never know when you'll need a yodeling pickle, but you will. They also have pretty, elaborately handmade cards, specialty wrapping paper, and pre-made bows that make the presentation of the gift rival whatever might be inside.

REAL MOTHER GOOSE
901 SW Yamhill St., 503/223-9510,
www.therealmothergoose.com
HOURS: Mon.-Thurs. 10 A.M.-5:30 P.M., Fri.-Sat. 10 A.M.-6 P.M., closed Sun.
Map 1

Part gallery and part retail shop, the Real Mother Goose has been a longtime staple in downtown Portland and in its other metro area locations. Whether you are just beginning to understand that a Gustav Klimt poster tacked to your wall with pushpins does not qualify as decorating or you are a serious collector, Real Mother Goose has pretty, distinctive elements in prices that range from $15 to several thousands of dollars. Whether it's ceramics, jewelry, woods, furnishings, fine art, blown glass, children's toys, or even wearable art, it's all here.

Gourmet Treats

Portland has a strong devotion to the Slow Food movement, which marries the enjoyment of food with a commitment to the community and the environment. When it comes to food, we like to take our time around here. Sometimes, that means making pasta from scratch or curing our own meats, but ultimately, we want our food to be delicious above all things. Portland is ripe with specialty shops that offer everything from picnic-friendly cheeses to salted chocolates and Northwest wines.

EDELWEISS
3119 SE 12th Ave., 503/238-4411, www.edelweissdeli.com
HOURS: Mon.-Sat. 9 A.M.-6 P.M., closed Sun.
Map 4

If you have spent any amount of time in Germany, Edelweiss will feel all too familiar to you: the narrow aisles filled with jars of mustard, pickles, and sauerkraut; the candy aisle with European sweets; the brusque, impatient service. Every inch of this store is crammed with sweets, treats, and authentic delicacies, many of which are made on-site, imported, or produced locally in the traditional European style. What's more, they have one of the best collections of imported European beers and wines in town,

Be sure to grab a number as you walk in the door. It gets crowded and the wait can be maddeningly long, but the selection in the deli case makes it all worthwhile. If you are a meat lover, don't be surprised if you get a little dizzy at the sight of all their handmade sausages, house-smoked meats, and house-cured bacon.

ELEPHANTS DELICATESSEN

115 NW 22nd Ave., 503/299-6304,
www.elephantsdeli.com
HOURS: Mon.-Sat. 7 A.M.-7:30 P.M., Sun.
9:30 A.M.-6:30 P.M.
Map 2

For Elephants, the word "delicatessen" doesn't even begin to cover it. They are part grocery, with an amazing array of cured meats, fine cheeses, olives, capers, anchovies, pickles, gourmet chocolates, and handcrafted caramels; but they are also a popular lunchtime

spot, catering company, and happy hour bar. It's a perfect place to stop and grab the makings for a simple gourmet picnic before you head out to Washington Park. Or check out the website and pre-order a basket with a perfectly paired bottle of Northwest wine.

FOOD FIGHT

1217 SE Stark St., 503/233-3910,
www.foodfightgrocery.com
HOURS: Daily 10 A.M.-6 P.M.
Map 4

This store is just one part of what is essentially a vegan strip mall. The veggie-centric grocery is next to Herbivore Clothing Company, and Sweet Pea Bakery, both of which share a desire to encourage a life free from the unnecessary use of animal products. Vegans and vegetarians can find everything from vegan health and fitness items to the delicious (locally made) NoFishGoFish soups and grab-and-go vegan nachos. You can also find a number of vegan household products, including shampoos, cleansers, and vegan cookbooks.

© GEOFFRY SMITH

A veritable chorus of cheeses awaits customers at Foster & Dobbs.

FOSTER & DOBBS

2518 NE 15th Ave., 503/284-1157,
www.fosteranddobbs.com
HOURS: Mon.-Sat. 11 A.M.-7 P.M., Sun. 11 A.M.-6 P.M.
Map 3

If Foster & Dobbs were a class, it would be called Gourmet 101. They have all the classics here, such as cheese, wine, chocolate, olives, and cured meats. If you are overwhelmed by the cheese selection, they can talk you through the flavor profiles, give you samples, and steer you toward the one that's perfect for you. Foster & Dobbs also holds regular classes that allow budding foodies to learn such necessary tasks as how to taste wine, make pickles, bake bread, use gourmet salts, and recognize a good port.

THE MEADOW

3731 N. Mississippi Ave., 503/228-4633,
HOURS: Sun.-Mon. 11 A.M.-6 P.M., Tues.-Fri. 10 A.M.-6 P.M.,
Sat. 10 A.M.-7 P.M.
Map 6

Salt takes on a whole new life at The Meadow, a boutique that specializes in gourmet sea salts, with a fine selection of chocolate, hard-to-find wines, bitters, and edible flowers such as apple blossoms and hibiscus. Before you do anything else, buy some of their salted chocolates, which hit the salty, rich, and sweet trifecta. Then, sample some of their alderwood-smoked salt or the Maboroshi Plum Salt. Ask for some advise on how to use the Vietnamese Pearl Sel Gris, or the Sel Rose curing salt, and you'll find that regular table salt is actually pretty harsh.

Before you leave, pick up a Himalayan Salt Plate, a pretty, translucent pink slab quarried straight from the Himalayan mountains that will revolutionize the way you cook.

PASTAWORKS

3735 SE Hawthorne Blvd., 503/232-1010,
www.pastaworks.com
HOURS: Mon.-Sat. 9:30 A.M.-7 P.M., Sun. 10 A.M.-7 P.M.
Map 4

For the denizens of Portland's Slow Food culture, a walk through Pastaworks is like food porn. Suddenly you are salivating, your pulse is racing, and you feel incredibly inspired to go home and cook something up. Maybe it's because of the fresh-made goat cheese ravioli, or maybe it's the lemon fig balsamic vinegar. Or, perhaps a gooey wedge of triple cream brie tips you over the edge as you consider pairing it with black truffle honey and pancetta. Whatever the source of your excitement is, Pastaworks has it. Of course, it's not terribly cheap, but then again, the good stuff rarely is.

PEARL SPECIALTY MARKET & SPIRITS

900 NW Lovejoy St. #140, 503/477-8604,
www.pearlspecialty.com
HOURS: Mon.-Sat. 10 A.M.-10 P.M., Sun. noon-7 P.M.
Map 2

Oregon's liquor laws can be pretty persnickety. You can't purchase hard alcohol in grocery stores, and the liquor stores close early and are often closed on Sundays. What's more, if you want to make a truly artisan-style cocktail with fancy bitters or gourmet olives, that usually means making several stops. Pearl Specialty Market & Spirits was given special permission by the Oregon Liquor Control Commission to be open seven days a week and maintain longer hours, as well as the right to sell things like chocolate, crackers, olives, cheese, caviar, cigars and champagne. Pearl Specialty also has an unbelievable selection of—get this—luxury water, in pretty, reusable decanters and Swarovski crystal–encrusted bottles.

SATURDAY FARMER'S MARKET

Portland State University in the South Park Blocks
between SW Harrison St. and SW Montgomery St.
HOURS: Apr.-Oct. Sat. 8:30 A.M.-2 P.M., Nov.-Dec. Sat.
9 A.M.-2 P.M.
Map 1

The biggest of many farmers markets in Portland, the Saturday market fills up the Park Blocks with as many as 250 produce stands, art booths, and food vendors. You can't get fruits, vegetables, and flowers any fresher than this, short of growing them yourself. The market is a great place to grab a bite to eat, listen to some music, or stock up on special handmade treats like fresh-smoked salmon from The Smokery, or lavender-infused jelly from Sundance Lavender Farm. For a special evening indulgence, pick up some of Rogue Creamery's world-class blue cheese, a bottle of Shy Chenin Blanc from Twist, and a Pearl Bakery baguette.

STEVE'S CHEESE

2323 NW Thurman St., 503/222-6014,
www.stevescheese.biz
HOURS: Mon.-Thurs. 11 A.M.-8 P.M., Fri.-Sat. 11 A.M.-6 P.M., closed Sun.
`Map 2`

Having grown up in a small Iowa farming community, Steve's Cheese owner Steve Jones has a deep appreciation for small, independent producers. Most of the cheeses he keeps on hand in his small Nob Hill shop are made by very small artisans. It's a much more hands-on approach that allows Jones to really get acquainted with the cheeses and their makers. Jones and his staff are knowledgeable and friendly and will assist you in choosing from the overwhelming array of choices, by asking you what you plan to eat or drink with your cheese and what your preferences are.

Vintage and Antiques

If you are looking for vintage treasures, there is no better destination than the Sellwood and Moreland neighborhood, better known as Antique Row. It's easy to lose a whole day there wandering up and down the sidewalks, sifting through memorabilia, costume jewelry, and curiosities. But Portland is full of places where everything old is new again—where you can find vintage fashions, old-school jewelry, and tchotchkes galore.

HOUSE OF VINTAGE

3315 SE Hawthorne Blvd., 503/236-1991,
www.houseofvintage.net
HOURS: Daily 11 A.M.-7 P.M.
`Map 4`

House of Vintage is a collective of more than 55 independent dealers all sharing over 13,000 square feet. This place is an absolute maze, but it is a wonderful cache of odds and ends. Give yourself plenty of time to explore, because you could easily spend hours wandering from room to room trying not to miss anything. Keep looking and you may just find a vintage lunchbox tucked into a curio cabinet, a kitschy table set for dinner with cute melamine dishes, or a diaphanous slip hanging from a wrought-iron gate. All you have to do is wade through the seemingly endless stacks of clothing, accessories, shoes, memorabilia, housewares, music, furniture, and tchotchkes.

MAGPIE

520 SW 9th Ave., 503/220-0920
HOURS: Mon.-Sat. noon-7 P.M., closed Sun.
`Map 1`

Near the heart of downtown is a darling little vintage shop where you can find that perfect get-up for a groovy 1960s-themed party, or a lovely *Mad Men*–style sheath dress. For all their style, and given the quality of items, the clothes at Magpie are remarkably affordable. In fact, you just might spend less on your dress or hat than you will on the martini you'll drink when you wear it. Magpie has a fantastic collection of vintage baubles, cigarette holders, and hats for the ladies, as well as a terrific collection of men's suits, vests, shoes, and coats. Before you leave, take a look at the jewelry selection up front. It is outstanding, and contains a number of new, modern pieces and many beautiful vintage pieces for both men and women.

NOUN

3300 SE Belmont St., 503/235-0078
HOURS: Tues.-Sat. 10 A.M.-7 P.M., Sun. 10 A.M.-5 P.M.
`Map 4`

Noun's motto is "a person's place for things," which is both cute and accurate. You may not *need* many of the things you'll find here, but you will want them. Check out the brand-new, retro-refrigerators that come in an old-fashioned palette of colors. Browse through the fun, eclectic mix of antique furniture, locally made jewelry, cards, buttons, and unique vintage items.

While you are there, swing by the back of the store and pick up a little tasty treat for yourself. Noun shares a space with Saint Cupcake, which specializes in you-know-what.

Pet Supplies

Portlanders love their pets, so much so that it is not uncommon to see a dog dining alongside his owner at a sidewalk café, or a cat being pushed through the grocery store in a just-for-pets stroller. Knowing this, local restaurants and bakeries began creating menus for their canine friends and baking up pet-friendly nibbles to hand out to four-legged patrons who stop in. Not to be outdone, boutiques began to spring up all over town offering high-end treats; locally made, recycled cat condos; organic beds; and even doggy-and-me fashions for the folks who want to take things that far.

Four-legged shoppers at LexiDog can be everything from a ballerina to a biker.

© HOLLYANNA MCCOLLOM

FUREVER PETS
1902 NE Broadway St., 503/282-4225,
www.fureverpets.com
HOURS Mon.-Fri. 10 A.M.-8 P.M., Sat. 10 A.M.-7 P.M.,
Sun. 10 A.M.-6 P.M.
Map 3

Whether you are shopping for cats or dogs, here you'll find a fun, whimsical selection of things that are reasonably priced. While most pet stores lean heavily on dog supplies, Furever Pets has the best selection of colors, toys, condos, and treats for kitties. Furever uses local products whenever they can, like their locally made catnip pillows, treats, and collars. Stop by the bakery counter at the front and pick out a handmade goodie for your dog, or check out the high-end handbags to carry around your small four-legged friend. The staff is quiet knowledgeable and loves pets. If you bring your dog with you, they will more than likely give him a treat. But don't worry, they will ask first.

LEXIDOG BOUTIQUE AND SOCIAL CLUB
416 NW 10th Ave., 503/243-6200, www.lexidog.com
HOURS: Mon.-Fri. 10 A.M.-6 P.M., Sat. 9 A.M.-6 P.M., Sun.
10 A.M.-4 P.M.
Map 2

At LexiDog Boutique and Social Club the standards are upped because they believe that every dog deserves to be spoiled. They host playgroups, birthday parties, and "Yappy Hours" when dogs and humans can mingle and drink wine (or water) while nibbling on snacks. The boutique has everything you could possibly want to pamper your pet, like comfy beds, bowls, and homemade treats that look good enough for human consumption. They also have rainwear, cozy hoodies, jeweled collars, tutus, and leather jackets. The shop caters to all sizes and breeds, but it's the small dogs that definitely have their day in this Pearl District shop.

URBAN FAUNA

235 NW Park Ave., 503/223-4602,
www.urbanfauna.com
HOURS: Mon.-Fri. 10 A.M.-7 P.M., Sat. 9 A.M.-6 P.M., Sun. noon-5 P.M.

`Map 2`

For the pet owner interested in unique items and accessories, try Urban Fauna. This store specializes in difficult-to-find, high-quality items from around the world. Urban Fauna offers obedience classes that can turn excessively energetic and unruly dogs into upright citizens, and they also have doggy daycare and grooming services for pets whose owners are on the go. They stock a number of chew-friendly toys, comfortable leashes, and cozy beds, as well as a good selection of high-quality food.

Not to worry about little Fluffy, though, as products in this store go way beyond man's best friend and cater to the needs of cats, birds, fish, and reptiles as well.

Shopping Centers and Districts

If you are looking to spend a rainy day indoors, or want to hit the mother lode of sales tax–free shops in one location, you may want to visit one of the city's shopping centers instead of wandering the streets. Here you will find all the major department stores and retail chains, as well as a few locally based boutiques.

SHOPPING CENTERS

BRIDGEPORT VILLAGE

7455 SW Bridgeport Rd., Tigard, 503/968-8940,
www.bridgeport-village.com
HOURS: Mon.-Thurs. 10 A.M.-8 P.M., Fri.-Sat. 10 A.M.-9 P.M., Sun. 11 A.M.-6 P.M.

`Map 7`

An upscale outdoor mall just 10 miles south of downtown, Bridgeport Village is a sprawling array of upscale shopping, dining, and entertainment. The 500,000-square-foot mall has popular retailers like Anthropologie, BCBG, Crate & Barrel, Urban Outfitters, and Cole Haan, plus a number of Portland-based boutiques. Parking can be a challenge here, but they do offer valet service for just $4 near the main parking garage.

LLOYD CENTER

2201 Lloyd Ctr., 503/282-2511,
www.lloydcentermall.com
HOURS: Mon.-Sat. 10 A.M.-9 P.M., Sun. 11 A.M.-6 P.M.

`Map 3`

On the north side of the river, you'll find Lloyd Center, a three-level indoor mall centered around an ice skating rink. You will find a number of major department stores here, such as Macy's, Nordstrom, and Sears, plus two major discount retailers (Marshall's and Ross Dress for Less). While you are there, drop by Captain Henry's on the bottom floor next to the rink. Pirates have a big following in Portland and this pirate-themed store takes things to the extreme.

PIONEER PLACE MALL

Four blocks bounded by SW Morrison St., SW 5th Ave., SW Taylor St., and SW 3rd Ave.
HOURS: Mon.-Sat. 10 A.M.-8 P.M., closed Sun.

`Map 1`

Inside downtown's side-by-side shopping towers, Pioneer Place, you will find a fairly walkable mall that houses such upscale retailers as Ann Taylor, Juicy Couture, Betsey Johnson, and Coach, as well as some affordable favorites like

Forever 21, the Gap, and J. Crew. There is a food court on the bottom floor and sky bridges over the streets to carry you between the two buildings or over to Saks Fifth Avenue next door.

SHOPPING DISTRICTS

Each Portland neighborhood has its own personality. From the polish of downtown Portland's Pioneer Mall to the vintage quirkiness of Southeast, there is something for everyone, providing you know where to look. Since most every establishment outside of the shopping centers is independently run, scoping out the gems can be a bit of a challenge. Pick up one of the free weekly papers (at most coffee shops and street corners) to find out what sales and events are happening that week, or check the resources at the end of this book for websites that offer further insight.

ALBERTA ARTS DISTRICT
Alberta Street between NE 12th Ave. and NE 33rd Ave.
Map 3

Sprinkled with galleries and artsy boutiques, Alberta Street is a perfect neighborhood to hit when you want to find something unique and inspiring. Once a month, when the street hosts an art walk called Last Thursday, these shops throw open their doors and invite guests to partake in special discounts, treats, and meet-and-greet opportunities with designers, artists, and special guests. Head over to Garnish, where local designer Erica Lurie displays her flattering feminine line, or paint a pot at Mimosa Studios.

It will take a bit of walking to find all the great boutiques along this strip, as they are scattered along a 20-block spread, but the street is always alive and vibrant with activity. If you are not a fan of crowds, avoid Last Thursday altogether and come in the afternoon when things are decidedly less chaotic.

DOWNTOWN
Bounded by W. Burnside to the north, I-405 to the east and south, and the Willamette River to the west
Map 1

Shopping in downtown Portland is remarkably

accessible, thanks to the proximity of most places and the affordable parking options. There are Smart Park garages located all over downtown where you can park for about $1.50 per hour and ample street parking for shorter trips. It is best to head near SW Yamhill between SW 3rd and SW 4th Avenues, where there are a number of parking options adjacent to the Pioneer Mall and other local shops. Hop on the MAX or the Streetcar if you want to venture to the west end of Downtown or the Pearl District.

HAWTHORNE AND BELMONT
SE Hawthorne Blvd. between SE 11th Ave. and 55th, SE Belmont St. between SE 31st Ave. and 60th Ave.
Map 4

Over on SE Hawthorne and SE Belmont Avenues, the vibe is laid-back and independent. This is the area where Portland's counterculture has put down its bohemian roots, opening up funky coffeehouses, indie music stores, and hip and inexpensive clothing stores. Weird isn't weird on these parallel streets (separated by five blocks), it's the standard. While Belmont appeals with its sweet charm and quiet devil-may-care attitude, Hawthorne is a bit more like San Francisco's Haight-Ashbury with its mash-up of hippies and hipsters.

NW 23RD AND NW 21ST AVENUE
NW 23rd Ave. and NW 21st Ave. between W. Burnside and NW Thurman St.
Map 2

Block-for-block, this district is Portland's prime shopping area. The Alphabet District is packed from A to Z (actually, from B to T is more accurate) with unique boutiques and a few high-end chain stores. Begin at West Burnside Avenue, where you will find Cost Plus World Market and Elephant's Delicatessen. Stroll down past Urban Outfitters, Restoration Hardware, and Pottery Barn to NW Glisan where the street really kicks into gear. Try to hit one side of the street and then double back to catch the other side before you head a few blocks over to NW 21st Avenue.

THE PEARL DISTRICT

Bounded by the Willamette River to the north,
W. Burnside to the The Pearl
Map 2

High-end boutiques, sophisticated salons, and
fashionable cafés mix together to make these
streets infinitely charismatic, particularly during the monthly art walk, First Thursday. This
is where you will find a number of Portland's
hottest boutiques, like Moule, Cheeky B,
Relish, and Nolita. It's also the home of the
iconic Powell's City of Books.

Shop for shoes at Imelda's and Louie's or
explore the art and street fashion of Lizard
Lounge. Don't worry if you get overwhelmed;
you can rest as often as you like in one of the
many cafés or martini lounges.

SELLWOOD AND MORELAND

Bounded by Highway 99W and McLoughlin Blvd. to the
north, the Portland city limit to the south, Highway 99E
to the east, and the Willamette River to the west
Map 5

Originally a city of its own, the Sellwood–
Moreland neighborhood was annexed back
in the 1890s, but still retains much of its
nostalgic allure. From the nation's oldest
operational amusement park, Oaks Park, to
the collection of shops that have given this
neighborhood the nickname Antique Row,
Sellwood–Moreland keeps a firm grip on the
past. Some two-dozen antique and vintage
stores populate 13th Avenue in Sellwood,
while West Moreland is home to a number
of antique malls.

HOTELS

If the most important things you look for in a hotel are a place to crash and a place to keep your things, your options are pretty unlimited in Portland. There are a number of reliable chains surrounding the airport that can be very affordable, particularly if you will be renting a car and don't mind navigating the freeways to get into town. Whether you prefer luxurious 5-star accommodations, the intimacy of a bed-and-breakfast, or want to meet some locals through a couch-hopping network, Portland's got a spot for you to lay your head.

Not surprisingly, the greatest concentration of hotels can be found downtown. After all, this is where most of Portland's public transportation system converges, where a number of performing arts companies perform every night, and where much of the city's commercial business takes place. Plus, with Portland State University, Oregon Health and Sciences University, and Lewis and Clark College all in the Southwest sector of town, downtown hotels are a particularly hot commodity, especially for visiting families and prospective students. For that reason, you will find everything from inexpensive motor lodge–style places to residential inns and luxury suites.

The best choice is really a matter of preference. Portland is home to a large collection of boutique-style hotels that offer an alternative to the occasional homogeneity of large chain hotel groups, as well as a peek at Portland's distinctive personality. Whether you're an artist, a foodie, a wine lover, or a rock and roll enthusiast, chances are there's a hotel that will feel like home (only, you know, better).

COURTESTY OF JUPITER HOTEL

HIGHLIGHTS

LOOK FOR 🌙 TO FIND RECOMMENDED HOTELS.

🌙 **Best Place to Snuggle with Your Four-Legged Friend:** If you travel with your dog, the pet-friendly **Hotel Monaco** is a good bet for keeping you both blissfully at ease – even employing an adopted canine as Pet Relations Manager to welcome guests of all sizes (page 153).

🌙 **Best Place to Feel Richer Than You Are:** One of the city's only 5-star hotels, **The Nines** is housed in the historic Meier & Frank building and outfitted with amazing art. The rooms, simultaneously cozy and chic, appear like they just stepped out of a Tiffany's blue box (page 153).

🌙 **Best Place to Fall Asleep in Class:** Once a rundown elementary school, **Kennedy School** is a real trip down memory lane. The classrooms have been converted into sweet,

affordable bedrooms, chalkboards still included (page 156).

🌙 **Most Charming Hotel:** A pretty little craftsman-style home in the popular Hawthorne and Belmont area, the friendly **Bluebird Guesthouse** offers an unfussy welcome (page 157).

🌙 **Best Hotel to Party All Night:** If Studio 54 were a hotel in Portland, it would be the **Jupiter Hotel,** a sleek and modern urban lodge where the parties often spill out into the courtyard (page 158).

🌙 **Best Dive Motel:** Not exactly known for luxury accommodations, **The Palms Motor Hotel** is to hotels what Pabst Blue Ribbon is to beer: simple, charmingly trashy, and iconic (page 158).

HOTELS

COURTESY OF THE JUPITER HOTEL

The Jupiter Hotel is positively pulsing with energy, and you are likely to see as many locals as out-of-towners spilling out of the sleek, high-design rooms.

PRICE KEY

$ Less than $75

$$ $75-150

$$$ $150-250

The rates can vary a lot by season, with the months between May and October often considered the high season. If you are not limited to a particular time for traveling, April can be affordable and the coldest days of the year have usually passed. The same is true of October and November, when the weather is still fairly mild and the rates have dropped. December, January, and February are great times to take advantage of low rates and super-saver specials, but these months usually bring with them the most inclement weather.

With bed-and-breakfasts, you can almost always get the best rate by calling directly instead of booking online. For hotels, it's best to check online rates and compare them against Hotwire (www.hotwire.com), Priceline (www.priceline.com), and Expedia (www.expedia.com). Online rates are often as much as half the regular rate, but be cautious because some hotels set aside their smaller or noisier rooms for online bookings. If you are concerned about it, call ahead.

Downtown
Map 1

ACE HOTEL **$**
1022 SW Stark St., 503/228-2277, www.acehotel.com

Ace Hotel, on the brink of downtown and the Pearl, has one of the most photographed lobbies in town. Whether it is for a fashion shoot, professional headshots, engagement photos, or an impromptu photo op with friends, the lobby just reeks of coolness. Friendly and affordable, this art-meets-music hotel is especially popular with creative professionals and international travelers. The rooms themselves are achingly hip—some even come equipped with turntables and vintage vinyl records! With enormous murals painted by hot local artists, vintage furniture, clawfoot tubs, flat-screen TVs, and custom-made Pendleton blankets, each room is unique. If you're a light sleeper, bring your earplugs or ask for a room away from the street.

THE BENSON HOTEL **$$**
309 SW Broadway, 503/228-2000,
www.bensonhotel.com

Simon Benson, a Portland lumber baron, visionary, and philanthropist (and the namesake for the all those sidewalk drinking fountains, the Benson Bubblers) opened The Benson (then The New Oregon Hotel) in 1913. It was a grand spectacle with a French Second Empire glazed terra-cotta and brick exterior, arched lobby windows, and mansard roof with dormers. The interior was no less grand, with carved Circassian walnut imported from the forests of Imperial Russia. Over the years, this hotel has seen a number of renovations and expansions, but still maintains remarkable beauty and opulence. The hotel has played host to a number of celebrities, sports figures, and politicians—and in fact, has bedded almost every U.S. president since Harry S. Truman.

COURTYARD BY MARRIOTT-CITY CENTER **$$**
550 SW Oak St., 503/505-5000,
www.marriott.com/pdxpc

Opened in May 2009, this 256-room Courtyard by Marriott enterprise was all too recently a vacated bank building. But after a major renovation, the new building is sleek, stylish, and designed to meet Gold LEED certification. So, it's a Marriott, but with a distinctly Portland twist. Furthermore, all of the artwork in the hotel was created by local artists. Paintings of local scenes adorn the hallways and lobby, and each guestroom features an original ceramic piece made by one of the graduates of the Oregon College of Art and Craft. The hotel offers many of the regular comforts one would expect at a Marriott, like smoke-free rooms, wireless Internet access, business services, complimentary lobby coffee, and valet parking.

EMBASSY SUITES DOWNTOWN 💲💲

319 SW Pine St., 503/279-9000,
www.embassysuites.com

If you have been to am Embassy Suites before, this one is going to seem just a little bit different. For starters, it is housed in the historic Multnomah Hotel building, one of the largest and most magnificent of its time. Built in 1912, in its heyday the Multnomah hosted a number of U.S. presidents, a Romanian queen, Charles Lindberg—and even Elvis Presley in 1957. During the 1960 presidential campaign, John Kennedy gave an impromptu speech here. The building was purchased and renovated 1995 to operate as an Embassy Suites with upscale, all-suite guestrooms, complimentary cooked-

to-order breakfasts, and afternoon manager's receptions with free alcoholic and non-alcoholic beverages and appetizers.

GOVERNOR HOTEL 💲💲💲

614 SW 11th Ave., 503/224-1236,
www.governorhotel.com

This historic hotel was built in 1909 and originally called the Seward Hotel, a "hotel of quiet elegance." With its ornate facade complete with art deco gargoyles and an interior that boasts Native American-inspired themes, rustic chandeliers, and rich wood textures, it certainly is elegant. The building was added to the National Register of Historic Places in 1985 and has served as the set for a number of films, including Madonna's *Body of Evidence* and *My Own Private Idaho*.

HEATHMAN HOTEL 💲💲

1001 SW Broadway, 503/241-4100,
www.portland.heathmanhotel.com

When it comes to luxury, the Heathman is really trying to corner the market. French

HOTELS

COURTESY OF HOTEL DELUXE

Classic Hollywood elegance is the name of the game at Hotel deLuxe, especially in the Marlene Dietrich suite.

press coffeepots and electric kettles in every room with Peet's coffee and loose-leaf teas? Complimentary L'Occitane products? MP3 players and free Internet? Blackout drapes? A menu that lets you choose your own mattress, with options like TempurPedic, pillow-top, and the oh-so-European featherbed? The historic hotel has a number of elegant touches and is popular for travelers looking to take in a little culture, especially since it's located mere steps away from the Portland Center for Performing Arts, the Portland Art Museum, and Arlene Schnitzer Concert Hall.

HOTEL DELUXE 🕏🕏

729 SW 15th Ave., 866/895-2094,
www.hoteldeluxeportland.com

If you have ever imagined yourself Bette Davis or Cary Grant, the Hotel deLuxe, at the edge of downtown Portland, has got your number. The former Mallory Hotel, which was built in 1912, has been carefully and respectfully restored, but still evokes the era of Hollywood's Golden Age. With richly detailed high ceilings, elegant columns, and crystal chandeliers, the hotel has a sophisticated elegance and a romantic ambiance. Each floor has a different theme based on Old Hollywood personalities and the rooms come equipped with luxurious amenities and menus that allow you to select your own pillow, choose an iPod pre-loaded with the music of your choice, and even order up a Torah if you prefer it over the Bible.

HOTEL LUCIA 🕏🕏

400 SW Broadway, 503/225-1717,
www.hotellucia.com

Throughout Hotel Lucia—in the guestrooms, lobby, and halls—you will find Pulitzer Prize–winning photographer David Hume Kennerly's odd and intriguing work. This downtown boutique hotel has 127 smallish guestrooms, each smartly decorated and appointed with pillow-top mattresses, high-threadcount duvets, pillow menus, CD players, plush robes, 24-hour room service, and Aveda bath products. If you are

COURTESY OF HOTEL MODERA

The elegant lobby of Hotel Modera, appointed with black walnut floors and Italian marble, shows little trace of its past as a cheap chain hotel.

traveling with a dog, you will find Lucia well equipped to host. The fourth floor is devoted to travelers with four-legged friends. Two notes of caution, however: The wireless Internet costs about $14 a day (but the staff is occasionally willing to waive that fee if you ask); Also, Lucia is an adults-only hotel, so guests must be 21 years or older.

HOTEL MODERA $$

515 SW Clay St., 503/484-1084,
www.hotelmodera.com

The fairly new Hotel Modera offers a comfortable, modern, attractive place to stay for people visiting Portland State University who wish to be downtown, but not smack dab in the middle of it. The beds are comfortable with pillow-topped mattresses, nice linens, and a fur throw that almost makes the whole stay worthwhile. Be sure to make use of the Tarocco blood orange bath products; they smell so good, you'll wish they were edible. There's a business center as well as free Wi-Fi, which works well in the hotel's pretty courtyard. They don't have a gym on-site, but will give you complimentary passes to the nearby 24-Hour Fitness if you are interested in working out.

◖ HOTEL MONACO $$

506 SW Washington St., 503/222-0001,
www.monaco-portland.com

This artsy hotel can be a lot of fun if you like art, wine, or free stuff. Every evening in the hotel lobby, they host wine reception with paints and canvases (in case you get inspired). Send your shoes out for a complimentary shoeshine while you take advantage of the free bike rental to explore the city. Work out in the 24-hour gym or browse the free Internet all night, knowing that the morning brings complimentary Starbucks coffee and tea service with free newspapers. If you bring your dog, there are a bevy of free things for him, too, like spring water and treats, a bed to sleep in, and "Dispose-a-scoop" bags. Didn't bring your dog? That's okay, Monaco will lend you a goldfish to keep you company during your stay (for free).

HOTEL VINTAGE PLAZA $$

422 SW Broadway, 503/228-1212,
www.vintageplaza.com

Wine lovers will feel right at home in this boutique hotel, which offers wine-themed accommodations in a majestic, 1894 downtown building. Each of the 117 rooms is named after an Oregon winery and decorated with rich color schemes reminiscent of Tuscany. Book one of the Garden Spa rooms if you can and you will enjoy a private patio with a two-person hot tub overlooking the city. The Starlight Room is another treat, with giant conservatory windows that allow you to stargaze while you sleep (assuming the weather is clear). Of course, staying in a wine-themed hotel has other perks, as well. In addition to having access to a remarkably extensive wine cellar for the attached Italian eatery, Pazzo, the hotel hosts a nightly wine reception where you can sample some of the Pacific Northwest's best.

MARK SPENCER HOTEL $$

409 SW 11th Ave., 503/224-3293,
www.markspencer.com

Centrally located between a number of downtown arts organizations, the Mark Spencer bills itself as Portland's "Hotel to the Arts." In fact, it's the hotel that a number of visiting artists take up residence in while performing in the city. The rates are remarkably reasonable given the hotel's proximity to both the hub of downtown and the Pearl District, and they also give you the opportunity to "name your own rate." Simply submit a proposed price and they will let you know if they can swing it. If they can't, they'll let you know when that rate might be available or will offer you the best price available for the date you would like to come.

◖ THE NINES $$$

525 SW Morrison St., 877/229-9995,
www.starwoodhotels.com

When your car pulls up to The Nines, you may wonder if there has been a mistake. Surely, you are not staying at Macy's. In fact, this 331-room luxury hotel occupies the top nine floors of the historic Meier & Frank Building, and

HOTELS

Macy's (which purchased the building from Meier & Frank) fills the building's lower five levels. The word of the day at The Nines is "posh," and that goes from the valet service to the bed that seems to swallow you in a heap of European linens. Interior rooms overlook the atrium, which is interesting if you like to people-watch, but otherwise rather ho-hum. Book an exterior room and you can enjoy views of the city and Pioneer Courthouse Square.

THE RIVERPLACE HOTEL $$

1510 SW Harbor Way, 503/228-3233,
www.riverplacehotel.com

The RiverPlace Hotel is especially suited for business travelers who want to be downtown, but need both a quiet space to work and a comfortable space to sleep. There's a 24-hour business center with computers and laptop ports, plus access to a printer, copier, and fax machine. The rooms are packed with a number of creature comforts, like 37-inch flat screen TVs, in-room DVD and CD players, L'Occitane bath products, plush bathrobes, and a coffeemaker with Stumptown coffee and Tazo tea. They also come equipped with complimentary high-speed Internet, a spacious Craftsman-style work desk, and an ergonomic office chair for finishing those big reports. Furthermore, the hotel is located right on the waterfront, which is a bit more peaceful than downtown and is a great place to jog before you head out to begin your day.

Northwest and the Pearl District   Map 2

THE INN AT NORTHRUP STATION $$

2025 NW Northrup St., 503/224-0543,
www.northrupstation.com

This hotel looks unassuming from the outside, but as soon as you enter you see that it is not your average hotel. First of all, it looks as if it were designed by Willy Wonka, right down to the giant glass jars filled with colorful candies that adorn all the tables in the lobby. The staff is friendly and energetic (perhaps due to prolonged access to all that candy?) and the entire place feels modern, fun, and trippy. If you're venturing out, the Inn at Northrup Station will provide free tickets for the Streetcar, which can take you downtown (where you can connect with the MAX to go practically anywhere) This is an all-suite hotel and most rooms come equipped with a kitchen—though there are plenty of Alphabet District restaurants nearby. Continental breakfast is free and usually includes pastries, cereal, fruit, bagels, and Tillamook yogurt.

PORTLAND INTERNATIONAL GUESTHOUSE $

2185 NW Flanders St., 503/224-0500,
www.pdxguesthouse.com

This sweet little guesthouse in the heart of the Alphabet District is a great place to stay if you're looking to save some money, but don't want to be far from the bustling heart of the city. With the five bed-and-breakfast-style private rooms that share two full bathrooms, it is a popular place for families who want to stay together. Here you will find free wireless Internet; a sitting room with a fireplace; a kitchen area with free coffee, tea, juice, and cereals in the morning; and Steven and Thomas, two of the nicest hosts in town, who live on-site and are regular travelers themselves.

SILVER CLOUD INN $$$

2426 NW Vaughn St., 503/242-2400,
www.silvercloud.com

Although this hotel is referred to as Silver Cloud Portland–Downtown, it is at the brink of Northwest Portland—about two miles away from downtown at the industrial edge of the Alphabet District. If you're a light sleeper, you may want to ask for a room away from busy Vaughn Street, but otherwise, the location is away from the bustle of the city, yet easily accessible by freeway and about six blocks from the main shopping and dining areas of NW 23rd Avenue. It's an attractive and comfortable

COURTESY OF INN AT NORTHRUP STATION

One of only a few hotels in the NW 23rd district, The Inn at Northrup Station is colorful and well-appointed with a fully equipped kitchen or wet bar in every room.

place. Silver Cloud has moderately spacious, clean rooms and mini-suites with free Wi-Fi, 42-inch plasma televisions, refrigerators, coffeemakers, and microwaves.

Northeast   Map 3

BLUE PLUM INN BED & BREAKFAST $

2022 NE 15th Ave., www.bluepluminn.com

Blue Plum Inn is a pretty, comfortable, and well-appointed house in Irvington that is just a short walk away from all the shops and restaurants that NE Broadway has to offer. There are two couple-sized guest rooms available and a suite that can be rented as one or two bedroom, accommodating up to four people. All rooms are equipped with a private bath, air conditioning, cable television, and bathrobes. Make sure to call to book your reservation for the best possible rates and get to know your hosts, Suzanne and Jonathan, because they are the real stars of the show. Breakfast is notoriously spectacular, and always made with fresh, local, organic ingredients.

DOUBLETREE LLOYD CENTER $$

1000 NE Multnomah St., 503/281-6111, www.doubletree.com

The best thing about this Lloyd District hotel is its location (and the warm chocolate chip cookies you get upon arrival). It's just across the street from Lloyd Center, where you'll find a number of department stores, boutiques, and dining options. It is also located right on the Red and Blue MAX lines, which means you can take the MAX directly from the airport to your hotel, or hop the train and head downtown, to the Rose Quarter, or to the Oregon Convention Center and never have to worry about finding parking. The rooms are, for the most part, spacious, clean, and comfortable, but book though an online discount website

COUCH SURFING PDX

Couch Surfing (www.couchsurfing.org) is an international non-profit hospitality exchange system that started in 2004. Couch Surfing is a web-based system that allows people to network with others who are willing to host strangers in their home for the duration of or a portion of their visit.

Portlanders are known for being fairly hospitable, so it is not surprising that the city is home to many surfers and "surfees." With well over 5,000 active members, it is the sixth most active city on the site. The city is positively brimming with options for the frugal traveler who doesn't mind spending some time getting to know a stranger. It's a great way to save money on your visit and get a local's insider perspective.

It is free to become a Couch Surfing member, but you have to register online and adhere to a mild security check, which basically means that you will be asked to submit personal references. There is also a personal vouching system, which allows previously vouched-for surfers to then vouch for others.

You are not required to host if you would like to surf, although it is strongly encouraged. The cost of staying is free, but in most cases, you are expected to provide your own food or at least compensate your host for the food you consumed. Usually, a stay is set up when a potential surfer logs in to post details about where they want to stay. People can then respond if they are in the area and feel they have space available. Negotiations are then made and details are agreed upon between the host and surfer prior to the latter's arrival.

While you are staying with your host family, it is best to pitch in as much as possible with dishes, cooking, and tidying up, although some hosts may not require it.

if you can because the difference in price can be astonishing.

EVERETT STREET GUESTHOUSE ❸

2306 NE Everett St., 503/230-0211,
www.everettstreetguesthouse.com

If the idea of a good bed-and-breakfast brings up images of fussy lace doilies, eerie smiling porcelain dolls, and teddy bears in tea hats, this is not the place for you. Everett Street Guesthouse is decked out in the style of a true Portlander, elegant, eclectic, and not the least bit pretentious. There are two rooms in the main house: the Wellfleet Room, which sleeps two people, and Sophie's room, a single. You can also rent the studio cottage, which is separate from the house and features a kitchenette, tiled shower, washer and dryer, television, wireless Internet, private patio garden, and a shared deck with the main house. Breakfast is not included in the price of your stay in the cottage, but you can add it for $7 per person. Everett Street has a two-night minimum for both the cottage and the other rooms. The proprietors also require a 50 percent deposit to book the room, and prefer cash or personal checks.

◖ KENNEDY SCHOOL ❸

5736 NE 33rd Ave., 503/249-3983,
www.kennedyschool.com

If you have ever fallen asleep in class, you know that it can be uncomfortable and embarrassing, but thanks to the McMenamin brothers—who have managed to build an entire business around salvaging old structures and turning them into cool pubs, theaters, and hotels—you're actually encouraged to do so here. This elementary school, which was built in 1915, was saved from probable destruction when the brothers decided to turn it into a fantastic hotel. Now the old classrooms have been stripped of their desks (but not their chalkboards) in exchange for comfy beds. Work out your kinks playing basketball or dodgeball in the gymnasium. Watch a movie in the old auditorium while sipping beer and noshing on pizza, or take a dip in the soaking pool. If you still feel guilty for nodding off, you can always send yourself to the Detention Bar for a little redemption.

LION & ROSE VICTORIAN BED & BREAKFAST ⑤⑤

1810 NE 15th Ave., 503/287-9245, www.lionrose.com

This breathtaking Queen Anne–style Victorian inn sits in Portland's historic Irvington District, surrounded by a number of stately Victorian homes. Each room has a distinctive, romantic flair, like the stately Edwardian bed frame and furniture you'll find in the Starina room, or the pretty, sun-drenched, turret-style sitting area in the Lavonna Room. Each room has a private bathroom, with the exception of the Avandel room, which has a dedicated bathroom and clawfoot soaking tub down the hall. The Lion & Rose offers two-course breakfasts and light refreshments in the afternoon or evening. If you're traveling with family you can opt for the Victorian Apartment, which sleeps up to six, has a kitchenette, dining table, bathroom, washer and dryer, wireless Internet, television, and an electric fireplace. The apartment will run you about $124–234 per night.

PORTLAND'S WHITE HOUSE ⑤⑤

1914 NE 22nd Ave., 503/287-7131, www.portlandswhitehouse.com

If you find yourself peeking around the corners to catch a glimpse of Barack Obama, don't be surprised. No, the 44th president hasn't stayed there, but the mansion does bear more than a passing resemblance to the "official" White House. But the grand portico and circular drive are just the beginning. The five guest rooms in the main house and the three rooms in the adjoining Carriage House are lavishly and meticulously decorated, each one a grand affair with fabulous linens, along with four-poster beds or magnificent canopies. The proprietors seem to go to painstaking lengths to ensure that your stay is superb, so if you like a hands-off approach, either mention it in advance or stay somewhere else.

HOTELS

Southeast   Map 4

⟨ BLUEBIRD GUESTHOUSE ⑤

3517 SE Division St., 503/238-4333, www.bluebirdguesthouse.com

This quaint and pretty guesthouse has seven guest rooms, each named for a different author, though not theme decorated. The one exception is the Elliott Smith room, which is (not surprisingly) located in the basement. Bluebird is located in Southeast Portland, a healthy walk from the adorable Clinton Street neighborhood and Hawthorne District. The decor combines vintage charm with modern character, lending to the place a cozy, at-home feeling that seems miles away from hotel life. Guests are allowed access to the sizable kitchen and refrigerator, with the understanding that they are responsible for their own clean-up. Robes, towels, washcloths, soap, shampoo and a hair dryer are all provided, and there is an iron and coin-op laundry machine in the basement.

THE CECILIA ⑤⑤

1334 SE 14th Ave., 206/245-5974, www.thececilia.com

If you are planning an extended stay or traveling with a small group, you may want to skip the hotels altogether. The Cecilia is a private condo in Southeast near the Hawthorne area with close access to downtown. It rents for $170–215 a night or $1,000–1,400 a week, depending on the time of year and number of people in your party. The beautifully decorated two-bedroom condo sleeps four, has a living room with a widescreen television, a washer and dryer, gourmet kitchen and dining room, a soaker tub, and a large covered porch. It's a good alternative if you want to avoid hotels but want more privacy than is typical at bed-and-breakfasts.

HAWTHORNE HOSTEL ⑤

3031 SE Hawthorne Blvd., 866/447-3031, www.portlandhostel.org

If you prefer a bohemian approach, Hawthorne

Hostel might be right up your alley. Located in the heart of one of the city's most youthful and dynamic neighborhoods, the Hawthorne Hostel is actively involved in the community, with potluck brunches every Sunday and summertime open mics or "bike in" movies in the backyard. The upkeep of the place tends to vary depending on the current staff, but everyone is friendly and easygoing. You can reserve a private room for about $48–58 a night or a shared dorm space for about $19–28. Sheets are included, but you'll need to make your bed every day and strip the sheets when you leave (it's a hostel, remember?); and you must pay extra to rent towels, so it's wise to bring your own. Also, it should be noted that there's a housecat. Though it remains in the common areas and is a short-haired cat, if you are sensitive to pet fur, you may want to skip this one.

JUPITER HOTEL $

800 E. Burnside St., 503/230-9200,
www.jupiterhotel.com

Oh, the Jupiter Hotel. It's the inner Southeast hub of the late-night crowd. It's the irresistible black sheep of Portland accommodations. It's not always as perfect as your fantasies might make it, but it comes darn close. It should be noted that the Jupiter is best experienced as a place to avoid sleeping. Throw your door open and interact with the other guests, who are likely to be spilling out of their own rooms and partying between the hotel and the attached Doug Fir lounge. The decor here is modern and sleek and the attitude is definitely no-frills fun. Those wanting to shake things up can take advantage of the Love & Lust package, which includes treats from Spartacus leathers, or enjoy VIP entrance to a concert at Doug Fir and two free drinks. Boozing all night and can't make it home? Jupiter has a special after-midnight check-in rate (subject to availability) where you can literally "get a room" for $59 plus tax.

North Portland   Map 6

THE PALMS MOTOR HOTEL $

3801 N. Interstate Ave., 503/287-5788,
www.palmsmotel.com

To be clear, The Palms motel is not exactly luxury accommodations, but if you appreciate even a little bit of kitsch, this little dive is calling your name. The neon sign, alive with monkeys and palm trees singing the praises of free HBO and Starz, is one of the most photographed signs in town. For all its tropical silliness, the Palms is practically a Portland icon. The motel is not all that bad, so long as you don't require high-threadcount linens and turn-down services, plus it's right on the Yellow MAX line, so access to downtown and the rest of the city is mere steps away. There's even a lime green "honeymoon suite" complete with a Jacuzzi tub for less than $100 a night—although, booking it for your *actual* honeymoon might send you straight into annulment. Best

© HOLLYANNA MCCOLLOM

The Palms Motor Hotel isn't exactly world-class, but the sign alone is worth the stay.

try booking something swankier for your first go around.

WHITE EAGLE HOTEL $

836 N. Russell St., 503/282-6810,
www.mcmenamins.com

The White Eagle is another McMenamins salvage job, but has the distinction of bearing one of the most sordid and storied pasts in Portland history. The legend dates back to the early 1900s, when the venue was commonly called "Bucket of Blood." Dock workers and railroad men would apparently stop in for a little pool, cigars, poker, and liquor, and if they played their cards right, a turn in the brothel or opium den upstairs. The hotel now rents inexpensive rooms (about $40–60 a night) that are unapologetically modest—and occasionally haunted. It's a fun, cheap way to spend the night in Portland, and you can watch some pretty legendary rock music in the saloon downstairs.

Greater Portland   Map 7

ALOFT $

9920 NE Cascades Pkwy., 503/200-5678,
www.starwoodhotels.com/alofthotels

Aloft provides a clean, fun, and affordable stay near Portland International Airport that is miles away from your standard airport stay. Service is quite personable and they seem perfectly equipped to give visitors who won't make it into the city a little taste of the downtown scene. Decor is modern and chic, with high-tech touches like free wired and wireless high-speed Internet access and a plug-and-play entertainment center to charge and play cell phones, laptops, and MP3 players on the 42-inch flat-screen television. You can choose between a 285-square-foot king room with one big bed or a 315-square-foot room with two queen beds. The fitness center, open 24 hours, is equipped with cardio and elliptical machines, plus free weights, exercise balls, and a splash pool. You can also visit re:mix, the in-house lounge, which offers a giant TV wall for game watching, billiards, and other games.

AVALON HOTEL AND SPA $$

455 SW Hamilton Ct., 503/802-5800,
www.avalonhotelandspa.com

Along the industrial but oddly serene south waterfront area of Portland, Avalon Hotel and Spa is an stylish and convenient alternative to staying in the city. One mile from the heart of downtown, the hotel is particularly suited for business travelers who want to maintain a steadfast routine of fitness, as the location provides easy access to a waterfront jogging area and a well-appointed gym. Parking will cost you $19 a night, but you may come and go as you please or take advantage of the free transportation to downtown. Rooms are luxurious and modern with fireplaces, high-speed Internet access, and comfy beds in all rooms, and private balconies and marble tubs in most.

RED LION HOTEL ON THE RIVER $$

909 N. Hayden Island Dr., 503/283-4466,
www.redlion.rdln.com

While decidedly removed from the core of Portland, the Red Lion Hotel on the River is located right off of I-5 and equidistant between Portland and Vancouver, Washington. The hotel boasts a handful of amenities that make it worthwhile to avoid the cost and chaos of downtown, like private balconies (some of which have lovely views of the Columbia River), a seasonal pool and Jacuzzi, a fitness center, tennis courts, boat dock, free high-speed wireless Internet, complimentary parking, and on-call airport transportation.

SHERATON PORTLAND AIRPORT HOTEL $$

8235 NE Airport Way, 503/281-2500,
www.sheratonportlandairport.com

If you want to stay near the airport, you can't

get much more convenient than the Sheraton. Besides being the nearest accommodations to the terminal, the hotel has a free shuttle that will run you to and from the airport, where you can pick up the Red MAX line and ride it into town. The staff is accustomed to dealing with last-minute arrivals and changes, so they are usually quite friendly to weary travelers. There's an on-site restaurant with 24-hour room service, a pool, an exercise room, a Jacuzzi, and sauna. The rooms are clean, comfortable, well appointed, and relatively quiet considering their proximity to the airport.

EXCURSIONS FROM PORTLAND

One of the great things about Portland is its proximity to some of the Pacific Northwest's most spectacular landscapes. With the slopes of Mount Hood to the north and the majesty of the ocean to the west, Portlanders relish the fact that they are always about an hour away from something spectacularly different than wherever they are. The terrain surrounding Portland is so diverse, in fact, that each year there is a relay marathon that begins at Timberline Lodge on majestic Mount Hood and ends one day later in Seaside, Oregon. For visitors, the diversity of landscapes is a bonus as well; when everything is so conveniently close, there is no need to choose between a ski vacation, a trip to wine country, or a stay in the city.

The Columbia River Gorge, which begins approximately 20 minutes east of Portland and extends for more than 100 miles, is a lush, breathtaking country, with numerous waterfalls, scenic drives, and a plethora of outdoor activities—like hiking, biking, golf, whitewater rafting, kayaking, and windsurfing.

Mount Hood is about 50 miles east/southeast of Portland, offering 4,600 acres of ski-able terrain and more than 1,200 miles of hiking trails. About 75 miles to the west, you will find the magnificent Pacific Ocean, and a flurry of quaint coastal towns with fun shops and fresh seafood.

A little closer to town (about 25 miles to the southwest), you will find Oregon wine country, where they grow, age, and bottle some of the best Pinot Noirs in the world.

© JEFF GUARDALABENE

HIGHLIGHTS

LOOK FOR **[C** TO FIND RECOMMENDED SIGHTS, ACTIVITIES, DINING, AND LODGING.

[C Best Place to Fly a Kite: With its wide, walkable beaches, the Oregon Coast has countless places where a blustery day can turn into a whole lot of fun. **Cannon Beach** is particularly popular, and the annual kite festival in April is a perfect time to test your flight skills (page 165).

[C Best Photo Op: "Majestic" is perhaps the word most often applied to **Multnomah Falls,** a 620-foot waterfall that plummets from Larch Mountain (page 167).

[C Best Place to Sing "Roll on, Columbia": The power of the Columbia River is never so evident as it is at **Bonneville Dam,** the place for which folk singer Woodie Guthrie wrote his famous song. The mighty facility features a fish hatchery and ladder, which Pacific salmon and steelhead pass through on their journey upstream to spawn (page 168).

[C Best Place to Sip a Future Star: Revolutionary **Carlton Winemakers Studio** houses 10 small artisan winemakers who share the eco-friendly space, equipment, and apparently, a talent for making phenomenal wines (page 174).

[C Best Place to Catch Flight Fever: The Wright Brothers had it. So did Howard Hughes. Catch the bug as you peruse the vehicles that got those guys airborne. From a replica of the first plane to the awesome heavy bombers of World War II and Hughes' remarkable "Spruce Goose," the **Evergreen Aviation and Space Museum** has it all (page 175).

[C Best Place to Go Sledding in the Summer: There's always a good patch of mountain to ride in the winter months, but **Mt. Hood Skibowl** also has some wicked happenings in the warmer months, like the wild concrete Alpine Slide, a 300-foot inner-tube course, and a 500-foot zip line (page 177).

PLANNING YOUR TIME

Each of these excursions from Portland can be done in a day if you travel by car. Of course, if you have the time to linger for an overnight or weekend, the possibilities are quite a bit more open. Depending on which portion of the coast you visit, you can spend just a couple of hours driving, or most of the day. Either way, for a trip to the Pacific, it is best to leave early in the day. Traffic to and from the coast and Oregon wine country can get particularly snarled on summer weekends, and both routes involve long stretches of scenic highway with few commercial areas. Be sure you make restroom stops when you can. You can easily visit most of the places you would like to see in wine country in one day, but the coast may be a little trickier. The roads between many of the coastal towns are scenic, but they are often winding, two-lane roads that don't provide for swift traveling. It is best to decide which town you would like to visit and spend a day focused on that town.

Traffic to the east depends largely on the time of year. As the snow piles up on the mountain, more and more people head up to take part in the fun. Through much of the winter season (particularly Dec.–Feb.), tire chains are a requirement, even on vehicles with four-wheel drive.

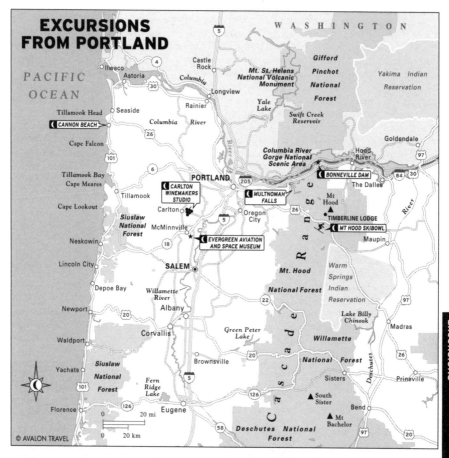

EXCURSIONS FROM PORTLAND

EXCURSIONS

The Oregon Coast

Oregon has more than 350 miles of coastline, much of it wild, jagged, and beautiful. The water remains fairly chilly (around 45–55°F in most places), and the coastal breeze makes for cooler climates—but the high basalt rock cliffs, long sandy beaches, and amazing tide pools make it a visitor's paradise.

Along much of the Oregon coastline, you can catch some serious whale-watching, as gray, humpback, and sperm whales migrate south toward Baja during their December pilgrimage

from the chilly waters of Alaska. Prime season for whale-watching is between December and March, so coastal hotels with prime spots for viewing book up fast.

SIGHTS
Astoria

At the tip-top of the Oregon coastline, you'll find Astoria, a historic spot where Lewis and Clark spent the winter of 1805–1806, holed up at **Fort Clatsop** (92343 Fort

Clatsop Rd., www.nps.gov/lewi, summer daily 9 A.M.–6 P.M., after Labor Day daily 9 A.M.–5 P.M., $3 adult, free for child under 15), which still stands today. The visitors center at Fort Clatsop National Monument has an exhibit built in 1955 and inspired by the expedition members' journals, as well as an interpretive center, gift shop, and an orientation film. In summer months, the center also features ranger-led programs and re-enactors in the fort.

Astoria has a lot of history for such a small town. In fact, don't be surprised if you recognize a lot of the landscape as you walk through the town. Astoria has been the filming locale for a number of movies like *Goonies, Overboard, Short Circuit, The Black Stallion, Kindergarten Cop, Free Willy, Free Willy 2, The Ring, The Ring Two,* and *Into the Wild.*

Both fishing and crabbing are popular sports in Astoria. **Let's Go Fishin'** (503/440-0912, www.letsgofishingoregon.com, $165 adult, $125 for child under 17, $100 crabbing) provides guided trips for salmon, steelhead, sturgeon, and crab at reasonable prices.

Seaside

A little farther down the coast, Seaside is one of the most popular tourist destinations on the northern coast. It hosts a number of annual events like the Miss Oregon contest, the Hood to Coast Relay After-Party, and Dorchester Conference, a convention of the Oregon Republican Party.

Just a short walk from Fort Clatsop National Monument is the **Seaside Aquarium** (503/738-6211, www.seasideaquarium.com), where you will find starfish, harbor seals, wolf eels, crabs, and a number of other Pacific sea creatures. You can also find a number of family-fun activities, like the carousel, arcades, miniature golf, bumper cars and boats, tilt-a-twirl, paddle boats, and canoes.

Tillamook

If you love cheese, the only place you really need to go on your Oregon trip is the **Tillamook Cheese Factory** (4175 Hwy. 101 N., 503/815-1300, www.tillamookcheese.com, summer daily 8 A.M.–8 P.M., after Labor Day daily 8 A.M.–6 P.M., free) in Tillamook. You

COURTESY OF OREGON COAST VISITOR'S ASSOCIATION

Come face to face with sharks, rockfish, and bat rays as you walk through one of the most popular exhibits at The Oregon Coast Aquarium in Newport, Passages of the Deep.

can tour the facility and find out how they make their world-class cheddar, plus—best of all—you can try endless samples of cheeses and 38 different kinds of ice cream.

The city of Tillamook is named for a Salish word that means "Land of Many Waters," and it's popular coastal fishing area today. There are seven rivers in Tillamook that are abundant with coho salmon and wild steelhead salmon, and the Nestucca, Nehalem, and Tillamook Bays are perhaps the most popular crabbing and clamming areas in the entire Pacific Northwest. Fishing guides like **Lee Darby's Guide Service** (503/351-0547, www.leedarbysfishing.com, $180 full-day trip) can take you out into the churning waters of Tillamook Bay, if you want to get your hands on a 30- to 100-pound sturgeon. If you just want to sightsee, charter boats such as **Garibaldi Charters** (503/322-0007, www.garibaldicharters.com, $40 for 2- to 3-hour tour) can take you out into whale-heavy waters for an up-close and personal look.

Cannon Beach

Cannon Beach is a handsome coastal town that is famous for its four-mile-long kite-friendly beach, its galleries and specialty boutiques, and iconic **Haystack Rock,** which rises 235 feet out of the sand and is occasionally accessible by foot during low tide. The city acquired its name in 1846, when a cannon from the U.S. Navy schooner *Shark* washed ashore just north of Arch Cape. Two more appeared in February 2008, having been buried in the sand for about a century and a half. These artifacts and others are on display at the **Cannon Beach History Center and Museum** (1387 S. Spruce St., 503/436-9301, www.cbhistory.org, Wed.–Mon. 1–5 P.M., free). Late spring is a great time to visit, with the spectacular **Puffin Kite Festival** (www.surfsand.com) in April and the annual **Sandcastle Competition** (www.cannon-beach.net/sandcastle.html) in May or June, depending on the year.

Newport

It's a 2.5- to 3-hour drive from Portland, but if you head over to Newport, you can fill an entire day strolling in the pedestrian-friendly historic Nye Beach district or shopping along the boardwalk—and still sneak in some time on the beach.

The Oregon Coast Aquarium (2820 SE Ferry Slip Rd., 541/867-3474, www.aquarium.org, summer daily 9 A.M.–6 P.M., after Labor Day 10 A.M.–5 P.M., $14.95 adult, $12.95 senior, $12.25 for child 13–17, $9.95 for child 3–12, free for child under 3) is located here. It's the home of more than 500 species of animals in both indoor and outdoor exhibits. Keiko (the whale of *Free Willy* fame) once lived here; when he left, his home was converted into Passages of the Deep, an exhibit that allows visitors to walk through acrylic tunnels surrounded by sharks, rays, and rockfish.

RESTAURANTS

Like sand in your shoes and windswept hair, **Mo's Clam Chowder** (www.moschowder.com, generally daily 11 A.M.–11 P.M., $6–10) is synonymous with a trip to the coast, and you can find locations in Cannon Beach, Lincoln City, and Newport. Since 1946, the company served Mohava "Mo" Niemi's recipe of New England clam chowder, made with locally raised Yaquina Bay oysters.

A great place to dine in Cannon Beach is **The Wayfarer** (1190 Pacific Dr., 503/436-1108, www.wayfarer-restaurant.com, Sun.–Thurs. 8 A.M.–9 P.M., Fri.–Sat. 8 A.M.–10 P.M., $20–28), where you can find a superb omelet made whatever is most fresh, like Dungeness crab, bay shrimp, or salmon—or maybe with Rogue Creamery blue cheese and local wild mushrooms.

In Seaside, you will find **Pig 'N Pancake** (323 Broadway St., 503/738-7243, www.pignpancake.com, daily 6 A.M.10 P.M., $7–10), a rather iconic Northwest greasy spoon. It's been in operation in Seaside since 1961, and the franchise has since expanded to Lincoln City, Cannon Beach, Astoria, Newport, and Portland.

Also in Seaside, you will find **Yummy Wine Bar & Bistro** (831 Broadway St., 503/738-3100, www.yummywinebarbistro.com, Thurs.–Mon. 3–9 P.M., closed Tues.–Wed., $10–20), a warm

EXCURSIONS

and inviting place off the main drag. It has a fantastic array of wines from around the world and a menu that changes regularly to emphasize local and organic items. The hours of operation change slightly with the seasons, so it's best to check before you go. For dessert, check out Zinger's Ice Cream Parlor (210 Broadway, 503/738-3939, www.zingersicecream.com) where every flavor is made from scratch.

In Newport, there are a number of local favorites, but **[** **Café Mundo** (209 NW Coast Rd., 541/574-8134, www.myspace.com/cafemundo, Tues.–Thurs. 4–10 P.M., Fri.–Sat. 4 P.M.–midnight, closed Mon., $10–15) tops the list for food, atmosphere, and overall creativity. The menu includes a number of fantastic pastas, sandwiches, salads, and espresso drinks, as well as some great Northwest wines and beers.

For elegant dining, **Saffron Salmon** (859 SW Bay Blvd., 541/265-8921, www.saffronsalmon.com, Thurs.–Tues. 11:30 A.M.2:15 P.M. and 5–8:30 P.M., closed Wed., $20–28) is located on a public pier on the west end of Newport's Historic Bayfront. They make good use of their proximity to the best seafood in the Northwest by buying direct, which means the salmon you eat for dinner might have been swimming in the Pacific when you woke up.

HOTELS

In Astoria, the **[** **Cannery Pier Hotel** (10 Basin St., 888/325-4996, www.cannerypierhotel.com, $189–525), as the name might suggest, sits on what was once the site of the Union Fisherman's Cooperative Packing Company Cannery. In operation since mid-2005, this boutique hotel rests atop a pier some 600 feet into the river, offering breathtaking views of the passing ships and storms rolling through the mouth of the Columbia.

In Seaside, try the **Gilbert Inn** (341 Beach Dr., 503/738-9770, www.gilbertinn.com, $69–229) a comfortable 10-room inn made cozy and romantic by classic Victorian decor. The inn is just one block from the beach and from the popular promenade.

The Ocean Lodge (2864 Pacific St., 888/777-4047, www.theoceanlodge.com,

$189–379) in Cannon Beach has spacious and comfortable rooms that have private oceanfront balconies with views of the sea and of Haystack Rock. The lodge is just a short drive from the shops and restaurants of downtown Cannon Beach, and is very close to great surf breaks as well as hiking and mountain bike trails.

Newport has a number of options. At **[** **Sylvia Beach Hotel** (267 NW Cliff Rd., 541/265-5428, www.sylviabeachhotel.com, $70–193), bookworms will feel right at home. There are no TVs, radios, or phones, but there are a number of books and reading nooks, and each room is decorated in the theme of a particular author, such as Edgar Allen Poe, J. R. R. Tolkien, and Dr. Seuss.

PRACTICALITIES
Information and Services

Before you go, check out **The Oregon Coast Visitors Association** (541/574-2679, http://visittheoregoncoast.com), where you can find advice on where to go and what to do, as well as links to the Chamber of Commerce and Visitors Association for each individual city along the coast.

Getting There and Around

From I-5, there are a number of routes that will take you to the Oregon Coast. Most of those routes are two-lane highways that wind though vast acres of trees, hills, and valleys. To get to the northern part of the coast, you can take Highway 30 along the south banks of the Columbia River through St. Helens and continuing on to Astoria.

Another popular route to the Pacific is Highway 26 (sometimes referred to in Portland as the Sunset Highway), which meanders west through Beaverton, Hillsboro, and Banks and continues on to Seaside. Both Highway 30 and Highway 26 connect with Highway 101 which runs north–south, parallel to the coastline, and passes through most of Oregon's coastal towns. Traffic can drag along Highway 101 on occasion, particularly as you pass through the larger towns like Lincoln City. Driving south along 101 makes for a lovely drive with the Pacific

Ocean at your constant right, but, if you are planning on visiting an area along the central part of coast, you might be better off finding a more direct route than this pretty, but arguably less efficient route.

You can get to the central coast by traveling south down I-5 and heading onto Highway 99 (Portland Rd. East). From there, head south towards Capitol Street and into downtown Salem. Follow the signs pointing towards Highway 22/Ocean Beaches, which will lead you over the Willamette River and out of the Salem. Stay on Highway 22 for approximately

25 miles until it intersects then turn left onto 18 and c coast. Follow Highway 18 t junction (about 25 miles) w south and head towards Li Bay, and Newport.

There are countless other routes to the coast that will inevitably lead you through a series of small towns and blink-and-you-miss-them communities. Once you determine which area of the coast you would like to visit, map your own roundabout route or check with the town's visitor's bureau for advice on how to get there.

The Columbia River Gorge

In about an hour or less from Portland, you can find yourself in the heart of the Columbia River Gorge, basking in the rugged natural beauty of the Columbia River, framed by sheer cliffs and majestic mountains. It's a beautiful drive, no matter how deep you get into it. Whether you are heading out to Hood River, stopping in Stevenson, Washington, or just checking out some historical landmarks, you will find plenty to do. There are countless outdoor adventures (like windsurfing, kiteboarding, rafting, mountain biking, and hiking) for those looking to get an adrenaline fix, but there is also a lot of places to kick back, sip a glass of wine, and enjoy the spectacular view.

SIGHTS
Crown Point and Vista House
You know you have arrived at the Columbia River Gorge when you see the unmistakable bluff that is Crown Point, a vantage point which was formed by a 14-million-year-old lava flow that now offers visitors a breathtaking view from 733 feet above the Columbia River. The **Vista House Visitors Center** (503/695-2230, www.vistahouse.com, daily 9 A.M.–6 P.M., free), an octagonal stone structure, was built as a memorial to Oregon pioneers. Its observation deck provides panoramic views that stretch on for nearly 30 miles, as

well as educational exhibits that relate the history of the area and the building.

Farther up the road, **Bridal Veil Falls State Park** (www.oregonstateparks.org/park_149. php) is located on the Historic Columbia River Scenic Highway and can be accessed off I-84 at Exit 28. There are two fantastic hiking trails here, the lower of which bears the same name as the park and will take you down to the base of the eponymous falls. The hike is just under one mile round-trip and includes a number of switchbacks. The upper Overlook Trail can be accessed about 20 yards west of the Bridal Veil Falls trailhead. It is a relatively short half-mile loop that will take you to the famous geologic edifice known as the Pillars of Hercules, a stately pair of basalt towers. Both trails are alive with native flora like trillium, lupine, bead lily, and bleeding heart, all of which are native— but so is poison oak, so stick to the path.

◖ Multnomah Falls
There are seemingly more waterfalls in this region than you could count (and it varies by season and rainfall levels) but none is more grand than Multnomah Falls (50,000 Historic Columbia River Hwy., Scenic Loop Dr., Bridal Veil, 503/695-2376, www.multnomahfallslodge. com, Summer daily 8 A.M.–9 P.M., Winter Mon.– Thurs. 10 A.M.–6 P.M., Fri. 10 A.M.– 8 P.M., Sat.

.–8 P.M., Sun. 8 A.M.–6 P.M., free), which ,uts from an underground spring on Larch .Mountain. The falls are a spectacular 620 feet tall, and broken into upper and lower falls, which can be traversed over by bridge. The view alone is worth the trip, but the multiple trails that are accessible from the falls make it all the more exhilarating. You can pick up a free trail map in the visitors center and navigate your way along the Larch Mountain Trail to the historic Benson Arch Bridge. The footbridge was built in 1914, and it is a popular place for a photo op with the breathtaking falls as a backdrop. You can continue on from there to the top of the falls or hike all the way up Larch Mountain Trail where the Cascade Mountains come into full spectacular view. The lodge at the base of the falls is where you will find the visitors center as well as a gift shop and the historic Multnomah Falls Lodge restaurant.

Sightseeing Tours

If you really want to get the lay of the land, book a trip aboard the **Columbia Gorge Sternwheeler** (503/224-3900, www.port-landspirit.com, June–Sept. Wed., $84 adult, $64 senior and child) or the historic **Mt. Hood Railroad** (www.mthoodrr.com), both of which allow you to sit back and enjoy the scenery (and, of course, take lots of pictures).

◖ Bonneville Dam

If anything were going to harness the power of the Columbia River, it has to be the Bonneville Dam (70543 NE Herman Loop, 541/374-8344, www.nwp.usace.army.mil, daily 9 A.M.–5 P.M., free admission), which spans the river and provides the area with power. The first powerhouse of the dam opened in 1937, in the midst of the Great Depression. The creation of new jobs and the luxury of affordable hydroelectric power are part of what inspired folk singer Woodie Guthrie to write the lines, "Thy power is turning our darkness to dawn. Roll on, Columbia, roll on." But, of course, the sheer command of the dam spoke volumes as well. Both the Oregon and Washington sides of the dam have a visitors center where you

can catch a tugboat or barge passing through the locks, or watch salmon, sturgeon, and lamprey as they swim through the fish ladders on their way to spawn. While the visitors center is open year-round, the months between April and September are most abundant with fish.

RECREATION
Kayaking

The Columbia River is a favorite spot for lovers of water sports. The **Kayak Shed** (6 Oak St., 541/386-4286, www.kayakshed.com) in Hood River can hook you up with whatever gear you will need for a wild river adventure. If you are an inexperienced kayaker, **Columbia Gorge Kayak School** (541/806-4190, www.gorgekayaker.com) offers both group lessons and private instruction. Two-day weekender courses will run you about $225. For rafting, try **Zoller's Outdoor Odysseys** (800/366-2004, www.zooraft.com), which takes passengers on thrill rides down the rapids of the White Salmon (half-day trip, $65 per person) and Klickitat (full-day trip, $90 per person).

Windsurfing

Few sports are more popular in the Gorge than windsurfing. **Hood River Waterplay** (541/386-9463, www.hoodriverwaterplay.com) offers windsurfing and kiteboarding classes for all levels of experience, plus equipment rentals and a thorough knowledge of the area–which makes them a great place to get wet, whether you are well versed or just starting out.

Fishing

For fishing, head to Laurance Lake, Drano Lake, Goose Lake, Lost Lake, or the mouth of Eagle Creek, where you won't battle with the currents as you will in the Salmon, Deschutes, and Klikitat Rivers. Or book a guided excursion with **Columbia River Fishing Guides** (1087 Lewis River Rd., Ste. 206, 360/910-6630, www.columbiariverfishingguide.com), based in Woodland, Washington. They will provide you with equipment, and claim they can guarantee you will catch a sturgeon, steelhead, or salmon.

Hiking

Hiking options abound in the Gorge, especially since it provides access the **Pacific Crest Trail** (PCT), which extends from the U.S. border with Canada all the way to Mexico. A good spot to access the PCT is the Herman Creek Trailhead, which provides a challenging but rewarding 16-mile hike up the Benson Plateau. Or, if you are looking for something a bit easier, try the Latourell Falls Trailhead, an easy two-mile hike past waterfalls, flowers, and streams. You can find detailed hiking plans and maps on Portland Hiker's Field Guide (www.portlandhikersfieldguide.org) to prepare you for your trip.

RESTAURANTS

Until you drive into some of the more populous towns like Hood River or Stevenson, Washington, your dining options are fairly limited to either home-style diner fare or romantic, elegant hideaways. If you aren't looking for anything fancy, swing by **Tad's Chicken and Dumplins** (1325 W. Historic Columbia River Hwy., 503/666-5337, www.tadschicdump.com, Mon.–Fri. 5–10 P.M. and Sat.–Sun. 4–10 P.M., $13–20), which is located in Troutdale along the Historic Columbia River Highway. As the name implies, they have a special penchant for comfort food, particularly their eponymous dish; like any roadside diner worth its salt, it does a mean fried chicken, too.

For a more elegant meal, try a longstanding Corbett restaurant, which fans of the *Twilight* series may recognize as the location where the memorable prom scene was shot. The ◖ **Viewpoint Inn** (40301 E. Larch Mountain Rd., 503/695-5811, www.theviewpointinn. com, Wed.–Sat. 11 A.M.–2 P.M. and 5–9 P.M., Sun. 9 A.M.–2 P.M. and 5–9 P.M., open Tues. in summer, closed Mon. year-round, $20–36) has served as an inn and restaurant since 1925, and played host to President Franklin D. Roosevelt and Charlie Chaplin long before the vampires moved in. The menu is rich, elegant, and romantic, with a focus on the Northwest bounty and seasonal favorites like wild salmon.

Just a skip over the river into Stevenson,

Washington, you will find a number of up-and-coming dining options, not the least of which is the **Cascade Room** (1131 SW Skamania Lodge Way, 800/221-7117, www. skamania.com, Mon.–Thurs. 7 A.M.–2 P.M. and 5–9 P.M., Fri.–Sat. 7 A.M.–2 P.M. and 5–9:30 P.M., Sun. 9 A.M.–2 P.M. and 5–9 P.M., $23–35), a fine dining restaurant housed in Skamania Lodge. Dinners boast such specialties as salmon, smoked pork loin, and roast prime rib of Washington beef, and breakfast and brunch are so good, even the oatmeal is worth writing home about.

For moderately priced burgers, sandwiches, beer, and wine, check out **Big River Grill** (192 SW 2nd St., 509/427-4888, www.bigrivergrill. us, daily 11:30 A.M.–9 P.M., $13–19), a popular spot with locals and passers-through that defines its cuisine as "High-End Roadhouse."

Also in Stevenson, a great spot to grab a microbrew and some grub is **Walking Man Brewing Company** (240 SW 1st St., 509/427-5520, www.walkingmanbrewing.com, Wed.–Fri. 4–9 P.M., Sat. 3–9 P.M., Sun. 3–8 P.M., $10–15). The house-made beers really take center stage here (particularly the Belgian red ale), but the artisan-style pizza isn't bad at all.

If you are looking for seafood, **3 Rivers Grill** (601 Oak St., 541/386-8883, www.3riversgrill. com, daily lunch and dinner, $12–24) has some of the best in the area. Located on Oak Street in Hood River, the place has a homey feel to it, with a deck area overlooking the river. In addition to some beautiful crab cakes, ceviche, and salmon dishes, they also have an award-winning wine selection.

Another master of Northwest cuisine and seafood is ◖ **Celilo Restaurant and Bar** (16 Oak St., 541/386-5710, www.celilorestaurant. com, daily 11:30 A.M.–3 P.M. and 5–9:30 P.M., $14–24) in Hood River. They're about as committed to supporting all things local as the sun is to shining, and the result is simple, expertly crafted food. You will want to make a reservation for Celilo (pronounced "Seh-LIE-low"), even if you have a small party, to ensure that you can take your time and that you will not have to sit at the bar.

Finally, as the evening winds down in Hood River, **Brian's Pourhouse** (606 Oak St., 541/387-4344, www.brianspourhouse.com, daily 5 P.M.–1 A.M., $15–22) is a great spot for a late dinner, or for drinks and appetizers. The small, Colonial-style, white clapboard restaurant stays open just a wee bit later than many other places in town, and the atmosphere is relaxed and enjoyable.

HOTELS

Oregon has a number of lodgings built around its numerous hot springs, and **◖ Bonneville Hot Springs Resort and Spa** (1252 E. Cascade Dr., North Bonneville, WA, 509/427-7767, www.bonnevilleresort.com, $179–499) is one of the most elegant, particularly if you're really looking to escape. Many rooms come equipped with their own private mineral-water hot tub, which overlooks the river canyon. The renowned 12,000-square-foot day spa has a number of treatments that utilize those therapeutic waters that form when water descends through the planet's cracks and fissures, gets heated by the earth's core, and is forced back to the surface.

Collins Lake Resort (88149 E. Creek Ridge Rd., Government Camp, 888/422-4776, www.collinslakeresort.com, $169–369) also offers all the luxuries you'd expect from a top-notch resort; its spacious, well-appointed, and comfortable chalets—complete with views of magnificent Collins Lake—really make this a favorite vacation destination.

◖ Skamania Lodge (1131 SW Skamania Lodge Way, Stevenson, WA, 509/427-7700, www.skamania.com, $189–389) also makes use of its beautiful surroundings, sitting proudly on a hill with a commanding view of the river and surrounding hills. The lodge is elegant and peaceful, with grand stone fireplaces, high rustic ceilings, and enormous picture windows.

Adjacent to the historic Columbia Gorge Hotel (which shuttered in February 2009, but reopened later that fall), **Columbia Cliffs Villas** (3880 Westcliff Dr., Hood River, 866/912-8366, www.columbiacliffvillas.com,

Skamania Lodge overlooks 175 wooded acres in the Columbia River Gorge.

$169–895) offers a wide variety of accommodations in 28 privately owned condominiums that range from one to three bedrooms. The Villas are great for families because they come equipped with lockout doors, which allow the space to be reconfigured as needed.

For families or those traveling on a budget, **Vagabond Lodge** (4070 Westcliff Dr., Hood River, 877/386-2992 www.vagabondlodge.com, $48–115) has clean, simple, and affordable rooms, many of which have stunning views of the Columbia River. All of the rooms have cable TV, microwaves, and a small fridge.

PRACTICALITIES
Information and Services
The **Columbia River Gorge Visitors Association** (www.crgva.org) provides maps and information on events, dining, accommodations, and shopping. They also have a trip planner called *Gorge Guide* with beautiful photos of the area, historical information, and travel tips for regions all throughout the Gorge.

Getting There and Around
Word to the wise: You will very likely get distracted while driving through the Gorge. With so many viewpoints, historic landmarks, unexpected waterfalls, and surprising panoramas,

it's natural to get a bit sidetracked, but that's half the fun. One of the best routes is the Historic Columbia River Highway (exit 17), the first planned scenic highway in the United States. The highway runs past a number of waterfalls (including the majestic Multnomah Falls) and photo stops like Crown Point and the Vista House. You can rejoin I-84 at exit 35, where you can cross over the Bridge of the Gods to the Washington side, or continue east to Hood River and access to Mount Hood.

If you are crossing the bridge (which was named for after a great Native American legend), you will need to pay a $1 toll. The bridge tollhouse is open 24 hours a day and serves as the emergency relay station for police departments on both sides of the river.

If you continue on to Hood River, which is about 45 minutes from Portland in good traffic, you can pick up the Mt. Hood Scenic Loop, a two-hour drive around the foot of Mount Hood over streams and through lush forests. From here, you can also drive the Fruit Loop, a collection of farms, orchards, vineyards, and wineries. There are easy-to-follow maps (which list Fruit Loop farms, attractions, and individual operating hours) available at the Hood River Visitors Center off Exit 63 on I-84.

EXCURSIONS

Oregon Wine Country

If you think the Portland metro area is scenic and green, you'll think Oregon wine country is exceptional. The vineyards of the Willamette Valley are situated between the Coast Range to the west and the Cascades to the east, nestled into a verdant landscape that is fragrant with spruce, fir, and pine.

The wine industry in Oregon is still remarkably young when you consider how much success it has had. It all began when David Lett of Eyrie Vineyards moved to the region in 1965 with some 3,000 clippings and grand intentions to make the most of the Willamette Valley's climate and latitude, which bear a striking

resemblance to that of Burgundy, France, Pinot Noir's ancestral home. Undeterred by his California counterparts, who scoffed at the idea of producing wine in a region that was so cold and wet, Lett planted the first Pinot Noir grapes in the Northwest, thus sowing the seeds for Oregon's future as a heavyweight in the wine industry.

It wasn't until the late 1970s that people really started to turn their eyes toward what was happening here. Nowadays, the Willamette Valley alone has over 200 wineries and 12,000 acres of grapes, and in these places, artisan wine makers have put Oregon on the international

NAVIGATING WINE COUNTRY

As you travel along Highway 99 West, the first major wine town you will hit is Newberg, home to George Fox College. Great wineries here include **Adelsheim** (16800 NE Calkins Ln., 503/538-3652, www.adelsheim.com, daily 11 A.M.–4 P.M.), which recently added a tasting room to their 190-acre vineyard at the base of the Chehalem Mountains. At **Rex Hill Winery** (30835 N. Hwy. 99W, 503/538-0666, www.rexhill.com, daily 10 A.M.–5 P.M.), you'll find 17 acres of Pinot Noir grapes and one wee little row of well-attended Muscat grapes.

Passing through Newberg, you can head west on Highway 240 to the quiet hamlets of Carlton, Yamhill, and Gaston, where you will find **Elk Cove Vineyards** (27751 NW Olson Rd., 503/985-7760, www.elkcove.com, daily 10 A.M.–5 P.M.). In 1974, Elk Cove became the first winery in the Yamhill-Carlton region to produce a commercial wine. This particular pocket of land is well protected by the Coastal Range, the Chehalem Mountains, and the Dundee Hills, which means slightly drier, more moderate growing conditions perfectly suited for cool-climate grapes like Pinot Noir.

Check out **Anne Amie** (6580 NE Mineral Springs Rd., 503/864-2991, www.anneamie.com, daily 10 A.M.–5 P.M.) or **WillaKenzie** (19143 NE Laughlin Rd., 503/662-3280, www.willakenzie.com, daily 11 A.M.–5 P.M.) for fine examples of how Pinot Noir thrives in such climates. In addition to the tasting room, Anne Amie also offers a guided tour for $30 per person, which includes a reserve tasting and Oregon Pinot Noir glass. Tours are offered daily beginning at 11 A.M., but you must call ahead to reserve a space.

This region is also home to **Carlton Winemakers Studio** (801 N. Scott St., 503/852-6100, www.winemakersstudio.com), where 10 small-but-savvy vintners work in the same space, each producing some of the region's most remarkable wines.

If you stay on 99 West as it passes through Newberg, you can head into the hills of Dundee.

Here you can visit **Sokol Blosser** (5000 Sokol Blosser Ln., 800/582-6668, www.sokolblosser.com, daily 10 A.M.–4 P.M.), a longtime giant of the Oregon wine industry, and soak up the landscape in their picnic area. There are many vineyards in this area and a smattering of excellent restaurants, so it's a good place to stop and grab a bite to eat as you head toward McMinnville, the largest city in Yamill County and the cultural center of the valley.

In McMinnville, you will find **Eyrie Vineyards** (1015 NE 10th Ave., 503/472-6315, www.eyrievineyards.com, Wed.–Sun. noon–5 P.M.), which was founded by the man affectionately known as "Papa Pinot."

Here are a few other great wineries to check out:

- **Argyle:** 691 Hwy. 99W, Dundee, 888-427-4953, www.argylewinery.com, daily 11 A.M.–5 P.M.

- **Bishop Creek:** 614 E. 1st St., Newberg, 503/487-6934, www.urbanwineworks.com, Wed.–Sun. 1–7 P.M., closed Mon.–Tues.

- **Chehalem:** 106 Center St., Newberg, 503/538-4700, www.chehalemwines.com, Thurs.–Mon. 11 A.M.–5 P.M., closed Tues.–Wed.

- **Dobbes Family Estate and Wine by Joe:** 240 SE 5th St., Dundee, 503/538-1141, www.dobbesfamilyestate.com, daily 11 A.M.–6 P.M.

- **Domaine Drouhin:** 6750 Breyman Orchards Rd., Dayton, 503/864-2700, www.domainedrouhin.com, Wed.–Sun. 11 A.M.–4 P.M., closed Mon.–Tues.

- **Erath:** 9409 NE Worden Hill Rd., Dundee, 503/538-3318, www.erath.com, daily 11 A.M.–5 P.M.

- **Torii Mor:** 18325 NE Fairview Dr., Dundee, 503/554-0105, www.toriimorwinery.com, daily 11 A.M.–5 P.M.

wine map thanks to incomparable vintages and revolutionary practices. According to the Oregon Wine Board (www.oregonwine.org), there are 72 grape varieties grown throughout the state, but only 15 of those varieties make up 97 percent of the vineyards in Oregon. At the top of that list is Pinot Noir. In fact, this region has been recognized as one of the premier Pinot Noir–producing areas in the world— which comes as no surprise to the Lett family. Apparently, they knew it all along.

WINERIES

Sokol Blosser (800/582-6668, www.sokol-blosser.com) is a pioneer in Northwest wine. The Sokol Blosser clan has been a part of the Oregon wine fabric since its first planting in 1971. Years later, Sokol Blosser is still family-owned and going strong, receiving accolades for both their vintages and their commitment to sustainability. Their 72-acre estate vineyards are located in the Dundee Hills, which makes for a lovely picnic spot, and their tasting room

is open 10 A.M.–4 P.M., with tours running every Friday, Saturday, and Sunday at 10 A.M. and noon (reservations are recommended, but not required).

The Four Graces (9605 NE Fox Farm Rd., www.thefourgraces.com) is a much younger vineyard at the northern entrance to Dundee. When the Black family purchased its 110-acre spot of land in 2003, it was fulfilling a lifelong dream to have a family-owned wine estate. Nowadays, people come from all around to sit in the historic farmhouse and sip extraordinary Pinot Noir, Pinot Gris, and Pinot Blanc. They are an enthusiastic and friendly bunch and are more than willing to welcome you into their tasting room (daily 10 A.M.–5 P.M.). You can also schedule a time to bring a group and meet one-on-one with the tasting room expert, Jason, who can explain how the happy trifecta of soil, climate, and topography combined with meticulous winemaking make for outstanding wines.

The original pioneer of the industry is the

© ANDREA JOHNSON

The 110-acre Black family estate at The Four Graces winery is where you'll find three of the top varietals grown in the region: Pinot Noir, Pinot Gris, and Pinot Blanc.

founder of **Eyrie Vineyards** (935 NE 10th Ave., McMinnville, 888/440-4970 or 503/472-6315, www.eyrievineyards.com), David Lett, who is affectionately known as "Papa Pinot." Lett planted the first Pinot Noir grapes in the Northwest, thus sowing the seeds for Oregon's future as a heavyweight in the wine industry. In 1975, Eyrie Vineyards produced the first Pinot Noir to successfully vie for recognition alongside the long-recognized Pinots of Burgundy, France. With that recognition came the acknowledgement of Oregon as the New World home for Pinot Noir. The Lett family is still at the helm of Eyrie and they still produce some of the most respected wines in the region. You can visit their tasting room (Wed.–Sun. noon–5 P.M., closed Mon.–Tues.) and sample for $5 per person, which is refundable upon the purchase of two bottles of wine.

Finally, if you really want an inside peek, call ahead and book a tour with **Domaine Drouhin** (6750 NE Breyman Orchards Rd., Dayton, 503/864-2700, www.domainedrouhin.com). Winemaker Véronique Drouhin-Boss uses the Burgundy method and she comes by it naturally. She is a fourth-generation winemaker who splits her time between Oregon and the other great wine region of the world, Beaune, Burgundy. The tour—a 60-minute walk through the vineyards and the four-story winery—is an exceptional peek into her process that culminates with comparative tastings between Oregon and Burgundy wines with water and cheese accompaniments.

Wine Tours

The best way to see wine country is to plan ahead, choose which places you want to see, and then map them out. Or, better yet, leave the driving to someone else and sign up for a tour with the likes of **Beautiful Willamette Tours** (877/868-7295, www.willamette-tours.com), **EcoTours of Oregon** (888/868-7733, www.ecotours-of-oregon.com), or **Wine Tours Northwest** (800/359-1034, www.wine-toursnorthwest.com). The benefit of opting for a tour is twofold: You do not have to designate your own driver, and you are often allowed to

tour places that are otherwise closed off to the public.

C Carlton Winemakers Studios

If you don't have enough time to tour a bunch of wineries, check out Carlton Winemakers Studios (801 North Scott St., Carlton, 503/852-6100, www.winemakersstudio.com, daily 11 A.M.–5 P.M.) where you can sample the wines of several up-and-coming winemakers. The studio is rather like a co-op, in that allows as many as 10 vintners at a time to share one state-of-the-art, gravity-driven, energy-efficient facility. The concept is a revolutionary way to encourage artisan winemakers to produce ultra-premium wines, while still promoting an eco-conscious, cost-friendly approach. For the consumer, that approach means that the wines produced within the studio have both the pedigree and palate of high-end wines, with the intimacy and price of a mom-and-pop vintner. What's more, you need not be a connoisseur to appreciate their space, or even be certain of what you are looking for. The airy, modern, and sleek studio tasting room has most of their in-house vintages on hand for tasting, providing a rare opportunity to explore the diversity of the region.

SIGHTS AND SHOPPING

When you need a break from sipping wine, Yamhill County has a number of other things to entertain you. Stop by **Red Ridge Farms** (5510 NE Breyman Orchards Rd., 503/864-8502, Wed.–Sun. 9 A.M.–5 P.M., closed Mon.–Tues., free), a family-owned herb and specialty plant nursery in Dayton. Nestled in the Red Hills, the farm has more than 300 varieties of herbs and other culinary, medicinal, and landscaping plants, including more than 100 types of lavender. It makes for some really pretty scenery. You can call ahead and have them prepare a picnic for you, or simply wander through the fragrant gardens. While you are there, be sure to browse through the shop filled with handcrafted items and garden-inspired gifts.

Shopping in and around McMinnville is also fun, and there are a number of great antiquing stops worth mentioning. **Lafayette Schoolhouse Antique Mall** (748 Highway 99W, Lafayette, 503/864-2720, www.myAntiqueMall.com, daily 10 A.M.–5 P.M.) has more than 100 antique dealers housed in a 1912 schoolhouse and 1930s era gymnasium. Also check out the **Downtown Historic District** and the **McMinnville Antique & Wine Gallery** (546 NE 3rd St., 503/474-9696, www.mcminnvilleantiqueandwine.com, Mon.–Sat. 11 A.M.–5 P.M., closed Sun.), where you will find vintage jewelry, linens, home decor, art, kitchen accessories, and clothing—as well as wine tasting from a handful of small, artisan wineries. Also in McMinnville, there are a number of galleries, restaurants, and independently owned boutiques and shops that specialize in handmade or locally produced items.

(Evergreen Aviation and Space Museum

The small town of McMinnville is home to the Evergreen Aviation and Space Museum (500 NE Captain Michael King Smith Way, 503/434-4180, www.sprucegoose.org, daily 9 A.M.–5 P.M., $26 adult, $24 seniors, $22 for age 5–16, free for child under 5), the biggest air and space museum west of the Mississippi. It's home to Howard Hughes's *H-4 Hercules,* a heavy transport aircraft more commonly known as the "Spruce Goose"—a name that Hughes detested. The newest section of the museum, which opened in 2008, has interactive flight simulators that allow you to practice landing the space shuttle, docking a Gemini capsule, or landing the Lunar Excursion Module on the surface of the moon. You can also catch a flick at the 3-D IMAX theater, see a 32,000-pound meteorite, or simply marvel at the amazing collection of military and civilian aircraft, spacecraft, and memorabilia. The museum offers docent-guided tours daily at 11 A.M. and 1:30 P.M.

RESTAURANTS

Nothing goes better with great wine than world-class dining, and this region has plenty of good spots to choose from. At the

Joel Palmer House (600 Ferry St., Dayton, 503/864-2995, www.joelpalmerhouse.com, Tues.–Sat. 5–9 P.M., closed Sun.–Mon., $29–37) the menu centers almost entirely around Northwest wild mushrooms. Once you have sampled the bounty of chanterelle, portobello, matsutake, and morel mushrooms, you will understand why. Try the Mushroom Madness menu, a prix-fixe meal ($75 per person) that includes six courses of fungus-y goodness.

(Tina's Restaurant (760 N. Hwy. 99W, Dundee, 503/538-8880, www.tinasdundee.com, Tues.–Fri. 11:30–2 P.M., daily 5–9 P.M., $22–30), on the other hand, is to wine what the Joel Palmer House is to mushrooms. Taking full advantage of their proximity to some of the best wineries in the business, they focus on artisan producers from the Willamette Valley and typically have about 60 local wines on hand. Wines by the glass are usually about $10–12 and are served in small one-and-a-half-glass carafes. It's a nice touch because it allows you the opportunity to share and sample different wines with different courses. The quiet, 50-seat restaurant serves up rustic French and Northwest cuisine using whatever is locally grown and in season, but they are particularly known for their roasted duck.

In Newburg, check out the **(Painted Lady** (201 S. College St., Newburg, 503/538-3850, www.thepaintedladyrestaurant.com, Wed.–Sun. 5–10 P.M., closed Mon.–Tues., $60–100), a popular spot for elegant meals and special occasions. The restaurant, which is housed in an old Victorian home, was named for the movement that sought to restore and revitalize Victorian and Edwardian homes by painting them in three or more contrasting colors and highlighting their architectural beauty. Both the menu and the setting seem to embody that ideal of using simple flourishes to highlight the beauty that is already there. Dishes are unpretentious, pretty, and well prepared. There's a regular and vegetarian menu each night, both of which feature a four-course, prix-fixe affair ($60 per person or $100 with wine pairings). In keeping with the elegance of the menu, the service at the Painted Lady is remarkably attentive as well, from offering a napkin to match your pants (thus preventing lint) to brushing the table between courses.

HOTELS

If you enjoy a good bed-and-breakfast, you are in luck. Wine country is ripe with them. **Dundee Manor Bed and Breakfast** (8380 NE Worden Hill Rd., Dundee, 888/262-1133, www.dundeemanor.com, $250), an Edwardian home that sits on five sprawling, manicured acres, comes with a bit more luxury than the average bed-and-breakfast. Guests are treated to a full gourmet breakfast, in-suite snacks, complimentary beverages, fleece robes, fresh flowers, and nightly turn-down service.

In Carlton, **The R.R. Thompson House** (517 N. Kutch St., Carlton, 503/852-6236, www.rrthompsonhouse.com, $150–245) is a good bet. Built in 1936, this bed-and-breakfast features two suites with sitting areas and satellite HDTV, as well as three sunny rooms with private baths and whirlpool tubs. A bonus for the non-morning people, the breakfast room has multiple tables, just in case you are feeling under-caffeinated or antisocial.

Honeymooners and couples looking to get away may want to check out the **Black Walnut Inn** (9600 NE Worden Hill Rd., Dundee, 866/429-4114, www.blackwalnut-inn.com, $295–495), which has been building a reputation as a romance-inducing escape since 2004. Located along the back roads of Dundee, the inn boasts incomparable views of the valley from most of the well-appointed rooms and suites. All of the accommodations here are spacious, cozy, and plush, with decor reminiscent of an Italian villa. Breakfast is a real delight. You may choose from four items each day, all of which are hearty, delicious, and straight from local farms.

Hotel Oregon (310 NE Evans St., McMinnville, 888/472-8427, www.mcmenamins.com, $50–135) is a unique spot to dine or stay thanks to the enterprising McMenamin brothers, who are responsible for 53 properties in Oregon and Washington—including a number of pubs, historic hotels, and movie

houses. This particular hotel, which has been around since 1905, has European-style rooms for as little as $50 a night, and suites with private bathrooms starting at $90. Hotel Oregon is known for its rooftop bar, which towers over old Main Street and offers a view of the Coastal Range and wine country.

Finally, the much-anticipated opening of **The Allison Inn & Spa** (2525 Allison Lane, Newberg, 503/554-2525, www.theallison.com, $295–1100) in September 2009 ushered in a new life to Oregon wine country, and further solidified the area as a destination spot. Located in Newberg, the inn occupies 155,000 square feet on 35 hillside acres. With 85 guest rooms, including 12 junior suites, seven one-bedroom suites, and a two-bedroom grand suite, The Allison is the largest luxury inn in the area. It also boasts a 15,000-square-foot spa and an 85-seat restaurant that serves Northwest cuisine, wine, and microbrews and provides 24-hour room service for guests.

PRACTICALITIES
Information and Services

Planning ahead for a trip to wine country is essential, because many wineries have limited hours and even more limited tour options. It's best to pick a few places and map out your day accordingly. A good resource for planning is the **Willamette Valley Visitors Association** (www.oregonwinecountry.org), a non-profit group that provides travel and tourism information for the entire Willamette Valley region. In addition to having an online calendar of events, they also have an interactive trip planner, a breakdown of area wineries, and descriptions of each of the area wine regions.

The **Willamette Valley Wineries Association** (www.willamettewines.com) is another good resource. They oversee more than 150 member wineries and tasting rooms in the valley and provide listings for recommended area restaurants and lodging options. Their website also features a map and a link to request their detailed brochure. If you are planning ahead, check out the **Oregon Wine Board** (www.oregonwine.org), which provides extensive looks into the history and horticulture of Oregon wines, notes on sustainability and craftsmanship, and tourism resources. From their website, you can request a comprehensive packet that includes an overview brochure about the industry, maps, and vineyard listings from the Willamette Valley and all over Oregon. There's a small cost, but they will mail the packet to your home so that you can get a head start on mapping out your trip.

Getting There and Around

It's not a long stretch of road that separates Portland from the hub of Oregon's Willamette Valley wine region. To get there, take I-5 southbound until you reach exit 289 (Sherwood/Tualatin), or detour through the Champoeg State Heritage Area by continuing south to exit 282A. Follow the signs to Butteville, and from there to Newberg and Highway 99W. Traffic can slow to a crawl as you pass through each of the small cities along the route, particularly during rush hour, so try to avoid traveling that stretch in the early morning or late afternoon.

Getting around Oregon wine country can be a challenge, thanks to rolling hills, gravel roads, and sporadic signage. But there are plenty of maps and tours that can help you navigate. If you are driving yourself, appoint one person as the map checker, who can be on the lookout for driveways and landmarks.

Mount Hood

The Cascade Mountain Range is like no other mountain range in the country. The range is part of the greater Pacific Ring of Fire, which is home to 452 active and inactive volcanoes—and is where about 90 percent of the world's earthquakes occur. Portland and the Cascade Mountains surrounding it have not seen much volcanic activity since Mount St. Helens blew its top in 1980, but seismologists and scientists are never quick to forget what lurks beneath those luminous peaks and glaciers. Even Mount Hood, which at 11,245 feet is Oregon's tallest peak, is considered a not-quite-dormant volcano. Try telling that to the locals who trek to the mountain all year long to ski and snowboard the 4,600 skiable acres, hike the numerous trails that wind their way through 1,200 miles of forests and wilderness areas, and enjoy the region's pristine rivers and lakes.

RECREATION
Downhill Skiing
◖ MT. HOOD SKIBOWL

Mt. Hood Skibowl (87000 E. Hwy. 26, 503/272-3206, www.skibowl.com, Mon.–Tues. 3–10 P.M., Wed.–Thurs. 1–10 P.M., Fri. 9 A.M.–11 P.M., Sat. 8 A.M.–11 P.M., Sun. 8 A.M.–10 P.M.) is one of three major ski resorts on Mount Hood, and America's largest night-skiing area. With the highest lift at 5,027 feet and the base lodge at 3,600 feet, it ranks lowest in elevation, but still has some of the steepest terrain on the mountain, with vertical drops of 1,500 feet. If skiing or snowboarding is not your thing, Skibowl has an adventure park that offers a number of warm-weather alternatives, such as an Alpine Slide, mountain bike park, hiking trails, disc and miniature golf, batting cages, bungee jumping, horseback riding, and zip-line trails.

TIMBERLINE LODGE

The beautiful Timberline Lodge (27500 E. Timberline Rd., 503/272-3158, www.timberlinelodge.com, daily 9 A.M.–4 P.M., night skiing Fri.–Sat. 4–10 P.M.) was the picturesque outdoor setting for the 1980 thriller *The Shining,* but don't worry. All those creepy things happened at a studio far away and there is no such thing as Room 237. Instead of scary ghosts, Timberline is famous for offering year-round resort skiing on the Palmer snowfield at 8,540 feet. Also, Still Creek Basin, Timberline's

PHOTO COURTESY OF TIMBERLINE LODGE

The historic Timberline Lodge offers year-round skiing.

newest network of trails, has eight alpine trails and a lift-served snowshoe and cross-country skiing trail.

MOUNT HOOD MEADOWS
Finally, with its steep terrain and abundant snowfall, Mount Hood Meadows (14040 Hwy. 35, 503/337-2222, www.skihood.com, Mon.–Tues. 9 A.M.–4 P.M., Wed.–Thurs. 9 A.M.–9 P.M., Fri.–Sat. 9 A.M.–10 P.M., Sun. 9 A.M.–9 P.M.), is arguably one of the most popular resorts in Oregon. The 11 chairlifts at Meadows run on 100 percent wind power, and provide access to the 2,150 acres of terrain on the southeast flank of Mount Hood. The Cascade Express lift will take you to the highest point at Meadows. At 7,300 feet, it is the access point to a handful of the 85 runs and the 1,700 vertical feet of terrain the resort has to offer.

Cross-Country Skiing
With the sprawling acreage of the Mount Hood National Forest on hand, there is some great cross-country skiing to be had. **Cooper Spur Mountain Resort** (10755 Cooper Spur Rd., 541/352-7803, Fri. 4–9 P.M., Sat. 9 A.M.–9 P.M., Sun. and holidays 9 A.M.–4 P.M.) has four miles of groomed track and up to 14 miles of ungroomed trail nearby. Track fees are small and you will need a wilderness permit to explore the backcountry. Permits are free and accessible via self-service at the trailhead.

Hiking
Hiking and backpacking are popular pastimes in the Mount Hood area. **Timberline Trail** is one of the best challenging but beautiful hikes. Constructed in the 1930s by the Civilian Conservation Corps, the trail loops near Timberline Lodge and Mount Hood Meadows, but is otherwise surrounded by wilderness. The 40-plus mile trail has a number of variations depending on where you start and what the season is, but the entire route takes about five or six days to complete. This and many other trails in the region present seasonal hazards that should be researched and prepared for such as hypothermia, landslides, unstable terrain, and risk of drowning. Portland Hikers (www.portlandhikers.org) is a good resource for information on terrain, seasons, and safety tips.

Fishing
If you would like to take in some fishing, there's no better spot to head than **Lost Lake** (www.lostlakeresort.org). On the north side of the mountain, this is a place of quiet serenity where motorboats are never allowed. The best fishing is along the shores, where aquatic insects are most prevalent and the lake's population of rainbow trout and steelhead appear trying to snatch a meal. There are no fees for using the lake or its surrounding forested areas, but a license is required for anglers over 14 years of age.

RESTAURANTS
Government Camp
Mount Hood has a few little gems when it comes to dining, some of them upscale and some of them decidedly not. Government Camp, the community that serves as the gateway for most of the area ski resorts, is a favorite stop on the way to or from the slopes.

Ice Axe Grill (87304 E. Government Camp Loop, 503/272-0102, www.iceaxe grill.com, daily 11 A.M.–10 P.M., $10–20) is a traditional pub that also happens to be the home of Mt. Hood Brewing Company. The menu consists of all the fare you would expect from any self-respecting pub, like burgers, sandwiches, salads, pizza, and beer-battered fish. But in a surprising turn from tradition, they also have a number of vegetarian dishes.

Another popular pub is **The Ratskeller** (88335 E. Government Camp Loop, 503/272-3635, www.ratskellerpizzeria.com, Mon.–Fri. 4–11 P.M., Sat. 11 A.M.–2 A.M., $8–10), a casual joint that specializes in pizza. "The Rat," as it is affectionately called, has one side devoted to family dining and another side with a bar, where you will find billiards, live music, and karaoke.

The 24-hour family-style restaurant at **Huckleberry Inn** (88611 E. Government Camp Loop, 503/272-3325, www.huckleberry-inn.com, daily 24 hours, $8–10) is a great place to stop for breakfast or if you want to treat yourself to a little coffee and pie. The food is homey and hearty here, and for good reason. Stacks of huckleberry pancakes or heaping plates of steak and eggs are sure to fuel you up for a day in the snow.

Feel like dining at 6,000 feet? The views are spectacular from Timberline Lodge and *Sunset* magazine recently named the lodge's ◖ **Cascade Dining Room** (27500 E. Timberline Rd., 503/272-3104, www.timberlinelodge.com, daily 7:30–10 A.M., noon–2 P.M., 6–8 P.M., $16–22) one of the top 10 mountaintop restaurants in the Pacific Northwest and Canada. The Farmer's Market Brunch runs every day 11 A.M.–3 P.M. and is practically worth the trip itself. Reservations are required for dinner, but breakfast and lunch are more casual and are first-come, first-served.

Welches

In Welches, **Altitude** (68010 E. Fairway Ave., 503/622-2214, www.altituderestaurant.com, Mon.–Sat. 7–11 A.M. and 5–9 P.M., Sun. 9 A.M.–2 P.M., $14–29) has classy but casual upscale dining in the ambient Resort at the Mountain. They are fairly new on the scene, but already making a name for themselves as a romantic anniversary spot.

The **Rendezvous Grill and Taproom** (67149 E. Hwy. 26, 503/622-6837, www.rendezvousgrill.net, daily 11:30 A.M.–9 P.M., $15–20) is perhaps a little less serious, but no less devoted to great food. They are particularly known for their desserts, but they cook a mean steak Oscar as well.

Also in Welches, **El Burro Loco** (67211 E. Hwy. 26, 503/622-6780, www.burroloco.net, $8–15) is a bright cantina with inexpensive but tasty food, fresh cocktails, and an extensive collection of microbrews and tequila.

You will find a number of other dining options nearby in the small communities of Brightwood, Rhododendron, and Zig Zag.

HOTELS

Accommodations abound up in the mountains, whether you are looking for a cozy cottage or a stately lodge. **Timberline Lodge** (27500 E. Timberline Rd., 503/272-3104, www.timberlinelodge.com, $110–290) is easily one of the most iconic longings in Government Camp. Rooms vary from positively dorm-like chalet rooms with bunk beds and bathrooms down the hall to the lofty private suites that sleep as many as eight people.

Right next to the Ice Axe and Mt. Hood Brewing Company in Government Camp, **Mt. Hood Inn** (87450 E. Government Camp Loop, 503/272-3205, www.mthoodinn.com, $159–179) is an affordable way to avoid the big lodge, but still be close to all the action. Resembling a hotel more than an inn, Mt. Hood Inn has three room types, from the basic deluxe room to the king spa room, which rents for as little as $179 a night. There's an indoor public Jacuzzi on-site as well, which is nice after you've been hitting the slopes all day.

If a bed-and-breakfast is more your style, check out the **Doublegate Inn** (26711 E. Welches Rd., 503/622-0629, www.doublegateinn.com, $139–169) in Welches. Every detail has been labored over here and the newly refurbished inn is practically oozing with cozy vibes. The rooms are beautifully appointed, and the largest features a king-size canopy bed, writing desk, full-size sofa, and a two-person soaking tub.

Also in Welches, you will find the beautiful

and modern **⊀ The Resort at The Mountain** (68010 East Fairway Ave., 503/622-3151, www.theresort.com, $173–569), a premier golf, ski, and meeting resort where you can occasionally hear the bagpipes play as they herald the sunset. The Resort was remodeled in 2008 and can now accommodate couples, families, outdoors enthusiasts, meetings, and event groups. It is, of course, popular for its proximity to the slopes, but it also has two restaurants, tennis courts, 27 holes of golf, a heated outdoor swimming pool, and a professional croquet court. Families can stay in the resort's enormous two- and three-bedroom villas, both of which have a full kitchen and dining room area, laundry facilities, private parking, and private decks. Standard rooms at The Resort at The Mountain can only be oxymoronically described as "basic luxury," with plush memory-foam mattresses, 42-inch plasma HDTVs, terrycloth robes, and environmentally friendly products.

PRACTICALITIES
Information and Services
You can find a plethora of up-to-date information about road conditions, snow fall, and weather online. For tips on travel and recreation, check out Mt. Hood Territory (www.mthoodterritory.com), which has maps, calendars, and recommendations on everything from activities to lodging. If you plan to take in a little Mother Nature, **Mt. Hood National Forest Headquarters** (www.fs.fed.us/r6/mthood) can provide you with maps, conditions updates, and details on permits and passes. Be sure to check with the Oregon Department of Transportation (www.odot.state.or.us/roads) before hitting the road to see if traction devices will be required to make it to your destination. It's also a good idea to check with the **Northwest Weather and Avalanche Center** (www.nwac.us) to be sure that conditions are safe, particularly if you plan to venture into the less-groomed areas.

All of the major ski areas have a regularly updated snow report, which will advise you on ski conditions, snow depth, and snowfall,

oftentimes providing live webcams of the lifts and slopes. You can visit the Timberline website (www.timberlinelodge.com) or call the snow line at 503/222-2211. The same goes for Mount Hood Meadows (503/227-7669, www.skihood.com) and Skibowl (503/222-2695, www.skibowl.com).

If you plan to hike or explore the backcountry, it's a good idea to rent a Mountain Locator Unit from one of the local mountaineering and outdoor shops or from Mt. Hood Inn (503/272-3205, www.mthoodinn.com). The device, which is exclusive to Hood, costs about $5 to rent and is worn on a sash across the chest. When activated, it sends out radio beacons to rescuers, giving them a better chance of finding you in the event of an emergency.

Getting There and Around
From Portland, take I-84 East as it passes through some of Oregon's most scenic natural wonders, like the Columbia River Gorge and Multnomah Falls. You can opt to take the Historic Columbia River Highway for a truly spectacular picturesque drive; it will reconnect with I-84 later on. Continue on I-84 to the town of Hood River, where you can visit a number of pretty orchards and vineyards. Next, continue on to Oregon Route 35, where you will soon connect with Highway 26, which passes through Sandy and on to Government Camp.

If conditions are poor, you might be better off skipping the scenic highways and taking the road more traveled. From I-84 East, take exit 16 (Wood Village/SE 242nd) and turn right, through the city of Gresham. Stay on SE 242nd south, and turn left onto SE Burnside, which becomes Highway 26, which passes through the small town of Sandy before continuing on to the mountain.

Sno-park permits are required for vehicles almost everywhere, including at the resorts. They are sold through various Oregon DMV offices (www.oregon.gov/ODOT/DMV/vehicle/sno_park_permits.shtml) and by permit agents in resorts, sporting goods stores, and other retail outlets. It will cost you about $3 a day or $20 annually.

BACKGROUND

The Setting

GEOGRAPHY

Situated approximately 110 miles from the Pacific Ocean, the city of Portland lies between the Cascade Mountain Range to the east and the Coastal Range to the west. The city, which is the largest in the state and one of the chief cities in the Pacific Northwest, is divided by the Willamette River, which flows into the Columbia River just to the north.

The land in the Willamette River Valley is agriculturally productive and for that reason, it was the desired destination of many pioneers who set out on the Oregon Trail in the 1840s. Although Portland is not often regarded as part of the Willamette Valley basin, it is well within the defining mountain ranges. Much of the area's fertility can be credited to its past, when massive ice dams in the prehistoric Glacial Lake Missoula in Montana repeatedly ruptured, each time flooding through eastern Washington and down through the Columbia River Gorge. It is estimated that during that time, much of the Willamette Valley, including Portland, was under several hundred feet of water—so much that only the West Hills, Mount Tabor, and Mount Scott were visible.

As Portland was beginning to blossom, the logging industry dominated the economy, and around 1847, the city experienced a growth so major that developers decided that they

© HOLLYANNA MCCOLLOM

needed more roads to encourage trade and to compete with the elder trading post upstream, Oregon City. Unfortunately, they discovered that as they cut down trees to make roads, the manpower needed to remove the stumps was stiflingly inadequate, forcing the arboreal remains to be left until workers could address them. To prevent wagon accidents and stumbling, locals began painting the stumps white for visibility, which aided pedestrians in traversing the notoriously muddy landscape and earned the city the nickname Stumptown.

Despite its distance from the waters of the Pacific, Portland has one of the busiest ports on the West Coast, as ocean shipments can reach the city by way of the Columbia and Willamette Rivers. There are also two interstate highways, several freight railways, and rail transit systems that serve the city, and numerous domestic airlines that fly through Portland International Airport.

By car, Portland is only 45 minutes from Salem, the state capitol, 1.5 hours from the ski slopes of Mount Hood, two hours from the Pacific Ocean, and about 3.5 hours to Seattle, Washington, or the Great Basin high-desert plateau in Bend, Oregon. But even within the city limits, Mother Nature is rarely more than five minutes or five blocks away. There are a number of botanical gardens, rose gardens, and arboretums; and Forest Park, with its 5,000 acres of alder, fir, cottonwood, maple and yew trees, is the largest wilderness park within a city in the United States.

CLIMATE

The weather in Portland is usually quite mild thanks to the White Mountains to the northwest, which keep snow from reaching the Portland metro area and keep the temperatures moderate. Fog and rain showers are common, but contrary to popular belief, it doesn't rain all the time. In fact, Portland receives about half of its annual rainfall between November and February. All told, it rains about 36–42 inches per year, with December and January being the wettest months.

The summer months are often mild and pleasant with temperatures that rarely top 90°F, a climate that often continues into the early months of fall. Winter begins late and usually extends into March, with one or two cold snaps that can last several days.

ANIMALS AND INSECTS

Of course, Oregon is the Beaver State, and while the state mascot is currently under environmental protection, you can still find the beaver in Pacific Northwest streams and rivers along with his cousins, the muskrat and nutria. Within the city itself you're more likely to see squirrels, chipmunks, raccoons, opossums, frogs, skunks, and the occasional mouse, garter snake, rat, or bat. Step into the wilderness of one of the parks or wildlife refuges and you might see deer, rabbits, otters, turtles, or possibly even a cougar or coyote.

Portland is heaven for bird-watchers and the city's numerous trees are populated by pigeons, blue jays, swallows, crows, hummingbirds, starlings, thrushes, warblers, woodpeckers, and wrens. When the weather is stormy at the coast, it's not uncommon for seagulls to come inland for a little respite, and when they get a little curious, it is not unusual for owls to set up residency in the rafters of a large building (such as the Oaks Amusement Park carousel) or home.

As far as pests and insects go, Portland is low on the radar. There are, of course, house flies, mosquitoes, honey bees, wasps, ladybugs, butterflies, and moths, all of which are small in comparison to the size they are in the southern and northeastern United States. Most of the spiders are harmless, and those that aren't (like the black widow) are extremely rare.

History

LEWIS AND CLARK AND THE EARLY SETTLERS

As Meriwether Lewis and William Clark neared the Pacific coast goal of their epic expedition across the United States, they were struck by the splendor of the region that would one day become Portland. But long before their journey would begin, Oregon was home to a number of Native American tribes. The mild climate and abundance of fish, game, and wildlife, coupled with the wealth of water sources—not the least of which are the Willamette River and the mighty Columbia—made the Willamette Valley a very rich area indeed. Native tribes such as the Multnomah and Clackamas based their entire economies and cultures upon the land and the water. Nearby Celilo Falls, for example, was a tribal fishing area on the Columbia River near what is now the border between the Oregon and Washington. This area, called Wyam after the tribe that inhabited it, was a hub of activity for fishing and trading that Lewis and Clark called a "great emporium…where all the neighboring nations assemble," until the completion of the nearby Dalles Dam flooded the falls and the neighboring village.

PETTYGROVE AND LOVEJOY'S LEGENDARY COIN TOSS

Portland wouldn't be what it is today if not for the collective $0.26 of Asa Lovejoy and Francis Pettygrove. Back in 1843, a Tennessee pioneer named William Overton and a Massachusetts lawyer named Asa Lovejoy steered their canoe down the Willamette River from Fort Vancouver toward Oregon City and stopped on the banks of what was then known as The Clearing. Knowing that a city would have to be established near the convergence of the Willamette and Columbia Rivers, Overton was certain that establishing a claim on the land would be a lucrative endeavor. Sadly, he lacked the $0.25 required to file a land claim.

Fortunately for Overton (and all the rest of us) Lovejoy made a deal with him. Lovejoy would pay the fee and in exchange share the 640-acre site with Overton. This suited Overton just fine and he set about building a homestead on what added up to about 16 blocks of land, but after a year, Overton decided to leave Oregon behind and depart for Texas. So, he sold his share of the claim to Pettygrove and the city as we know it began to evolve.

When the founders of this budding city discussed what to name it, however, they hit a snag. Pettygrove wanted to name the city after his hometown, Portland, Maine, and Lovejoy thought it only proper to name it after his home of Boston, Massachusetts. They agreed to flip a coin and after heads came up two of the three times the penny was tossed, Pettygrove had won. The coin used in this legendary meeting has come to be known as "the Portland Penny" and is currently on display at the Oregon Historical Society.

PORTLAND'S NOT-SO-PRETTY PAST

As the city grew into a lively port town, so did the traffic of ne'er-do-wells. By the late 19th century, a constant influx of sailors, loggers, sheepherders, ranch hands, and vagabonds meant a growing need for saloons and boarding houses. Sadly, even the most practical intentions soon fell victim to vice. Brothels and opium dens began to spring up all over town, and visiting them often led to robbery, kidnapping, or death. One notorious tradeswoman of the time was simply known as Sweet Mary. Mary cleverly avoided the usual legalities of owning a brothel by housing hers on a barge that floated to whichever quadrant of the city offered the least attention from the law. The police and vice squads couldn't do much about it since her placement on the river meant that she wasn't officially under anyone's jurisdiction.

It was during that time, however, that

WHAT'S THAT YOU SAY?

There are so many nicknames for Portland, it's hard to keep track of them all. The city also has a number of catchphrases that are helpful to know so you don't get offended if someone asks you if you have seen "Big Pink."

- **Beervana:** With all the fantastic microbreweries and artisan beermakers in town, this designation makes sense. Portland is a beer lover's heaven.

- **The Benson Bubblers:** Those public drinking fountains you see on the street corners were named for philanthropist Simon Benson. And in case you were wondering, it is safe to drink from them. The water comes from the same municipal source as the rest of the city's drinking water and is not recycled back into the fountain.

- **Big Pink:** This term refers to the 43-story boxy pink building at SW 5th and Burnside Street.

- **Bridgetown:** There are a total of 11 bridges that keep Portland cars, buses, bikes, and people moving.

- **The City of Roses:** The city comes by this nickname naturally. People figured out a long time ago that Portland has the ideal climate for growing roses. It wasn't long before the International Rose Test Garden

was established and an annual festival was planned to celebrate this fact.

- **The Couve:** Vancouver, Washington, just over the I-5 bridge. It is also occasionally (and less kindly) referred to as Vantucky.

- **DIY:** Do-it-Yourself. It's more than a crafty way to get things done in Portland; it's a way of life. The phrase is part of the city lexicon and stands for creativity, invention, and tenacity.

- **Keep Portland Weird:** This phrase, which was introduced to the city by the iconic record store Music Millennium, is everywhere, from bumper stickers to buildings. In Portland, the focus is one celebrating self-expression and self-reliance. The only thing that is considered truly weird or suspicious is abject normalcy.

- **Lake O:** This refers to Lake Oswego, an affluent suburb south of the city.

- **Little Beirut:** Portland has always been pretty blue, politically speaking, and when President H. W. Bush visited the city in the early 1990s, he was met with so many protesters that he and his staff dubbed the city Little Beirut.

- **NoPo:** This term refers to North Portland.

Portland's more notorious reputation developed, as it came to be known as the "Unheavenly City" or the "Forbidden City." Despite the fact that the United States Constitution had declared slavery illegal, countless intoxicated or naive men came to Portland only to be kidnapped or tricked into captivity and sold into slave labor on merchant ships.

Throughout much of downtown, particularly in Old Town, there is a maze of underground tunnels that were used to trap and transport unsuspecting souls to their doom. There was money in it for the sort of guy who was willing to swindle, drug, or beat his victims into

submission—and no one was more notorious for it than Joseph "Bunco" Kelly. Legend has it that Bunco once swiped a wooden statue from a local cigar shop and sold it to a ship's captain as a drunken sailor. During Prohibition, bars that wanted to allow patrons to drink and gamble moved their operation to the tunnels, which provided some protection from the law, but only served to increase the possibility of capture.

Still to this day, there are hints about Portland's disreputable past, trap doors leading to bars, human-sized holding cells, mysterious artifacts, and rumors of ghosts still inhabit

There are a number of other neighborhoods that have tried to adopt this method of nicknaming (SoWa for the South Waterfront, FoPo for Foster-Powell), but NoPo is the only one that has really caught on.

- **PDX:** Yes, it is the airport code for the city, but it is also a well-recognized shorthand epithet for the city.

- **Pill Hill:** This is Oregon Health and Sciences University, which looms above the city in Portland's west hills.

- **P-Town:** Nothing fancy here, just an affectionate pet name used by locals.

- **Puddletown:** With 36–40 inches of rain per year, this name is self-explanatory.

- **Rip City:** Portlanders can thank basketball announcer Bill Schonely for this nickname. The play-by-play man was known for his creative exclamations during the Trail Blazers games, and this one became a rallying cry for the team and eventually a city moniker.

- **The Schnitz:** Slang for the Arlene Schnitzer Concert Hall.

- **Slabtown:** This nickname refers back to the days when Portland had a reputation for mischief. Sailors or young ladies caught unawares were likely to end up being shipped off to a life of slavery or to end up dead on a concrete slab.

- **Snob Hill:** This term affectionately refers to Nob Hill, or the shopping districts on NW 21st and NW 23rd Avenues.

- **Stumptown:** This nickname was first meant as an insult when the forested landscape was rapidly cleared to make way for growth. The stumps were not cleared and became hazards when traveling through the mud or dark. Eventually, the stumps were painted white, which made for a scene that rather resembled a graveyard.

- **The Sunset Highway:** Otherwise known as Highway 26 West, a lovely name for the road that jams up bumper-to-bumper during rush hour each weekday.

- **Zoobombers:** These daredevils take a weekly wild ride down the hills of Washington Park on kiddie bicycles that they carry with them on the MAX to the Oregon Zoo stop. It is not intended to be an aggressive act, and the zoobombers are mostly regarded with bemusement. There's a sculpture on the corner of 13th and West Burnside where the participants stack their bikes with joyful abandon.

the underground tunnels, a veritable warren of deception and despair.

THE MCMENAMINS KINGDOM

In addition to owning nearly 60 brewpubs, microbreweries, music venues, historic hotels, and theater pubs, and being one of the top 50 largest craft breweries in the United States, Mike and Brian McMenamin are rather like historians. A number of their restaurants, pubs, and hotels are salvaged historical buildings that have colorful pasts as mortuaries, poor farms, vaudeville houses, churches, and elementary schools. The "McBrothers" have a reputation for breathing new life into buildings that would have otherwise met with a wrecking ball, while still holding on to the venues' original charms. Given the nature of their business, the brothers take history pretty seriously, and their kingdom (as they call it) employs a full-time historian to dig up and preserve stories, like that of a prostitute killed by her jealous lover at the White Eagle Hotel, or that of the Zakojis, a family of Japanese immigrants who owned Hotel Louie (the McMenamins newest endeavor) long before it became a notorious bathhouse.

OREGON ON FILM

Oregon is blessed with a beautiful landscape, which filmmakers have long sought because of its versatility. If some of the scenery you encounter looks familiar, don't be surprised. Here's just a sampling of the films that were made in Oregon:

- *Bandits:* This comedy starring Bruce Willis, Billy Bob Thornton, and Cate Blanchett was filmed all over Oregon. The bank robbery scene was filmed in the small town of Silverton, residential scenes were shot in West Linn, Lake Oswego, and Oregon City. The Broadway Bridge and Crown Point State Park in Corbett also make appearances.

- *Body of Evidence:* The movie, which featured Madonna and Willem Dafoe, was largely considered a clunker, but many scenes in this erotic thriller were filmed in Portland, including a number of scenes at the Governor Hotel.

- *Come See the Paradise:* This historical drama set before and during World War II is about the treatment and internment of 100,000 Asian Americans. The movie starred Dennis Quaid and was filmed in Astoria, Portland, and the Willamette Valley.

- *Coraline:* Neil Gaiman's creepy-cool story of a plucky young girl who wishes for better parents was painstakingly animated in the Portland stop-animation studio Laika.

- *Drugstore Cowboy:* This film, which was Gus Van Sant's second, starred Matt Dylan and Kelly Lynch. It was filmed in and around areas such as the Nob Hill Pharmacy on NW Glisan, and the Irving Apartments near NW 21st and Irving. While set in the 1970s, there are a number of buildings that appear on screen which were not built until the 1980s.

- *Elephant:* Another Gus Van Sant film, *Elephant* was filmed in 2002 at Whitaker Middle School (which has since been torn down) and followed the actions of a pair of teen shooters who opened fire on their classmates. The film starred real Oregon high school students instead of professional actors.

- *Feast of Love:* This film starring Morgan Freeman, Greg Kinnear, Radha Mitchell, and Selma Blair was set at Portland State University, but filmed at Western Seminary and Reed College.

- *Fire in the Sky:* This 1993 alien abduction movie starring D. B. Sweeny, Robert Patrick, and Henry Thomas was filmed in Oakland, Oregon, near Ashland and Roseburg. It was based on the real-life accounts of the main character, Travis Walton.

- *Five Easy Pieces:* The classic Jack Nicholson movie was filmed in Eugene and Florence, Oregon, as well as in the city of Portland. The infamous diner scene was filmed at a Denny's restaurant in Glenwood, Oregon.

- *Free Willy* and *Free Willy 2:* Both of the Keiko adventure movies were filmed in Astoria and Cannon Beach, Oregon. Later, the orca would find a temporary home in Newport's Oregon Coast Aquarium.

- *The Goonies:* The classic 1980s coming of age film was filmed in Astoria and Cannon Beach, Oregon. The main character's home still stands on 38th Street (visit on foot if you go).

- *The Hunted:* Directors of this film starring Benicio del Toro and Tommy Lee Jones picked Portland because they needed a lot of rain for filming. Sadly for them, Portland was visited by an unusually dry spell that lasted several weeks.

- *Into the Wild:* This adaptation of the John Krakauer book starred Emile Hirsch, Marcia Gay Harden, and William Hurt. The graduation scene was filmed at Reed College.

- *Kindergarten Cop:* "It's not a tumor!" Yup, that scene and many others were filmed at John Jacob Astor Elementary School in Astoria. The Bayview Motel on Marine Drive, the Sefare restaurant on Industrial Street, and Ecola State Park (near Cannon Beach) also played significant roles.

- *Maverick:* This 1994 Western comedy starred Mel Gibson, Jodie Foster, and James Garner. It was filmed in the Columbia River Gorge, and near Beacon Rock on the Washington Side of the Gorge.

- *Men of Honor:* The Cuba Gooding, Jr. film about the first African American U.S. Navy diver filmed some restaurant exterior shots in Portland.

- *Mr. Holland's Opus:* The Richard Dreyfuss film about a composer who agrees to teach music in order to support his family was filmed in and around Grant High School in Northeast Portland.

- *My Own Private Idaho:* Gus Van Sant's sad film about two young men on a journey of personal discovery was set in Van Sant's hometown and favorite locale, Portland.

- *National Lampoon's Animal House:* This iconic college frat film, which set up a lifetime of imitators, was filmed at the University of Oregon in Eugene.

- *One Flew Over the Cuckoo's Nest:* Ken Kesey's amazing story of life in a mental ward was filmed in the Oregon State Hospital in Salem, a mental institution that is operational to this day.

- *Paint Your Wagon:* The 1969 Clint Eastwood musical movie was filmed in Baker City, in eastern Oregon.

- *Paranoid Park:* The Gus Van Sant film about a teenage skateboarder who accidentally kills a security guard was set in and filmed in Portland, in particular, the Burnside Skatepark, the Willamette River, and the Steel Bridge.

- *The Shining:* The exterior of Timberline Lodge served as the setting for this 1980 horror film about an ill-fated family that agrees to serve as winter caretakers for a ski lodge. While the interior of the hotel was not used for filming, the hotel still asked the filmmakers to change the room number mentioned in the book (217) to 237, a room that doesn't exist at Timberline.

- *Short Circuit:* Number 5 came alive in Oregon. The 1986 comedy starring Ally Sheedy and Steve Guttenberg was filmed in Astoria, Portland, the Cascade Locks, and other portions of the Columbia River Gorge.

- *Sometimes a Great Notion:* The 1970 film, starring Paul Newman and Henry Fonda, is an adaptation of Ken Kesey's moving novel about the Oregon logging industry and its effects on the Stamper family. Though the film is set in the fictional Wakonda, Oregon, you can see much of the Central Coast, including the Siletz River, Yaquina Bay, and the city of Newport.

- *Stand by Me:* Much of Rob Reiner's quintessential coming-of-age story was filmed in Lane County, near Eugene, including the infamous pie-eating contest where Lardass Hogan got his revenge.

- *Twilight:* The wildly popular vampire movie, which was adapted from Stephanie Meyer's series was set in the fictional town of Forks, Washington, and filmed in various locations around Oregon and Washington. The prom scene was filmed at the View Point Inn in the Columbia River Gorge.

- *Untraceable:* This thriller starring Diane Lane as an FBI agent on the hunt for a serial killer was filmed in a number of Portland locales, including Oaks Amusement Park and the Broadway Bridge.

- *What the Bleep Do We Know!?:* This documentary-style film about quantum physics and human consciousness was filmed at The Bagdad Theater on Hawthorne, in the Pearl District, and in the MAX tunnel, which serves as the Washington Park Zoo stop.

PORTLAND TODAY

Looking around Portland today, you can see that the city is changing, because somehow, the city never lost its pioneering roots or its desire to build or re-create something from nothing. Early efforts in city planning from some of the city's founders ensured that there would always be plenty of green space even in the most urbanized areas. That is why there are big parks, small parks, tree-lined streets, and rooftop gardens all over the city. Some of these spaces are meant for play and some for reflection, but all encompass that need to mix the Pacific Northwest love of nature with a need for growth and progress. Whether its dogs scampering through the off-leash area of Overlook Park, kids splashing through the fountain at Jamison Square, or a performance of *King Lear* under the trees in Laurelhurst Park, these green spaces are valuable and well used.

The city has also seen quite a bit of urban development of late. Twenty years ago, the Pearl District was little more than abandoned warehouses and railroad tracks. Today it's a bustling neighborhood full of world-class restaurants and more galleries than you can shake a paint brush at. Mississippi Avenue was falling into disrepair before an influx of creative youthful energy turned it into an artsy, eco-focused, and affectionate community. The same can be said for the Alberta Arts District, but perhaps on a much grander scale. Spread throughout the city there are neighborhoods that despite being interconnected, bear a personality and style all their own. In every district, there are funky, unique, and elegant shops, top-notch restaurants, and stylish bars. Getting to all those neighborhoods is a snap, since the transportation system has evolved along with the city a little more each year with the streetcar, light rail, and bus system providing yet more car-free access to the metro area. Since the transportation system was built around the idea of urban growth and city planning, it has thus far been a pretty happy marriage.

Cycling is hugely encouraged and supported

COURTESY OF TRAVEL PORTLAND

The pretty Pearl District was once made up of just warehouses and train tracks.

throughout the city with bike lanes, paths, and parks that oftentimes lead to vantage points where, on a clear day, sparkling water and distant mountains are an awesome sight to behold.

The locals, for the most part, are very friendly and willing to point you towards the best cup of coffee, plate of fries, or hamburger in town, but their opinions are likely vary as much as the weather. One thing is certain, however: Portlanders are all about self-expression, self-sufficiency, and the pursuit of the next best story. It might be about that amazing gnocchi from that shop down the street, the next project we are working on, or that artist we met while touring First Thursday. Every experience seems to be treated as if it is ripe with possibility. That is why chef-owned restaurants are so much more common than franchises and why you will find them around almost every corner. Almost all of them pride themselves on using local fresh ingredients and tailoring the menu to what's in season.

© JOSH OAKHURST

Portland Center Stage, the city's second oldest theater company, is now housed in the historic First Regiment Armory building.

Government and Economy

GOVERNMENT

The city of Portland leans largely to the left of the political scale. In 2009, there were 341,962 registered voters and 206,412 of those were Democrats. The city as a whole tends to be fairly progressive, with the mayor, four city commissioners, and a city auditor at the helm. In fact, Portland's system of government is one of the few things it is not progressive about as a city. Of all the large cities in the United States, Portland has the last remaining commission form of government. Under the commission structure, the officials elected to represent Portland constitute the legislative body of the city and are, as a group, responsible for taxation, appropriations, ordinances, and other general functions. Each commissioner is assigned a responsibility to one aspect of municipal affairs, like public works, public affairs, or public safety. All city officials, including the mayor, are elected to serve four-year terms, with elections being spaced out every two years so as not to inadvertently fill a council with inexperienced members.

The mayor and city commissioners make up the city council, which carries out its duties in accordance with the laws of the state and the Portland City Code and Charter, and are primarily responsible for making laws which govern the city of Portland. And while the council is accountable for legislative policy and for keeping Portland running like a well-oiled machine, the auditor keeps the council in line with the system of checks and balances. Both city and state law allow Portlanders the right to initiate legislation through the proper processes or even to refer legislation that has passed through city council to a vote of the people.

© HOLLYANNA MCCOLLOM

Portland's City Hall was erected in 1895.

ECONOMY

Early in its history, Portland's economy was largely dependent on the rivers that flowed through it. The Willamette and Columbia Rivers provided access to the Pacific Ocean, and their deep waters meant that the city was well placed to become a nucleus for logging, farming, and fishing. When the city was selected as the West Coast terminal for the U.S. mailing ship *The Petonia,* it seemed like the city was well on its way to becoming a major part of the nation's economy. But disaster struck in 1873 when a fire reduced 22 downtown blocks and parts of Chinatown to ashes. To add insult to injury, another fire had occurred just eight months earlier when anti-Chinese arsonists set ablaze three city blocks, with a loss estimated at about $2 million. Despite the devastation, the city began to rebuild and this time with only cast iron, brick, and stone. By the turn of the 19th century, the construction of the transcontinental railroad that linked Portland to the East Coast caused the population to swell to 90,000 people.

Today, the city's economy is quite different and the technology and research industries are leading the pack. In fact, Intel, Providence Health Systems, and Oregon Health and Sciences University are the city's top employers, followed at a distance by Fred Meyer, the Kaiser Foundation, and Legacy Health System. Despite having significant layoffs in the early part of 2009, the health and tech industries continue to dominate the economy for the entire state, and the Portland metro area in particular. Even within those fields there has long been a focus on utilizing sustainable practices whenever possible and devising eco action plans when practices weren't readily available. For a long time, this focus on the environment gave Portlanders a reputation for being tree-hugging hippies, but now that the city is poised to become the leader in green technology and sustainable practices, things are looking even brighter. Cities all over the world are turning to Portland to find out how they can conserve energy and resources without diminishing their way of life. Mayor Sam Adams and the current

SYMBOLS OF THE OREGON SPIRIT

- **Bird:** The medium-sized blackbird with a distinctive yellow belly is known as the **Western meadowlark,** a state symbol shared with Kansas, Nebraska, Wyoming, North Dakota, and Montana. Portland has its own symbolic bird, the Great Blue Heron, which can be spotted in some of the wetlands and nature conservatories.

- **Animal:** The industrious **American beaver** is right at home in a state known for logging, but the semi-aquatic rodent is considered a pest in some parts of the world.

- **Flower:** The **Oregon grape** is an evergreen shrub that has pretty yellow flowers in late spring that form into clusters of purple berries that resemble grapes. They may look tasty, and the birds sure like them, but don't be tempted to try them yourself. While not poisonous, they are extremely tart. Portland's city flower is, of course, the rose.

- **Tree:** The hills and parks of Oregon are abundant with **douglas fir** trees, the second-tallest conifer in the world (second only to redwoods). The tree commonly lives for 500 years and sometimes as long as 1,000.

- **Fish:** The **chinook salmon** is born in freshwater and may spend anywhere between one and eight years in the Pacific Ocean before returning to their birth waters to spawn. The fish was a highly valued part of Native American culture.

- **Rock:** Similar to geodes, **thunder eggs** are formed within rhyolitic lava flows. They look like plain Jane baseball-shaped rocks on the outside, but once split in half and polished, they reveal pretty layers of agate, jasper, and opal.

- **Nut:** In 2008, Oregon produced 34,000 tons of **hazelnuts.** These popular nuts are not only quite tasty, they are also a super-food, rich in protein and unsaturated fat with significant amounts of thiamine, vitamin B6, and fiber.

- **Mushroom:** The delicious **Pacific golden chanterelle** is distinguished by its fluted martini glass shape, apricot smell, and mild peppery taste. They commonly grow under pine, beech, or birch trees and can be found from July until the first frosts.

- **Fruit:** Superior growing conditions in the Hood River Valley make it the top **pear** producer in the United States. The Anjou pear, in particular, thrives in the warm sunny days and crisp, cool nights.

- **Beverage:** The Oregon dairy industry contributes over $600 million to the state's economy, so it's no surprise that **milk** takes top honors in the beverage department. Although, there is a push right now to make beer the statewide drink.

- **Dance:** We all did it in gym class, do-si-doing with that awkward kid who had two left feet. But the **square dance** reflects on Oregon's pioneer heritage and the friendly, spirited nature of it was deemed a part of the Oregon character.

- **Motto:** The Latin phrase *Alis Volat Propriis,* which means, **"She Flies With Her Own Wings"** was adopted in 1854, changed about one hundred years later and then re-adopted in 1967 to reflect the state's independent spirit. The city of Portland has its own motto, "The City That Works."

- **Song:** The state song, *Oregon, My Oregon,* was written for a contest in 1920 by John Andrew Buchanan and Henry Bernard Murtagh. The first verse of the song honors the early settlers and the pioneers of the Oregon Trail. The second verse praises the natural beauty of the land.

city council have pushed to develop a new economic strategy that will brand Portland as the nation's most sustainable city. Along with that program come economic incentives and training programs for workers in targeted industries (like health, technology, and manufacturing), which Adams hopes will set Portland up as the leader in the global green economy.

The Rose Society and the Rose Festival

Portland's annual Rose Festival is quite the event and it's all thanks to the Rose Society, which was founded in 1888 by Georgiana Pittock, the flower-loving wife of *Oregonian* publisher Henry Pittock. But it started long before that, when in 1837, the first rose plant was brought to Oregon and presented to Anna Maria Pittman, the bride of missionary Jason Lee and the first white woman to be married, give birth, die, and be buried in Oregon. After much of the mission was destroyed by a fire years later, pioneer and legislator John Minto salvaged the rose and transported it to his home. The plant flourished in Portland's climate and thanks to Minto's willingness to share clippings, the city soon fell in love with the thorny beauty.

In an effort to teach and encourage amateur gardeners to plant and cultivate roses, a group of Portlanders decided to form a society which would one day become the oldest of its kind in the United States. While the city's first rose show occurred in 1889—a tradition that is still practiced during the festival to this day—the first official Rose Festival didn't happen until 1907.

In the early days of its existence, a king, Rex Oregonus, was chosen to rule over the festival. His identity (masked by a gigantic beard) was kept secret until being revealed at an annual celebratory ball. In 1914, the king was replaced by a queen, a socialite chosen from Portland's elite. The tradition continued until 1930, when the city decided to let each of the area high schools choose a representative from their senior class to serve as a Rose Festival princess. One year later, the title came with a college scholarship. Nowadays, the princesses (sometimes called "ambassadors") are not chosen for their beauty and social status; instead, they must have a minimum grade-point average of 2.75 and demonstrate exemplary citizenship. As ambassadors for their schools and the city, who now receive $3,500 for the honor, they are evaluated for their character, communication skills, and presence.

Education

Oregon students historically exceed national averages for math and verbal on their Scholastic Aptitude Test (SAT) scores. For dozens of years, Oregon and Washington have held the top two positions among the 23 states that test at least 50 percent of their high school graduates. There are more than 600 schools and 21 districts within the Portland metro area, and a number of secular and religiously affiliated private schools at the primary, secondary, and high school level.

The Portland metropolitan area is richly endowed with educational resources, including some of the best colleges in the nation. It is a bit of a chicken and egg question because it is hard to define which came first, the prevalence of smart, creative, and educated citizens, or the schools to entice them here. Whatever the cause, Portland boasts a number of colleges, universities, and trade schools.

Portland State University (PSU) is a public university in the heart of downtown, and is the fastest-growing school in the Oregon University System. At the outset, PSU was mainly a liberal arts college, but the university has since added doctorates in Mathematics, Biology, Chemistry, Computer Science, Applied Psychology, Engineering and Technology Management, Mechanical Engineering, and Sociology. Since the university is located in an urban area, traditional college housing is fairly limited, but there are a number of affordable apartments in the area. PSU's mascot is the Viking, and as part of the Big Sky Conference, and the Viking football team got a lot of attention when Jerry Glanville, who coached for 21 years in the NFL, became the 12th head coach in the history of the Portland State program.

Located in southeast Portland, **Reed College** is a private, independent, liberal arts college that is known for its disproportionately high number of graduates who go one to earn their PhD and/or Masters. The university has a distinct reputation for liberal, progressive, and anti-establishment leanings. In order to graduate, all students have to complete an intense year-long thesis project that will eventually become a part of the college's permanent research library. Upon completion of the senior thesis (which usually culminates in the form of a "thesis parade"), students must also pass an oral exam that focuses on their thesis, but may also include questions about any course previously taken. The official mascot of Reed College is the Griffin, but the unofficial mascot is the legendary Doyle Owl, a roughly 280-pound concrete bird that has been continuously stolen and re-stolen since 1913.

Lewis and Clark College is a private, liberal arts school in Southwest Portland that offers degrees in Arts and Sciences, the Law, and Education and Counseling. The students who attend Lewis and Clark are often globally minded, environmentally conscious thinkers, so it was no surprise when the college became the first campus in the country to comply with the Kyoto Protocol's emission targets in 2003, and just two years later became the first private institution in Oregon to sign the Talloires Declaration, a 10-point action plan created in France for incorporating sustainability and environmental literacy in teaching, research, operations, and outreach at colleges and universities.

The **University of Portland** (UP) is a private Roman Catholic university located in North Portland. It is affiliated with the Congregation of Holy Cross and is a sister school to the University of Notre Dame. It is the only school in the state that offers a college of arts and sciences; a graduate school; and schools of business, education, engineering, and nursing in one location. The UP mascot is the Portland Pilots, and their women's soccer team received a lot of recognition when they won the 2002 and 2005 Division I NCAA Women's Soccer Championships.

There are two other smaller religiously affiliated colleges in the city that seem to draw a lot of students to the city. **Concordia University** in Northeast Portland is a small Lutheran college with an enrollment that tops out at around 1,700 students each year. Though it is a private college, it is open to students of any faith who wish to pursue any of the 18 undergraduate majors. **Warner Pacific College** is a private liberal arts school in Southeast Portland that is affiliated with The Church of God and offers 19 majors, four areas of pre-professional study, and 25 minors for traditional students and adults seeking to further their education later in life.

Of course, given the city's love of art and food, it's no surprise that Portland has three colleges of art (**The Art Institute of Portland, Oregon College of Art and Craft,** and **Pacific Northwest College of Art**) and a culinary school that is considered to be top notch **(Western Culinary Institute)**. The city also happens to have a world-class teaching hospital and research center that draws in students, scientists, and patients from across the country and around the world. **Oregon Health Sciences University** currently has five schools in Medicine, Nursing, Dentistry, Science and Engineering, and Pharmacy, and is the only place in Oregon that grants doctoral degrees in Medicine, Nursing, and Dentistry.

Healthcare

The state of the healthcare system in Portland is a hot-button issue and Oregon has the fastest-growing rate of uninsured constituents in the nation. The downturn in the economy has had some effect on that and so has the influx of wealthy retirees and out-of-state transplants who have driven a deeper wedge between the haves and the have nots. While there is some animosity about the increased gentrification of older Portland neighborhoods and the accompanied increase in cost of living, locals and city officials are attempting a number of creative ideas to ensure that all Portlanders are protected from the rising cost of medical care.

People and Culture

In 2008, the population of the state of Oregon was estimated at 3,791,060. Of those, 19 percent lived in Multnomah County—the smallest of Oregon's 36 counties—which encompasses Portland, Gresham, Fairview, Troutdale, Wood Village, and portions of Lake Oswego. In July 2008, the city's population swelled to 575,930, a 1.33 percent increase over the previous year. The population of the metro area (which includes the surrounding five counties) is projected to reach 2.8 million by 2025.

The median age for Portland metro area residents is 36, with 44 percent of the population aged 15–44 years and 14 percent or residents over 60 years of age. While it has been said that Portland is "the whitest city in America," the statement is a bit hyperbolic. As of the latest census estimate, the city is about 77 percent Caucasian, 5.9 percent African American, 6.8 Asian or Pacific Islander, and 10 percent Hispanic.

In 2009, *Marie Claire* magazine declared that Portland was 10th on the list of top cities to find single guys. This claim, whether there is a great deal of truth to it or not, is largely due to Portland's status as a destination for the youthful creative class. More and more each week, people are coming to Portland to work and live life outside of the lines. Creative types like artists, chefs, and even engineers and scientists always have been lured by the city's tolerant, off-center way of life, and their presence has had a lasting effect on the economy, the lexicon, and the overall personality of the city. The city has long been called a big small town because it is easy to meet people, and also quite easy to find solitude if you seek it. People tend to be pretty easygoing, helpful, and more focused on the success of the community than on individual success.

CHINATOWN

Chinese immigrants have been in Portland almost as long as the city founders, and most were brought here to build bridges, tunnels, and railroad beds, and work in the mines, salmon canneries, and textile industries. The numbers in Portland continued to grow each year between 1850 and the early part of the 1880s despite the Chinese Exclusion Act, which was the first federal law to ever be passed banning an ethnic group from entry into the United States based on the fear that they would be an endangerment to the public. In 1885 and 1886, however, the population of Chinese immigrants mushroomed due to the expulsion of immigrants from Seattle, Tacoma, and Olympia in neighboring Washington. At the time, the Pacific Northwest was facing an economic downturn and the Chinese were blamed for taking jobs away from Americans and driving the average wage down. Although the city of Portland had not yet chosen to expel the Chinese, the immigrants were forced from outer communities into what was essentially a ghetto, an area that was notorious for kidnappings (through the Shanghai Tunnels), opium dens, and brothels. While Chinatown had those less attractive qualities, the neighborhood also had a strong sense of community, with barbershops, grocery stores, schools, and restaurants.

Today, Chinatown residents and property owners are struggling to overcome the neighborhood's reputation as a haven for crime, homelessness, and drug abuse, and they are also struggling to maintain a sense of community. With proposed development that includes large-scale grocery stores and higher-end restaurants, the proponents of Chinatown are eager for the opportunity to clean up the streets, but cautious about a development plan that might force out the very families and businesses that have maintained the spirit of Chinatown.

AFRICAN AMERICAN CULTURE

Ask most locals about the earliest recorded history of African American culture in Portland

© HOLLYANNA MCCOLLOM

This 12-foot bronze statue, which stands between Burnside and Couch Streets, was a gift to the city from Chinese businessman Huo Baozhu.

and you are likely to get a variety of answers. What most people don't realize is that there was an African American community that thrived as far back as the early 1900s near the spot where Union Station still stands today. Job opportunities at the railroads stimulated a small population growth within Portland's black community. People came from all over the United States, and particularly the South, as part of the Great Migration to work as Pullman porters, Red Caps, cooks, waiters, and shop laborers. The Portland Hotel, which was located at the present site of Pioneer Courthouse Square, was another big draw. More than 70 black men were brought up from the Carolinas and from Georgia to work in the hotel as service positions for what would become a major hub of the city's business and social activity.

Between 1850 and 1900, Portland's African American population increased from about a dozen to 775—not a staggering number, but enough to support two churches, a handful of businesses, and a newspaper. Along with those newcomers (many of whom migrated from

the South during the Great Migration) came a hardworking sense of spirit and a community alive with barbershops, restaurants, pool halls, haberdasheries, and hotels. On Sundays, the Golden West Hotel, which was owned by a black man named W. D. Allen, became a gathering spot of sorts when services at the nearby Mt. Olivet Baptist and Bethel AME churches let out. Dressed in their Sunday best, people would congregate in the Chinese restaurant, Turkish bath, barbershop, gambling room, gymnasium, and ice cream parlor and share stories.

In the early part of the 1900s, the African American community faced less discrimination than it would come to face in later years. In 1906, black people were allowed to vote and serve as jurors. Black children shared classrooms with white children and whites and blacks sat side-by-side in restaurants. In 1894, Charles Hardin became the first African American man to join the police force, and by 1915, he was the first black man to be made sheriff's deputy. When work was scarce, many

HOW TO TALK LIKE A LOCAL

If there is one thing that will mark you as a tourist (a term sometimes even applied to people who have lived in Portland for several years), it's the mispronunciation of several key words and phrases. A Portlander may not correct you if you get their name wrong, but call the state "Oree-Gone" and you are likely to get an earful. Here are a few phrases and tips on how to speak like a native.

- **Aloha:** This suburb of Beaverton is just a few miles west of Portland and far from the Hawaiian islands. Unlike the island greeting, the name of this community is pronounced *Ah-LO-wa*.

- **ART:** The acronym for Artists Repertory Theatre. However, if you say, "art," when referring to them, everyone will know you are either a neophyte in the arts or that you aren't from around here. It's *A-R-T*.

- **Clackamas:** This is the name of a Native American tribe that once inhabited this area, and is now one of the major Oregon counties. It is pronounced *CLACK-uh-mas*.

- **Couch Street:** We're not talking about furniture. This street is named after John H. Couch, one of the city founders. It is pronounced *Cooch*, which rhymes with pooch.

- **Eugene:** The city to the south is referred to as *Eu-GENE*, not *EU-gene*.

- **Glisan Street:** This street in Northwest and Northeast Portland was named for Dr. Rodney Glisan, a doctor for the U.S. Army in the 19th century. The good doctor's name was pronounced *Gliss-an*, but for reasons unbeknownst, the street name is pronounced *Glee-san*.

- **Marquam:** It's a double-decker bridge in Portland named after Philip Marquam, a state legislator and Multnomah County judge. It's pronounced *MARK-um*.

- **Multnomah:** It's a county, a waterfall, and a Native American tribe, and it's pronounced *Mult-NO-mah*.

- **OMSI:** The acronym for Oregon Museum of Science and Industry is treated like a word, *AHM-zee*, and almost never pronounced in full.

- **Oregon:** There are only two acceptable pronunciations: *OR-uh-gun* or *OR-ee-gun* – and the last one is pushing it.

- **Sauvie Island:** This pretty area about 10 miles northwest of Portland boasts a number of U-pick farms and a wildlife refuge, and is alternately referred to as *SAW-vee* or *SO-vee*.

- **Schuyler Street:** This Northeast Portland street can claim that it is loaded with beautiful historic homes, but it can't claim that it rhymes with "ruler." In fact, the street name is pronounced *Sky-ler*.

- **Tigard:** This suburb of Portland is not a buddy of Winnie-the-Pooh. It'ss pronounced *TIE-gard*.

- **Weidler:** The street in Northeast Portland is pronounced *WIDE-ler*.

- **Willamette:** This word comes up a lot. Whether you are referring to the river that divides the city, the alternative weekly newspaper, or a number of other things, it is pronounced *Wil-LAM-met*. It should never rhyme with confetti.

African American men began to explore the opportunity of owning a small business, and in turn began to shop in and patronize only community-owned businesses as a means of economic survival. For many years, it worked. By 1920, 8 percent of Portland's African American community owned or operated their own business, a statistic that was almost unheard of at the time.

But the tide began to turn as more European immigrants began to settle in Portland. Housing discrimination forced most African

Americans to settle near the industrial area on the east side of the Broadway Bridge, where you will now find Memorial Coliseum and the Rose Quarter. The Great Depression, too, was devastating to the African American community. Within a year, most of the black-owned businesses were forced to close their doors, including the Golden West Hotel. Jobs became even more difficult to come by, with racial tensions rising every day.

Today, little remains of the area that was once so alive with the city's first African American leaders. The Golden West Hotel still stands, but now serves as transitional housing for homeless, mentally ill individuals. The African American community is largely centered in the Albina area, which includes the Boise, Concordia, Eliot, Humboldt, Piedmont, Sabin, Vernon, King, Alberta, and Woodlawn neighborhoods. In many of those neighborhoods, the threat of gentrification has spurred conflict and conversation. The liberal-minded tendencies of Portlanders helps a little, but even the best of intentions can have negative results. It's a bit of an uphill battle but the city and organizations like Urban League of Portland and National Association for the Advancement of Colored People (NAACP) are helping to preserve the community and promote equality, and encourage a healthy rate of growth and development.

THE LGBT COMMUNITY

The city of Portland has long had an active gay community, and has one of the strongest feminist and lesbian communities in the United States. The history of the community dates back to World War II, when the city received countless traffic in and out of town from lonely soldiers, sailors, and war industry workers away from their families and friends. During that time, though the gay and lesbian community was still fairly closeted, the beer parlors, vaudeville houses, bars, and hotels were willing to look the other way while same-sex curiosities were explored and thrived. One such spot, the Music Hall, became a popular hangout for lesbians and was known to put on a pretty remarkable drag show. The club received a lot of attention when the sin-busting Mayor Dorothy McCullough Lee (1949–1953) attacked it most vociferously with liquor license queries and investigations. She did not succeed in shutting the venue down, but did manage to drive the drag act out of town.

At that time, there were gay rights organizations popping up all over the West Coast in major cities like Seattle and San Francisco, but Portland had no such movements toward encouraging pride and establishing rights. In spite of the community's lack of effort, however, gay men and lesbian women continued to flock to the more laissez-faire Portland after being chased out of other cities. In fact, the Portland police department tended to leave suspected gay hangouts alone. When Commissioner Stanley Earl wanted to shut down the Harbor Club in the late 1950s, it was the police that talked him out of it, suggesting that it was better to have homosexuals gathered in one place rather than scattered throughout the city.

Things reached a bit of a boiling point in 1964 when the papers began to run numerous headlines about "homosexual rings" that preyed upon children. Mayor Terry Schrunk was determined to crack down on bars that catered to gay men and lesbians, and formed the Committee for Decent Literature and Films to stop the production of publications that depicted homosexual activity. That summer, an *Oregon Journal* columnist stated to the police that the "unmentionables" were numerous in Portland, and that the number of gay and lesbian bars had inflated from three to ten. He assured the police that some local businessmen promised to take "vigilante action" against them in order to restore the civility of the city. Also that year the Portland City Council asked the Oregon Liquor Control Commission (OLCC) to revoke the liquor licenses of all the city's suspected gay and lesbian bars. The licenses were revoked, but quickly renewed when the OLCC admitted that the bars were operating within the law. After that, the city and the police department were largely unmotivated to continue pressuring the gay and lesbian venues.

Throughout the tough periods in the 1960s, Portland still did not have much in the way of activism for the gay and lesbian community, but there was little need for it. Portland was essentially wide open.

The LGBT community in Portland these days is far more active; and the complacency about city-wide or nationwide activism seems to have worn off. Organizations like the Portland Area Business Alliance, Basic Rights Oregon, Northwest Gender Alliance, and the Q Center are working overtime to ensure that the city stays "wide open," but smartly so. The election of mayor Sam Adams, the city's first openly gay mayor of a major American city, sparked a lot of attention and further confirmed Portland as a gay-friendly city.

But there are a number of other reasons why the city is so attractive to the gay community. The city is socially conscious and progressive with a number of organizations that offer everything from financial to emotional support, HIV/AIDS education and assistance, and networking opportunities and social activities. Portland also offers domestic partnership registration. While Multnomah County made a decision in 2004 to allow such unions, it wasn't until the passage of the Oregon Family Fairness Act and its subsequent signing by Governor Kulongoski that the domestic partnership system was made legal by the state of Oregon. Under that ruling, same-sex couples are now allowed to enjoy many of the things that they would have otherwise been denied, like hospital information, mortgage loans, and parental rights.

ESSENTIALS

Getting There

BY AIR

Portland International Airport, which goes by the call sign PDX, is the number one airport in the state of Oregon. It has direct connections to major airport hubs throughout the United States, plus non-stop international flights to Canada, Japan, Mexico, and the Netherlands. While the airport does have service from some smaller airlines like JetBlue (www.jetblue.com) and Hawaiian Airlines (www.hawaiianair.com), PDX is a major hub for Alaska Airlines and Horizon Air, and serves as a maintenance facility for Horizon Air. The route between PDX and Seattle-Tacoma International Airport is considered the 19th busiest air route in the world, in terms of flights per week, thanks to a number of travelers who prefer to skip the sometimes slow I-5 crawl (otherwise known as "the slog").

PDX has won a number of awards for its accessibility, courtesy, security, and amenities. Most visitors are pleased with the number of shops like Broookstone, Powell's Books, and Nike, where they can pick up last-minute supplies or gifts. Stores are not allowed to charge more than their off-site locations would charge, and as always in Oregon, everything is sales-tax free. There are a number of great places to grab a bite to eat or a drink as well. Locals love to stop by Good Dog/Bad Dog, Gustav's

Pub & Grill, Laurelwood Brewing Company, or Pizzacato, all of which are favorites in town as well.

To and From the Airport

The pick-up area for taxis, airport shuttles, parking shuttles, and town cars is located outside baggage claim in the center of the terminal's lower roadway. A few hotels offer complimentary shuttle service to and from the airport, but many are located prohibitively far from the center of the city. However, Portland's light rail system, MAX, picks up at the south end of the terminal and you can ride straight into the heart of downtown for about $2.30 per person. There are plenty of cabs to hail if you prefer to take one in, but cabs are expensive in Portland and it will run you about $30 and possibly as much as $70. A towncar service, like **Pacific Cascade** (888/869-6227, www.towncar.com), can be cheaper (about $35–60) if you arrange ahead of time. Just make sure you give them your flight number when you make the reservation so they can track any delays or cancellations.

Car Rental

All the major national car rental companies have outposts at PDX, so whatever your preference is, you can find it here. If you can wait until you get into town, you can always set up an account with **Zipcar** (503/328-3539, www.zipcar.com), a popular rental service in Portland that stashes cars all over the city. Reserve the one nearest to you and return it to the same spot when you are done. All the gas and insurance are included.

BY CAR

From Portland International Airport, head southwest on Airport Way to I-205 South and turn right onto the freeway. Follow I-205 to exit 21B to merge onto I-84-West and US 30-West to Portland.

If you are continuing to downtown Portland,

take the I-5 exit on the left that leads to Salem and Beaverton, and keep right as you take the exit marked "City Center." Follow the signs to merge onto the Morrison Bridge and into downtown Portland.

BY TRAIN

Portland's historic Union Station is served by three Amtrak passenger trains that has three daily departures between Seattle and Portland, and daily service to Vancouver, British Columbia. The Amtrak Cascades travels along the pretty countryside of the Pacific Northwest and British Columbia, and offers reclining seats; laptop computer outlets; bicycle, ski and snowboard racks; and regional food, local wine, and microbrews from the Bistro car.

Amtrak's Coast Starlight operates daily, connecting Los Angeles, San Francisco, Portland, and Seattle. This train has both a coach section (with optional at-seat meal service) and sleeping cars, and an Arcade Room with a selection of arcade-style video games.

Amtrak's Empire Builder route takes you through the Lewis and Clark Wilderness, beginning in Portland and heading east to Chicago. Stops along the way include Spokane, Whitefish, Glacier National Park, Minot, Minneapolis, and Milwaukee.

BY BUS

The **Greyhound bus terminal** (550 NW 6th Ave., 503/243-2361, www.greyhound.com) is located next to the Amtrak Station at the edge of Old Town. Greyhound offers connecting services all over the United States for reasonable rates, and often combines with Amtrak to reach destinations otherwise unreachable by train. The station is one of many along the I-5 corridor that connects Bellingham, Seattle, Salem, Eugene, and much of California. There are also select affiliate routes that can get you just about anywhere in the United States.

Getting Around

Portland is often thought of as a very European city. People here like to walk, bike, and utilize the various systems of public transportation available. In fact, the city as a whole encourages it. Many venues along the MAX or streetcar lines offer discounts to patrons who show their TriMet ticket. Neighborhoods that are particularly bike-heavy (like Mississippi Avenue, Alberta Street, Belmont Street, and Hawthorne Street) are equipped with plenty of bike lanes and places to park and lock up your bike. Most Portland neighborhoods are extremely walkable and have wide, pedestrian-friendly sidewalks with easily recognizable, wheelchair-accessible crosswalks.

The public transportation system in Portland is known for being just about as easy to use and reliable as a system can get. It's a safe, reliable way to get around on the weekdays, but becomes a little more complicated on weekends and holidays as it all but stops running after 2 A.M. So, if you are planning on staying out past last call, plan to take a cab or walk. For areas that are particularly congested when it comes to parking (like the Pearl District or NW 23rd), it is best bike there or ditch your car in a Smart Park (www.portlandonline.com/smartpark) lot and use the MAX or streetcar.

PUBLIC TRANSPORTATION
TriMet Buses
Nearly all of the TriMet buses and some of the C-TRAN (a system that serves Vancouver, Battleground, Hazel Dell, Camas, and Washougal, Washington) buses congregate at the transit mall on 5th and 6th Avenues downtown. Buses stop every three to five blocks, with one bus stop location per block. Northbound buses travel along 6th Avenue and southbound buses travel along 5th Avenue. Each bus stop is assigned a Stop ID number, which will be posted on the bus stop sign or on the schedule in the stop's bus shelter. You can use TriMet's Transit Tracker system (503/238-7433) by entering the Stop ID number when you call. The system will tell you exactly how long it will be before the next bus arrives.

MAX
Portland is particularly proud of its Metro Area Express, or MAX, system. TriMet and the city of Portland worked to integrate transportation needs with land use planning to give the city a longer-term plan for urban growth, energy resources, and environmental concerns. For this reason, MAX is a popular, affordable, and efficient way to get from place to place in the metro area. The Red Line runs about 25 miles from the Beaverton Transit Center to the Portland International Airport. The Blue Line begins at the Hatfield Government Center in Hillsboro and runs about 33 miles, well into Gresham. The Yellow Line, which is currently the shortest, runs about seven miles from the Portland Expo Center to SW 10th Avenue downtown. The newest MAX line, the Green Line, runs from Clackamas Town Center to Portland State University.

The Streetcar
The Portland Streetcar (www.portlandstreetcar.org) is a little more lightweight than the MAX line, but essentially serves the same purpose, which is to connect the various quadrants of town and encourage people to take public transportation instead of cars. Unlike MAX, the streetcar runs with the traffic and must obey signals, so it is obliged to cover shorter distances than its big brother. The streetcar (which arrives about every 12–15 minutes) runs from Legacy Emmanuel Hospital in NW Portland to SW Lowell and Bond at the South Waterfront District and the base of the OHSU Aerial Tram. The streetcar will not automatically stop at every stop, as the MAX does. If you would like to indicate your desire to stop, push the yellow strip or the stop button to let the operator know. The fare for the streetcar is the same as MAX or TriMet, and you can use your TriMet ticket or transfer as proof of

payment. If you wish to purchase a ticket for the streetcar, you can do so at the fare box on board.

Portland Aerial Tram

The tram (www.portlandtram.org), a $57 million project that opened in February 2007, can accommodate up to 78 passengers on each of the Swiss-made silver cabins. When the weather is clear, the view is spectacular, offering a vista that includes Mount Hood, Mount St. Helens, the Willamette River, and the city's downtown skyline. The tram takes about three minutes to travel 3,300 feet up to Oregon Health and Sciences University (OHSU) at the top of Marquam Hill, a rise of 500 feet in elevation. OHSU foot much of the bill for the construction of the tram, which has served as a valuable link between the main campus on the hill and the new Center for Health & Healing at South Waterfront.

You must purchase a round-trip ticket to ride, which will cost you $4 (children under six and bicycles ride free). The ticket machine will not take dollar bills, but it will take quarters and credit or debit cards.

TAXIS
Broadway Cab

Broadway Cab (503/227-1234, www.broadwaycab.com) and Radio Cab have been neck and neck for decades in Portland, and very little has changed now except that Broadway (in the iconic yellow cab) has added six Toyota hybrids to their fleet of more than 200 cars. It is part of their long-term goal to replace all their cars with vehicles that use sustainable or alternative fuels. As with all the cab companies in Portland, it is best to book a taxi ahead if you are on a schedule.

Radio Cab

Radio Cab (503/227-1212, www.radiocab.net) has been driving Portlanders around since 1946 and they are still one of the most popular numbers dialed after last call. If you are planning at least 24 hours in advance, you can book your trip online. Radio Cab (the black and white tuxedo cabs) has a state-of-the-art system for dispatching, so the response can be pretty quick. Ask your dispatcher for an estimate when you call.

PDX Pedicab

If you happen to be downtown or in the Pearl District, PDX Pedicab (503/839-5174, www.pdxpedicab.com) may just be your best (and most fun) way to get around. This bike-powered, rickshaw-style vehicle can transport two or three people comfortably (they have canopies and lap blankets) and quickly. You can hail one if you happen to see an empty one, or call dispatch to have one sent. They operate Monday–Friday 10 A.M.–midnight and Friday–Saturday 10 A.M.–3 A.M. The drivers are fun, knowledgeable, and safe, and are oftentimes able to tell you a lot about the city. If you're feeling adventurous, you can also book a Pedicab tour of Old Town, where you will be given a recorded audio history of the city's most scandalous section of town.

The aerial tram takes passengers on a scenic trip to the west hills and OHSU.

DRIVING

Driving in Portland can be a bit confusing at first, and it's simpler if you look at a map before you drive so that you can navigate the many one-way streets and sudden on-ramps to bridges and freeways. There is no need to panic. For one thing, even if you get lost, you are still likely to be only a few minutes away from your destination, and if you accidentally land yourself on a bridge or freeway, it is still pretty simple to take the nearest exit and follow the signs back to where you were.

One notable frustration is that once you are in downtown Portland, it is nearly impossible (and often illegal) to make a left turn. To avoid the frustration of going too far and having to backtrack, turn right a few streets early and C-turn yourself back in the right direction.

If you are heading into Southeast Portland and have to pass through or near Ladd's Addition, here's hoping you packed a lunch, because you may be there for a while. This neighborhood is notoriously confusing, so again, consult a map before you drive. Seeing the grid of the area from overhead can make the crazy turns and broken-up streets more navigable.

BIKING AND WALKING

Portlanders love to bike and walk, which may come as a surprise considering the fickle weather in the Pacific Northwest. Even in the winter, cycling remains one of the top methods for locals to commute from place to place. For that reason, the streets (and drivers) tend to be respectful of cyclists and pedestrians.

Downtown, the blocks are approximately half the size of a normal city block, with public art, fountains, and parks scattered throughout the urban areas. In the Pearl District and Northwest, the streets are numbered in one direction (ascending order from the waterfront) and run alphabetically in the other direction using the names of famous Portland historical figures, like Couch, Davis, Everett, Flanders, and so on. Burnside Avenue divides Portland by the north and south, the Willamette River divides the city by the east and west.

Portland has arguably the nation's most progressive support system for bike transportation, thanks to the wide, clearly marked bike lanes on most major commuter routes; municipal bike racks; and access to most bridges. TriMet has created space for bikes to be taken on the MAX trains and their buses are equipped with bike racks on the front, which makes traveling long distances on a bike that much more feasible.

If you prefer to explore on foot, you can pick up a walking map at most downtown hotels, at the Visitor's Information & Services Center in Pioneer Courthouse Square (701 SW 6th Ave. at Morrison St., www.travelportland. com), and at Powell's City of Books (1005 W. Burnside St., www.powells.com). Cyclists will find the Bicycle Transportation Alliance (www.bta4bikes.org) and Bike Portland (www. bikeportland.org) to be good resources for bike routes, repair shops, and bike-related events.

WHEELCHAIR ACCESS

All of Portland's buses and MAX trains are equipped with lifts, ramps, and special seating. The seating near the entrances of both the bus and MAX is reserved as priority seating for seniors and people with disabilities. Both the MAX and the streetcar have a ramp that extends out for easier boarding, and the buses have either a boarding ramp or power lift. Seniors and passengers with disabilities may qualify for the "Honored Citizen" rate of $0.95 for a two-hour ticket.

Conduct and Customs

UMBRELLAS

The quickest way to mark yourself as a tourist is to pop open an umbrella when it rains. For native Portlanders, a hooded jacket is all you need to ride out the inconsistent weather. Given that the average rainfall in a year is about 36 inches, it may seem like madness not to rely on an umbrella, but there's method in it. For one thing, the rain is often accompanied by a good deal of wind and an umbrella doesn't fare well in such circumstances. Also, the weather changes so often that you may only need protection from the rain for a few moments before a sun break passes through. Finally, when you have a cell phone in one hand, a latte in the other, and laptop bag on your shoulder, an umbrella just becomes cumbersome.

SHOPPING BAGS

As a means of keeping the city even more environmentally minded, city officials are trying to discourage the use of plastic shopping bags within the city limits. There has been talk of taxing the bags, or perhaps banning them altogether. The best thing to do is bring your own reusable bag and consolidate purchases whenever possible. You can purchase a reusable bag at all grocery stores, at Powell's Books (www.powells.com), and a number of other stores all over the city.

DRINKING SUSTAINABLY

Portlanders love their coffee. While a cup or two of Stumptown a day is not a bad thing, cups, lids, and coffee sleeves add up to a lot of trash—even if it is made from recycled materials. So, bring a travel mug with you and you'll end up fitting right in with the locals. What's more, a number of places will give you a discount on your cup of joe if you bring your own container.

The same is true for bottled water. The tap water in the city comes from the Bull Run Reservoir, one of the purest drinking-water sources in the world. Go ahead and fill your Nalgene or stainless steel water bottle right from the tap. Cover your bottle with stickers and people will assume you have lived here all your life.

PUMPING GAS

Oregon and New Jersey are the only two states where self-serve gas is banned. You will not be allowed to pump your own gas, even if you have been doing it your whole life and you are in a hurry. If you try to do so, you could get smacked with a pretty hefty fine. The Oregon law has been amended to allow motorcyclists to pump their own gas, but an attendant must still be there to remove the nozzle and replace it when the fueling is finished.

STRIP CLUBS

Thanks to a liberal free-speech clause in the state constitution and several rulings by the state Supreme Court, Oregon strip clubs and other sex-oriented businesses are practically untouchable. Portland has more strip clubs per capita than anywhere else in the world (including Las Vegas), or at least it did until the tiny town of Springfield, Oregon, opened its seventh club—knocking Portland off the top seat. Inside the 50-plus Portland clubs, pretty much any kind of no-contact nude performance is allowed; with the sheer number of strip clubs in town, that means you can see a vast array of sizes, styles, ages, and shapes.

While in some cities, the industry is treated as thing that gets whispered about, Portland tends to be rather unabashed and unapologetic about it. The clubs that are most popular are the ones that embrace the Portland ideal of self-expression and individuality. In these clubs, the dancers are not likely to look like models out of a gentlemen's magazine, but will instead be tattooed, pierced, and might be wearing tube socks instead of fishnets.

TIPPING

While always a hotly debated issue, tipping is customary in Portland. For services such as haircuts, manicures, pedicures, and massages, 15–20 percent is acceptable, or 25 percent if there were extra services or special attention given. Ten percent or less is appropriate if the services are poor.

Servers in Portland make minimum wage, but pay taxes on their tips and must oftentimes share their tips at the end of the night with kitchen staff, bussers, and dishwashers. About 20 percent is standard, or 15 percent if the service is underwhelming. Anything less than can be construed as insulting, particularly if it is not accompanied by an explanation to the management or the server.

SMOKING
Smoke-Free in 2009
It was a big battle that finally ended on January 1, 2009, when all Portland bars and restaurants went smoke-free. Some places were relieved by the ban, others were angry and are still a bit sensitive about it. Some places saw it as an opportunity to expand, remodel, or make changes to accommodate both their smoking and non-smoking customers. Until such accommodations can be made, it is not uncommon to see a gaggle of smokers huddled outside their favorite bar.

Where You Can Still Smoke
You can smoke 10 feet or more away from any building, which means most sidewalks, parks, and the waterfront are places where it is okay to light up. One notable exception, however, is Pioneer Courthouse Square. Smoking is not allowed on that entire block and you will be asked to put it out or leave if you don't comply.

As far as bars go, there are still a number of places that have smoke-friendly patios and decks, but they are likely to be crowded with displaced smokers. EastBurn (www.theeast-burn.com) has outdoor heaters, swinging chairs, and miniature fire pits built into the tables, and the Lucky Devil Lounge (a strip club) has a heated, covered patio with a pool table. There are more than 50 restaurants and bars in the metro area that have heated patios for smoking. If you want an updated list or details on the venues, check out the Bar Fly website (www.barflymag.com), which offers reviews and round-ups of the bar scene.

CITY HOURS
While Portland might seem to be the antithesis of New York, the city isn't exactly sleeping when the sun goes down. If you intend to do some boutique shopping, you'll want to get it done early since most shops close around 6 or 7 P.M. Shopping malls and department stores stay open until only 9 P.M., except during holidays; and most music stores and bookstores stay open until at least 10 or 11 P.M. Bars and restaurants are usually bustling around this time, however, because Portlanders tend to be more interested in spending time together and sharing good food than they are with working. The prime dinner hour is around 7–8 P.M., but for particularly popular places, it is not uncommon to see a line forming when the venue opens around 5 P.M. For most venues, things stay busy until about an hour before last call, particularly on the weekends. Around 2 A.M., it's time to go home, or head to an all-night diner like the **Doug Fir Lounge** (830 E. Burnside St., 503/231-9663, www.dougfir-lounge.com) or **The Roxy** (1121 SW Stark St., 503/223-9160).

Tips for Travelers

TRAVELING WITH CHILDREN

Portland is a great city for children and the locals tend to take their kids everywhere they go, from gallery openings to dinners at four-star restaurants. If you would like to take your child along on one of the many art walks in the city, skip First Thursday in the Pearl, which caters more to the over-21 crowd and focuses more on the appreciation of art than it does on frivolity. Instead, opt for Last Thursday on Alberta, where the art tends to spill out onto the street along with tall bike riders, performers, stilt walkers, and impromptu parades.

The city is also chock-full of things to do with children that won't bore parents out of their skulls—like Oregon Museum of Science and Industry (www.omsi.edu), the Oregon Zoo (www.oregonzoo.org), and the World Forestry Center (www.worldforestrycenter.org), which is more fun than the name implies. While you are here, check out Metro Parent (www.metro-parent.com) for an updated calendar of family events and tips on what the hottest kid-friendly places are.

SENIOR TRAVELERS

Portland is becoming a particularly popular place for people to retire because it offers the excitement and variety of city life, but still retains a sense of small-town charm and security. Seniors also enjoy Portland because the streets, parks, buses, and trains make the city very navigable, which in turn encourages a healthy, active lifestyle that places very little demand on the individual.

TriMet tickets are only $0.95 for those 65 or older (with proof of age); a two-week unlimited pass goes for $13. Many of the local theaters and movie houses offer discounted rates and mid-week matinees for seniors.

GAY AND LESBIAN TRAVELERS

Portland has a vibrant and active Lesbian Gay Bisexual Transgender (LGBT) community, and, in fact, has one of the most active lesbian communities in the United States. *Just Out* (www.justout.com) is the city's free weekly newspaper devoted to the LGBT community

© HOLLYANNA MCCOLLOM

The Oregon Museum of Science and Industry is an adventure no matter what your age is.

PAWS ON PDX

Traveling with your pooch is easier than you think. Walk down the sidewalk of any Portland neighborhood and one thing is certain: Portlanders love their dogs. Dogs have been unofficially welcomed at restaurant patios and sidewalk cafes for years, but lately, some establishments are taking the needs of their canine customers very seriously.

Come summertime in the Park Blocks and the Pearl District, you will find welcoming bowls of water set near entryways and sidewalk cafés. Frequenters of Portland Farmers Market and Portland State University dog owners also appreciate Shemanski Fountain (between SW Salmon and Main), a triangular sandstone structure that features three small drinking basins, placed low so that passing dogs can quench their thirst.

If you ask most dog owners about their favorite dog-friendly establishments, chances are, the **Lucky Labrador** (915 SE Hawthorne Blvd., 503/517-4352, www.luckylab.com) is at the top of the list. With three area locations, the Lucky Lab caters to dog owners' desires to enjoy a pint on the covered patio while spending time with their favorite pooch.

Other restaurants, such as **Berlin Inn German Restaurant and Bakery** (3131 SE Powell, 503/236-6761, www.berlininn.com) and **Tin Shed Garden Café** (1438 NE Alberta, 503/288-6966, www.tinshedgardencafe.com) offer special doggie menus with whimsical items made to order for your best friend. **Paragon Restaurant** (1309 NW Hoyt St., 503/833-5060, www.paragonrestaurant.com) in the Pearl District also loves dogs, and is happy to accommodate them on the patio when weather allows. They will even bring out some water and house-made "cookies" for Fido to enjoy. For dessert, head over to **Pop Culture** (900 NW Lovejoy St., #160, 503/477-9172, www.pcyogurt.com), where you can pick up a cool treat for your dog and yourself as well. Pop Culture serves healthy active-culture yogurt, not the chalky stuff that was popular a decade ago. For just two bucks, you can get some healthy doggie yogurt with doggie treat garnish.

When the dogs need to stretch their legs, there are plenty of parks for them to run and mingle with other dogs. Some of the most popular off-leash areas are in **Gabriel Park** (SW 45th and Vermont), **Normandale Park** (NE 57th and Halsey), and **Chimney Park** (9360 N. Columbia Blvd.). According to Portland Parks & Recreation, however, there are areas for off-leash playtime in 32 Portland parks.

When it's time to check in, there are a number of hotels who will roll out the welcome mat for your four-legged friend. **Hotel deLuxe** (729 SW 15th Ave., 503/219-2094, www.hoteldeluxeportland.com) will charge a small fee per day, but stock your room with food and water bowls, a pet bed, a squeaky toy, a bag of treats, and clean-up baggies. Upon check-in, you will also find a personalized note, addressed to your pooch, that outlines the hotel pet policy, offers up a list of things to do that are pet-friendly nearby, and best of all, includes a pet-focused room service menu.

Wherever you go, there are many options for bringing your pooch out to play, especially in the warmer months when many restaurants have open patios. Whether you are looking for relaxation, refreshment, or sport, there are a number of places to please both the two-legged and four-legged Portlander. The elegant **Benson Hotel** (309 SW Broadway, 503/228-2000, www.bensonhotel.com) offers a roof overhead for dogs of any size for no extra fee. Call ahead to book and make sure you advise them that you will be bringing your pet. Your dog will be accommodated with a foam pet bed, collapsible water dish, squeaky toy, and a rawhide chew bone upon arrival.

Finally, the two hotels that probably get the most attention for being pet-friendly are **Hotel Vintage Plaza** (422 SW Broadway, 800/263-2305, www.vintageplaza.com) and **Hotel Monaco** (506 SW Washington St., 503/222-0001, www.monaco-portland.com), both Kimpton hotels. Dogs are treated like royalty to the extent you allow (and are willing to pay for). You will be greeted with complimentary amenities, such as treats, food bowls, water, a mat, a bed, and clean-up bags; but you can also set up dog-walking service, pet massage, veterinary services, and grooming.

and it is a great resource for what's happening and where.

In mid-June, Portland celebrates the community with its annual Pride Festival, wherein people from all walks gather along the waterfront for food, drinks, entertainment, and one of the city's most colorful parades (second only to the Grand Floral Parade during the Rose Festival). All told, there are a number of festivals, arts organizations, and performance groups that are particularly popular among the gay community. Along with Film Action Oregon, the Portland Lesbian & Gay Film Festival produces an annual showcase of feature, documentary, and short films that are made by, about, or for people in the LGBT community. Another big event, the annual Red Dress Party (www.reddresspdx.com), draws thousands of revelers (all of whom are required to wear a red dress) to party all night as a fundraiser for programs that support gay youth, as well as people living with HIV/AIDS and other serious diseases.

There is very little of Portland that is not gay-friendly, and while you won't find a nightlife scene that rivals that of New York or San Francisco, there are plenty of hotspots for lesbians and gay men, whether you prefer to dance all night or share a quiet, romantic meal. A good resource is the Gay Yellow Pages (www.pdxgayyellowpages.com), which catalogs gay-owned or gay-friendly restaurants, bars, businesses, and services.

TRAVELERS WITH DISABILITIES

Particularly in the former industrial areas, like Old Town and the Pearl District, Portland has not always been the most accessible city, but things are improving at a rapid pace. The TriMet system is very accessible, with seating, ramps, and lifts on all of the buses and MAX trains; braille signage at all MAX stations; and ticket machines with both audio and visual instructions. TriMet also has a special service called **LIFT** (503/802-8000), which offers prearranged public transportation service for people who are unable to use buses or MAX due to a disability or disabling health condition. The cost is comparable to that of the regular transit fares.

One way to know if a place is accessible before you go is to check Where's Lulu (www.whereslulu.com), a free, online database where Portlanders can rate and review places based on their services and accessibility. If you want to know whether or not Bagdad Theatre & Pub has wheelchair-friendly tables (they do), you can find out using their search engine. The website also filters for criteria such as whether nearby public transit options exist, whether braille signs are present, and whether aisles and hallways are wide and easy to pass through.

TRAVELING WITH PETS

Portland is a tremendously dog-friendly town. Many downtown hotels, like Hotel Monaco (www. www.monaco-portland.com) and Hotel Vintage Plaza (www.vintageplaza.com) have in-house pet-relations managers (a.k.a. dogs), and will accommodate your pet at no additional charge. Along with your regular accommodations, some will even provide food bowls, pet beds, water, treats, and toys for use during your stay, but you can go all out and book a pooch pampering package that includes massage and keepsake gifts.

Want to take your buddy out for a bite to eat? Portland has pet-friendly restaurants in spades. **Lucky Labrador** (915 SE Hawthorne Blvd., 503/236-3555, www.luckylab.com) is a P-Town favorite for beer drinkers who hate to leave their dog at home; so is the **Tin Shed** (1438 NE Alberta St., 503/288-6966, www.tinshedgardencafe.com), where they'll not only welcome your dog, they'll serve him too. The special doggy menu includes (among other things) Kibbles-n-Bacon Bits, a blend of rice and free-range hamburger, for about $5. Or, if you are strolling through the Pearl District, you can stop by **Cupcake Jones** (307 NW 10th Ave., 503/222-4404, www.cupcakejones.net) and pick up a doggy cupcake. Pups (and cats!) love the sweet treats, made fresh daily by owners Lisa Watson and Peter Shanky using oats, nuts, and bananas.

© HOLLYANNA MCCOLLOM

Dogs and diners sit side by side at the Lucky Labrador.

Health and Safety

HOSPITALS AND PHARMACIES

Portland is home to Oregon Health Sciences University (OHSU), which has been recognized several times over by *U.S. News and World Report* as one of the best hospitals in the world, and is considered one of the top research and teaching facilities in the United States. OHSU is the place where Gleevec, an anti-cancer medication, was discovered and developed.

This is also the home of Doernbecher Children's Hospital, which provides the region's widest range of children's healthcare services, serves as the primary center for OHSU pediatric programs, and boasts a kids-only emergency room with a specialized pediatric staff. OHSU and Doernbecher reside in Portland's west hills (affectionately known as Pill Hill) and are easily accessible by car, bus, or aerial tram (www.portlandtram.org).

Other notable hospitals in the area are Legacy Health System (www.legacyhealth.org) and Providence (www.providence.org), both of which have a number of hospitals and clinics around the Portland metro area.

If you have a pet emergency, there's no better place to take your pet than DoveLewis (www.dovelewis.org), a clinic that employs board-certified critical care specialists who provide emergency care, observation, and treatment. The clinic is fully equipped and staffed to provide state-of-the-art intensive care medicine around the clock.

You can pick up prescriptions at a number of grocery stores, such as Safeway (www.safeway.com) and Fred Meyer (www.fredmeyer.com), as well as at drug stores like Rite Aid (www.riteaid.com) and Walgreens (www.walgreens.com).

EMERGENCY SERVICES

In the case of an emergency, you can reach a dispatcher for police, fire and rescue, and paramedic services by dialing 911 from any phone. To reach the Portland Police Department's non-emergency line, dial 503/823-3333.

CRIME AND HARASSMENT

Thanks to the number of walkable streets in Portland, it is relatively safe to be out, even at night, so long as you keep alert and stay in areas where people are congregating.

Of course, every city has crime, but for the most part Portland's rate is relatively low and seems to be centered in outer Northeast, Southeast, and North Portland (close to the airport and Vancouver, Washington). With the growth of neighborhoods like Mississippi Avenue and the area surrounding the Wonder Ballroom on NE Russell Street, crime has largely been pushed out by the bustling crowds.

In the heart of downtown and on a number of the well-trafficked streets, you will find a lot of homeless people, but they are generally non-confrontational. If you feel you're in danger, call 911. If you find someone to be of concern, call the Downtown Clean & Safe Patrol Officers (503/224-7383), who are very good at dealing with public drunkenness, disorderly behavior, and aggressive street youth.

Information and Services

MAPS AND TOURIST INFORMATION

The best place to find maps and get information on what's happening in and around Portland is at the Visitor Information and Services Center (701 SW 6th Ave. at Morrison St., 503/275-8355, www.travelportland.com), which is located in the center of downtown at Pioneer Courthouse Square. In addition to having a comprehensive calendar of local events, the center offers brochures, maps, and itinerary-planning assistance.

COMMUNICATION AND MEDIA
Phones and Area Codes

All land lines in Portland should have either the 503 or 971 area code. You must use all 10 digits in order to place a call.

While the number of payphones in the city has dramatically decreased with the advent of the cell phone boom, there are still a few located in prominent public spots, like in shopping centers and on some street corners. The cost of making a local call is $0.50 and you can call any of the Portland metro area cities for free (Tigard, Tualatin, Beaverton, etc.).

Internet Services

Thanks to the Personal Telco Project's (www.personaltelco.net) initiative to provide free Internet access to the city, virtually all of downtown Portland and, in fact, much of the city, has free Wi-Fi access. You can check the Personal

Stumptown Coffee is a haven for coffee lovers looking to pick up a little Wi-Fi.

COURTESY OF TRAVEL PORTLAND

COFFEE AND CONNECTIONS: 10 GREAT COFFEEHOUSES WHERE YOU CAN GET WI-FI

Albina Press: On the north side of town, Albina Press (4637 N. Albina Ave., 503/282-5214) is a popular spot to grab a cup of Stumptown coffee made by one of their award-winning baristas. The café is always bustling with energy, but there are some cozy couches available if you can catch one. Albina is also pretty laptop friendly, since they have an abundance of outlets to refuel.

Backspace: This Internet café (115 NW 5th Ave., 503/248-2900, www.backspace.bz) has a lot going for it. The multi-use space is open until 11 P.M. or midnight most nights, and gets pretty crowded and noisy at times. They have lots of places to settle in and work with a number of outlets and PCs to rent by the hour. They serve Stumptown coffee, Hot Lips pizza, and an array of vegan and vegetarian food.

Coffeehouse Northwest: This quiet little place with the unassuming name (1951 W Burnside St., 503/248-2133, www.coffeehousenorthwest.com) has some of the best coffee and hot chocolate around. There are a couple of larger tables for gathering, but mostly, the place is lined with small tables and outlets, perfect for plugging in and getting down to business.

Costello's Travel Caffé: This European-style coffeehouse (2222 NE Broadway St., 503/287-0270, www.costellostravelcaffe.com) has only one couch, but they have a number of tables and the space is pretty open and accommodating. The Caffé Umbria coffee is good, and the food is even better. The quiche is homemade and changes daily and the scones are arguably some of the best in the city.

Fresh Pot: There are two Fresh Pots in town, but the Mississippi Avenue café (4001 N. Mississippi Ave., 503.284-8928, www.thefreshpot.com) holds some truly undeniable charm. It was the set of the 2007 film *Feast of Love*, a film that seemed to capture the coffee shop's inherently welcoming vibe.

Sip & Kranz: The name of this café (901 NW 10th Ave., 503/336-1335, www.sipandkranz. com) literally means to "sip slowly and gather around," so it makes sense that it would be a good place to get cozy and relax. They serve Stumptown coffee and baked goods from Nuvrie Pastries. Internet access is free and they have plenty of outlets to plug into.

Stumptown Coffee: There are a number of venues around that call themselves Stumptown, and even more places that serve their signature roast, but the downtown Stumptown (128 SW 3rd Ave., 503/295-6144, www.buystumptowncoffee.com) is the perfect fit if you are someone who works best while a constant cacophony of noise surrounds you. They have a number of tables where you can take up residence as you sip some perfectly brewed Hairbender blend.

Three Friends: This lovable little neighborhood café (201 SE 12th Ave., 503/236-6411) is spacious and friendly and always seems to have plenty of tables, chairs, and couches to go around. They serve Stumptown coffee (are you sensing a pattern here?) and DragonFly chai. The service is cheerful, but never in that way that makes you suspect they have been sampling the espresso too much.

Townshend's Alberta Street Teahouse: If coffee is not on the menu for you, but you still need to caffeinate and send out those Facebook updates, head over to Townshend's (2223 NE Alberta St., 503/445-6699, www.townshendstea.com). The wall of tea is both pretty to look at and wonderfully fragrant, and the whole place is outfitted with comfortable couches and overstuffed chairs, as well as tables and chairs for more serious working.

Urban Grind: There are two locations for Urban Grind; the Northeast location (2214 NE Oregon St., 503/546-0649, www.urbangrindcoffee.com) is shockingly spacious, with ample seating and lots of natural light. They also have a separate kids room that is accessible through a small door that has been painted like the trunk of a tree.

Telco page or WiFi PDX (www.wifipdx.com) to find where the real hotspots are. Pioneer Courthouse Square is a great spot to pick up free access and, if you don't mind sitting on a bench or the steps, there are a number of places where you can grab a seat. Another hotspot is in the South Park Blocks, where you can hunker down in the shade or grab a bench. You can always find access at one of the many local coffee shops, like Sip & Krantz (901 NW 10th Ave., www.sipandkranz.com) and Stumptown (128 SW 3rd Ave., www.stumptowncoffee.com), and at some of the chain coffee stores. (Starbucks does not have free Internet access.)

If you need a computer, check out Backspace (115 NW 5th Ave., www.backspace.bz), a coffee shop and gallery with a number of computers available for use (for rent by the hour) in the back room. Fuel Café (1452 NE Alberta St.) also has computers, which they are happy to let you use for free if you are a paying customer.

Mail and Messenger Services

Most downtown hotels offer mail services, but if you need a post office, you can find one downtown at 1505 SW 6th Avenue, in the Pearl District at 715 NW Hoyt Street, and in Northeast Portland at 815 NE Schuyler Street, just to name a few.

If you need courier service, you have a number of options. Magpie Messenger Collective (www.magpiemessenger.com) can deliver anywhere in the greater Portland area for about $5–40, depending on distance and urgency. Rose City Delivery Service (www.rosecitymessengersvc.com) is another great option. They are a family-owned local business that hires the highest number of women of any company of its kind. Their employees are friendly, well informed, and prompt.

Newspapers and Periodicals

An effective way to plan a tour of Portland is to consult many of the local media outlets for tips on what's getting the most buzz. Publications like the *Oregonian, Willamette Week, Portland Mercury, Portland Monthly* and *Just Out* present regular shout-outs to their favorite spots.

Furthermore, since each publication has its own particular niche, it is easy to determine which editorial voice fits best with your persona.

The *Oregonian* is Portland's oldest daily newspaper and is the largest paper in Oregon and the Pacific Northwest in terms of circulation. The *Oregonian* publishes a weekly Arts and Entertainment guide on Fridays, which includes calendars and reviews for film, theater, dance, and classical music. It can be found on newsstands and is also available on the web at www.oregonlive.com.

Portland Monthly is the city's full-color, glossy magazine, which covers the arts, fashion, entertainment, and dining. It particularly caters to the mid- to upper-class demographic of the city. It is available on newsstands and online at www.portlandmonthlymag.com.

Willamette Week is a free alternative weekly that can be picked up in the blue boxes on street corners and in coffee shops, bars, and restaurants all over the city. The content in print is also accessible online (www.wweek.com), along with expanded blogs from the writers and editors of the publication. It features reports on local news, politics, and culture with music previews, performing arts reviews, and gallery write-ups. It has a strong liberal bent, with touches of sarcasm and sharp humor.

The *Portland Mercury* has many similarities to *Willamette Week* in terms of coverage, distribution, and political leanings. The *Mercury* tends to push the envelope a little further and occasionally adopts a sillier, more mocking tone than its sharp-tongued competitor. You can find the *Mercury* online at www.portlandmercury.com and in white boxes that are oftentimes placed alongside the blue boxes of the *Willamette Week*.

Just Out is Portland's life and culture biweekly newspaper serving the lesbian, gay, bisexual, and transgender community. It has a small web presence (www.justout.com) and distributes in a number of bars, restaurants, and coffeehouses, as well in as free distribution boxes all over the city. *Just Out* often has news stories and opinion pieces related to current events as they effect the demographic and profiles of prominent Northwest people who are living within the LGBT community.

El Hispanic News is the oldest Hispanic publication in the Pacific Northwest, providing national, international, and local news and opinions, along with its sister publication *más,* which features local, national, and international talent, culture news, reviews, and events.

The *Skanner* (www.theskanner.com) is a newspaper that is published in Portland and Seattle for the African American community, focusing on news, entertainment, business, and sports. You can find a free copy of the newspaper at a number of newsstands and coffeehouses around town, or read it online. Similarly, the *Asian Reporter* (www.asianreporter.com) is a free weekly paper that includes international, regional, and local Asian news. It too is available for free from newsstands and street boxes, or you go to their website to download a PDF copy.

Finally, *Exotic* is a free, monthly, full-color glossy magazine. It focuses for the most part on sexual, musical, and pop culture subjects, and primarily serves Portland's booming sex industry. It contains occasionally explicit articles on local tattoo artists, exotic dancers, and sex workers; industry-related stories; and advertising that focuses on adult businesses, nightclubs, and music. *Exotic* is available at most strip clubs, some nightclubs, and a few select street boxes around town.

Radio and Television
TALK RADIO

Portlanders are big fans of National Public Radio's Oregon station, OPB (91.5 FM). One of the popular local shows is LiveWire!, a one-hour radio variety show recorded in front of a live audience that includes witty speakers, musical performances, and readings. It is essentially Oregon's version of Prairie Home Companion that airs weekly at 7 P.M.

For talk radio, there's the locally-owned KBOO (90.7 FM), a volunteer-powered, non-commercial, listener-sponsored, full-strength community radio that emphasizes cultural awareness and the arts. On the AM dial, there's KEX (1190 AM), a news radio station that airs a number of syndicated shows from the likes of Rush Limbaugh, Dr. Laura Schlessinger, Mike Huckabee, and Dave Ramsey. KXL Radio (750 AM) airs the syndicated shows of Bill O'Reilly, Michael Savage, Brian Berger, and Bob Brinker, as well as the locally produced, nationally syndicated show by talk host Lars Larson. KPAM is another popular talk radio program that has garnered awards for breaking news coverage, traffic reporting, sports, and overall excellence. KPAM (860 AM) has a decidedly conservative propensity and airs popular programs like that of Sean Hannity and local right-wing commentator Victoria Taft. Another noteworthy station is KPOJ (620 AM), which was the first Air America affiliate to be owned by Clear Channel Communications. They feature non–Air America syndicated host Ed Schultz. Through Schultz, KPOJ was the first station to call its format "progressive talk," a tag that is often used to describe that particular type of liberal-leaning program. Finally, if you're looking for sports, turn to KKTG (95.5 FM), an all-sports radio station owned by Paul Allen, who also owns the Portland Trail Blazers.

MUSIC STATIONS

For classic rock, Portlanders turn to KGON (92.3 FM). For a mix of modern and classic rock, go to KUFO (101.1 FM), where you will find shock jocks on Wednesdays and head-banging music all day. For alternative rock, the favorite is KNRK (94.7 FM), which plays a lot of local musicians, in addition to indie rock and favorites from the 1990s. You can find Top 40 hits on KKRZ (100.3) and on The Buzz (105.1 FM). There's soul, blues, and rap on KKJM (107.5), soft rock on KKCW (103.1 FM), and oldies on KLTH (106.7 FM). For country music, turn to KUPL (98.7 FM) and KWJJ (95.5 FM); and for classical music, you can turn to KQAC (89.9 FM), as well as a number of the aforementioned talk radio stations.

TELEVISION STATIONS

- KATU 2 (ABC)
- KOIN 6 (CBS)
- KGW 8 (NBC)
- KOPB-TV 10
  Oregon Public Broadcasting (PBS)
- KPTV 12 (FOX)
- KPXG 22 (ION)
- KRCW-TV 32 (The CW)
- KUNP-LP 47 (Univision)
- KPDX 49 (MyNetworkTV)

RESOURCES

Suggested Reading

HISTORY AND GENERAL INFORMATION

Boehmer, Gabriel. *City of Readers: A Book Lover's Guide to Portland.* Portland: Tall Grass Press, 2007. City of Readers is a "literary umbrella," that encompasses all things loved and adored by Portland's literati, such as bookstores, libraries, landmarks, lectures, authors, and titles. A self-proclaimed bookworm who got married at Central Library in Downtown Portland, Boehmer compiled a comprehensive directory of the city's bookstores and provides excellent chapters on the authors and titles that have defined the city, and the best places to find solitude among many (in other words, great places to read). Borrowing its title from the city's monolithic bookseller, Powell's City of Books, the guide is a love letter to a city where book lovers can read with relish and share with enthusiasm.

Granton, Shawn and Beaty, Nate. *The Zinester's Guide to Portland: A Low/No Budget Guide to Visiting and Living in Portland, Oregon.* Portland: Microcosm, 2007. This locally produced biannual book targets anyone who is looking to experience Portland on the cheap, or discover those sometimes hidden gems and hard-to-find happenings. The book offers a glimpse into the city's history and local lore, offering up a low- to no-cost guide to bars, bookstores, coffeehouses, restaurants, record stores, video stores, thrift stores, performing arts spaces, and more. Their way is not simply to tell you where you should go, but telling you why you want to and giving you the story behind the story whenever possible. The book is illustrated with fantastic line drawings of P-Town landmarks as depicted by the authors and some other notable local artists. The book is broken down by the five main P-Town quadrants and the outer neighborhoods like St. Johns, Kenton, and Sellwood, and also includes a section that will help the reader navigate the city's bus system and bike culture with aplomb.

Lansing, Jewel. *Portland: People, Politics, and Power, 1851–2001.* Corvallis: Oregon State University Press, 2005. This ambitious work covers more than 150 years of Portland's political and economical past, from the days when the excessive logging of a new city in the Pacific Northwest earned it the nickname Stumptown to the 21st century and the bustling, progressive city that we know today (but still occasionally call Stumptown). Lansing served as an elected city auditor, so she knows all too well how the city government works. Lansing's well-researched and lively book gives an insightful account of the mayors of our past, from ambitious Hugh O'Bryant, the city's first mayor, to the savvy and persuasive Vera Katz. Lansing highlights the political, business, and cultural forces that have shaped the city—once a hotbed of corruption and vice—into the cultural metropolis we know today.

Stanford, Phil. *Portland Confidential: Sex, Crime, and Corruption in the Rose City.* Portland: Westwinds Press, 2004. It's no secret that Portland has a few skeletons in its historical closet, and this account of the city's colorful past takes you right into the dark and mysterious heart of it. Written by former *Portland Tribune* columnist Phil Stanford, the book shows us the Portland of bygone days when prostitution, gambling, and drug running were de rigueur. By the 1950s, underworld kingpin James "Big Jim" Elkins was ruling over the city's vice industry, and just happened to have most of the police force and the local political movers and shakers on his payroll. Loaded with photographs and newspaper clippings of the time, Stanford's book seeks to expose our dirtiest little secrets, and show its readers the landmarks that still stand where it all went down.

FICTION AND MEMOIRS

Palahniuk, Chuck. *Fugitives and Refugees: A Walk in Portland, Oregon.* New York: Crown Publishing, 2003. This book from the author of the best-selling novel *Fight Club* is part travelogue and part memoir as the author reveals some of the city's most interesting (and sometimes terribly unattractive) landmarks, historical moments, and bits of culture. Go behind the doors of sex clubs; learn about the annual rampage of Santas; find out where you can mingle with the dead; and discover the not-so-secret location of Palahniuk's tonsils.

Sampsell, Kevin. *Portland Noir.* New York: Akashic Noir, 2009. A series of short stories from some of the Pacific Northwest's most exceptional writers, *Portland Noir* takes the reader through the underbelly of the Rose City with stops at the Shanghai Tunnels, Powell's Books, Pirate's Cove, Voodoo Doughnut, and many other all-too-familiar places for local readers. This book is a dirty, pretty depiction of the weird, wonderful world otherwise known as the City of Roses. With funny stories of petty mischief, haunting tales of tragedy, and mysterious tales of violence, it's a deliciously dark read.

Internet Resources

INFORMATION AND EVENTS
City of Portland
www.portlandonline.com
This is the official website for the city of Portland, with links to information on current city and state politics, top news stories, and visitors information. Here you will find maps, calendars, and facts about public transportation, city planning, and city services.

Eventful
www.eventful.com/portland
Eventful enables its community of users to discover, promote, share, and create events such as concerts, markets, store openings, political rallies, fundraisers, sporting events, readings, and more.

Oregon Beat
www.oregonbeat.com
Oregon Beat is a weekly calendar with links to exhibits, lectures, festivals, sporting events, tours, performing arts events, gallery showings, and special food and wine affairs.

PDX Pipeline
www.pdxpipeline.com
PDX Pipeline is a word-of-mouth-fueled website that has up-to-date listings for concerts, festivals, fundraisers, restaurant events, and gallery showings. They do regular promotions through social media and provide links to a number of the city's most popular venues.

Travel Portland
www.travelportland.org
Travel Portland is the city's official visitor's association and has a comprehensive website

with an events calendar, resources, special offers, historical accounts, and in-depth profiles on what makes the city great. You can also visit them in person at Pioneer Courthouse Square (503/275-8355), where you can pick up the annual *Travel Portland* magazine, an insider's guide to the city.

NEWS
Oregonian
www.oregonlive.com
Portland's oldest newspaper is online with extensive "real-time" news coverage, and in-depth reports on sports, entertainment, and local culture.

Portland Mercury
www.portlandmercury.com
One of Portland's most popular weekly sources for the dish on news, music, art, theater, fashion, and food has an active web presence with the particular tongue-in-cheek style we have come to expect from them.

Portland Monthly
www.portlandmonthlymag.com
This monthly full-color glossy lifestyle magazine focuses on news and general interests. On their website, you can catch the first few paragraphs of the articles from their most current issue and find comprehensive listings on restaurants, theaters, shops, and galleries.

Portland Tribune
www.portlandtribune.com
The *Tribune* is best known for its coverage of issues local to Portland and the state of Oregon, as well as its extensive coverage of local high school, college, and professional sports teams, with concentration on the NBA, Pac-10, Big Sky Conference, and West Coast Conference.

Willamette Week
www.wweek.com
Much like the *Portland Mercury,* the *Willamette Week* provides savvy, sometimes sardonic coverage of local news, politics, and culture. Their website provides extended coverage of

the articles that appear in print and offers updates stories, reviews, listings, calendars, and classifieds.

HISTORY
Lewis and Clark Trail
www.lewisandclarktrail.com
This comprehensive website details the historic trip that explorers Meriwether Lewis and William Clark made from Pennsylvania to the Pacific Ocean. You can read quotes from their journals about their first glimpse of Portland and see what remains of their stay in this area.

Oregon Historical Society
www.ohs.org
The Oregon Historical Society (which is also a museum) has a number of studies on their website that offer insight into the history of Portland and the state of Oregon, like the Oregon History Project, which explores the history of the state through the perspectives of the people who helped shape it; and Timeweb, an interactive timeline that uses over 800 records from the society's archival collection to tell the story of Oregon over time.

Portland History
www.pdxhistory.com
Portland History is a scrapbook of the past, with vintage postcards and pictures of the city from the earliest days when pioneers began to make their homes. You can find pictures of Portland's streetcars of the 1870s, when they were powered by horse, and a number of hotels that were open at the turn of the 19th century that are still in operation today.

NOTEWORTHY BLOGGERS
Culturephile
www.portlandmonthlymag.com
Lisa Randon spent five years running the Ultra PDX blog (www.ultrapdx.com), which showcased art, fashion, music, performance, visual arts, and dance; and as the associate editor of *Portland Spaces* magazine, Randon has the pedigree to be called an expert in the field. In

August 2009, she started Culturephile, which "chronicles the vibrant world of Portland arts, its movers and makers" and the site is already proving to be a very viable voice on the scene.

Dave Knows: Portland
www.portland.daveknows.org
A native Portlander and lover of beer, soccer, basketball, books, pinball, and other such things, Dave maintains a blog that is especially helpful for information on Portland sports (such as Timbers soccer and the Trail Blazers) and any festival that involves beer.

Extra MSG
www.extramsg.com
Nick Zukin of foodie favorite extramsg.com posts ultra-detailed reports about the meals he eats at the city's most popular diners, taquerias, *pho* joints, sandwich shops, and more. He is particularly known for highlighting those hole-in-the-wall places that have the kind of food people would swim through shark infested waters to have.

Followspot
www.followspot.blogspot.com
This blog spotlights Portland theater with interviews, articles, and reviews in 50 words or less. Since it caters to both the theater-going public and theater artists, commentaries alone can become quite informative and occasionally quite heated.

Food Carts Portland
www.foodcartsportland.com
This blog is a virtual guidebook on where to find the best food carts and what to eat once you get there. The blog is easily navigated with categories by cuisine types and specific locations, and it provides frequently updated listings of carts with a map to guide you.

Geek in the City
www.geekinthecity.com
Self-proclaimed geek Aaron Duran rants about all things geeky, dweeby, nerdy, and cool, such as games, comics, movies, music, and pop culture. His website features a geek-centric calendar with links to comic book releases, movie premieres, game nights, and shows. Duran is a freelance writer and media producer who is a regular guest on various Portland radio programs.

id Magazine
www.idmagazineor.com
Pronounced "eye-dee," id Magazine is a monthly publication for the LGBTIQ community of Portland and Oregon (which, according to id, stands for Lesbian Gay Bisexual Transgender In-Transition and Queer). It is distributed online, with short runs of hard copies that feature local businesses, community events, the arts, and entertainment.

Our PDX
www.ourpdx.com
This round-up-style blog acts as a conduit to many of the other great writers in town with links to the reviews, inside stories, and insights that are helping shape the city. They read everything they can, click their mouse, pluck out the gems and put them on their site, thereby saving you the trouble of reading 100 blogs to find the good stuff. They also offer up their own opinions, insights, and pointers whenever possible.

PDX Plate
www.pdxplate.com
This gastronomical adventure of a site is both knowledgeable and well traveled around this fair city. They were gutsy enough to compile a list of 100 things that are must-eats for Portland and they regularly put together useful lists on topics such as great late-night dining, recession-proof drinking, and eating local.

PDX Sucks
www.pdxsucks.com
A parody website meant to call up the days when Portland was just a big small town with "Rants from the Tree-Hugging, Birkenstock-Wearing, Dope Smoking, Red-Headed Sustainable Stepchild of the Pacific Northwest." The site has regular podcasts with interesting

Northwest people and write-ups about what's happening around town.

Portland Food and Drink
www.portlandfoodanddrink.com

This restaurant review site was born out of a frustration that many venues were receiving overly glowing and not entirely honest reviews. The site rates restaurants on a star system after visiting no less than three times. They also have a menu section, where you can view the menus of more than 100 restaurants and bars.

Silicon Florist
www.siliconflorist.com

This blog highlights the websites and startups in the Portland area that might otherwise be missed amid the mighty giants of the Silicon Forest (thus the references to flowers, not trees). Founder Rick Turoczy enthusiastically gives readers news and events straight out of the city's blossoming tech scene.

Urban Honking
www.urbanhonking.com

Urban Honking is Portland-based hub of more than 80 active bloggers who post articles about everything from writing and visual art to music to movies. UrHo (as it is affectionately called) began as a web magazine and then exploded as its web presence and readership grew. The site now hosts an annual competition, The Ultimate Blogger, which is inspired by reality TV contests, wherein participants engage in challenges and then post the results in their individual blogs.

Index

Sights Index

Restaurants Index

Nightlife Index

Shops Index

Hotels Index

www.moon.com

DESTINATIONS | ACTIVITIES | BLOGS | MAPS | BOOKS

MOON.COM is ready to help plan your next trip! Filled with fresh trip ideas and strategies, author interviews, informative travel blogs, a detailed map library, and descriptions of all the Moon guidebooks, Moon.com is all you need to get out and explore the world—or even places in your own backyard. While at Moon.com, sign up for our monthly e-newsletter for updates on new releases, travel tips, and expert advice from our on-the-go Moon authors. As always, when you travel with Moon, expect an experience that is uncommon and truly unique.

MOON IS ON FACEBOOK—BECOME A FAN!
JOIN THE MOON PHOTO GROUP ON FLICKR

MAP SYMBOLS

	Expressway	◖	Highlight	✗	Airfield	⚑	Golf Course
	Primary Road	○	City/Town	✈	Airport	ⓟ	Parking Area
	Secondary Road	⊚	State Capital	▲	Mountain	⬢	Archaeological Site
═ ═ ═ ═ ═	Unpaved Road	⊛	National Capital	✦	Unique Natural Feature	▮	Church
- - - - - -	Trail	★	Point of Interest			⬢	Gas Station
·············	Ferry	•	Accommodation	⫝	Waterfall		Glacier
═⚊═⚊═	Railroad	▼	Restaurant/Bar	⬥	Park		Mangrove
	Pedestrian Walkway	■	Other Location	⬛	Trailhead		Reef
⫿⫿⫿⫿⫿	Stairs	⋀	Campground	⛷	Skiing Area		Swamp

CONVERSION TABLES

°C = (°F - 32) / 1.8
°F = (°C x 1.8) + 32
1 inch = 2.54 centimeters (cm)
1 foot = 0.304 meters (m)
1 yard = 0.914 meters
1 mile = 1.6093 kilometers (km)
1 km = 0.6214 miles
1 fathom = 1.8288 m
1 chain = 20.1168 m
1 furlong = 201.168 m
1 acre = 0.4047 hectares
1 sq km = 100 hectares
1 sq mile = 2.59 square km
1 ounce = 28.35 grams
1 pound = 0.4536 kilograms
1 short ton = 0.90718 metric ton
1 short ton = 2,000 pounds
1 long ton = 1.016 metric tons
1 long ton = 2,240 pounds
1 metric ton = 1,000 kilograms
1 quart = 0.94635 liters
1 US gallon = 3.7854 liters
1 Imperial gallon = 4.5459 liters
1 nautical mile = 1.852 km

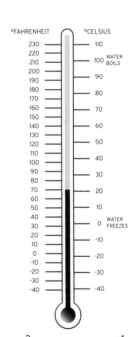

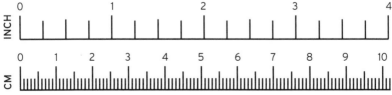

MOON PORTLAND

Avalon Travel
a member of the Perseus Books Group
1700 Fourth Street
Berkeley, CA 94710, USA
www.moon.com

Editor: Elizabeth Hollis Hansen
Series Manager: Erin Raber
Copy Editor: Ellie Winters
Graphics Coordinator: Darren Alessi
Production Coordinator: Darren Alessi
Cover Designer: Darren Alessi
Map Editor: Albert Angulo
Cartographers: Lohnes & Wright, Kat Bennett,
 Albert Angulo, Chris Markiewicz, Brice Ticen

ISBN-13: 978-1-59880-194-1
ISSN: 2153-3741

Printing History
1st Edition – May 2010
5 4 3 2 1

Text © 2010 by Hollyanna McCollom.
Maps © 2010 by Avalon Travel.

Front cover photo: *Transcendence* by artist Keith Jellum, © www.reflexstock.com
Title page photo: © Hollyanna McCollom

Interior color photos: page 2 Courtesy of Travel Portland; page 18 (inset) Courtesy of Portland Saturday Market, (bottom left) Courtesy of Travel Portland, (bottom right) © Jeff Guardalabene; page 19 © Kim Nguyen; page 20 Courtesy of Travel Portland; page 21 (top) Courtesy of Travel Portland, (bottom) Courtesy of Pioneer Courthouse Square; page 22 © Jeff Guardalabene; page 23 Courtesy of Portland Art Museum; page 24 Courtesy of Travel Portland

Printed in Canada by Friesens

KEEPING CURRENT

If you have a favorite gem you'd like to see included in the next edition, or see anything that needs updating, clarification, or correction, please drop us a line. Send your comments via email to feedback@moon.com, or use the address above.